Kon H. YANG

The
Communicator's
Commentary

Ecclesiastes,
Song of Solomon

THE COMMUNICATOR'S COMMENTARY SERIES
OLD TESTAMENT

Lloyd J. Ogilvie

General Editor

The Communicator's Commentary

Ecclesiastes, Song of Solomon

David A. Hubbard

WORD BOOKS, PUBLISHER • DALLAS, TEXAS

Library of Congress Cataloging-in-Publication Data
Main entry under title:

The Communicator's Commentary.
    Bibliography: p.
    Contents: OT15B. Ecclesiastes, Song of Solomon/by David A. Hubbard
    1. Bible. O.T.—Commentaries. I. Ogilvie, Lloyd
John. II. Hubbard, David A., 1928–
BS1151.2.C66 1986 221.7'7 86–11138
ISBN 0–8499–0763–2 (V. OT15B)

Printed in the United States of America

5 6 7 8 9 9 AGF 9 8 7 6 5 4

To
the memory of
William Sanford LaSor

Teacher
Colleague
Friend

Contents

Editor's Preface

God has called all of his people to be communicators. Everyone who is in Christ is called into ministry. As ministers of the manifold grace of God, all of us—clergy and laity—are commissioned with the challenge to communicate our faith to individuals and groups, classes and congregations.

The Bible, God's Word, is the objective basis of the truth of his love and power that we seek to communicate. In response to the urgent, expressed needs of pastors, teachers, Bible study leaders, church school teachers, small group enablers, and individual Christians, the Communicator's Commentary is offered as a penetrating search of the Scriptures of the Old and New Testament to enable vital personal and practical communication of the abundant life.

Many current commentaries and Bible study guides provide only some aspects of a communicator's needs. Some offer in-depth scholarship but no application to daily life. Others are so popular in approach that biblical roots are left unexplained. Few offer impelling illustrations that open windows for the reader to see the exciting application for today's struggles. And most of all, seldom have the expositors given the valuable outlines of passages so needed to help the preacher or teacher in his or her busy life to prepare for communicating the Word to congregations or classes.

This Communicator's Commentary series brings all of these elements together. The authors are scholar-preachers and teachers outstanding in their ability to make the Scriptures come alive for individuals and groups. They are noted for bringing together excellence in biblical scholarship, knowledge of the original Hebrew and Greek, sensitivity to people's needs, vivid illustrative material from biblical, classical, and contemporary sources, and lucid communication by the use of clear outlines of thought. Each has been selected to contribute to this series because of his Spirit-empowered ability to help people live in the skins of biblical characters and provide a "you-are-there" intensity to the drama of events of the Bible which have so much to say about our relationships and responsibilities today.

The design for the Communicator's Commentary gives the reader an overall outline of each book of the Bible. Following the introduction, which reveals the author's approach and salient background on the book, each chapter of the commentary provides the Scripture to be exposited. The New King James Bible has been chosen for the Communicator's Commentary because it combines with integrity the beauty of language, underlying Hebrew and Greek textual basis, and thought-flow of the 1611 King James Version, while replacing obsolete verb forms and other archaisms with their everyday contemporary counterparts for greater readability. Reverence for God is preserved in the capitalization of all pronouns referring to the Father, Son, or Holy Spirit. Readers who are more comfortable with another translation can readily find the parallel passage by means of the chapter and verse reference at the end of each passage being exposited. The paragraphs of exposition combine fresh insights to the Scripture, application, rich illustrative material, and innovative ways of utilizing the vibrant truth for his or her own life and for the challenge of communicating it with vigor and vitality.

It has been gratifying to me as editor of this series to receive enthusiastic progress reports from each contributor. As they worked, all were gripped with new truths from the Scripture—God-given insights into passages, previously not written in the literature of biblical explanation. A prime objective of this series is for each user to find the same awareness: that God speaks with newness through the Scriptures when we approach them with a ready mind and a willingness to communicate what he has given; that God delights to give communicators of his Word "I-never-saw-that-in-that-verse-before" intellectual insights so that our listeners and readers can have "I-never-realized-all-that-was-in-that-verse" spiritual experiences.

The thrust of the commentary series unequivocally affirms that God speaks through the Scriptures today to engender faith, enable adventuresome living of the abundant life, and establish the basis of obedient discipleship. The Bible, the unique Word of God, is unlimited as a resource for Christians in communicating our hope to others. It is our weapon in the battle for truth, the guide for ministry, and the irresistible force for introducing others to God.

A biblically rooted communication of the gospel holds in unity and oneness what divergent movements have wrought asunder. This commentary series courageously presents personal faith, caring for individuals, and social responsibility as essential, inseparable dimensions of biblical Christianity. It seeks to present the quadrilateral gospel in its fullness which calls us to unreserved commitment to Christ, unrestricted self-esteem in his grace, unqualified love for others in personal evangelism, and undying efforts to work for justice and righteousness in a sick and suffering world.

A growing renaissance in the church today is being led by clergy and laity who are biblically rooted, Christ-centered, and Holy Spirit-empowered. They have dared to listen to people's most urgent questions and deepest needs and then to God as he speaks through the Bible. Biblical preaching is the secret of growing churches. Bible study classes and small groups are equipping the laity for ministry in the world. Dynamic Christians are finding that daily study of God's Word allows the Spirit to do in them what he wishes to communicate through them to others. These days are the most exciting time since Pentecost. The Communicator's Commentary is offered to be a primary resource of new life for this renaissance.

It has been very encouraging to receive the enthusiastic responses of pastors and teachers to the twelve New Testament volumes of the Communicator's Commentary series. The letters from communicators on the firing line in pulpits, classes, study groups, and Bible fellowship clusters across the nation, as well as the reviews of scholars and publication analysts, have indicated that we have been on target in meeting a need for a distinctly different kind of commentary on the Scriptures, a commentary that is primarily aimed at helping interpreters of the Bible to equip the laity for ministry.

This positive response has led the publisher to press on with an additional twenty-one volumes covering the books of the Old Testament. These new volumes rest upon the same goals and guidelines that undergird the New Testament volumes. Scholar-preachers with facility in Hebrew as well as vivid contemporary exposition have been selected as authors. The purpose throughout is to aid the preacher and teacher in the challenge and adventure of Old Testament exposition in communication. In each volume you will meet Yahweh, the "I AM" Lord who is Creator, Sustainer, and Redeemer in the unfolding drama of his call and care of Israel. He is the Lord who acts, intervenes, judges, and presses his people into the immense challenges and privileges of being a chosen people, a holy nation. And in the descriptive exposition of each passage, the implications of the ultimate revelation of Yahweh in Jesus Christ, his Son, our Lord, are carefully spelled out to maintain unity and oneness in the preaching and teaching of the gospel.

This is the second volume in the Communicator's Commentary which has been authored by Dr. David A. Hubbard. In the preface to his first work on Proverbs, I noted that most readers will already have been impacted by his ministry of scholarship and leadership. As the years pass, this becomes even more inevitable. David Hubbard continues to be in demand throughout the world as a teacher and preacher. His prolific writings span the range from technical scholarship to popular encouragement. For more than twenty-five years he has been professor of Old Testament and president of Fuller Theological Seminary in Pasadena, California. He continues to lead Fuller into increasing prominence as a center for the training of pastors, missionaries, and psychologists—and as an academy for top-notch evangelical scholarship.

Although Ecclesiastes and the Song of Solomon stand juxtaposed in the Bible and bear the common label of wisdom literature, "at first glance there seems to be a great fixed gulf" between them, as Dr. Hubbard notes in his preface. They treat a wide spectrum of human experience, from the pangs of new love to the despair of mid-life crisis. Yet both texts speak to the profound questions of our day: What is life really for? Is there any real meaning to my existence? How can I experience true love? Who am I as a sexual person? Thus, as communicators, we accept the responsibility of conveying the truths of Ecclesiastes and the Song of Solomon in our contemporary culture.

But this is not a simple task. Not only is there a gulf between Ecclesiastes and Song of Solomon but even more so between their world and ours. The beauty and power of ancient images and poems will be lost on us, unless we are assisted by one whose expertise stretches across the centuries. David Hubbard is this person. "I have tried," he explains, "to build a bridge between what the text meant to its first hearers and what it means to God's people today." His effort has proved, once again, to be most successful.

Recently, one of our seminarians at Hollywood Presbyterian Church had the good privilege of taking one of Dr. Hubbard's classes at Fuller Seminary. This student raved in glowing terms about the lectures: "Every word matters. He helps me to understand what the original text really meant. His grasp of scholarship is overwhelming.

And he even challenges me to consider the relevance of the biblical text for our world and my ministry." This review aptly describes this commentary as well. Once again I am grateful to David Hubbard for his outstanding work as a scholar, a pastor, a leader, and a valued contributor to the Communicator's Commentary. He exemplifies excellent communication while helping us to imitate him as we work with these timely and challenging Old Testament books.

LLOYD OGILVIE

Author's Preface

The Bible is a book of life. It not only tells where life comes from, but it also discloses what life is about. It was a happy choice of God's Spirit to inspire and preserve for Holy Scripture the two books whose messages occupy these chapters. At first glance there seems to be a great fixed gulf between Ecclesiastes and the Song of Solomon. One sparkles with the poetic imagery of lovers full of admiration and desire; the other is often gray in its contemplations of life's enigmas. Yet we could not do without either of them, since the window of life that each opens to us is indispensable. We need the reminder of how hard it is for mere mortals to make sense of God's mysteries, as Koheleth tried to do, and we need the encouragement to find meaning and delight in love as did the lovers in the Song. In fact, their celebration of covenant-love may be viewed as an illustration of two of the Preacher's proverbs:

> Two are better than one,
> Because they have a good reward for their labor.
> For if they fall one will lift up his companion.
> But woe to him who is alone when he falls,
> For he has no one to help him up.
> Again, if two lie down together, they will keep warm.
> But how can one be warm alone?
> Though one may be overpowered by another,
>   two can withstand him.
> And a threefold cord is not quickly broken.
> *Eccles. 4:9–12*

And especially,

> Live joyfully with the wife whom you love all the days of your vain life which He has given you under the sun, all your days of vanity; for that is your portion in life. . . .
> *Eccles. 9:9*

15

Present-day students of Ecclesiastes and the Song are well-supplied with up-to-date commentaries. I have profited immensely from those works listed in the Bibliography (p. 349) and have sought to acknowledge their contribution throughout the text though it is impossible to give full credit for their impact on my own comments. At the same time, I have tried to make my own way through the lyrics of the Song and the musings of the Preacher. I have aimed to build a bridge between what the text meant to its first hearers and what it means to God's people today. Neither side of that task is easy. Ancient oriental literature is still puzzling to us modern Westerners despite our possession of wonderful tools for solving the puzzle bit by bit. This means that whatever pulsing exhilaration one feels in finishing a commentary is matched, if not surpassed, by the nagging uncertainty as to how much one is helping or misguiding the reader. We do our best and rejoice in that, realizing our limitations and praying that future students of these books will do much better.

My thanks go to the institutions and organizations where parts of this material were tested in lectures and seminars: The Divinity School of Acadia University in Nova Scotia, Southeastern Baptist Theological Seminary, Nazarene Theological Seminary, a Pastor's conference of the Christian Reformed Church. My gratitude is due also to the hundreds of pastors and thousands of students who over the past thirty years have been forbearing hearers and caring critics of presentations on these books. Some of the material on the Preacher has been adapted from my *Beyond Futility: Messages of Hope from the Book of Ecclesiastes* (Grand Rapids: Wm. B. Eerdmans, 1976). My office team has rallied around this project with its usual efficiency and good will. Vera Wils deserves special recognition. She retired recently after twenty-two years of service to Fuller Seminary, the last seven as my assistant. Denise Schubert has taken her place. Shirley Coe has been a ready helper. Dr. John McKenna has been key not only in handling the mechanics of the project but also in sharing his knowledge of the books, particularly Ecclesiastes. David Sielaff, who leads the word-processing crew at Fuller, has been a model of efficiency and accuracy in deciphering the illegible and emending the unintelligible.

Ruth, my wife, has again been a patient encourager of this work. Her loving companionship for forty-two years has been a treasure beyond words.

The dedication gives me opportunity to recognize the contributions made to my life by Dr. William Sanford LaSor (1911–1991). He was my first teacher of Hebrew and other Semitic languages. His example of thorough, patient research and warm-hearted teaching left indelible marks on me. His friendship and collegiality through nearly three decades at Fuller have been a fundamental support of my ministry. With this dedication come my love and thanks to Betsy LaSor and their children, Betsy Jr., who passed away while the book was in its final stages, Sandy, Fred, and Susan.

Abbreviations

AB	Anchor Bible
AV	Authorized Version
Heb.	Hebrew
JB	Jerusalem Bible
LXX	Septuagint Greek Version
MT	Masoretic Text of Hebrew Bible
NASB	New American Standard Bible
NEB	New English Bible
NIV	New International Version
NKJV	New King James Version
RSV	Revised Standard Version
TEV	Today's English Version
Vulg.	Vulgate Latin Version

Introduction to Ecclesiastes

"Come, learn from me," the Preacher beckoned. We do not know his name. The Jews called him *Koheleth*, the one who addressed a congregation. The Greeks translated it *Ecclesiastes*. Both words are titles not names. They speak of a task he performed, of a role he played. He probably had appointed himself. What official group would have selected such an outspoken, controversial, contrary-minded leader to be their Teacher? Yet individuals and groups for centuries have answered his beckoning, have sat at his feet to listen, ponder, argue, and learn.

Creation, time, meaning, work, profit, piety, death, joy, grace, freedom, vanity—these are his themes. Nothing trivial or trite among them. To understand any would exhaust the wisdom of Solomon. In fact Koheleth reached back to Solomon's experiences of wisdom, pleasure, and achievement and used them as the core of his curriculum. And they make an incredible learning experience.

The Importance of Ecclesiastes

Wisdom literature comprises a narrow section of the Old Testament when compared with the Law, the history, the Psalms, and the prophets that loom so large on its pages. And Ecclesiastes is only one brief burst of wisdom compared to the prolonged salvos of heavy artillery found in Proverbs and Job. Yet that short, sharp volley has riveted the attention of countless generations of men and women who have wanted to learn life clearly and live it wisely. We do well to join them, and for several reasons.

The Baffling Character of the Book

Few Old Testament writings have produced such a flurry of opinions as to how they should be read, and what they mean, as Ecclesiastes. The ancient Preacher blazed a trail of obscurity in communication that too many of us as his modern progeny have followed. Trying to puzzle out the major themes of his message is a task tantalizing, frustrating, and important. Coping with his style, weighing his contradictions, tracing his arguments, deciphering his imagery, trimming his exaggerations—those tasks have vexed yet challenged all who have unrolled the Teacher's brief scroll. The book lies before us like a chest full of puzzles, testing us afresh each time we open the lid. Partial success is all we can hope for, but that's the case in most of what we do.

The Scriptural Role of the Book

Ecclesiastes is, has been for more than two millennia, and will continue to be, a part of Scripture. There are only sixty-six such parts. This can mean nothing less than that we must take each with great seriousness. Ecclesiastes may not be Genesis, Isaiah, Acts, or Ephesians but it *is* part of God's Word, demanding our attention, insisting on our study, compelling our involvement. God's purposeful providence was not absent when this book was chosen for the canon. No interloper slipped it into the sacred collection while God's back was turned. What God has joined together—Koheleth, as the Jews called the Preacher, and the other sixty-five books—let no one put asunder, whether by intent or neglect. Our commitment to the whole counsel of God is suspect if we omit from our circle of interest any part of the received and preserved and prescribed list of biblical writings.

The Present Usefulness of the Book

Turn a secular and reasonably intellectual audience loose on the Bible and if they can riffle their way through the Old Testament far enough, they will latch on to Ecclesiastes as their kind of stuff. It will speak to their needs, march to their cadence, give voice to their outlook. Koheleth's question, "Does life have meaning?" is their question. Besides, his dread of death captures their mood precisely. As Bishop Fulton Sheen once said, *death* is the taboo of modern society as *sex* was the no-no of the Victorian era. How do we define taboo? A taboo is what genteel people do not discuss at tea parties. Can you hear the cups rattle and see the starched collars wilt, if someone in Belgrave Square asked a Victorian matron about her sex life? The same sense of dread would shroud a party in Beverly Hills if someone injected, "I hear Shirley has cancer. How long do you think she'll live?" The death rate in Beverly Hills, like everywhere else, is: 100 percent, and Koheleth insists that we recognize that. Furthermore, his warnings about overvaluing the techniques of wisdom or the pleasures of materialism have volumes to say to our modernity—

where most of us are yuppies at heart, though we prefe
label on others. The Old Testament offers no clearer
our generation with our foibles than the twelv
Ecclesiastes.

The Message of Ecclesiastes

The lack of agreement among commentators on the basic thrust of
the Preacher's message is both startling and intriguing. It is startling
because in the overall reading of most biblical books a strong consensus has developed in the past few decades. Ecclesiastes is the
exception. It is intriguing because the sleuthing has been intense, and
numbers of mature and able scholars have spent years combing
through the text to break its code, with remarkably diverse results.
The challenge is both compelling and humbling to all who tackle it.

Three major issues confront us readers as we attempt to discover
the gist of Koheleth's message. The first is the meaning of the theme
word—*hebel*, variously translated vanity, futility, meaninglessness,
mystery, enigma, absurdity, irony, brevity, and the like. Just how
pessimistic is the word? The sweeping *vanity verdicts*, which open
and close the Book and punctuate its sections in almost every chapter, if taken by themselves, give the impression of unrelieved gloom.
Yet this impression is modulated markedly when we grasp the
Preacher's words on God's grace which gives us joy as our human
portion, when we hear the Words of Advice that lay out ground rules
for coping with life despite the shroud of vanity that hangs over it,
and when we read his urgings to fear God in the midst of uncertainties and injustices in our world.

In other words, whatever *hebel* means, it is not a label for nihilism. It
does not mean that life has no purpose and will bear no fruit. God
may seem distant; God is by no means absent. To the contrary, God's
presence is to be reckoned with at every turn. Times and seasons are
in God's hands (3:1–9). God's person mandates brevity in prayer, integrity in offering sacrifices, faithfulness in keeping vows (5:1–7).
God is the Creator who commands us to rejoice in the gifts that sustain us day by day. God is to be obeyed, feared, and remembered
(12:1) throughout the brief days of our sojourn under the sun.

Hebel stands more for human inability to grasp the meaning of
God's way than for an ultimate emptiness in life. It speaks of human

ᴛitation and frustration caused by the vast gap between God's knowledge and power and our relative ignorance and impotence. The deepest issues of lasting profit, of enlightening wisdom, of ability to change life's workings, of confidence that we have grasped the highest happiness—all these are beyond our reach in Koheleth's view.

The second major issue to be grappled with in our reading of Ecclesiastes is how much the Preacher is stating his own opinions and how much is he refuting those of his colleagues. The whole "royal experiment" (1:12–2:26), with its tests of the values of wisdom and pleasure, seems to be geared to undercut the naive importance placed on them by members of his society. The relative worth of wisdom and pleasure the Preacher readily acknowledged. They deserved to be branded as *vanity* only when they were overvalued. Indeed, the degree to which they were overvalued and corrupted into virtual absolutes provoked his startlingly strong denunciations of them. The meaning of the tests, then, should be seen not so much as the fruit of Koheleth's personal search as it is the means by which he taught his lessons to others trapped in the fatal mistake of seeking life's purpose where it could not be found and thereby missing life's center where God had placed it—in the calm acceptance of God's timing for life's events and God's spacious provision of life's simple joys.

The third major issue to be tackled is the relative emphasis to be placed on the two dominant formulas which stitch the Book together: the *vanity verdict* and the *alternative conclusion* which urges Koheleth's students to take daily joy in God's ordinary gifts of food, drink, work, and love. The *vanity verdict* seems to be the dominant note. It occurs more frequently, and, above all, it is the *sweeping conclusion* which sounds the Book's theme at the beginning (1:2) and summarizes it at the end (12:8). The *alternative conclusion* (see at 2:24 in the commentary) occurs six times and is reinforced by other notes of joy (e.g.,: 11:9–10).

In a sense these two motifs, *vanity* and *joy*, set the rhythm for the Preacher. They are more complementary than contradictory. Each must be heard in terms of the other. *Vanity* marks the limits of our ability to understand and change the way life works. It salutes in its gloomy way the sovereignty of God whose mysteries are to us unfathomable. *Joy* brings relief in the midst of frustration. It announces that God's puzzling clouds of sovereignty carry a silver lining of grace. That grace, expressed in the daily supply of our basic needs, gives us freedom to fear God, not to hate God.

Vanity is the main theme as tone, style, and frequency dictate. It had to be, because Koheleth's countrymen were in such dire danger of blaspheming God and perverting their humanity by arrogance. Koheleth shouted *vanity* loudly and pounded it heavily to get their attention. But his mission was more than negative. It had crucial lessons to teach about joy, grace, obedience, and gratitude. Pointedly, repeatedly, and winsomely it taught them. Faithful communicators of biblical reality will do the same.

The Interpretation of Ecclesiastes

Four assumptions determine the ways the Book is treated in this commentary. Assumptions they are, because none of them is a certainty that lies beyond scholarly dispute. They represent approximately the points of view of a significant number of students of the Book, though it is no exaggeration to say that there may be less agreement about the interpretation of Koheleth than there is about any other biblical book, even the Revelation of John! The reader, therefore, has high incentive to test each assumption while putting it to use. As in all biblical interpretation, the final court of appeal is the text itself.

Assumption One: Ecclesiastes Has Crisis As Its Motivation.
The crisis is the product of at least two influences: the Preacher's *historical setting* and the Preacher's *intellectual climate*. The crisis can be understood as the vacuum caused by the seeming absence of God in Koheleth's time and the overarching arrogance of religious teachers who sought to fill that vacuum with simple formulas for happiness and mechanical explanations of divine behavior. To point out the nature of the crisis and to suggest the way beyond it, the Preacher taught and wrote his book.

1. *The Preacher's historical setting* helped shape the crisis. All evidence points to a "late colonial period" in Jewish history for the Preacher's ministry. The final decades of the two centuries of Persian dominance (400–330 B.C.) or the early stages of the Seleucid regime (300–250 B.C.), the Syrian part of Alexander's fragmented empire, are the era in view. Even without pin-point precision, it is safe to reckon that the southern kingdom of Judah had gone nearly three centuries without independence, while the northern territory of Israel had felt the boots of conquerors for over four hundred years—Assyrians,

Babylonians, Persians, and Greeks in a sequence that put almost unbearable pressure on the faith of the covenant people. If we lay that time line—three hundred to four hundred years—on the history of our continent, it will mark off a period about as long as Europeans have lived on the banks of the St. Lawrence or the coast of Virginia.

What could this mean for large segments of the citizenry but loss of power, only faded memories of independence, absence of a sense of either national history or national destiny? This historical setting had all but robbed the people and most of the leaders of the vibrant sense of life before God that pulsates in the Psalms and prophets.

2. *The Preacher's intellectual climate* helped shape the crisis even more than his historical setting. The forces that make for spiritual renewal were at a low ebb. We can guess that the *priests* had increasingly degenerated into religious functionaries who barely observed the letter of the Law, let alone the spirit of it. Malachi more than a century earlier had spotted this trend and argued against it. We have little evidence that *prophets* were active to recall people to covenant loyalty and revive their hope in a salvation still to come. And *apocalyptists* such as the authors of the Book of Enoch and Fourth Ezra had not yet arrived on the scene in full force to alert the people to their special chosenness and to forecast with mystic symbols the downfall of the heathen and the vindication of God's people. Nor had renewal and protest communities such as the one at Qumran been formed to relight the torch of hope, faith, and discipline.

What we do see, and what Koheleth seemed to know best, is a *wisdom movement*, staffed by heirs to the wise who left their stamp on the Book of Proverbs and the Psalms of wisdom (for example, Pss. 1, 34, 37, 49, 73, 112, 127, 128, 133). The intensity with which the Preacher hammers at premises of the wisdom movement suggests that it was strongly institutionalized and therefore well defended. Its stock in trade was traditional formulas which cabined divine freedom, oversimplified the complexities of life, and frequently promised what they could not deliver. We may describe the tension between conventional wisdom and Koheleth in terms of a breakdown for him of the accepted patterns of cause and effect. To the earlier teachers prosperity was a de facto proof of righteousness. Good conduct inevitably meant long life. Koheleth says No. Both injustice and death sever that neat tie between responsible behavior and desirable outcomes (see 1:18; 2:15–16; 3:16;: 7:15, for starters).

The end result of this historical despair and intellectual narrow-ness was a *sterile religiosity* that could spawn only an accompanying secular hedonism. With their true spiritual goals abandoned, large segments of the populace, especially the upper-classes to whom Koheleth probably belonged, sought satisfaction in material and sen-sual pleasures made possible by their commercial enterprises (2:1–11). Whether in its pious (5:1–7) or its secular guise, this arro-gance became the object of Koheleth's unmasking. Divine freedom and the limits of human understanding were at stake for him as for the author of Job. Both lived in the midst of crisis. The old formulaic tools, which they knew so well and had earlier used, were now shat-tered on the anvil of personal experience; and the scattered fragments had to be reforged into better instruments in order to deal with life as it really is.

A recent interpretation (Loader, *Polar Structures*, pp.: 125–31), re-fines and details the crisis along the following lines. First, post-exilic Jews found God pushed into the distance partly by their circum-stances, as already noted, and partly by the increasing awe in which they held the one God. This awe avoided the name *Yahweh* and more and more used substitute expressions—Heaven, the High, the Maj-esty, the Glory—to describe and address him. In all this, the sense of his imminent presence and involvement in their lives was dulled. Second, a vacuum ensued as God was perceived to be increasingly remote. They felt God too far removed to communicate with them, or for them to have ready access to Him. Third, into this vacuum were brought numbers of *intermediaries*; among the chief were *wisdom*, treated as a personality virtually separate from God (an extravagant interpretation of Prov.: 8), the *Word* or *voice* of God (Heb. *bat-qôl*), the *Spirit*, the *Name*, and the *Shekina*. These biblical expressions of God's person took on what was virtually a life of their own. Fourth, the gap was thus bridged between the people and the remote deity, who was in touch with his flock through these intermediate manifestations of his power. Thanks to these intermediaries, the tension caused by the remoteness of God was not fully felt by many of the people. Cer-tainly, the conventionally wise experienced no crisis. Fifth, the Preacher, however, did feel it. He shared the prevalent sense of remoteness but found no place for the intermediaries. Sixth, instead, he lived in ten-sion between the older wisdom on which he was reared and the overdogmatizing (Loader calls it "fossilization") of that wisdom which he could not accept. It is that tension, or something like it, that accounts for the remarkable assaults of Koheleth on the teachings of his colleagues and his persistent attempts to show a better, if more modest, way. In any case, we understand him best, if we see *crisis as his motivation.*

Assumption Two: Ecclesiastes Has Continuity As Its Method
1. The Preacher is a wise man occupied with the *role and meaning of wisdom* (see: 12:9–11). It is one of his prime subjects, mentioned something like fifty times. To dig deeply into it was his firm intent, and its ultimate elusiveness became his sharp frustration (8:16–17). It was a chief point of his interaction with his fellow sages. The differences between their handling of the topic and his became a main bone of contention. They saw wisdom as the absolute answer; he viewed it as the insoluble problem (7:23–24).

2. The Preacher, in continuity with the wise, believes in the *centrality of the created order.* The order, power, beauty, and justice of the creation were at the heart of how the wise saw life, as the Book of Proverbs illustrates. Not only was wisdom present at the creation as Yahweh's playful offspring (see Prov. 8), but wisdom was also to be discerned in the patterns of animal life, so that industry could be learned from the ant (Prov. 6:6–8) and cooperative togetherness from the locusts (Prov. 30:27). Beyond that, the creation, charged as it was with Yahweh's power and presence, was the arena of blessing or punishment depending on whether human behavior was wise (i.e., righteous) or foolish (i.e., wicked). Koheleth saw creation from a somewhat different angle but held it no less important. With no apparent doctrine of covenant or redemption to sustain him, he clung tenaciously to his view of God as Creator (12:1) and argued for the constancy of that order (1:4–11) and the fixity of its times (3:1–8).

3. Like the other sages, the Preacher gleaned his *knowledge from experience.* He does not do battle with the purveyors of conventional wisdom or the practitioners of hedonism using weapons of special revelation. He does not cite Moses' Law (by "commandments" at the end of the book, his pupil does not mean the Ten Words of the Pentateuchal law); he does not appeal to prophetic audition or apocalyptic vision. He says continually "I saw," or "I found," in the reflections, a staple literary form of his, based on his eye-witness observations. And he counters their experience-grounded proverbs with "antiproverbs" of his own coining, equally derived from experience. To put it in the technical

language of philosophy, it was not their *epistemology*, their way of discovering truth, that he questioned but the selectiveness of that epistemology, which failed to look at life from all sides and then tended to form absolute conclusions on the basis of limited data.

4. The Preacher's *means of arguing* were identical to those of the conventional teachers. Virtually every literary form that he uses is found in the books of Proverbs and Job before him, and the apocryphal writings of Sirach and Wisdom (not to speak of the New Testament words of Jesus and James) after him.

Reflections or personal observations (see Prov. 7:6–23) are a main pillar in Koheleth's structure of arguments. They picture what he "sees," "says to himself," and "finds" or "concludes" as he examines firsthand life's opportunities, puzzles, and injustices.

Summary appraisals (Prov. 1:19) help to punctuate the sections of the Preacher's arguments and describe the inadequacy of the search or the enigmatic nature of its results. Most common of these is the *vanity verdict* (1:17; 2:11, 23, 26; 4:4, 16; 6:9, etc.).

Proverbs or "sayings" (see the large collection in Prov. 10:1–22:16) are voiced in the indicative mood and make their points by describing how life works not by commanding what should be done (4:12; 5:10).

Comparisons (see Prov. 26:3,: 8; 12:9; 17:1) are a subspecies of proverbs that do their work by lining up the point to be made with an illustration of it: what dead flies do to fancy ointment is precisely what a little folly does to one's reputation for wisdom (10:1). "Better" (Prov. 15:17) is a key to comparison in many sayings (7:1–3).

Admonitions (Prov. 1:15–16; 3:1–2) are commands, either positive or negative, that tell a person what (or what not) to do and often give a reason introduced by "for" or "lest" (7:9; 12:1, 12–14).

Parables or brief instructive stories are used to illustrate foolish or tragic situations like those of the young king who rises to power on a tide of popularity and in turn is forgotten when his successor replaces him (4:13–16), and of the man, poor but wise, who saves a city from attack and is then cast aside and remembered no more (9:13–15).

Allegory, along with its sustained use of imagery (see Prov.5:15–23), may or may not occur in Koheleth depending on the interpretation of: 12:3–5. If the "keepers," "strong men," "grinders," "almond tree," "singing birds," and "grasshopper" are figures of speech, then the passage is an allegory of old age. See, however, the commentary for another, more literal, rendering.

Rhetorical questions (Prov. 6:27) are worded so as to leave the hearer no option as to an answer (3:9; 8:4).

Numerical sayings (Prov.: 6:16–19; 30:15–16, 18–19, 21–23, 24–28, 29–31) use a formula where a number is stated and then followed by another number one unit higher (x, x + 1). The force conveyed is something like "good and better" or "enough and more than enough": two are better than one and three is even better (4:9–12); dividing an investment in seven portions is safe enough but eight is even safer (11:2).

Beatitude and *woe cry* (Prov. 3:13–14; 23:29; for both, see Luke: 6:20–26) occur side by side, demonstrating their function as contrasting terms— "trouble to you" = woe; "happy are you" = beatitude (10:15b–17).

The Preacher's use of such forms is not just a matter of strategy, fighting the enemy with his own weapons. It is a matter of necessity. Given his times, his setting, his training, and the state of his faith, these techniques of discerning reality through observation were all he had. So steeped is Koheleth in the ways of wisdom, it is probably accurate to call his entire book a *māshāl* (see on: 12:9), a lesson, a piece of instruction, an extended proverb, if you will, on what life means and does not mean. We shall not catch who he is or how he thinks unless we see *continuity in his method*.

Assumption Three: Ecclesiastes Has Conflict As Its Mood

A recent suggestion for labeling the opposing sides in this conflict is apt: it is a contest between Koheleth's "protesting wisdom" and the "dogmatized wisdom" of the conventional teachers (Loader, *Polar Structures*, p. 123). If this analysis of the polarities—the placing of opposing views side by side in a dozen or so themes and an equal number of literary forms—is even half right, the conflict is the core of the book.

1. *The value of everything good* is a major issue in the conflict. Wisdom, wealth, achievement, pleasure are not seen by the Preacher as ultimate foundations on which to ground one's life. When treated as absolutes, they cave in under the weight of expectation placed upon them and become clear examples of life's seeming futility. However precious the authors who assembled the Book of Proverbs deemed wisdom to be, its value for Koheleth was only relative. Certainly, it is better than folly but cannot legitimately be peddled as the chief key to life. There is too much mystery beyond its reach, too much divine freedom beyond its ken.

2. *The outlook on the creation* is another issue of conflict. We have already seen how the traditional wisdom treasured the creation as a school of wisdom and a court of justice. For Koheleth, however, it seemed locked into fixed routines. Even more, it was so totally regulated by the decree of God that human choice and endeavor left no impact on it. It revealed not so much the *glory* of God, which the Psalmist celebrated, as the *constancy* of God who, like a tight-fisted and thin-lipped helmsman, seemed to control all our times and seasons.

3. *The views of death* sharpened the conflict. The sages saw it as the release of the human spirit to make its home with God. "How do you know?" queried Koheleth (3:19–21). "Can you prove that human destiny after death differs from that of dogs?"

4. *The matter of divine justice* was a further point of debate. The older teachers assumed a just universe governed by a just God. The younger Preacher peppered this proposition with case studies based on his own investigation which convinced him of inexplicable elements of whimsy and caprice in the divine order (8:10–14; 9:1–3).

5. *Definition of the good* became one of the points of fiercest controversy. Koheleth was convinced that both the wise and the seekers after fame, wealth, and pleasure had higher hopes for satisfaction and fulfillment in life than his reading of it warranted. "Scale back your expectations," was his counsel. He repeated it six times in the various forms of the *alternative conclusion* (2:24–26; 3:12–13, 22; 5:18–20;: 8:15;: 9:7–10). "Find joy in ordinary activities of life by seeing them as gifts of the Creator—ordinary activities like eating, drinking, working, and making love to your spouse. See these normal human pursuits as marks of the Creator's grace. Our appetites for them are his work; the opportunity to enjoy them is an act of his goodness." Since no automatic cause-effect relationship is available to Koheleth, for him well-being must be a direct, intentional gift of God to each person.

Koheleth saw the world differently from his colleagues. For him it was a world less tidy, more cramped, less friendly, and less promising than conventional wisdom assumed. *The conflict was constant*—and at very basic levels of life. It permeates the book and accounts more than any other factor, for its prevalent mood.

Assumption Four: Ecclesiastes Has the Canon As Its Mooring

Ecclesiastes' acceptance in the Hebrew Bible was not altogether smooth. Some rabbis were as puzzled by its contents as we are. But just decades before the Christian era, Hillel's positive verdict carried the day over Shammai's doubts. Questions lingered among Christians for at least four centuries. But since then Koheleth's work has sat securely among the books of wisdom preserved in the Scripture and wants to be seen, as do all other books, in terms of what it offers to the faith and life of God's people.

1. *The basic unity of the book* contributes to our understanding of its role in the Canon. One of the gains in scholarship over the past two decades is a tendency to look at biblical writings as we now have them, in completed form. Of course, we want to learn as much as possible of how they were formed, what stages can be discerned in their composition, what sources may have contributed to their make-up. But it is even more important to grasp the message, role, and purpose of the book as a whole.

Apart from the final verses (12:9–14), where a disciple of Koheleth describes the Preacher's work and admonishes its young readers, the book can be understood as a unity and has been thus understood with more and more consensus among contemporary scholars. But its unity can be comprehended only as we understand its method of arguing. It begins with the announcement of its basic conclusion: everything in life is futility (1:2), in the sense that it has been overvalued and cannot be fully understood or depended on as ground for security, satisfaction, or hope. That theme is illustrated with a whole chain of evidence drawn from Koheleth's personal observations—the four Demonstrations (1:4–2:26; 3:1–4:16;: 5:13–6:12;: 8:10–9:12). It is reinforced with clusters of proverbs—the three collections of Words of Advice (5:1–12;: 7:1–8:9;: 9:13–12:8)—that show the emptiness of conventional wisdom and that counsel the hearers in how to make the best of life, hard as it is. And it is punctuated with the six *alternative conclusions* that urge the people to set modest expectations for themselves and enjoy God's simple, everyday gifts of food, drink, work, and love. It concludes as it began with the *vanity* (or "futility") *verdict*. Some such picture of the unity of Ecclesiastes sets the stage for our discussion of its contribution to the Canon. See the Outline below for the full development of the book's unity and movement.

2. *The restoration of balance* is one of Koheleth's services to the believing community. Proverbs, as a literary genre, necessarily oversimplify and overgeneralize. "Haste makes waste" and "he who hesitates is lost" cannot both be true in every circumstance. Each

claims absoluteness by its form. But we can only use each rightly when we know the proper occasion. And there is some evidence that the conventional teachers had so crystalized their understanding of order in the universe that they squeezed out all possibility of divine surprise, even though the Book of Proverbs maintains a steady awareness of the possibility of such surprise (see especially chap. 16). They reduced God's activity to the patterns of their formulas and felt they could thus predict and control human destiny by consistent use of their own teachings.

Koheleth rightly saw that life was more complex and God more free than their dogmas allowed. Like Job, he helped to restore balance in a situation where the truths of the Book of Proverbs had been overinterpreted and overplayed. One scholar's recent comparison is apt: Koheleth's warnings were to wisdom's exaggerations what James' strictures were to the excessive applications of Paul's doctrine of grace.

3. *The limits of empirical understanding* is another canonical emphasis of the book. Personal investigation, acute observation, and perceptive analysis of how life works do provide valuable insight. Because creation has a basic order to it, patterns can be discerned, generalizations can be drawn, and valuable lessons can be learned and taught. Indeed much of the accumulated wisdom of the human family over the millennia has been garnered just this way.

But it is not enough. That is part of what Koheleth teaches us. The methods of wisdom, whether plied by the conventional sages or the more radical ones, cannot probe to the heart of life. Its full meaning lies beyond their reach. The mysteries of God's ways for the human family, the matters of what may lie beyond death, the wonder of worship and fellowship with God—these all call for insight that experience alone cannot provide. Neither the wise conventions nor the more acute perceptions of Koheleth can catch the crucial issues. But their failure to do so is itself an important lesson. It readies us for the role of other forms of revelation.

Koheleth, then, plays a part important for his own day, as well as for ours, in offsetting the extremes of wisdom's claims and demonstrating, by his own inability to make a brilliant breakthrough in the recovery of life's major purposes, the limits of any method of learning based on observation alone. This part—balance and limitation—I would call his *interim* role in the canon. He sharpened issues for his peers as well as for us. And we can be grateful beyond words that the God of the Proverbs who can be so regularly counted on has also shown us himself as the God of Job and Koheleth, rich with surprises, sovereign in his hiddenness, replete with purposes that our limited ingenuity can only guess at.

4. *The preparation for the gospel* is Koheleth's *ultimate* gift to the canon. His *verdict of vanity* is a comment that anticipates Paul's:

> For the earnest expectation of the creation eagerly waits for the revealing of the sons of God. For the creation was subjected to futility, not willingly, but because of Him who subjected it in hope; because the creation itself also will be delivered from the bondage of corruption into the glorious liberty of the children of God. For we know that the whole creation groans and labors with birth pangs together until now.
>
> *Rom. 8:19–23*

The Preacher shows just how vain was the vanity ("*futility*," v. 20) to which the creation was subjected as it awaited the manifestation of the sons and daughters of God.

Such futility, clutching at the vitals of the old creation and choking off its glory, could only be dealt with by the wonders of the new creation which God sent the Son to inaugurate. That Son, Word of God incarnate, came as prophet, priest, servant, king. But he came also as *wise man*. And thus he stands in continuity with the conventional and radical sages in the questions that he raises and the methods that he uses. But he couples all of these with the prophetic and eschatological vision that lifts his perspective to realms and ranges beyond their reach. In fact, a major role that he plays—this divine Son—is to solve the puzzles left still tangled when the earlier wise had done their best.

This canonical perspective that assigns Koheleth both his interim and his ultimate roles will govern the flow of this commentary. The outlook of the older wise man in Proverbs, the probings of the younger sage in Ecclesiastes, and the affirmations of the Greater Wise Man of the Gospels—these will be the perspectives to be tested. The reader should note that the *interim* contribution of Koheleth, the message designed for his own time, comprises the bulk of the Commentary discussion. In each main chapter this is introduced by a contemporary illustration of the situation Koheleth addresses. These introductions aim to serve as seed thoughts for preaching and teaching the materials in the book and suggesting some application to current needs. Koheleth's *ultimate* contribution is hinted in the epilogues to the chapters under the heading "The Greater Wise Man." The epilogues seek to deal with Ecclesiastes in the total context of the Christian canon of Scripture–both Hebrew and Greek. Communicators, then, have the options of (1) dealing with the message of the Book as Koheleth presented it and viewing it within its historical and theological setting in Jewish life after the Exile or (2) pursuing the themes of Ecclesiastes on into the New Testament to see how Jesus both affirmed them and led his people beyond them. Only a fool would downplay the importance of wisdom as the biblical writers dispensed. But there came a time, as the hymn writer recognized, when a Greater Wise Man summoned the allegiance of all who ponder in order to teach:

> Sages leave your contemplations,
> Brighter visions beam afar;
> Seek the great Desire of Nations,
> Ye have seen His natal star:
>
> Come and worship, Come and worship,
> Worship Christ, the newborn king.
> *James Montgomery*
> *(1816)*

An Outline of Ecclesiastes

Introduction: 1:1–3
- A. Title: 1:1
- B. Theme: 1:2–3
    1. Sweeping conclusion of *"vanity"*: 1:2
    2. Guiding question on *"profit"*: 1:3
I. First Demonstration of Theme: 1:4–2:26
- A. Introductory Poem: 1:4–11
    1. Constancy of creation: 1:4–8
        a. Cycles of nature and the stability of earth: 1:4
        b. Sun's journey: 1:5
        c. Wind's movement: 1:6
        d. Rivers' flow: 1:7
        e. Human response: 1:8
    2. Absence of novelty: 1:9–11
- B. Reflections on a Royal Experiment: 1:12–2:23
    1. Anguish of wisdom: 1:12–18
        a. Preacher's self-introduction: 1:12
        b. Account of Preacher's quest for wisdom: 1:13
        c. Negative summary appraisal: 1:14
        d. Proverb confirming the appraisal: 1:15
        e. Preacher's self-evaluation: 1:16
        f. Account of Preacher's quest for understanding: 1:17a
        g. Negative summary appraisal: 1:17b
        h. Proverb confirming the appraisal: 1:18
    2. Frustrations of pleasure: 2:1–11
        a. Decision to search for pleasure: 2:1–a
        b. Negative verdict against pleasure: 2:1b–2
        c. Description of search: 2:3–8
        d. Positive results of search: 2:9–10
        e. Negative verdict against pleasure: 2:11
    3. Lack of permanence: 2:12–23
        a. Wise and fool both die: 2:12–17

          b. Proverb against verboseness: 5:3

      3. Faithfulness is better than fickleness: 5:4–7

          a. Admonition on paying vows: 5:4–5

          b. Admonition against lying about vows: 5:6

          c. Admonition to fear God: 5:7

  B. Caution Toward Government: 5:8–9

      1. Conspiracy of the bureaucracy: 5:8

      2. Complicity of the king: 5:9

  C. Restraint of Greed: 5:10–12

      1. Proverb against love of money: 5:10

      2. Proverb about expenses rising with income: 5:11

      3. Proverb about the restlessness of the rich: 5:12

IV. Third Demonstration of Theme: 5:13–6:12

  A. Reflection on Risks of Bad Investments: 5:13–17

      1. Nothing left for son to inherit: 5:13–14

      2. No joy in life for the broken parent: 5:15–17

  B. *Alternative Conclusion*: 5:18–20

      1. Joy in the commonplace: 5:18

      2. Ability to enjoy heritage as a divine gift: 5:19

      3. Importance of being occupied with joy: 5:20

  C. Reflection on Frustrations of Fraud or Theft: 6:1–9

      1. Introduction of observation: 6:1

      2. Content of observation: 6:2

      3. Further thoughts on observation: 6:3–6

          a. Dissatisfaction is worse than death: 6:3–5

          b. No length of life can outweigh frustration: 6:6

      4. Proverbs confirming observation: 6:7–9

          a. Sheol has an insatiable appetite: 6:7

          b. Sheol has a leveling quality: 6:8

          c. Sheol prompts us to live now: 6:9

  D. Sayings on the Limits of Human Freedom: 6:10–12

      1. No one can contend with God: 6:10

      2. Wordy arguments make things worse: 6:11

      3. We cannot understand present or future: 6:12

V. More Words of Advice: 7:1–8:9

  A. Sobriety Is Better than Levity: 7:1–7

      1. In the face of death: 7:1–4

      2. In the face of injustice: 7:5–7

  B. Caution Is Better than Rashness: 7:8–10

C. Wisdom Is Better than Folly: 7:11–12
D. Resignation Is Better than Indignation: 7:13–14
E. Integrity Is Better than Pretentiousness: 7:15–22
    1. Observation on unsuitable rewards: 7:15
    2. Admonition against extremes in behavior: 7:16–18
    3. Summary saying on the fear of God: 7:18
    4. Implications of the fear of God: 7:19–20
        a. We value wisdom: 7:19
        b. We acknowledge sin: 7:20
    5. Admonition to patience when spoken against: 7:21–22
F. Reflections on Human Limitations: 7:23–24
    1. Confession of failure in test for true wisdom: 7:23–24
    2. Summary of the test's intensity and breadth: 7:25
    3. Statement of one discovery: dangers of a grasping woman: 7:26
    4. Elaboration on the search and discovery: 7:27–28
    5. Generalization on the contrast between people as God made them and as they are now: 7:29
    6. Boast of wise man's success despite seeming failure: 8:1
G. Admonitions on Respect for Authority: 8:2–9
    1. Admonition to obey the king: 8:2
    2. Admonition not to revolt against the king: 8:3
    3. Four proverbs on authority: 8:4–7
        a. King's power is absolute: 8:4
        b. Rebellion should wait for the right time: 8:5
        c. Waiting is hard when disaster seems imminent: 8:6
        d. Even kings can't read the future: 8:7
    4. Proverb on certainty and untimeliness of death: 8:8
    5. Concluding observation on oppressiveness of power: 8:9
VI. Fourth Demonstration of Theme: 8:10–9:12
A. Reflections on the Mysteries of Divine Justice: 8:10–14
    1. Wicked receive attention; righteous are forgotten: 8:10
    2. Delays in sentencing cause laxity toward righteousness: 8:11
    3. God will ultimately set things right: 8:12–13
B. *Alternative Conclusion*: 8:15
    1. Joy in the commonplace: 8:15a
    2. Promise of its endurance: 8:15b
C. Reflections on the Mystery of All Divine Activities: 8:16–17
D. Reflections on the Universality of Death: 9:1–6
    1. Timing of death unconnected to human conduct: 9:1–4a

2. Proverb on importance of life: 9:4b
3. Poem on importance of life: 9:5–6
E. *Alternative Conclusion*: 9:7–10
 1. Joy in the commonplace: 9:7–9
 2. Nothing in the grave: 9:10
F. Reflections on the Mysteries of Divine Providence: 9:11–12
 1. Sayings on time and chance: 9:11
 2. Sayings on human limitations: 9:12
VII. Closing Words of Advice: 9:13–12:8
A. Guidelines to Practicality: 9:13–10:20
 1. Reflection on wisdom's virtue and fragility: 9:13–18
  a. Story of Wisdom, effective yet forgotten: 9:13–16
   (1) Introduction: 9:13
   (2) Story: 9:14–15
   (3) Koheleth's reaction to story: 9:16
  b. Proverbs praising wisdom yet warning of its limits: 9:17–18
 2. Sayings on dangers of folly: 10:1–3
  a. Metaphor on folly's ability to spoil good achievements: 10:1
  b. Literal descriptions of foolish behavior: 10:2–3
 3. Sayings on kings and citizens: 10:4–7
  a. Admonition to calmness in court: 10:4
  b. Observations on royal folly: 10:5–7
 4. Sayings on the consequences of carelessness: 10:8–11
 5. Sayings on the consequences of unguarded speech: 10:12–15
 6. Sayings on the foibles of the ruling class: 10:16–20
  a. Woe to a land with an unfit ruler: 10:16
  b. Beatitude to a land with disciplined leaders: 10:17
  c. Sayings on dangers of laziness: 10:18
  d. Saying on risk of excessive festivity: 10:19
  e. Admonition on danger of demeaning nobility: 10:20
B. Principles of Financial Investment: 11:1–8
 1. Admonitions to diversity: 11:1–2
  a. Take a risk: 11:1a
  b. Expect a return: 11:1b
  c. Divide the risk: 11:2a
  d. Hedge against disaster: 11:2b
 2. Examples of lessons learned from observation: 11:3–4
  a. Cloud: 11:3a
  b. Trees: 11:3b

      c. Wind: 11:4a
      d. Cloud: 11:4b
    3. Examples of what cannot be learned from observation: 11:5
      a. Wind: 11:5a
      b. Womb: 11:5b
      c. Conclusion: 11:5c
    4. Admonitions to timely action: 11:6
      a. Sow seed: 11:6a
      b. Do not withhold: 11:6b
      c. Reason: you don't know how growth works: 11:6c
    5. Conclusion on enjoying life: 11:7–8
      a. Saying on life's joy: 11:7
      b. Admonition to remember that death is coming: 11:8
  C. Ground Rules for the Young: 11:9–12:8
    1. Admonitions to joy: 11:9–10
      a. Live life of joy: 11:9a–b
      b. Motivation: God will judge: 11:9c
      c. Avoid life of pain: 11:10a–b
      d. Motivation: youth is brief: 11:10c
    2. Admonition to faithfulness: 12:1–7
      a. Call to remember: 12:1a
      b. Motivation: death is certain: 12:1b–7
        (1) Literal description of old age: 12:1b
        (2) Figurative description of old age: 12:2
        (3) Dramatic description of funeral: 12:3–5
        (4) Figurative description of death: 12:6
        (5) Literal description of death: 12:7
    3. Summary of book: sweeping conclusion: 12:8
Conclusion: 12:9–14
  A. Description of Teacher's Discipline: 12:9–11
    1. Method of preparation: 12:9
    2. Chief aims: 12:10
      a. Elegant words: 12:10a
      b. Truthful words: 12:10b
    3. Impact on students: 12:11
  B. Admonitions on Student's Duty: 12:12–14
    1. Beware of misleading books: 12:12
    2. Fear and obey God: 12:13
    3. Motivation: judgment is certain: 12:14

CHAPTER ONE

First Demonstration: Theme and Introduction

Ecclesiastes 1:1–11

Their question stopped me in my tracks. They had not put it to me that way before. Perhaps it was a drawn look on my face, or perhaps it was the fact that I was five minutes late to class that prompted the students to ask me the question. "Students" I call them, though they were actually pastors—friends and colleagues of mine in ministry— who were taking a special course at the seminary to sharpen their skills and expand their understanding.

They had sensed that I was troubled, and they gave me opportunity to talk about it with the question, "Had a good day?" A good day? I could have wept. I had just concluded an extended phone call that seemed to unravel a project I had been working on for three months. Just when I thought I had the whole pattern put together, it fell apart at my feet.

A "good day?" they had asked. And with moist eyes I shared the deep futility that I was feeling.

Futile days we can expect from time to time. Some of what we plan will miscarry. Paths that look promising will fade out and force us to backtrack. Pillars that we lean on will collapse and send our hopes tumbling down on us.

When sickness strikes or financial reverses hit, futile days may stretch into empty weeks or months. There have been times when we heaved huge sighs as we ripped December's page from the calendar and welcomed a new year that offered better days than the old.

Days, weeks, months, even years can be tinged with or stamped by futility. Life's complexion is almost never totally free of blemishes. It does have its bleak side. But the Preacher in the Book of Ecclesiastes

41

painted it in consistently dark tones, as a warning to those who na-
ively were trying to understand it and arrogantly were seeking to
change it. His opinion was not that life—the way his contemporaries
were living it—was basically and usually good, with occasionally
painful exceptions. To the contrary, he announced, life, the way you
are going at it, can only be labeled good when you do not look at it
closely. Offering that closer look at their wrongheadedness and sharing with them how to be content in the midst of uncertainty was his
mission.

INTRODUCTION

The *Title* of the book speaks volumes despite its leanness and brevity.

> 1 The words of the Preacher, the son of David,
> king in Jerusalem.
>
> *Eccles. 1:1*

"*Words*" means something like "official collection of teachings."
Sages like Agur and Lemuel (Prov. 30:1; 31:1) and prophets like
Amos (1:1) and Jeremiah (1:1) had sets of their proverbs and oracles
so labeled by those who collected and preserved them for posterity.
How the author and other wise teachers went about their work is de-
scribed with some detail in the conclusion (12:9–10).

"*Preacher*" translates a Hebrew word that stems from a root meaning "congregation" or "assembly" (*qāhāl*), the standard term for the
gathering of Israel for political or religious purposes (Deut. 31:30; 1
Kings 8:14, 22, 55; 12:3). We cannot be sure of the precise meaning of
qōhelet. In form it is a feminine participle used to denote an office or
the person who held the office. A couple of examples are found in the
list of names in Ezra 2:55, 57: *Sophereth* = scribe; *Pohereth-Zebaim* =
"tender of gazelles." English parallels would be names like Penman
or Fowler.

If Koheleth (using the more common English spelling) is an officer
of the congregation, what is his role? Convening it? Addressing it?
Instructing it? Based on the contents of his *words*, we can probably
answer, "all of the above." And, on the basis of some uses of a similar
word in the Syriac, we may well add a note of "arguing" or "debat-
ing" in the presence of the congregation.

One thing seems sure: *Preacher* is the pen name to describe the part played by the book's author. It depicts an *"office"* he assumed for the sake of his pedagogical task and not his acknowledged authority over his people. Yet he does not picture himself as an ordinary preacher. *"Son of David"* and *"king in Jerusalem"* claim a connection with the royal family and help to account for the tradition that identifies the author as Solomon, whose contributions to Israel's wisdom movement are well attested (Prov. 1:1; 10:1; 25:1; 1 Kings 4:29–34; 10:1–9). But in contrast with Proverbs and Song of Solomon (1:1; 3:7, 9, 11; 8:11–12), Ecclesiastes never mentions Solomon by name.

The obliqueness of the reference to David's *"son"* (which to his audience could mean any of his descendants, not just his immediate offspring) is apparently part of a literary device that uses a "Solomonic" background to underscore the Preacher's points about the limits of wisdom, power, and pleasure which other wise men had extolled. This royal guise is sustained through chapter 2 of the book and then is discarded. Its force is powerful. The Preacher, who himself is named only at the beginning (1:1, 12), in the middle (7:27), and again at the close of the book (12:8-10), dons the robe of the royal paragon of wisdom to expose the weaknesses of the teachings of those who named Solomon as their patron and mentor. Having made his point in what James Crenshaw has called "The Royal Experiment" (1:12–2:26), the Preacher casts aside the Solomonic garb and seeks to let his arguments carry their own weight.

The *theme* is stated in two ways: (1) a *sweeping conclusion* (v. 2) that all of life is marked by mystery ("*vanity*") and (2) a *guiding question* (v. 3) that wonders whether all our human attempts to understand and improve our lot will have any lasting value. The relationship between the conclusion and the question will be dealt with in the course of the comments.

The conclusion brackets the entire book and wraps it in the mood of mystery (see 12:8, where 1:2 is repeated virtually verbatim). This mystery is akin to irony, because it is full of surprises. We find it where we least expect it. Values that we treasure prove false; efforts that should succeed come to failure; pleasures that should satisfy increase our thirst. Ironic futility, futile irony—that is the color of life as seen through the Preacher's eyes. So frequently does life turn out the opposite of our expectations that "absurdity" (Fox) is one term used to describe Koheleth's estimate of it.

43

Main point

Throughout his twelve chapters the author argues one main point—it is incredibly difficult for us as human beings to gain a grasp of life that will take us *beyond futility*. This is the meaning of the famous pronouncement with which his book begins:

> 2 "Vanity of vanities," says the Preacher;
> "Vanity of vanities, all is vanity."
>
> *Eccles. 1:2*

Strong language the Preacher used, language reinforced by repetition and summed up in the sweeping generalization expressed in *"all"*. *Everything* is so utterly puzzling that it looks empty, hollow, futile. Life is not what it seems, not what we want it to be. Not only is everything *vanity*, but it is the vainest kind of vanity, the most futile brand of futility. The expression conveys a superlative quality. As "Song of Songs" means the finest song, and as "king of kings" points to the greatest king, so *"vanity of vanities"* means that the full meaning of life is totally beyond our reach; our quest for understanding is marked by the worst sort of futility.

The Hebrew term *hebel* is a catchword that stitches together the text of Ecclesiastes, occurring thirty-eight times and found in every chapter except chapter 10. In this commentary we shall ordinarily use words like "mystery," "enigma," or even "futility" to avoid the ambiguity of "vanity" which in English may also suggest pride. The most common uses of *hebel* are in the clauses often called the *vanity verdict*: *"all is vanity"* (1:2, 14; 2:11, 17; 3:19; 12:8) and "this also was/is vanity" (2:1, 15, 19, 21, 23, 26; 4:4, 8, 16; 5:10; 6:2 [without *"also"*], 9; 7:6; 8:10, 14). Several of the latter set of clauses are modified by *"and grasping for the wind"* (2:17, 26; 4:4, 16; 6:9) which intensifies the sense of puzzlement at the workings of life and our human strivings to make sense of them.

The strong words of the Preacher were prompted by his disagreement with his fellow wise men. Their teachings were full of promises about the possibilities of wealth, security, happiness, and blessing. Koheleth, the Preacher, objected. He thought that the other teachers were promising more than life could produce. They were misleading their students with the unrealistic dreams that they painted. They failed at two points in particular: they tried to predict God's ways without due respect for the mysteries involved; and they ignored the fact of death which cut short their plans and left their wealth to others.

44

In argument after argument the Preacher tried to expose the blind spots in the teachings of these traditional wise men and to discourage his own pupils from building their lives on values doomed to collapse. To make his points, he deliberately attacked the beliefs and opinions of his society. Ideas they had cherished and customs they had practiced he exploded as vapid, vanishing, and vain.

Is there *"profit"* in work? That was Koheleth's *guiding question*, the second half of his statement of theme, the logical follow-up to his thesis that everything in life is stamped with vanity:

> 3 What profit has a man from all his labor
> In which he toils under the sun?
>
> *Eccles. 1:3*

This verse compresses into two lines a number of Koheleth's favorite terms. *"Profit"* (Heb. *yitrôn*), found nowhere else in the Old Testament, is used ten times by the Preacher (1:3; 2:11, 13 [twice]; 3:9; 5:9, 16; 7:12; 10:10, 11). In most of these occurrences the sense is *absolute* and describes profit, success, or desired results. In 2:13 and 10:11, the force is *comparative* and should be translated as the "advantage" that one thing has over another. Though the origin of the term must have been in economics, describing material or monetary profit—the "bottom line"—its use in Koheleth is more general and includes "contentment" and "complete satisfaction." Graham Ogden has suggested that it points to a lasting satisfaction that "transcends this present earthly experience" (p. 23) and is "wisdom's reward both here and after death" (p. 29). We cannot be certain that the term carries quite that force in a book that makes so much of death's finality, especially in its closing thoughts (11:9-12:8).

"Man" (Heb. *'ādām*) reaches back to the creation account in Genesis 1–2 and embraces the whole human family. "Person" may be the best translation of it. It does not focus on any single individual nor is it usually restricted to the masculine gender. The question of ultimate satisfaction pounds within every human chest. That life is hard is not doubted. The pressing universal issue is whether the harshness of human existence has an adequate payoff in the long run.

"Labor" or *"toil"* (Heb. *'āmāl*), a dominant term in the book, is found in its verbal form (Heb. *'āmal*) eight times (1:3; 2:11, 19, 20, 21; 5:16, 18; 8:17; half of these passages have *'ādām*, "person," as their subject, while three are linked to the toiling of the Preacher); the noun

is even more frequent, occurring twenty-two times and in all but three chapters. In Psalm 25:18 it describes mental and emotional agony ("pain" in NKJV), while its physical force is present in Psalm 127:1 ("labor"). Both meanings are found in Koheleth, though the emotional thrust seems more prominent. "Life's strains in general" is the paraphrase offered by Fox (p. 38), while Ogden interprets it as speaking "both of the action of working as well as of the outcome of such work" (p. 30). Its background seems to be the curse on Adam, though Genesis 3:17 employs a different term (Heb. ʿiṣābôn) for "toil." This side of the fall, human toil is more taxing and less satisfying than the Creator meant it to be.

"Under the sun" is an ancient Semitic description of life as it is carried out in this world. In the Old Testament, only Koheleth uses it. And use it he does—twenty-nine times! Its sister-phrase—"under heaven" (lit. "under the heavens")—crops up three times (1:13; 2:3; 3:1). Both terms picture the universality of the Preacher's perspective. Though a son of Israel, he uses a wide canvas to depict human life in general. Anywhere one goes, the uncertainty, injustice, futility, and fixity of life will be evident. And so will be the finality of death. Bleeding through this theme of universality is a tinge of the note of limitation. "Under the sun" reinforces the senses of unchangeableness and inscrutability that permeate the book. God in heaven does what we cannot change and knows what we cannot fathom. Life "under the sun" and "under the heavens" is ever and always for human beings a life with virtually insufferable limits.

Taken together, the theme verses (vv. 2–3), with their sweeping conclusion and guiding question, set the tone of the book. The "vanity" or "futility" which the conclusion portrays is at root (1) our human inability to understand life's enigmatic mysteries and (2) our impotence to change the realities that need changing. These connotations of hebel come clear in the proverb whose role is to encapsulate the meaning of "vanity:"

> What is crooked cannot be made straight,
> And what is lacking cannot be numbered.
>
> Eccles. 1:15

The "profit" is the projected gain that we could enjoy were we able to grasp the baffling mysteries and bring the needed changes. Is this *"profit"* as hopeless a goal as it seems? That is the question that guides the Preacher's experiments and findings as the book unfolds.

The *"labor"* is both the mind-blowing thought that goes into our efforts to unravel life's enigmas and the backbreaking effort expended in our attempts to change the way life works. The ardor of this task is accented in (1) the repetition of the basic Hebrew root (*'ml*) as both noun and verb—*"labor"* and *"toils,"* (2) the use of *"all"* which picks up the inclusive note of verse 2, *"all is vanity"* and restates it, and (3) *"under the sun"* which tells us that the tasks of understanding and changing life are both pervasive and perturbing.

Work does not really make an ultimate difference in life. We do not fully subdue the earth, despite all our trying. We till and rake and plant and water; we build our dams, develop our lakes, reshape the contours of our land—but in the long run the earth wins the struggle. It wears us down—generation after generation—while we improve it slightly and sometimes despoil it badly.

Here the Preacher hit the opinions of his fellow wise men full in the face. For centuries they had been extolling the profits to be found in hard work. It was a key to personal success and to national stability. They taught generations of disciples with words like these:

> He who tills his land will be satisfied with bread,
>   but he who follows frivolity is devoid of
>   understanding.
>   *Prov. 12:11*

Work, not idleness, is what pays off—and work, not talk, does the same, according to the older teachers:

> In all labor there is profit,
>   but idle chatter leads only to poverty.
>   *Prov. 14:23*

Concerning any gain in toil, the Preacher queried to sharpen the issue. "In all toil there is profit," the wise men had taught. What they prized, he questioned; what they valued, he called empty. At least half of the chapters in Proverbs contain teachings on work as an indispensable endeavor on which survival of persons, families and communities depended. Yet Koheleth wondered and worried about work's value.

And we can see why. Much of our toil is monotonous routine that never really ends. You think you have all the dishes washed and from a bedroom or a bathroom there appears, as from a ghost, another dirty glass. And even when all the dishes are washed, it is only a few hours until they demand washing again. So much of our work is cyclical, and so much of it futile. We shape plans that collapse; we pinch out savings that shrink; we toil for promotions that others get; we leave our goods to governments or heirs that squander them.

Yet we have to go on working. Even the discouraged Professor, as we might call Koheleth, did not advocate giving up work and waiting for death to come. Thinking as much as he did and writing a substantial book are at least as taxing as digging ditches or harvesting grapes.

First Demonstration

The statement of the theme (vv. 2–3) is followed immediately by the first demonstration of it: a series of observations which examine some of the most highly prized attributes of life, including knowledge and pleasure, as well as some of its most painful experiences, such as death and toil (1:4–2:26). But before tackling those specifics, the Preacher takes a sweeping look at the natural world in which human life takes place (1:4–11).

4 One generation passes away, and
   another generation comes;
   But the earth abides forever.
5 The sun also rises, and the sun goes down,
   And hastens to the place where it arose.
6 The wind goes toward the south,
   And turns around to the north;
   The wind whirls about continually,
   And comes again on its circuit.
7 All the rivers run into the sea,
   Yet the sea is not full;
   To the place from which the rivers come,
   There they return again.
8 All things are full of labor;
   Man cannot express it.
   The eye is not satisfied with seeing,
   Nor the ear filled with hearing.
                              Eccles. 1:4–8

Symbols of constancy they have become—the sun, the wind, the streams. Their course is set; their path is determined; their pace is fixed. No human effort can make them different; no human surprise can be extracted from them. To catch the nuances of the poem (1:4–11) that follows the theme verses, we need to look at its context and its structure.

The *context* suggests that it is both a prologue to the Preacher's "royal experiment" that occupies the text from 1:12 to 2:26 and a poetic comment on the intimidating task of trying to find *"profit"* (1:3) in the massive human endeavors to understand life and change it where needed. As *prologue,* this poem announces the changeless nature of the creation which is immune to all efforts to interfere with its fixed cycles and relentless dependability. And it anticipates the dominant theme of God's iron-fisted control of reality and destiny summarized in the terse proverb of 1:15 and expanded in the famous poem on *time* in 3:1–8. As *comment* on 1:2–3, the poem addresses the human quest to break through the barriers of *"vanity"* and by the costly *"labor"* of mind and hand gain control of reality's helm to turn its ship toward the haven of lasting *"profit."* Its meaning is blunt and simple: you will not be able to induce significant change in the course of life because creation itself is stamped with an indelible pattern that brooks no human alterations.

The *structure* amplifies this message (see Whybray, p. 39).

Introduction: endless repetition of creation's activity	v. 4
Illustrations of repetition	vv. 5–8
sun	v. 5
wind	v. 6
sea	v. 7
Summary of this endless activity	v. 8a
Impact of illustrations on human observers	v. 8b–d
indescribable	v. 8b
incomprehensible	v. 8c–d
to eye	v. 8c
to ear	v. 8d
Conclusion: absence of any possibility of innovation	vv. 9–11
Denial of novelty	v. 9
Rejection of claims to novelty	v. 10
Failure of memory	v. 11

The introductory verse 4 is not easy to understand. *Generations* (Heb. *dôr*) usually describes a human lifetime, shared with a circle of contemporaries like that of Noah who was "perfect in his generation" (Gen. 6:9). The context in 1:4–11, however, dealing with components of nature, suggests that more than human life is in view. *Dôr*, used only here by the Preacher, may mean "cycles of activity in the whole creation" and embrace the actions of the sun, wind and sea as well as human birth, life, and death. Its close cousin *dûr* is translated "around" in Isaiah 29:3 and "ball" in Isaiah 22:18 (NIV). "Circle" seems to be the root meaning. The repeated rounds of activity, among which are the three depicted in verses 5–7 and summarized in verse 8a, leave the *"earth"* unruffled. It too is part of the stability of God's created pattern.

"Earth" can have other meanings: "land" as opposed to water (Gen. 1:10), "nation" or "national territory" ("land of Shinar," Gen. 10:10), or even "humanity as a whole" (Gen. 11:1), the option adopted by Fox (p. 171). If the approach to context and structure which I have taken is correct, however, the spotlight in verse 4 is not on the durability of the human family, as remarkable as that is, but of the planet itself, the arena affected by the specific illustrations of constancy in the verses that follow.

In grammar, vocabulary, and pronunciation, verse 4 sets the tone for verses 5–7. The verbs are participles, conveying the idea of perpetual motion: the generations keep coming and going, the earth keeps abiding (lit. "standing," v. 4), the sun keeps rising and setting (v. 5), the wind keeps blowing and circling (v. 6), the rivers keep running (v. 7). And the key words "going" (*"passes away"*) and "coming" dominate the descriptions of motion. "Coming" (*"comes"*) is the same Hebrew word (*baʾ*) which reads *"goes down"* in verse 5. "Going" (*"passes away"* in v. 4) translates the Hebrew word (*hōlēk*) that dots the rest of the passage, twice describing the movement of the winds (v. 6), and three times the flow of the rivers (v. 7). Even the repetitions of sound are used by the Preacher to tie together verses 4–8 and confirm the sense of constancy: the *ô* sound (long *ō* as in hope) is heard five times in verse 4 and fourteen times in the verses that follow.

The picture of the creation's stability is comprehensive. (1) It embraces the four essential elements of earth, sun, wind, and water. (2) It ranges to all points of the compass—the east-west orbit of the sun, the south-north circuit of the wind. (3) It catches the unending dependability (a) of the *"earth"* which abides *"forever"* (Heb. *l^e^{c}ôlām*), that is, as far ahead as anyone can imagine and beyond; (b) of the *"sun"* which sets nightly into the Western Sea (as the Hebrews called the Mediterranean) and races back under the earth to spring forth in solar glory over the eastern steppes of Bashan, Gilead, and Moab, never faltering in its course; (c) of the *"wind"* which swirls in all directions (*"south"* and *"north"* in v. 6 balance the implied east-west movement of the sun in v. 5; prevailing winds in the Holy Land were normally west winds from the Mediterranean and, periodically, the *ḥamsîn* or *sirocco* which blew hot and dry from the east), yet always returns to its starting point to begin its swirling again; and (d) of the *"rivers"* (called *wadis* by the Arabs; LXX calls them "winter streams") which dump their water into the sea and the next year have an abundant supply to do it again.

The *summary* line (v. 8a) is not easy to translate. *"Full of labor"* is probably a better reading than the usual "wearisome" (NASB, NEB, JB, NIV). The emphasis should be on the continuity of the tasks, not their fatiguing results. The Hebrew root (*yg^c*) describes chores of building cities and growing crops in Joshua 24:13 and Isaiah 62:8. Two recent commentators suggest meanings like "busy activity" (Whybray, p. 39) and "toiling along toward some goal" (Ogden, p. 32). *"All things"* is the preferred meaning of a phrase that could also mean "all words" (Fox, p. 333; Loader, p. 21). It refers to the cycles of nature depicted in the previous verses. The point of the summary is to encapsulate in one phrase the repetitive, dependable constancy of creation's changeless pattern.

The human response to it (v. 8b-d) is threefold as the parallel structure shows: a man cannot describe it in words; an eye cannot see it clearly enough to turn away satisfied; an ear cannot ever be filled to the brim with hearing about it. The mystery expressed in the *verdict of vanity* with which the Preacher began (v. 2) is reaffirmed here. The *"labor"* of trying to grasp life's meaning and change its directions (v. 3) is an unending task, beyond the reach of human comprehension. We can paraphase verse 8 like this:

> All these things toil along toward their goal,
> Our tongue cannot describe them accurately,
> Our eye cannot see them clearly,
> Our ear cannot hear them fully.

The poem (1:4–11) concludes with a strong denial (vv. 9–11) that new things happen in life—whether in creation or personal history—to break the pattern of constancy described in the preceding verses.

> 9 That which has been is what will be,
> That which is done is what will be done,
> And there is nothing new under the sun.
> 10 Is there anything of which it may be said,
> "See, this is new"?
> It has already been in ancient times before us.
> 11 There is no remembrance of former things,
> Nor will there be any remembrance of things
>   that are to come
> By those who will come after.

Eccles. 1:9–11

The denial is based on two arguments: ". . . there is nothing new under the sun" and "there is no remembrance of former things . . . " (Eccles. 1:9, 11).

Any notion of novelty is an illusion, based on limited perception (v. 10) or faulty memory (v. 11). For Koheleth to call something *"new"* in this world of ours (*"under the sun"*; see on v. 3) is to display an appalling lack of knowledge of what has gone on in the past (*"ancient times"*; lit. "the ages which were before us") and perhaps to insult the sages of bygone days who *"already"* knew about such things. Furthermore, the claim to discover something new may be an instance of faulty memory (v. 11), whether of previous events or people. The Hebrew term can mean either (RSV reads "things" with NKJV; NIV reads "men"). The sages themselves would not be remembered even though they had taught what they deemed deathless wisdom to their pupils (2:16). *"Already"* (v. 10; Heb. *kᵉbār*) is a favorite word of the Preacher. He alone uses it in the Old Testament. Often it underscores his view that no change is possible because the matter has *"already"* and unalterably been settled (2:12, 16; 3:15, 4:2, 6:10; 9:6, 7).

How sharply that opinion clashed with the words of Israel's prophets and psalmists! They looked forward to new things God has yet to do—call his people by a *new* name (Isa. 62:2), create a *new* heaven and a *new* earth (Isa. 66:22), establish a *new* covenant (Jer. 31:31), put a *new* spirit in the midst of his people (Ezek. 11:19), give them a *new* heart (Ezek. 36:26). And they urged their people to sing *new* songs as the new things happened (Pss. 33:3; 96:1; 98:1).

They also encouraged their followers to remember what God had done for them in their history past and to live in the light of those deeds. The word for "memory" (*"remembrance"*; Heb. *zikkārôn*) is used to mark memorable events in Israel's history like the memorials of the Exodus (12:14) and the entry into Canaan (Josh. 4:7). The verb that forms its root (Heb. *zākar*) is found frequently in Deuteronomy to highlight Yahweh's rescue of Israel and their consequent call to obedience (Deut. 5:15; 7:18; 8:2, etc.).

It is the mark of the depths of the spiritual crisis in Koheleth's day that the joy of such memories and the hope of God's newsmaking interventions in the lives of his people had been lost. Without these twin anchors in past and future the Preacher had to do the best he could to help the people stay on a steady course. It was part of the mission of the greater Wise Man to enact new things and call the people to magnificent memories.

Epilogue: The Greater Wise Man

What do the life and teaching of Jesus have to say about the issues raised in these introductory verses? Ecclesiastes' place in the Christian canon nudges us to ask this question.

We who work daily need to know more about the importance and value of labor than the Preacher has told us. Concern that human endeavor not be overvalued has caused him to put more emphasis on the sweat of it than on its fruit.

We who are dependent on the creation for survival and are mandated to be stewards of its resources have to gain a fuller perspective on its importance and our relationship to it. Surely Koheleth's poem that features its stability is not the whole story.

We who are heirs to the magnificent history of God's revelation and redemption want to know more about the possibilities of remembering the old days and hoping for the new things than Ecclesiastes allowed for. His outlook locked us into the present only, and life without past or future is a bed too short and a cover too narrow for us to be comfortable in. How can we move beyond the apparent futility of work? How can we find true, lasting profit in our labors?

In the deeds and words of a later, Greater Wise Man, we find our answers. Part of the gospel's good news is that our work—even though routine and tedious—need not be futile. Jesus had, as part of his mission, the purpose of taking us beyond futility to profit in our work.

Perhaps that is why he came as a carpenter (Mark 6:3). Tools he knew how to handle. Orders from customers he had to fill. Wood and iron were the stuff he worked with. His knuckles felt knicks and his fingers held blisters. The Son of God entered our human labor crew. Shoulder to shoulder he toiled with the rest of us. Doing God's will entailed doing menial work. He did it with diligence and delight.

And he linked his daily work to the work beyond work—the doing of the Father's will and the trusting of the Father's power. He urged his hearers to engage in this same spiritual work: "'Do not labor for the food which perishes, but for the food which endures to everlasting life . . . '" (John 6:27). And more positively, "'This is the work of God, that you believe in Him whom He sent'" (John 6:29).

To trust Jesus for rescue from our sins, to trust Jesus for guidance for our lives, to trust Jesus for power in our service—that is the work of God, the work beyond work, the true work in which all our work becomes profitable.

When it comes to creation, Jesus again had good news for us. His very birth in our kind of manger and our kind of flesh told us about creation—the place where God's love and care are at work. Not a frustration to our welfare but a means of our sustenance, not just evidence of life's constancy but witness to God's glory—that is creation as Jesus treated it. Spiritual stories from seed and soil (Mark 4:1–20), fatherly care of sparrows and lilies (Matt. 6:25–34), kindly transformation of water to wine at a wedding (John 2:1–12)—Jesus, the Lord of creation, was at home in what he had made. And we can be too.

But his miracles sometimes took us to the creation beyond creation: the new creation, the wonder of the coming age. As Lord of the sea, he subdued creation's turbulence (Mark 4:35–41). As Lord of disease, he healed creation's woundedness (Mark 5:21–43). As Lord of demons, he defeated creation's enemies (Mark 3:20–27). As Lord of death, he determined creation's outcome (John 11:1–44). And by his resurrection he has led his people into the realm of the new creation where God's will is fully done and God's glory clearly seen.

And what about history? Nothing new? Is history headed nowhere? Nothing worth remembering? Is history a stagnant heap of oblivion?

No is the answer which Jesus' good news shouts to those questions. History still has its surprises, and Jesus' appearance in human flesh was one of them. New covenants, new commandments, new persons, new heavens and new earth are all yet to come. Jesus entered our history to teach us to remember and hope. He pointed to a past worth recalling in his death and resurrection; he depicted a future worth anticipating in his church and his return.

The three glorious tenses of Christian living are dramatized at the communion table. There we remember the past's ultimate exodus, Christ's shed blood and broken body; there we wait for the future's ultimate innovation, Christ's victorious return; there we pledge ourselves to the present's ultimate privilege, demonstrating Christ's love to all with whom we have to do.

Futile days and futile weeks we may have, where life loses its glue and turns leaky at the seams. But a futile life will not be our lot. Christ's news is too good to let that happen. Life is filled with meaning because he is making all things new—beginning with us.

CHAPTER TWO

First Demonstration: Anguish of Wisdom

Ecclesiastes 1:12–18

I hated to dampen their sparkling spirits, but I had to help them face reality. Year after year I went through the experience. It was during the time I served as a teacher at Westmont College in Santa Barbara. Each fall I had the privilege of addressing the entering class, eager as they were to savor their new experience, zealous as they were to pursue their course of learning.

I hated to weigh down their buoyant minds, but I had to help them see what they were in for. What do you want to get out of college? I would ask them. Spiritual inspiration? Great! I am all for it, but if that is your main goal you should go to summer conferences and deeper life retreats. What do you seek in college? Fun? Good times? Friendships? Recreation? Fine, I would answer, but you would find all of them in your local country club—and for far less money. What is it you are looking for in these halls of learning? Information? Facts? Knowledge? Excellent! I heartily approved, but would you not do better to buy a comprehensive encyclopedia and memorize its data in the comfort of your own home?

I could not guarantee that the bright, bubbly men and women in the freshman class would gain spiritual inspiration, wholesome recreation, or useful information, though I hoped and prayed that their cup would be filled with these daily. What I did guarantee was something quite different, something totally unexpected. "You can be sure," I promised them, "that one thing will happen to you, if your college education really takes: your capacity for suffering will increase."

Here I had the wise Preacher on my side. He knew full well the pains inherent in the pursuit of wisdom and knowledge. He begins his task of demonstrating the futility of life as his countrymen lived it by exposing the weaknesses inherent in their quest for understanding and their claims to have garnered it.

> 12 I, the Preacher, was king over Israel in Jerusalem.
>
> 13 And I set my heart to seek and search out by wisdom concerning all that is done under heaven; this burdensome task God has given to the sons of man, by which they may be exercised.
>
> 14 I have seen all the works that are done under the sun; and indeed, all is vanity and grasping for the wind.
>
> 15 What is crooked cannot be made straight,
> And what is lacking cannot be numbered.
>
> 16 I communed with my heart, saying, "Look, I have attained greatness, and have gained more wisdom than all who were before me in Jerusalem. My heart has understood great wisdom and knowledge."
>
> 17 And I set my heart to know wisdom and to know madness and folly. I perceived that this also is grasping for the wind.
>
> 18 For in much wisdom is much grief,
> And he who increases knowledge increases sorrow.

Eccles. 1:12–18

A look at the *structure* of this paragraph will help us catch the force and movement of its content:

A.	Preacher's self-introduction	v. 12
	B. Account of his quest for understanding	v. 13
	C. Negative summary appraisal	v. 14
	D. Proverb confirming the appraisal	v. 15

A'. Preacher's self-evaluation   v. 16
 B'. Account of his quest for understanding   v. 17a
  C'. Negative summary appraisal   v. 17b
   D'. Proverb confirming the appraisal   v. 18

The balance between the two sections is obvious. The repetition of each component serves to highlight the quest, the credentials of the Preacher, and the negative results of the investigation. Each half emphasizes one specific point more than the other. The first half describes more fully the nature of the search (v. 13). The second half amplifies the Preacher's credentials, especially his achievements in garnering *"great wisdom and knowledge"* (v. 16).

As for its *context,* this passage makes quite plain what was intimated in the introductory section (vv. 2–11): our human inability either to catch the meaning of life and how it works or to change life in ways that make it more profitable. These verses look ahead as well as back, setting the stage for the search for pleasure (2:1–11) on which the "Solomonic" Preacher embarks once he comes up empty-handed in his adventure with wisdom.

With a jolt these words must have hit Koheleth's students. The contradiction between these negative summary appraisals (vv. 14, 17b) with the proverbs that supported them (vv. 15, 18) and what was normally taught about wisdom was arresting, to say the least. We do not have to leaf far in the Book of Proverbs to feel the sting of this contradiction:

> Happy is the man who finds wisdom,
>   And the man who gains understanding;
> For her proceeds are better than the profits of silver,
>   And her gain than fine gold.
> She is more precious than rubies,
>   And all the things you may desire cannot
>   compare with her.
> Length of days is in her right hand,
>   In her left hand riches and honor.
> Her ways are ways of pleasantness,
>   And all her paths are peace.
> She is a tree of life to those who take hold of her,
>   And happy are all who retain her.
>   *Prov. 3:13–18*

The dividends promised from an investment in wisdom are lavish indeed: long life, riches, honor, pleasantness, peace, happiness. No one can vote against any item in that list. It is more than we dare ask from the most generous Santa Claus in life.

What the Preacher has said in his own abrupt, almost gruff way is that there is another side to wisdom that coats it with irony. Far from producing all that happiness and prosperity, wisdom has several handicaps with which those who quest after it must reckon.

To make this point dramatically the Preacher, using the literary device of *self-description,* donned the royal robes of Solomon and put himself into the experience of the great king. "I, the Preacher, was king over Israel in Jerusalem" (1:12). A possible translation is "I am the Preacher (Koheleth); I was king. . . ." The practice of royal self-introductions is amply documented in the royal literature of Egypt and Phoenicia. In fact, the Ten Commandments begin with the same formula: "I am the Lord your God . . ." (Exod. 20:2). The Preacher assumed the role of Solomon for two reasons. First, Solomon's wisdom was celebrated. If any person had enough wisdom to assure him blessing and happiness, Solomon did. His prayer to God had been this:

> "Therefore give to Your servant an understanding heart to judge Your people, that I may discern between good and evil. For who is able to govern this great people of Yours?
>
> *1 Kings 3:9*

God's answer was a resounding yes to Solomon's request:

> "Behold, I have done according to your words; see, I have given you a wise and understanding heart, so that there has not been anyone like you before you, nor shall any like you arise after you.
>
> *1 Kings 3:12*

Koheleth's second reason for playing the part of Solomon in this passage is that the people who most needed the message were ardent disciples of Solomon. They esteemed him as the founder and patron of their whole movement. He it was whose "wisdom excelled the wisdom of all the men of the east, and all the wisdom of Egypt." He it was who "spoke three thousand proverbs" and whose "songs were one thousand and five" (1 Kings 4:30, 32).

So Koheleth began to speak as though he were Solomon to prove his case that wisdom was not the solution to all human problems, as the other, older wise men had sometimes implied: *"And I set my heart to seek and search out by wisdom concerning all that is done under heaven; . . . I have seen all the works that are done under the sun; and indeed, all is vanity and grasping for the wind"* (Eccles. 1:12–14).

Investigating the data of life was the normal task of a wise man. Habits of animals, patterns of plants, customs of tribes or families or persons—these were carefully analyzed so that general rules for human behavior could be learned and taught. Again it was Solomon who had pioneered this path by probing curiously into every area of life: "Also he spoke of trees, from the cedar tree of Lebanon even to the hyssop that springs out of the wall; he spoke also of animals, of birds, of creeping things, and of fish" (1 Kings 4:33).

As psychologists, sociologists, and anthropologists today look over the shoulders of biologists and zoologists to gain insights into human behavior, so the whole range of creation and experience was the laboratory for Koheleth and his colleagues. These fellow wise men understood the Preacher's methods of investigation.

The search combined all the necessary ingredients. It was *deliberate.* Koheleth gave it the intense focus of his mind and will, as *"set my heart"* suggests (see 1:17; 7:21; 8:9, 16; 9:1). He was not dabbling; he was desperate, committed to find out what life was like if it drained the last gram of tears, sweat, and blood from his dedicated frame. The search was also *thorough.* The verbs confirm this. *"Seek"* (Heb. *dārash*), used only here in Ecclesiastes, elsewhere describes the passion with which Judah is to pursue justice (Isa. 1:17) and, even more importantly, how Judah is to direct their full attention to God in quest of pardon and reconciliation (Isa. 55:6). *"Search out"* (Heb. *tûr*; see 2:3; 7:25 where *"wisdom"* is again the object) connotes a deep and sharply focused investigation for which words like "delve" and "probe" are fitting. The method of the quest is *appropriate—"by wisdom"* (Heb. *ḥokmâh*). This is the broadest, most comprehensive term the Hebrews had for intellectual, spiritual, and practical understanding. It can be roughly defined as the "art of success," the combination of insight gained by observing how life works, of organizing carefully all information available, of applying it prudently to personal and communal life, and of seeking to find the will and hand of God in all human circumstances.

In short, it was the best possible tool with which to explore life's meaning.

The exploration is *wide-ranging: "all that is done under heaven"* is its laboratory and its target. *"Under heaven"* (see also 2:3; 3:1) is virtually a synonym for *"under the sun"* (see on 1:3). *"All"* recalls the comprehensive expressions of futility and toil in 1:2–3. The search is *obligatory,* so the second half of verse 13 seems to suggest. The search itself is the *"grievous* (Heb. *rāʿ,* lit. "evil"; here "harsh," "dangerous," "frustrating") *task"* or "business," a word (Heb. *ʿinyān*) used only by Koheleth in the Old Testament with overtones of exertion and labor that stem from its root (Heb. *ʿānāh* which is translated *"exercised"* in this verse). Used ten times in the book, it is accompanied by the adjective *rāʿ* three times—here, in 5:14, where the phrase refers to a business *"misfortune,"* and in 4:8 where it complements *"vanity"* in a summary appraisal: *"grave misfortune."* The sense of obligation is conveyed by *"God has given"* (Heb. *nāthan*). This verb, with God as subject, is sprinkled throughout the book (2:26; 3:10, 11; 5:18, 19; 6:2; 8:15; 9:9; 12:7). Sovereign grace is its connotation most of the time, though the note of sovereignty is heard louder than the note of grace in this passage. It is the Preacher's term to express his conviction that the events in our lives are "givens" and that we do well to accept them as such from God's hand, though we may not always like what we get.

So much for the nature of the quest as detailed in verse 13. *"I have seen"* (v. 14) introduces the findings. This verb (Heb. *rāʾāh*) is used more than twenty times in the book to stress the Preacher's firsthand observations—his scientific investigations, if you will. As a trained wise man he drew his lessons from experience as well as reflection. "See" can have both meanings (in v. 16 it is translated *"understood"*). Here as frequently (see 1:16; 2:24; 3:16, etc.), *"I have seen"* introduces the Preacher's conclusion or *summary appraisal.* The thoroughness of the quest (see on v. 13) is reaffirmed in the *"all"* that links verses 2, 3, 13, and 14 and the *"under the sun"* that continues the mood of verses 3 and 13. *"Works that are done"* combines a verb and noun of the same root (Heb. *ʿāśāh*), which occurs over sixty times in the book. The terms are general and encompass a wide circle of human and natural activity. If they are to be given a more precise meaning here, the context seems to connect them with human efforts to understand life's mysteries and to change life's inequities.

It is of deeds wherever they are done and whatever their nature that Koheleth pronounces his verdict: *"all is vanity"* (see 1:2). The interpretative embellishment *"grasping for the wind"* frequently accompanies *hebel* (2:11, 17, 26; 4:4; 6:9) and likens the futile attempt to snatch meaning from life to a shepherd's (the root for "grasp" is Heb. *rā͑āh*, to feed, tend, lead sheep, the term used in Ps. 23:1) hopeless effort to corral the *"wind"* as he would herd a flock into the fold.

Not the lack of wisdom, but the presence of wisdom was what bothered Koheleth. He found what he had sought, and it proved futile. Far from being the solid rock on which a sound life could be built, wisdom was as insubstantial as a vapor, as undependable as a breeze. Reach to clutch it, and the movement of your hand blows it away. Think you have it, and it seeps between your fingers.

This dreadful conclusion about the limitations of wisdom was based on two reasons. First, *wisdom cannot change reality.* That is the meaning of the *proverb* which reinforces the conclusion of verse 14. *Counter-proverb* may be a better name for it. It is the first occurrence in the book of a literary device for which Koheleth is famous: the use of a proverbial form to teach a lesson opposite to what Israel's teachers would usually say. Their word centered in the competence and effectiveness of wisdom. Here (v. 15) the message is the impotence of wisdom when faced by the fixity of life (see on vv. 4–11).

Much of what is wrong with life is not wisdom's fault; it is just the way things are. Full of injustice, stamped by suffering, plagued by weakness, terrorized by crime, life has so much wrong about it that wisdom stands by powerless to do more than observe. Think of the massive problems that confront our huge cities: treasuries on the edge of bankruptcy, numbers of the homeless growing to alarming levels, education perplexed about its directions, crime rates soaring to vulture heights. Wisdom is much better able to analyze the trends than it is to prescribe the solutions. Our wise man must have had this in mind when he wrote these puzzling words:

> What is crooked cannot be made straight,
> and what is lacking cannot be numbered.
>
> *Eccles. 1:15*

Wisdom may finger the problem but it cannot straighten out what is crooked nor count what is simply not there. Wisdom cannot change reality. This depressing idea is repeated later in the book and reminds us that its message is one of the Preacher's major themes:

> Consider the work of God;
> For who can make straight what He has made
> crooked.
>
> *Eccles. 7:13*

"*Made straight*" translates a root (Heb. *tāqan*) that describes the orderly way that the Sage arranged the proverbial sayings that were the curriculum of his teaching (12:9). Later Jewish scribes used the word for the handful of corrections they made in the biblical texts to soften language they deemed irreverent. "*Crooked*" crops up again in the funeral description which closes the book (12:3), where a slightly different form of the verb is read "*bow down*" in the picture of a grief-laden gesture of mourning. This physical use of the root (Heb. *ʿāwat*) adds to the note of permanence in the proverb.

The *self-description* (v. 16) with which the second half of the paragraph begins is designed to heighten the picture of wisdom's grievous limitations, when pitted against the profound riddles and obstinate realities of life.

> 16 I communed with my heart, saying, "Look, I
> have attained greatness, and have gained more
> wisdom than all who were before me in Jerusalem.
> My heart has understood great wisdom and knowl-
> edge."
>
> *Eccles. 1:16*

The Preacher ponders—"*communed with my heart*" means "talked to myself" (2:15)—the problem as though he were Solomon himself and comes to the conclusion that the answer to his perplexity is not more wisdom. In "*wisdom*" (see on 1:13) his degree came *summa cum laude*. "*Greatness*" speaks of both the fact and the reputation (see also 2:4, 9). This is not deluded self-aggrandizement but publicly acknowledged achievement. "*All in Jerusalem before me*" is a stage-prop for the Solomonic guise. Taking it literally is awkward, given the fact that of the Israelite kings only David ruled there before Solomon and did not capture Jerusalem until the eighth year of his reign (2 Sam. 5:1–10). "*Knowledge*" (Heb. *daʿat*) is coupled with "*wisdom*" to make the picture of discernment and learnedness as inclusive as possible. In wisdom literature the two are often linked (1:18; 2:21, 26; 7:12; 9:10; 12:9; see also Prov. 1:2–7). The tie between *"wisdom," "knowledge,"* and the *"fear of the Lord"* suggests that *"knowledge"* is more than mere information but centers in the comprehension of God's will and ways and includes elements of obedience, akin to those stressed by prophets such as Hosea (4:1, 6; 6:3, 6; for prophetic use of wisdom notions and language, see Hos. 14:9). *"Heart"* points to the combined use of mind and will in the quest for knowledge. Biblical Hebrew has no specific words for mind or brain. Thinking and understanding and deciding are all done by the *"heart."*

Verse 17a rehearses in briefest terms the *account of the quest* detailed more fully in verse 13. The new ingredient is *"madness and folly"* a common pair in Koheleth (2:12; 7:25; 10:13). Though each term may be used separately—*"folly"* (Heb. *siklûth* or *siklûth*, the usual spelling, 2:13; 10:1), *"madness"* (9:3)—the two together indicate that to be foolish is not just to lack knowledge or to have a low I.Q.; it is to behave badly, wildly, out of phase with the patterns that make for responsible conduct and positive contributions to society. "Crazy fool" is Koheleth's label for those who so behave. Taken together, *"wisdom"* (see 1:13) and *"madness and folly"* constitute the whole range of learning about human behavior. Koheleth's pursuit of life's meaning left no viewpoint unexplored. Not only did he examine the extremes listed in verse 16 but every option in between. Stating the poles is a graphic way of embracing the whole catalog of possibilities from cover to cover. *Merism* is the name of this literary device. We shall meet it again in the poem about *time* in 3:1–8.

As thorough as the search had been, its results, restated briefly in the summary appraisal, are flatly negative:

> 17 I perceived that this also is a grasping for the wind.
>
> *Eccles. 1:17b*

"Perceived" is literally "I knew" or "came to know," the same root as that of *"knowledge"* in verse 16. It often conveys understanding gained from personal experience and is parallel here to the *"I have seen"* of the first summary appraisal in the paragraph (1:14). *"Grasping for the wind"* is a slightly different Hebrew form of the phrase

used in verse 14. No difference in meaning is discernible. This alternate form (Heb. *ra'yôn rû'h*) occurs at 2:22 and 4:16.

Wisdom cannot change reality. That was its first drawback discovered by the Preacher. But wisdom can increase sorrow. That was Koheleth's second reason for doubting the value which the older wise man had credited to wisdom. With life as crooked and as lacking as it is, wisdom only calls attention to the sour notes; it cannot bring the singing into tune. If the choir cannot carry their parts, if the rhythm and the pitch are faulty, if the words are pronounced sloppily, it is better for the people listening not to be trained musicians. If they are, they will agree with the Preacher's second *counter-proverb* (see v. 15):

> 18 For in much wisdom is much grief,
> And he who increases knowledge increases
> sorrow.
> > *Eccles. 1:18*

The wiser they are in things musical, the more a bad performance will pain them. The more they learn about life's tragedies, the greater will be their anguish. This is what I tried to put across to those fledging students eager to flex their wings in college. Wisdom and knowledge in themselves will not satisfy. By exposing life's sorry sides, they may actually increase our pain. Both the process of acquiring wisdom—the combination of midnight oil, grueling sweat, and smarting scars—and the results of wisdom bring *"grief"* (or "vexation" as *ka'as* may be rendered; see 2:23; 7:3, 9; 11:10). "Ignorance is bliss" is not an altogether facetious line of wisdom. *"Sorrow"* (Heb. *mak'ab*; 2:23) speaks of stinging, pounding pain. Its root (*kā'ab*) describes the excruciating aftereffects of adult circumcision (Gen. 34:25), while the noun expresses the terrible agonies of Jerusalem's destruction in Lamentations 1:12, 18.

My teacher and predecessor as president of Fuller, Edward John Carnell, illustrated the pathos of this proverb with a story of a philosopher whose life in the 1930s was made desperate by the Great Depression. Out of a job because his college could not meet its payroll, the professor went to the railway yard on a moonless night and clambered into an open boxcar. Fatigued from exertion and anxiety, he settled on his bedroll and went to sleep. When he awoke he became conscious of the sounds, smells, and touches of a flock of sheep that had been herded into the dark cavern while he lay sleeping. The swaying of the boxcar and the rhythmic clatter of steel wheels on steel tracks told him that the train was moving at full tilt. Immediately the terrifying thought struck him: Omaha was the next stop. Ahead lay the unloading of the sheep one by one beneath a low door, the sharp smack of the club that rendered the sheep unconscious and the trip to the slaughter house. What would happen to him as each step in the ritual unfolded? The sheep had a rather comfortable ride to Omaha, protected by their ignorance of destination and purpose. The philosopher knew more, and he died a thousand deaths along the route:

> For in much wisdom is much grief,
> And he (or she) who increases knowledge increases
> sorrow.

As doubtful as the Preacher was about attaching too much importance to wisdom, he did not suggest that it was better to be ignorant or foolish (2:13–14). In fact, he used keen wisdom to show us what wisdom could not do. He proved how much he valued wisdom while he demonstrated the limits to its value. He pointed out its substance by the wisdom he used to argue for its futility.

And he did us a service. It is easy for us to confuse a wise man with a smart aleck. They are not the same. But he did not take us far enough. It remained for another Wise Man—a Wise Man who was not only a wise preacher but a wise Savior—to take us beyond the fringes of wisdom to its solid core.

Epilogue: The Greater Wise Man

More wisdom than Solomon knew was found in Jesus the Christ: for the Queen of Sheba "came from the ends of the earth to hear the wisdom of Solomon; and indeed a greater than Solomon is here" (Matt. 12:42). Through his wisdom we move beyond futility to a true wisdom, a wisdom from above (James 3:17).

Wisdom can change reality—that was part of the startling news that Jesus brought to light. Wisdom as Jesus revealed it was not the product of deep study, but of strong commitment. It was not written on a scroll, but emblazoned on a cross.

The cross, with its power of forgiveness; the cross, with its wisdom of love can make the crooked things of life straight and can add to life what it lacks. What the best of human wisdom could not do, Jesus Christ—the power and wisdom of God—has done (1 Cor. 1:18–25). He has settled our debt to God; he has charted our direction in life; he has sorted out our confused values; he has freed our enslaved spirits.

Reality has been changed. Only God was wise enough to change it. True wisdom was not only Jesus' instruction about right and wrong, but Jesus' commitment—a commitment to death—to make us right where we were wrong. The change in our reality has brought a change in our welfare. Hear these assuring words: "He [that is, God] is the source of your life in Christ Jesus, whom God made our wisdom, our righteousness and sanctification and redemption" (1 Cor. 1:30 RSV). These are the words that make for happiness—not the long life, honor, wealth, peace, and blessing the older wisdom offered.

These words—righteousness, sanctification, redemption—ring with the notes of relationship. They tell us that God has brought us out of our slavery into his family; he has cleansed us of our pollution and made us fit for his fellowship. We have come to terms with God because of Christ's commitment to us. That is the meaning of happiness; that is the path of wisdom.

CHAPTER THREE

First Demonstration:
Frustrations of Pleasure

Ecclesiastes 2:1–11

A day at the county fair—I suppose that was the dream of all of us as youngsters. With pulses racing, voices rising, and eyes darting, we would push our way through the crowds to our favorite booths. What an array of them to choose from! And what a wealth of wonders those stalls sheltered! Snow cones, caramel apples, chocolate fudge, homemade ice cream, cotton candy, deep dish apple pie, long ropes of licorice—these were only a sampling of the delights that beckoned for our attention and bargained for our pennies.

That was just the beginning. The county fair was much more than a massive sweet shop. It was also a vast marketplace of homemade goods. From handknit sweaters to patch quilts, from home-canned peaches to farm-churned butter, from carved wood figurines to kiln-baked candlesticks, the labors of a thousand hands were on display.

And so was the produce of the fields. From the pens and sheds behind the booths there sounded the chorus of the livestock. Mooing cows, braying donkeys, neighing horses and bleating sheep all blended in a barnyard cantata. But it was not for their music that the animals were on display. It was the richness of the milk, the thickness of the wool, the squareness of the shoulders, the soundness of the legs that the judges inspected. White, red, and, especially, blue ribbons were the praise the farmers waited for.

At night the air was filled with entertainment—the rhythm of the square dance, the circling lights of the Ferris wheel, the crack of the target rifles, and especially the blazing, dazzling radiance of the fireworks. It was an evening worth staying up late for.

A cafeteria of pleasure, an emporium of entertainment the county fair was—and still is in some towns. It offers in the confines of one place and in the span of a few days a summary of our human delight in food, play, competition, and achievement. For small boys and girls of all ages it was the highlight of the year.

The wise Professor would have enjoyed the county fair. He would have understood the intrigue with which a fair can put its noose around our hearts and bind us to its attractions.

Pleasure was part of the agenda he set for himself; it was a key course in his curriculum to understand life. After he tested wisdom and found out that its contribution was limited because it had the power to increase human suffering but not the power to change reality, he turned next to pleasure to see what depths of meaning he could find in it. Again he put himself in Solomon's place, mindful that no one else in Israel's long history had greater power, wealth, and leisure to give the search for pleasure its full play.

THE LURE OF PLEASURE

Speaking for Solomon, the Preacher described his search, as his "royal experiment" continues:

2:1 I said in my heart, "Come now, I will test you with mirth; therefore enjoy pleasure."

Eccles. 2:1a–b

The quest for wisdom's worth (1:12–18) was external: the search ranged far and wide and examined everything in its purview from how wisdom works to the foibles and dangers of mad folly (1:17). The test of pleasures was internal: the Preacher, as earlier (1:16), was talking to himself (*"my heart,"* 2:1). The imperatives *"come now"* and *"enjoy pleasure"* (lit. "gaze at or reflect upon what is good") are addressed to *"my heart,"* which is also the *"you,"* the object of *"I will test."* *"Test"* (Heb. *nāsāh*; see 7:23) occurs in a number of familiar contexts: Yahweh's test of Abraham in his willingness to offer Isaac (Gen 22:1); Ahaz's refusal to show his faith in Yahweh by testing him for victory over the northern coalition of Ephraim and Syria (Isa. 7:12); Daniel's test of his loyalty and that of his comrades in

Nebuchadnezzar's court (Dan. 1:12, 14). The point of the test is to find out whether pleasure is as good as it is cracked up to be, and especially to answer the question, will I find more satisfaction in pleasure than in wisdom? Do *"mirth"* (lit. "joy"; Heb. *śimḥāh* a theme word of Koheleth, used about seventeen times altogether in verbal, adjectival, and nominal forms: 2:1, 2, 10, 26; 5:20; 7:4; 8:15; 9:7 are the occurrences of the noun) and *"pleasure"* (lit. "good"; Heb. *ṭôb;* see 2:3, 26; 12:14 for representative uses; frequently the word means "better" in a comparative proverb; see on 4:3, 6, 9, 13) provide a positive answer to the *guiding question* (1:3) about profit from all our efforts? The lengthy, varied list of activities that served as components of the "test" (vv. 3–11) shows what broad and encompassing terms *"mirth"* and *"pleasure"* are in this passage.

Only after he had announced the futile results of his pilgrimage did he take time to rehearse its stages.

> 1 ... but surely, this also was vanity.
> 2 I said of laughter—"madness!"; and of mirth,
> "What does it accomplish?"
>
> *Eccles. 2:1c-2*

The negative verdict (vv. 1c-2) comes in two parts. The first is general, repeating the note of *"vanity,"* futility, or mystery (see on 1:2, 14). The second part is specific, directed pointedly at the components of the test: *"mirth"* (Heb. *śimḥāh*) and its synonym *"laughter"* (Heb. *śᵉḥôq,* 7:3; 10:19). The latter he dismisses with a sarcastic label: *"madness,"* out-of-control conduct marked by mindless babbling; the Hebrew word is close kin to the noun in 1:17. The former he banishes with the rhetorical *"what does it accomplish?"* to which his assumed obvious answer is "nothing"!

We must not let the bluntness of his conclusion—pleasure is empty—blind us to the lure of pleasure. You can be sure that the wise man enjoyed himself a good bit while working toward his negative conclusion.

After all, part of pleasure's lure is that it offers to _heighten our senses._ We are created to enjoy a tender touch, a tasty morsel, a tangy beverage, a graceful figure, a delicate perfume. From the standpoint of our senses, we might conclude that pleasure is what we were made for. The Preacher sought to test that view of life by abandoning himself to pleasure. He gave his senses every chance to thrill and tingle, to stir and soothe. Would he uncover life's full purpose by arousing his sensitivities? He thought it worth a try:

> 3 I searched in my heart how to gratify my flesh with wine, while guiding my heart with wisdom, and how to lay hold on folly, till I might see what was good for the sons of men to do under heaven all the days of their lives.
>
> *Eccles. 2:3*

The wise man's very language suggested how difficult the human quest for meaning is. The *good* (v. 1) in life—what is really worth going after—was not at all apparent. Therefore, the Preacher had to "search" diligently (see on 1:13 for the force of the verb *"searched"*). Furthermore, there are severe limitations placed on our humanity (*"sons of men"* surely includes both genders): it is lived *"under heaven"* (see *"under the sun,"* 1:3; also 1:13), subject to the terms laid down by God; and one of those terms is that life lasts only a few days (lit. "the number of the days of their lives"; see 5:38; 6:12 where *brevity* also seems to be the point).

These factors, then, compounded the problem. The existence of good was questionable. There was only an earthly environment in which to seek it. And the time for seeking was short. No wonder that the Teacher plunged into the search with full vigor!

Like an eager boy at the county fair, pockets bulging with six months' allowances, he roamed from booth to booth tasting the goodies designed to heighten the senses. Again he was willing to dabble with *"folly"* (see on 1:17) so as not to rob himself of any potential pleasure. At the same time his mind (*"heart"*) was *"guiding"* as would a shepherd a flock (Heb. *nāhag*, Exod. 3:1). With *"wine"* he cheered (the Heb. verb *māshak* usually means to "draw out" or "continue"; here the idea must be to "refresh" or "stimulate," though the precise connection to the root meanings is hard to catch) his body (as *"flesh"* here indicates) while dulling his feelings of anguish or despair (2:3).

Pleasure has another lure: it offers to *lift us above the routine.* So much of our living seems bound to the ordinary. It is hobbled by the patterns we learned in childhood; it is grooved by the habits we de-

71

veloped as teenagers; it is fettered by the cords of conformity our culture puts upon us and kept on a narrow track by the duties of our daily jobs. Often we long to kick over the traces and bolt off on our own free course.

Pleasure lets us do that. Temporarily we can hang our inhibitions in the hallway and go to the party without them.

And not all pleasure is sheerly sensuous. The Preacher spoke of pleasure in his accomplishments. Extraordinary achievements provide delight as they lift us above the routine:

> 4 I made my works great; I built myself houses,
> and planted myself vineyards.
> 5 I made myself gardens and orchards, and I
> planted all kinds of fruit trees in them.
> 6 I made myself water pools from which to
> water the growing trees of the grove.
>
> *Eccles. 2:4–6*

Useful, attractive, productive works these were, and satisfying. They began with a dream, took seed with a plan, started to bud as the building and planting began, and came to full flower in the grandeur of a palace and the verdure of a garden.

The account of Solomon's achievements in 1 Kings puts more emphasis on the Temple (chapters 5, 6, 8) than on his own house. Yet there is ample evidence that he indulged himself as well in the splendor of his own palace, which took thirteen years to build (1 Kings 7:1), almost twice as long as the Temple (1 Kings 6:38). The inventory of his building enterprises is impressive, and its extravagance probably contributed to the ultimate breakaway of the Northern tribes under Jeroboam (1 Kings 12). Listed in 1 Kings 7 among the edifices whose construction he sponsored were these: (a) his own house (v. 1), (b) the house of the forest of Lebanon (v. 2), (c) the hall of pillars (v. 6) and, the hall of judgment (v. 7), (d) two other courts—one for him and one for his Egyptian wife, Pharaoh's daughter (v. 8), (e) fortifications around Jerusalem, Hazor, Megiddo, and Gezer (9:15), (f) whole cities like Gezer, Lower Beth Horon, Baalath, Tadmor (9:17–18), and (g) storage cities or encampment for chariots and cavalry (9:19).

A hallmark of royalty from time immemorial has been the planting of *"gardens"* (Song of Sol. 4:12; 5:1; 6:2, 11), *"vineyards"* (Song of Sol. 8:11), *"orchards"* (Heb. *pardēsîm* is borrowed from a Persian word which is also the source of "paradise"), and ornamental groves. *"All kinds of fruit trees"* echoes the fertility of Eden without the forbidden fruit (Gen. 1:11, 29).

In a land that had neither major rivers, such as the Nile or Tigris, nor adequate annual rainfall, the leaders had to exercise ingenuity in building aqueducts and reservoirs (v. 6). The Bible notes such enterprises in Hezekiah's day (2 Kings 18:17), as well as Nehemiah's (2:14). Zeal in husbandry is the theme of a story preserved by the great Roman statesman and orator, Cicero. It describes an encounter between Cyrus II, a Persian prince, son of Darius II, and Lysander, a distinguished general from Sparta. When Lysander visited Cyrus about 408 B.C., the Persian showed him a well-ordered grove of stately trees and noted that he himself had planned and planted it. Lysander cast an eye on Cyrus' robe adorned with gold and jewels, then looked around at the splendid park. His remarks, as transmitted by Cicero, were these: "With good reason, Cyrus, men call you happy, since in you good fortune (the bejeweled robe) has been joined with virtue (the will and wisdom to plant well)."[1] From long before Nebuchadnezzar's hanging gardens to the latest blossoming of the White House cherry trees, heads of state have been delighted to be known as patrons of horticulture.

Solomon, as Koheleth represents him, devoured voraciously all these delights and many others:

> 7 I acquired male and female servants, and had servants born in my house. Yes, I had greater possessions of herds and flocks than all who were in Jerusalem before me.
>
> 8 I also gathered for myself silver and gold and the special treasures of kings and of the provinces. I acquired male and female singers, the delights of the sons of men, and musical instruments of all kinds.
>
> 9 So I became great and excelled more than all who were before me in Jerusalem. Also my wisdom remained with me.
>
> 10 Whatever my eyes desired I did not keep from them.
>
>> I did not withhold my heart from any pleasure,
>> For my heart rejoiced in all my labor;
>> And this was my reward from all my labor.
>>   *Eccles. 2:7–10*

The test of pleasure moves beyond its occupation with construction and horticulture (vv. 4–6) to personal wealth and sensual pleasures (vv. 7–8). *"Acquired"* here means "purchased," though slaves were sometimes collected as trophies of war. Israelites were not normally allowed to be held permanently as slaves (Deut. 15:12–18), though there were shocking violations of this prohibition (Amos 2:6; 8:6; Jer. 34). *"Servants born in my house"* are the children of the slaves in whom the owners took special delight and toward whom they exercised special responsibility as prized possessions (note Abram's relation to Eliezer, Gen. 15:1–4).

The *"herds"*—large animals like cattle and oxen—and *"flocks"*—small animals like sheep and goats—were additional signs of luxury, given the fact that commoners subsisted on grains, fruits, and vegetables and ate very little meat. They saved their animals for work, milk, and wool. The list of Solomon's daily provisions shows why he had to maintain such an enormous drove of livestock (1 Kings 4:22–23). The picture of unparalleled possessions is reminiscent of Job's wealth (1:3). On *"all who were in Jerusalem before me,"* see 1:16. There, here and again in 2:9, its force is superlative (see 1 Kings 10:23, for a similar hyperbole). It means "unparalleled" and highlights the thoroughness and validity of the royal tests—whether of wisdom or pleasure.

The account of material wealth (v. 8) is a brief summary of Solomon's annual take (1 Kings 10:14–17). Koheleth lists *"silver"* along with *"gold,"* while the record in Kings discounts the value of *"silver"* (1 Kings 10:21). The relative value of silver and gold seemed to vary throughout Israel's history. In the earlier periods silver was worth more because its sources in Persia and Asia Minor were less accessible than the gold mines of southern Arabia and East Africa (Gen. 13:2; 24:35). This may account for the fact that silver is usually mentioned first, when the two metals are listed side by side.

"Special treasures" is an inclusive term for wealth of any kind, including probably ivory, jewels, perfumes, spices, rare textiles, along with the precious metals mentioned. All of these were used as gifts to royalty or tribute paid by the officials of one nation to those of another from whom they sought favors. Such courting of the king's good graces seems to lie behind *"kings"* and *"provinces"* (v. 8), though the grammar here is a bit awkward. Some interpreters read *"provinces"* as "prefects" in the light of a proposed meaning in Ugaritic.

The lavish wealth purchased substantial side benefits which Koheleth enumerates as he draws the list of specifics to a close. The *"singers"* were used for banquets and parties within the court. *"Delights,"* in keeping with its use in Song of Solomon 7:6, must have an erotic meaning—"sexual pleasures" that men (the sexual context encourages a masculine meaning to *"sons of men"*) enjoy. The term (Heb. *ta$^{c a}$nugôt*) has a more general meaning like "pleasant," "comfortable," or "cozy" when applied to the homes of evicted women in Micah 2:9. *"Musical instruments"* is a translator's guess, an attempt to tie the puzzling Hebrew words *shiddāh* and *shiddôt* to the clearer mention of "singers" both *"male"* and *"female."* Most recent translators connect the Hebrew root with the word for breast (Heb. *shōd*; Job 24:9; Isa. 60:16; 66:11) or with an Akkadian word for "woman" and read it as an expansion of the sexual *"delights"*: "harem" (NIV), "concubines" (RSV, NASB), a translation that accords with the Solomonic inventory of love partners—seven hundred wives, three hundred concubines (1 Kings 11:3).

If verses 3–8 describe the specific steps in the Teacher's pleasure test, verses 9–11 summarize its results. Its *positive* effects are sketched in verses 9–10. They raise for us a question about the delight of high accomplishment. Few societies have driven themselves harder to achieve than has America's. Who are the men and women we admire? The pace setters and the record breakers. Our list of heroes begins with persons who started with nothing and amassed great fortunes, who overcame hardship to rise to prominence, who shook off obscurity and rocketed to fame. Vicariously we savor their accomplishments to the last morsel. The pleasure of those who succeed helps to feed those who watch.

Who of us would not like to write a description of our achievements like the Preacher's in verse 9? It reaches back to 1:16 and restates the highpoints of that evaluation: his greatness and excellence (the same Heb. roots *gādal* and *yāsaph* are used both places), his "wisdom," which was not only abundant (1:16) but abiding (*"remained,"* the same Heb. word which describes the stability of the earth in 1:4), his superiority to his predecessors.

And who of us would not privately, if not publicly, gloat over the privileges described in verse 10? *"Eyes"* and "mind" (*"heart"*) were set free to make their choices with no one saying, "don't!" "wait!" or "not that!" *"Pleasure,"* also translated *"mirth"* (2:1), is the blank check whose limits and joys the Preacher set out to test in 2:1. The task itself was brimful of joy. *"Labor"* looks back to 1:3 and speaks not only of all the ardor involved in the undertakings but also of the quest for profit itself, as verse 11 will make clear.

"Reward" (Heb. *hēleq*; see 2:21; 3:22; 5:18, 19; 9:6, 9; 11:2) is one of Koheleth's theme words and is variously translated "heritage," "share," "portion," "serving." It connotes the "part" or "lot" which is given to a person to make the best of. Its root meaning is to divide, as an inheritance is divided among several children—hence "heritage" or "legacy": Yahweh is the heritage of Aaron's sons, who are given no permanent share of the land (Num. 18:20), and, in turn, the people are Yahweh's legacy (Deut. 32:9). The "portions" into which the land is divided in Joshua's day are another use of the term (Josh. 18:5, 6, 9). The idea is that we have a fixed lot or portion in life and ought to be content with it and not ask for more. Frequently in Koheleth the hand of God is seen as a source of the dividing. "I found pleasure in my search for pleasure" is the Preacher's initial verdict. He has demonstrated well the lure of pleasure. But he is not yet finished with his summation.

THE SNARE OF PLEASURE

Despite the high excitement and the quiet satisfaction which the pursuit of pleasure gave "Solomon" (Eccles. 2:10), the wise man, after "facing up" to the issues and results (*"looked on,"* v. 11, is lit. "turned to face"), branded the whole quest as futile. That is to say, the ultimate meaning in life, the highest good to which we should give ourselves, is not pleasure. Koheleth's last words on the subject were essentially the same as the first—except that they were even more doubtful about the values of what so many people lived for:

> 11 Then I looked on all the works that my hands
>   had done
> And on the labor in which I had toiled;
> And indeed all was vanity and a grasping for
>   the wind.
> There was no profit under the sun.
>
> *Eccles. 2:11*

"My heart found pleasure in all my toil," the Preacher admitted, yet *"all was vanity."* He knew the lure of pleasure, and he knew its

snare. He had found that *pleasure promises more than it can produce.* Its ←
advertising agency is better than its manufacturing department. It
holds out the possibility of exquisite delight, but the best it can perform is titillation. It seeks to tickle the human spirit but cannot probe
its depths. It daubs iodine on human wounds when what is needed is
surgery. It may distract us from our problems by diverting our attention, but it cannot free us from those problems.

This *negative* verdict (v. 11) supersedes the positive one (vv. 9–10)
and encapsulates most of what has already been noted in the theme
verses (1:2–3) and the two previous summary appraisals (1:14, 17c).
The search for meaning was laden with toil (*"labor,"* 1:3). Its results,
once held up to the light of full-faced consideration, were that the all-
encompassing mystery of life's meaning (*"vanity,"* 1:2, 14) was still
impenetrable, as elusive to human means of investigation as trying to
ride herd (*"grasping,"* 1:14, 17a) on the wind, and that any measurable
and lasting positive results (*"profit,"* 1:3) in our hide-bound world
(*"under the sun,"* 1:3) were a lost cause. The verbal links between 2:11
and 1:2–3 serve to bracket this section (1:2–2:11) and prepare for the
next variation on the theme in 2:12–26.

Living for pleasure has another snare. *Pleasure satisfies only during* ←
the act. Repetition is the key to pleasure. One drink, one sexual fling,
one contest won, one project accomplished, one wild party—none of
these, nor all of them put together, can be enough to bring satisfaction. The quest for pleasure is like eating salted peanuts; it is
impossible to stop after the first bite. One bite leads to another because the first leaves no lasting impact. To reflect on the delights of
the first peanut is far less gratifying than to reach for the second. Far
from comforting us, each act of pleasure leaves us thirsty for the next.
One of the wealthy celebrities of our generation has acknowledged
this: "My attention span is short, and probably my least favorite
thing to do is to maintain the status quo. Instead of being content
when everything is going fine, I start getting impatient and irritable.
For me the important thing is the getting, not the having."[2]

One other snare needs mentioning. *The pursuit of pleasure results
in either boredom or frustration.* Put simply, if we gain the pleasure we seek, we soon become tired of it. If we do not gain it, we are
filled with disappointment. Those who give themselves to pleasure are often bored; those who wish they could and cannot are often
bitter.

When pleasure's snares are examined we can see why the Preacher reached his negative conclusion. If you are looking for a foundation on which to build your life, do not count on pleasure. It does not have the permanence to sustain you. One or two days a year are all we can take even of something as beckoning as the county fair. What a hollow and futile life it would be to be locked within its gates permanently! The booths, contests, and amusements that seem so enticing on rare occasions would cloy and nauseate us as a steady diet.

Epilogue: The Greater Wise Man

It was a good warning that the Preacher gave us: even the richest, wisest, most accomplished of us will end up in futility if pleasure is our aim. To move beyond futility we must go another route.

It was Jesus—the greater than Solomon—who showed us the way, and it is a way that stands in sharp contrast to the Preacher's path of pleasure.

Pleasure there will be, Jesus promised, but it is not found by those who make seeking it their chief aim. True happiness will not come *apart from sharing Christ's suffering.* Who are the happy and blessed ones? Jesus' answer was plain: those who are poor in spirit, who mourn, who are hungry and thirsty for righteousness, who are persecuted for Christ's sake as they take up their cross and follow him (Matt. 5:1–12).

And the true joy that Jesus promised will not be found *apart from serving Christ's purposes.* Not food, not drink, nor raiment are our ultimate concern. "For after all these things the Gentiles seek. For your heavenly Father knows that you need all these things. But seek first the kingdom of God and His righteousness, and all these things shall be added to you" (Matt. 6:32–33). To do God's work was why Christ came. There is no path beyond futility that does not merge with Christ's own way.

And most important, the true pleasure that Jesus promised will not be ours *apart from loving Christ's person.* When it comes down to it, what gives us fullest pleasure is not recreation, entertainment, or accomplishment. It is fellowship. It is the intimate sharing of time, thoughts, experiences, and feelings with those for whom we care. Dutiful slaves and graceful dancing girls, charming gardens and lavish buildings, rich food and challenging games—all of these are no competition for the sheer delight of time spent with One we love.

Beyond futility—to pleasure? Only when we can give the right answer to the question that Jesus posed to Peter: ". . . do you love Me more than these?" (John 21:15). To give the wrong answer is to be as foolish as a grown man who lingers over cotton candy at the county fair when his wife is waiting at home with the promise of intimate and satisfying love.

NOTES

[1] Vernon K. Roberts, ed. *Ancient Quotes and Anecdotes* (Sonoma, Calif. Polebridge Press, 1989), pp. 199–200.)

[2] Donald Trump, *Trump: Surviving at the Top* (New York: Random House, 1990).

CHAPTER FOUR

First Demonstration: Lack of Permanence

Ecclesiastes 2:12–26

They were a wonder of the ancient world, and forty-five centuries after their building we sons and daughters of a modern era still gaze at them in awe. The pyramids of Egypt, especially those at Giza, just outside of Cairo, are massive monuments to ancient technology. They demonstrate what can happen when a great civilization bends its back to achieve its purposes.

The Great Pyramid of the Pharaoh Khufu is staggering in size. Nearly five hundred feet tall, it contains some 2.3 million blocks of stone, each of which weighs at least two tons. Many comparisons have been used to try to convey an accurate impression of its vastness. One scholar has suggested that within its base there would be room for the great Italian cathedrals of Florence, Milan, and St. Peter's in the Vatican, as well as St. Paul's Cathedral and Westminster Abbey in London. One of the most striking comparisons comes from Napoleon's time. While some of his generals climbed to the top of the Great Pyramid, the Emperor waited below calculating the mass of stone in the three pyramids that jut up from the Giza plateau. When his generals descended, Napoleon is said to have greeted them with this startling announcement: If all the stone in the three pyramids could be exported to France it would serve to build a wall ten feet high and one foot thick around the entire realm of France.

Why these massive pyramids? What purpose did they serve the pharaohs who used thousands of workmen and decades of time in their building? Their aims were not just architectural. They had one chief goal in view as they emptied their coffers of gold, quarried their reserves of stone, preempted the skills of their engineers, and lashed at the backs of their laborers—they, the noble pharaohs of the Old Kingdom, were *desperate to deal with death.*

Memorials the pyramids were, massive tributes to the memories of departed monarchs. As memorials they served well. Still dominating the Nile to the east and the desert to the west, they remind all who see them of the awesome majesty of Egypt's bygone emperors. Memorials are one way of dealing with death. Large and lasting monuments confront later generations with the heroes of the past. We Americans have done just that with the beautiful stone tributes to the legacies of our presidents like Washington, Jefferson, Lincoln, and Kennedy.

But Egypt's pharaohs had more in mind than memorials as they sought to deal with death. Here several things must be noted: first, the shape of the pyramid was probably patterned after the impression one gains in looking at the rays of the sun fan out from their single source as they shine on the earth; second, the pharaohs of Egypt considered themselves as incarnations of the sun-god Ra; third, the ancient Egyptians believed that the dead had to be transported to the other world by some vehicle or conveyance (often a boat). When these points are put together, it seems reasonable to conclude that the chief purpose of the pyramid was to serve as a ladder, or better, a staircase, to enable the departed king to make the steep ascent to his heavenly home. The pyramid, shaped like the falling rays of the sun, became the means by which the king returned to the sun, whence he had come to earth to rule among the men and women of Upper and Lower Egypt.

A desperate attempt to cope with death the pyramids were. Some kings spent most of their reign to prepare for its end.

Their giant tombs, then, are symbols of the transitory nature of their lives. Whatever we accomplish, whatever our station, however long we live—the end is the same, death. Its certainty is a constant reminder to commoner and king alike of our impermanence. The Preacher would have understood the pyramids and the kings who conceived them, because he too carried on all his labors in the shadow of death.

In fact, one of the compelling evidences in his argument about the futility of the things people depend on is the certainty of death. We use our wisdom and our resources to build sand castles that we deem attractive, and death like a giant bully stalks life's beaches and with a poke here and a kick there destroys the works of a lifetime.

The Preacher, playing the role of Solomon, continued his testing of the claims of the various candidates who were saying, "Vote for me, and I will show you life's meaning." *Wisdom's* credentials had been examined and found deficient, because wisdom cannot change reality; it can only seek to understand it; and, in understanding how bad reality can be, wisdom serves to increase our suffering (1:12–18). *Pleasure's* platform was also inadequate, despite the lavish campaign promises (2:1–11). Pleasure leads to frustration or boredom, because it provides satisfaction only during the moment that pleasure is being enjoyed and not beyond it. If we taste pleasure, we are soon bored; if we do not, we are often frustrated.

Next, then, the Preacher embarked on this final step in his First Demonstration of life's insoluble enigmas (1:4–2:26). He had Solomon explore the relationship of wisdom and folly to see whether one is really worth more than the other. Solomon assumed that his verdict would be accepted because no one who followed him would have greater opportunity or better resources to make such tests.

In *structure* this last section (2:12–26) is comprised of three subsections:

No ultimate difference between the wise and the fool	2:12–17
No final assurance that labors will last	2:18–23
No better solution than to enjoy the commonplace	2:24–26

Each segment begins with reflections on what counts or does not count in life, and each ends with a summary appraisal of the puzzling futility of any chosen path: *"for all is vanity and grasping for the wind"* (2:17); *"this also is vanity"* (2:23); *"this also is vanity and grasping for the wind"* (2:26). The verdict not only punctuates the three sections but provides interim conclusions within them: *"This also is vanity"* (2:15, 19); *"this also is vanity and a great evil"* (2:21). The further the Preacher proceeds in his royal experiment the more frequently he snaps out his negative evaluation. He seems to feel the need to press life's limitations more keenly as he drives his First Demonstration of the main theme (1:2–3) to its conclusion.

THE WISE AND THE FOOLS—ONE FATE

The first subsection (2:12–17) heads in a positive direction and then takes a sharp turn at verse 14b. Its movement can be analyzed along these lines:

Introduction of next stage of quest	2:12
Announcement of positive findings	2:13

proverb of confirmation	2:14a
counter-conclusion	2:14b
Personal reflection on fate of fools and wise	2:15a–c
complaining question	2:15d
negative conclusion	2:15e–f
explanation of conclusion	2:16
Final reaction—hatred of life	2:17

The ultimate reality of death makes wisdom's worth only relative.
> 12 Then I turned myself to consider
> Wisdom and madness and folly;
> For what can the man do who succeeds the king?—
> Only what he has already done.
> 13 Then I saw that wisdom excels folly
> As light excels darkness.
> 14 The wise man's eyes are in his head,
> But the fool walks in darkness.
> Yet I myself perceived
> That the same event happens to them all.
> *Eccles. 2:12–14*

As important and thorough as was the test of pleasure, the Teacher's basic concerns centered in the value of wisdom. There his search began (1:13), and to that search he now returns. Nothing in human experience lies outside its scope. With intensity bordering on compulsion he wants to comb through all the intellectual and existential questions that make life tick or keep it from ticking. That range is summed up in the merism of *"wisdom"* (see at 1:13) as one pole and *madness and folly* (see at 1:17) as the other. We should note that madness and folly are not two separate ideas but combine to emphasize the wildest, craziest kind of folly. *Hendiadys* (lit. "one through two") is the Greek term used to describe this literary device where two terms coalesce to fortify one idea. *"Turned myself"*—the same Hebrew verb read *"I looked"* in verse 11—both links this section to the pleasure-quest and marks the transition to the final step in the "royal experiment."

The question and answer which close verse 12 are baffling indeed. They can be translated quite easily, though the verb *"can do"* is not found in the Hebrew text and is usually supplied by the translations (NASB, JB, RSV, NIV). It is not the translation but the intent of the passage together with its role in the context that makes it difficult. What is Solomon's point? Several possibilities have been suggested. First, he may be claiming that his research has been so competently and thoroughly executed that there is little left to be done by the *"man"*—here *'ādām* (see at 1:3) is both singular and masculine in force—who *"succeeds"* (lit. "comes in after") him. Second, he may hope he has set a pattern of diligent investigation that his heir will carry on. Third, he may assume that the successor may be an "ignoramus" (Fox, p. 334) utterly unsuited for such intellectual labors. Choice one seems out of harmony with the context, which is quite pessimistic about the quality and character of Solomon's successor (2:19). Choices two and three come out about the same place: Solomon has done his work so efficiently that it is unlikely that anyone who comes after will make significant improvements in it, even though it is strongly presumed that pursuit of wisdom was a constant duty of kings. A *"foolish king"* was a menace (4:13); the king's unquestionable authority made wisdom essential (8:2, 4); royal wisdom kept the whole court doing the right things at the right time (10:16–17).

At first glance, the findings from the royal detective work seemed positive (v. 13). *"Excels"* translates the familiar *yitrôn* (see on 1:3), with its notes of "advantage" or "profit." It suggests that there is an undeniable plus to *"wisdom"* that is much more than a slim percentage of income over outgo. The comparison to the differences between *"light"* and *"darkness"* is dramatic (Amos 5:18, 20): *"light"* speaks of "safety," even "salvation" (Ps. 27:1); *"darkness"* equals "danger," even "disaster" (Joel 2:2; Mic. 7:8).

Koheleth grasps for a proverb to cinch his point (v. 14a). The *"wise man"* has 20-20 vision in both *"eyes"*; the *"fool"* (Heb. *kᵉsîl*, used nearly fifty times in Proverbs and eighteen times in Koheleth, is the stock word to describe the irresponsible behavior of someone who cannot or will not do and say the things that honor God's will for decent and constructive human behavior) is blind as a bat. *"Walks"* describes his whole way of life—how he conducts himself, makes his choices, relates to others, works in his community (Ps. 1:1; John 8:12). *"Darkness"* (see at 2:13) marks his character, conduct, and destiny as disasters.

For a brief moment, it looks as if the quest has come to its "Eureka!" its grand "Aha!" It sounds as though the guiding question of 1:3 has found its satisfying answer: There is profit for the human toil of delving into life's mysteries. *"Wisdom"* is the answer. We stand ready to applaud the outcome, watch the curtain drop, and cheer the Preacher as he takes his final bows.

But he gives us no opportunity to do that. The proverb (v. 14a) does not leave him convinced. His experience and reason combine (*"I myself perceived"* translates the Heb. root *yādaᶜ*; see at 1:16) to point to a counter-truth which makes all that he has affirmed about *"wisdom"* relative, not absolute. The counter-truth is *the universality of death*. To Koheleth's way of thinking, wisdom's profit was temporary, cut short by *"the same event that happens to them all."* *"All"* should be translated "both," embracing the wise and the fool (*"all"* has this same meaning in 7:18). *"Event"* and *"happens"* derive from the same Hebrew root (*qārāh*). Other Old Testament uses suggest that these events that happen are beyond the control of those who experience them but may turn out to be part of God's plan: the strange happenings of Joseph's brothers in the court of Egypt (Gen. 42:29); Ruth's random choice of Boaz's field as her gleaning place (Ruth 2:3); Mordecai's painful knowledge of Haman's plot that was about to happen to the Jews (Esther 4:7); the *"time and chance"* that change the lives of the swiftest, strongest, wisest, most skilled persons we know (Eccles. 9:11).

Death as a "happening" looms large in Koheleth (3:19; 9:2). As dreadful as death is, the Preacher uses the fact of it to teach humility and simplicity to his hearers. That "happening" (*"event"*) like all others is much more in God's hands than ours. Its reality ought to chasten our pride and humble our self-sufficiency. *"Happens,"* by the way, is to us moderns a very understandable way of speaking of death. One of my friends remarked recently that he and his wife often plan for their personal futures with clauses like, "If anything happens to me. . . ." What they really mean is, "If I die first."

The ultimate reality of death dampens the enthusiasm of the wise.

Given the choice of being wise or being foolish, one would choose wisdom as one would prefer bread to stone or cheese to chalk. Yet wisdom lacks permanent worth, because of death's relentless presence. Death is the "one event" that catches both foolish and wise.

> 15 So I said in my heart
> "As it happens to the fool,
> It also happens to me,
> And why was I then more wise?"
> Then I said in my heart,
> "This also is vanity."
>
> Eccles. 2:15

What he had perceived as being universally true Koheleth now applies personally to himself—*"it also happens to me."* This reflection casts a whole new light on his work. *"Why"* here, as often in the Psalms (10:1; 22:1; 43:2), suggests a complaint. The force of the question can be read, "I should not have spent my time and effort in garnering wisdom. Death makes futile (*"vanity"*) my whole life's work."

Beyond that, *the ultimate reality of death wipes out the memory even of the wise:*

> 16 For there is no more remembrance
>   of the wise than of the fool forever,
>   Since all that now is will be
>   forgotten in the days to come.
>   And how does a wise man die?
>   As the fool!
> 17 Therefore I hated life because the work that
> was done under the sun was distressing to me, for all
> is vanity and grasping for the wind.
>
> *Eccles. 2:16–17*

We toil to build our little pyramids of remembrance, our modest monuments to our wisdom, and death sweeps over the terrain like a hot, dry sirocco and turns our pyramids into sand dunes—all of which look alike.

"No more remembrance" takes us back to the poem which set the stage for the actions of the First Demonstration (1:4–11). There (1:11) it clinched the argument that real change in life is impossible, since our opinion that something new has arrived on the scene is based only on our faulty memory. Everything "new" has occurred before; we just do not remember it. Likewise, verse 16 hammers home, our wisdom brings no lasting advantage to life since it too will be erased from the memories of those who come when we are gone. *"Forget"* (Heb. *shākah;* see Hos. 2:13) often means more than mere lapse of memory. It suggests that the record and impact of our existence will be wiped out, as though we had never lived. Death is the great eraser as Koheleth clearly laments:

> And they (the dead) have no more reward,
> For the memory of them is forgotten.
>
> *Eccles. 9:5*

"All" in verse 16 means *"both"* (NIV, JB). The context, as in verse 14, makes clear that the antecedent is *"wise"* and *"fool,"* "both" of whom will be *"forgotten"* as the days go by. As *"why"* in verse 15 signals a *complaint,* so *"how"* (Heb. *ʾêk*) in verse 16 marks a *lament:* "How the mighty have fallen" (2 Sam. 1:19). The question, *"And how does a wise man die?"* is not a straightforward query, as though Solomon wanted information. It is a wail of grief over the lack of any real difference in the ultimate destinies of the wise and the foolish. The lament introduces the verb *"die"* in the book. The softer term *"happens"* (2:14–15) gives way to the stark and painful reality of death. The verb (Heb. *mût*) bobs up periodically in the various arguments (3:2, 19; 4:2; 7:17; 9:4–5), and the noun (Heb. *māwet*) appears in 7:1, 26; 8:8; 10:1. Their frequency, along with "event" or "happening" (see at 2:14–15), shows us how almost compulsively the Preacher's attention was fixed on the questions of ultimate destiny.

Indeed it sounds as if death had him by the nape of the neck and was shaking the joy of life out of him. *"I hated life"* is incredibly strong language for a wise teacher whose basic vocation was to find and teach the key to success in life. What would it take to get Zubin Mehta, Itzhak Perlmann, or Beverly Sills to start an interview with the explosive declaration, "I hate music"? In Scripture only the laments of Job (chap. 3), Jeremiah (20:14–18), and Lamentations reach the depths of despair expressed in verse 17, which repeats Koheleth's vocabulary of pain and frustration: *"distressing,"* damaging to the point of disaster (1:13); *"work that was done,"* the all-embracing expression for human efforts to make sense of life and to improve our lot in it (1:14); *under the sun* (a dominant phrase in this segment: vv. 17, 18, 19, 20, 22), the universal yet earthbound context of human endeavors (1:3); *"vanity,"* the perpetual mystery which blocks our understanding of life (1:2); *"grasping for the wind,"* the elusiveness of any real comprehension of how life works (1:14).

The similarities in wording between 2:17 and 1:14 testify to the Preacher's inability to make headway in his quest for understanding. If he was in a hole at the beginning of the search, he has only dug himself in deeper as he comes to the close of his First Demonstration. The specter of death is the new reality, and he is hard-pressed to cope with that and retain any zest for life.

Our Labors and Our Skills—One Destiny

The second subsection of our passage (2:18–23) moves Solomon beyond the threat of death—the *"same event"* suffered by wise and fool alike (2:14–16). Its theme is the follow-up question: what becomes of the fruit of all our labor and skill when death "happens"? "It is left to someone else whose worthiness and competence are unknown qualities," is the painfully simple and simply painful answer.

Solomon's look at the impact of death, the ultimate reality, drives on toward its doleful finale. Death makes wisdom's worth only relative and thus dampens the enthusiasm of the wise for their calling. And death has one other vicious whim: *it leaves all of our accomplishments for others to use:*

> 18 Then I hated all my labor in which I had toiled under the sun, because I must leave it to the man who will come after me.
>
> 19 And who knows whether he will be wise or a fool? Yet he will rule over all my labor in which I toiled and in which I have shown myself wise under the sun. This also is vanity.
>
> 20 Therefore I turned my heart and despaired of all the labor in which I had toiled under the sun.
>
> 21 For there is a man whose labor is with wisdom, knowledge, and skill; yet he must leave his heritage to a man who has not labored for it. This also is vanity and a great evil.
>
> 22 For what has man for all his labor, and for the striving of his heart with which he has toiled under the sun?
>
> 23 For all his days are sorrowful, and his work burdensome; even in the night his heart takes no rest. This also is vanity.
>
> *Eccles. 2:18–23*

The movement of this segment flows something like this:

Conclusion about the futility of labor	2:18
elaboration of the conclusion	2:19
personal confession of despair	2:20
general observation of grounds for despair	2:21
rhetorical question lamenting the despair	2:22
Summary of the grounds for despair	2:23

The mood of the passage is unrelieved depression. Listen to the language: (1) *"I hated"* (v. 18) sets the tone for what follows as it continues the theme of what preceded (v. 17), a link-word in every sense of the term; (2) *"who knows"* (v. 19) rings with the frustration not of gray uncertainty but of black certainty—"no one knows" is its thrust; (3) *despaired* (Heb. *yāʾash*, v. 20) smacks of hopelessness, describing the intense suffering and depression of Job (6:26) and the utter absence of hope entailed in Judah's persistent idolatry (Isa. 57:10, "There is no hope"; Jer. 18:12, "That is hopeless!"); (4) *"sorrowful"* days (v. 23) sobs with the cries of lament (see 1:18); (5) *"burdensome" "work"* or "business" (v. 23) moans with vexation (see on *kaʿas* in 1:18); (6) *"no rest"* (v. 23) tosses and turns with anxiety, as the *"heart"* ("mind") seeks futilely to unwind the tangled threads of life; (7) *"vanity"* (vv. 19, 21, 23) pounds through the passage drumming home the totally baffling nature of the wise man's quest (see on *hebel*, at 1:2); (8) its negative verdict is measured by the doubly doomful *"great evil"* (v. 21), pointing to a catastrophe of massive dimensions (see on the adjective *raʿ* at 1:13; 2:17); here the form is the noun *rāʿāh* found fourteen times in Ecclesiastes. Though it is Hebrew's most general term for "wrongdoing" or the "harm" that flows from it (7:14–15; 8:11), the Preacher's outlook sometimes colors the meanings he gives it—injustice or folly and the pains they cause (5:13, 16; 6:1; 10:5), mishaps beyond one's control (9:12; 11:2), hardship in general (8:6; 11:10; 12:1).

The keenness of the depression is in direct proportion to the ardor of Koheleth's labors. These verses perspire with the recollection of how hard he has worked to probe life's mysteries and find meaning in them: (1) the root words for *"labor"* or *"toiled"* (Heb. *ʿāmāl* and *ʿāmal*; see on 1:3) are found nine times, and in five of the six verses (vv. 18–22); (2) the intellectual nature of the quest has made it all the more draining—the two verbs in verse 19, *"I toiled . . . I have shown myself wise,"* combine to form one idea, "I worked at this with all the wisdom I have" (on this use of *hendiadys* see comments on 2:12); (3) this idea is expanded (v. 21) with the use of three synonyms which reinforce each other to suggest the incredible amount of mental labor that Solomon poured into his work—*"wisdom"* (Heb. *hokmâh*; see at 1:13), *"knowledge"* (Heb. *daʿat*; see at 1:16), *"skill"* (Heb. *kishrôn*) which means shrewd or canny activity that leads to success or profit (see 4:4; 5:10 for noun; and 10:10; 11:6 for verb, *"prosper"*); (4) *"striving of his heart"* (v. 22) suggests an effort to solve the mystery as single-minded as is the shepherd's desire to keep the flock together; its other uses in Koheleth (1:17; 4:16, *"grasping for the wind"*) may add here a further note of frustration.

The heart of Koheleth's depression is caused by his realization that what he has accomplished is to be left to someone else. Having given a nod to that subject in verse 12, he has now returned to face it head on. The thought takes shape in stages. First (v. 18) the wise man loathes the idea of leaving to another person all the fruit of his diligent toil. *"Labor"* here must stand for the results of the work not just the doing of it. Hence it must embrace all the projects outlined in the quest for pleasure described in 2:1–11: parks, buildings, singers, concubines, together with all the trappings of government. The focus is personal in verse 18: *"I must leave . . . after me."* Solomon cannot take it with him, and his contributions will soon be forgotten (v. 16). The total result will be as if he had never lived.

In the second stage of his reflections (v. 19), the Teacher faces the very real possibility that a *"fool"* (see on 2:14) may succeed him on Israel's throne (*"rule;"* Heb. *shālaṭ*, "exercise power or dominion"; 8:9; Esther 9:1) and, thereby, hasten the dissolution and oblivion of his mighty works. Whether Koheleth is pointing a finger at the failure of Rehoboam's efforts to wield the Solomonic scepter (1 Kings 12), we cannot be sure, but that is certainly a possibility. The combination of foolishness and power is one that Koheleth dreads—and rightly so (4:13; 9:16-17; 10:16–17).

In the third stage (v. 21) the Teacher looks away from his own situation to the more general human scene where the fruits of diligent physical and mental exertion become the *"heritage"* (Heb. *ḥēleq*, "portion" or "lot"; see at 2:10) of persons who have made no contribution to it. That this should be so makes no sense at all and ought not to happen, as *"vanity"* and *"great evil"* declare.

The price of such achievement is so insufferably high that some permanent result ought to remain. Wise though he is, the Teacher offers no idea of what he would choose to happen to his legacy. He may hanker for eternal life; he has no confidence that such a state exists. He may long to set the terms by which future generations would behave; he knows, if he knows anything at all, that to do that is God's responsibility, not his. So he reflects on life's conundrums, and the more he reflects the more he laments the way things are.

Futile and senseless it is to pay the demanding price to acquire goods and wealth. We cannot take them with us—the wise man knew that. But what pained him even more was that an entirely unworthy heir might gain the comfort and glory.

No biblical passage paints a grimmer picture of what it costs to succeed on human terms and how fragile that success is. Strain, toil, pain, vexation, insomnia—this is the currency with which we pay for success that we can neither fully gain nor truly keep.

We spend all our human resources, and we borrow against energy we do not have, to build our pyramids by which to be remembered. Then death, our common destiny, slips into the scene, erases our name from the cornerstone, and engraves in larger letters the name of someone less deserving. Our expensive legacy of wisdom and work has been stripped from us by death, the consummate swindler.

Eat, Drink, and Work—One Source of Joy

Death is a haunting reality diminishing the value of wisdom, erasing the memory of even the wise, and transferring our hard-earned gains to persons unsuited for them. All this the wise man made clear. Yet he did not counsel his pupils to give up on life. Instead, he came to an *alternative conclusion* that modest enjoyment was possible. Three words of advice expressed this conclusion.

First, *enjoy life as you can:*

> 24 Nothing is better for a man than that he
> should eat and drink, and that his soul should enjoy
> good in his labor. This also, I saw, was from the hand
> of God.
> 25 For who can eat, or who can have enjoyment,
> more than I?
>
> Eccles. 2:24–25

God, to Koheleth, was not an absentee landlord. He was a gracious Provider, apart from whom we would not have either the basic staples of life or its simple delights. The God of grace has given us freedom to enjoy his daily gifts. What we are not free to do is to presume on his grace or predict our own future, so we enjoy life as we can.

②

Submit

➔ The second word of advice was this: *surrender to God's decisions:*

> 26 For God gives wisdom and knowledge and
> joy to a man who is good in His sight; but to the
> sinner He gives the work of gathering and collecting,
> that he may give to him who is good before God. This
> also is vanity and grasping for wind.
>
> *Eccles. 2:26*

God it is who determines what kind of lot we have in life. And he does this on the basis of his evaluation of us. His decisions are final, though it is our duty to seek to please him. Since he alone knows what is best for us, we must surrender to his decisions and make the best of the lot he sends us.

③ ➔ This final word of counsel summed up the wise man's opinion: *Do not expect anything better*. We only brand life's results as vanity—as futility—if we hope for too much. It is false optimism that wounds us, according to the Teacher. If we try to guarantee our own permanence, if we try to build timeless pyramids through wealth, wisdom, pleasure, or achievement, we are doomed to futility. If we take God's gifts and decisions as they come and do not try to outwit God, we can snatch a measure of enjoyment from each day.

➔ This *alternative conclusion*, so simple and direct when compared to the grandiose experiment which is its setting, serves to wrap up the entire argument from 1:2 to 2:23. What it says, in effect, is that all our efforts to grasp the larger picture of God's plan for the world and our lives will come a cropper. What Solomon could not do with all his wealth, power, leisure, station, and wisdom, we surely cannot do with our puny resources. Hence we must look at life from an entirely different angle. To fail to do so is to continue to crack our heads against its unbending mystery and rigidity.

In various forms this conclusion is the heart of the book, the key to its purpose and positive message. It breaks through the gloom persistently and brings its gentle light just at those places where life's puzzles seem to have left us most in the dark. The accompanying chart is an attempt to track the similarities, differences, and thematic movement among the six instances where this *alternative conclusion* occurs.

Koheleth's *Alternative Conclusion*

Text	Context	Form	List of Good Things	Mention of Grace	Additional Thought
2:24–26	End of First Demonstration: *Death* happens to all; all toil is left to someone else.	Nothing better than	Eat, drink, enjoy good in work.	This is from hand of God.	God will reward those who live this way. Yet *how* is a mystery (*"vanity"*) (2:26).
3:12–13	Middle of Second Demonstration: God is sovereign over human events; we have to accept God's timing and cannot change it.	I know nothing better than	Rejoice, do good, eat, drink, enjoy fruit of labor.	It is a gift of God.	God's unchangeable sovereignty over the world (3:14–15).
3:22	Middle of Second Demonstration: *Death* happens to human beings and beasts alike.	I perceived nothing better than	Rejoice in his works.	That is his lot (*"heritage"*).	Future is impossible to discern; hence the focus on present work (3:22c).
5:18	Middle of Third Demonstration: *Death* robs us of any profit.	Here is what I have seen: It is good and fitting	Eat, drink, enjoy fruit of labor.	Life is a gift of God; its simple joys are our lot (*"heritage"*).	Celebrating God's gifts will keep us from worrying about the pain of life's brevity (5:19–20).
8:15	Middle of Fourth Demonstration: *Death* catches us all, and not always in circumstances that reflect our wickedness or justness.	So I commended enjoyment; because nothing is better than	Eat, drink, be merry.	Days which God gives	Joy of simple things will last longer than other things.
9:7–10	End of Fourth Demonstration: *Death* catches us all. The dead know nothing, have no hope.	Go!	Eat with joy, drink with a merry heart, live joyfully with the wife whom you love, work zestfully now.	God has accepted your works.	Do now what needs doing, for the grave offers no opportunity for wisdom or work (9:10).

A few comments of comparison on these alternative conclusions are sparked by the chart. First, they occur always in the sections of the document that we call Demonstrations and not in the Words of Advice (see Outline, p. 33). They are so central to Koheleth's major argument that at least one conclusion is found in each of the four Demonstrations. They comprise the major positive evaluation and instruction in the book and bear the personal stamp of Koheleth, as the *Form* column indicates: *"I know"* (3:12), *"I perceived"* (3:22), *"I have seen"* (5:18), *"I commended"* (8:15).

Second, the conclusions encapsulate the best alternative we have in trying to take life as it comes and in coping with its dilemmas, mysteries, frustrations, and injustices. *"Nothing better than"* drums this home in its quartet of occurrences (2:26: 3:12, 22; 8:15). The practicality of life's simple, basic activities sets them apart from all our fantastic and inaccessible human dreams of fathoming life's uncertainties and changing its inconsistencies. Food, drink, work, and love are a list of human necessities, and they are within the reach of most of us whatever our ability or station.

Third, the thread of *joy* that winds through these passages changes the mood of the entire book. It is not the moanings of a person battered by life's hardships nor the sighings of a person baffled by life's riddles. The book, as influenced by these conclusions, is the account of the simple, sober, chastened enjoyment that finds pleasure in the everyday tasks and blessings which come our way. Koheleth heeds his own warnings about the mindless frivolity of fools (7:2–6). Giddiness and gladness are not the same thing. But then neither are sobriety and pessimism. Sobriety can walk hand in hand with joy. Joy and pessimism journey in opposite directions.

Fourth, the source of these modest yet genuine blessings, fraught with what one hymn writer called "solid joy and lasting treasure," is the gracious hand of God. Notes of grace run through the whole cantata as a reminder that, mysterious as the hand of God may be in the crucial events of human life, that hand is extended in grace to us as God's creatures in the provision of the simple delights that sustain us. Seeing God's hand in the ordinary provisions which are our lot or *"heritage"* fuels our faith to trust that hand in times when its purposes may be hidden.

Fifth, each conclusion is followed by an additional thought that reinforces it or explains further its validity. A common theme in these addenda is the need to focus on the present rather than the future: (1) God has a system of righteous rewards but how he distributes them is filled with mystery (2:26); (2) the future, like the rest of life, is determined by God; our task is not to try to change that future but to fear and obey God in the present by receiving and using his gift of life's necessities (3:14–15); (3) no one can bring us back after death to participate in the future; our lot is to do our best in the present (3:22); (4) we acknowledge God's grace by receiving his daily gifts and not worrying about how painful or fleeting our days may be (5:20); (5) the daily joy of God's simple gifts is more lasting than grand schemes and fanciful dreams that we are prone to bet our lives on (8:15); (6) since the grave is not a workshop or study, we should do now what God calls us to do as well as we possibly can (9:10).

Finally, each statement of the conclusion is prompted by the sense of the inevitable sovereignty of God, especially as that sovereignty shows itself in the certainty of death. Long-term hopes carried great risk for the Preacher. The better way was to enjoy each day as God gave it and to make the best of God's common gifts of food, drink, work, and love. So doing may not have solved life's mysteries but it did put his students in touch with life realities—their basic needs, their reachable joys, their experiences of grace, their human mortality.

A few brief notes on 2:24–26 may prove helpful at this point. Thematically the verses are bound together by the accounts of the work of God. God's "hand" determines what sustenance and what enjoyment of it we have (v. 24). The prominence of "good," found twice in both verses 24 and 26, echoes the "very good" of the creation story (Gen. 1–2). It suggests that we should take the same delight in God's gifts which we help come into being by our labors as God took in his work on the six days in which he labored to form the creation. When applied to the person who gains rewards (v. 26), "good" may hint that such persons suit his purposes and contribute to his plan as did the various stages of his creative activity. For some uses of "good" that ring with joy, see Psalms 50:23; 59:10; 91:16.

This affirmation is reinforced by the rhetorical question whose demanded answer is "no one" (v. 25): all human nourishment and "enjoyment" are derived from and determined by God. "Enjoyment" (Heb. yāḥûsh) would usually mean "hasten" but here seems to derive from a Ugaritic verb that means "rejoice." An alternative suggestion reads it as "fret" or "worry" as in Job 20:2—*"anxious"* (Fox, p. 188). If the latter interpretation is correct, the question of verse 25 provides a transition to verse 26 where the way in which God metes out either food or fretting is contemplated. *"More than I"* should be translated "apart from him" (RSV) or "without him" (NEB, NASB, NIV), continuing the focus on *God's* activity from verse 24 and supplying the subject of the verb *"gives"* in verse 26. *"More than I"* would awkwardly reintroduce Solomon and his role as the prime example of one who has been blessed by God's hand.

The mystery of God's grace is the theme of verse 26. He treats the person who is *"good"* with the blessings that lead to success and satisfaction. Note that *"wisdom"* (see 1:13), *"knowledge"* (see 1:16), and *"joy"* (see 2:1) are viewed more as gifts than achievements. The gift given to the *"sinner,"* however, is the frustration of handing over what he has accumulated to the one whom God deems good, with the result that he has no lasting fruit from his labors. Not defined here are the meanings of *"good"* and *"sinner"* (for this pair, see also 7:20; 9:2, 18). Interpretations have ranged from "lucky" and "unlucky" to "righteous" and "wicked." The emphasis seems not to be so much on outward conduct as on inner attitude. The words *"in His sight"* and *"before God"* (Heb. *lᵉpānāyw*, "before his face") are used both places. They may be the key. Divine reward or judgment, as the Preacher saw them, were based on criteria which were always clear to God but not always clear to the recipients' neighbors. God's hand conducted life's opera but from a score which even the wisest could not read.

If our interpretation is anywhere close to what Koheleth meant (and this is just one of his sayings that are virtually unfathomable), then his verdicts of *"vanity"* (see 1:2) and *"grasping for the wind"* (1:14) are a sigh and groan at the mystery of God's ways. Direct our lives and reward our ways, God does. But the manner, terms, and outcomes are much better known to him than to us. We do what we can do by taking the gifts he gives and enjoying them for all they and we are worth.

Epilogue: The Greater Wise Man

This *alternative conclusion* has a lot of merit to it. It keeps us from tacking our hopes to the crepe paper of tomorrow's wishes. It stirs us to seek joy in God's daily gifts. But it does little to help us face the ultimate reality of death. It has no power to assure us of the permanence we crave.

It took the Greater Wise Man to do that. He replaced death as the ultimate reality when he said, "I am the resurrection and the life. He who believes in me, though he may die, he shall live" (John 11:25). Resurrection is a triumphant solution to the problem of permanence. It takes us out of death's hands and places us under the power of a Savior who is himself the resurrection, the master of death.

As recreated persons, we will carry out a permanent mission—we will love and worship God through all eternity. Long after the biting sands, chipping winds, and acid rains have eroded the strong pyramids that guard the Nile, the resurrected people of God will live on to enjoy rich fellowship with their Maker and to praise the name of him who fully and finally has dealt with death.

CHAPTER FIVE

Second Demonstration: Absence of Freedom

Ecclesiastes 3:1–15

In some ways the red book is the most important piece of equipment in my office. About the size of a church hymnal, it sits in a prominent place on Denise's desk. Denise is my assistant, and, like Vera and Inez before her, she is the keeper of that red book. If I call her, she will automatically pick up the book and bring it to my inner office, so that together we may consult it.

To some extent that book stands between us and utter confusion. It tells us which Tuesday to have lunch with a bishop, which Thursday to take the 8:45 A.M. flight to Chicago for a conference, which Monday the Seminary board will meet—and a thousand other things.

The red book on the desk contains our calendar for the year. In it all appointments are recorded—often months ahead of time. Once the schedules are set, that book comes close to being the governor of our lives. It sets the times by which we do things; it controls with almost rigid regularity our comings and goings.

And in so doing, it greatly limits our freedom. We cannot face each day with the open question, what shall we do? We have to face it with the closed question, what have we already committed ourselves to do? Whatever regulates our time curtails our freedom.

That was the struggle the Preacher faced in one of his most famous passages. For him life was a red book in which all the key events were written by the hand of God with the result that men and women had freedom neither to alter them nor completely understand them.

Futility, the Preacher called this lack of freedom. Futility—because our plans are limited, our ability to change our schedules is confined, and our potential for affecting our destiny is almost nil.

THE OLDER ADVICE: CONTRIBUTE TO YOUR DESTINY

This grim conclusion that freedom is limited put the Preacher at odds with many of the other wise men, particularly those whose sayings have been collected in the Book of Proverbs. They were much more optimistic: "contribute to your destiny" was their motto. They advised their pupils to discover life's great principles and head in their direction.

By hard work they believed that they could make a contribution to their destiny:

> He who has a slack hand becomes poor,
> But the hand of the diligent makes one rich.
> He who gathers in summer is a wise son;
> But he who sleeps in harvest is a son who causes shame.
>
> *Prov. 10:4–5*

The implication was clear: if we do the right thing at the right time and do it well, we can shape our own prosperity.

Similarly, the wise teachers of Proverbs had taught their pupils that by *sound choices* they could contribute to their destinies:

> The wisdom of the prudent is to understand his way,
> But the folly of fools is deceit.
>
> *Prov. 14:8*

And again:

> Without counsel, plans go awry,
> But in the multitude of counselors they are established.
>
> *Prov. 15:22*

Or this:

> Plans are established by counsel;
> By wise counsel wage war.
>
> *Prov. 20:18*

Diligence was one way to influence the future, and discernment was another. One of the qualities of a sound choice was to determine the right time for something to be said or done. In this way time could be used to advantage; its tides could be harnessed to carry their ship forward to their destiny:

> A man has joy by the answer of his mouth,
> And a word spoken in due season, how good it is!
> *Prov. 15:23*

Generations of young men and women were nurtured on this type of advice. They sought to know the right season for what they said, and they believed that hard work and sound choices would pave their path to success. And then the Teacher in Ecclesiastes challenged everything they had been taught.

Koheleth's Counsel: Submit to God's Determinations

The wise men in Proverbs had urged their students to humility. They should not take God's ways for granted:

> There are many plans in a man's heart,
> Nevertheless the Lord's counsel—that will stand.
> *Prov. 19:21*

But Koheleth argued that more than humility was needed. Total submission to what God had determined was the best that one could do.

The mystery, difficulty, even futility of trying to catch life's hidden meaning, and especially of trying to change life's destined course, that was the reality that the Preacher was seeking to demonstrate. The persistence of that mystery he had affirmed repeatedly in the *theme* (1:2), the *guiding question* (1:3), and the several stages of the First Demonstration (1:4–2:26).

Now he sets aside his Solomonic robe in which he pursued the "royal experiment," and changes the literary style from prose to poetry—balanced in form and held together by the constant repetition of *"time."* These changes in voice and form mark the beginnings of his Second Demonstration (3:1–11) in which the thoroughly frustrating matter of probing life's meaning is evidenced in God's control of all events.

100

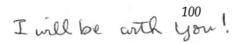
I will be with you!

Twice before, this theme has been noted. It was developed implicitly in the introductory poem (1:4–11) on the dependability and stability of the creation: the predictable journey of the sun, the repeated circuits of the wind, the ceaseless pouring of water into the sea. It was stated more specifically in the pivotal proverb quoted to show the narrow confines within which wisdom moves:

> What is crooked cannot be made straight,
> And what is lacking cannot be numbered.
>
> *Eccles. 1:15*

God's planned time was the first evidence he offered in his argument.

1 To everything there is a season,
A time for every purpose under heaven:
2 A time to be born,
    And a time to die;
A time to plant,
    And a time to pluck what is planted;
3 A time to kill,
    And a time to heal;
A time to break down,
    And a time to build up;
4 A time to weep,
    And a time to laugh;
A time to mourn,
    And a time to dance;
5 A time to cast away stones,
    And a time to gather stones;
A time to embrace,
    And a time to refrain from embracing;
6 A time to gain,
    And a time to lose;
A time to keep,
    And a time to throw away;
7 A time to tear,
    And a time to sew;
A time to keep silence,
    And a time to speak;
8 A time to love,
    And a time to hate;

101

> A time of war,
>   And a time of peace.
>   9 What profit has the worker from that in which
> he labors?
>
> *Eccles. 3:1–9*

In this poem the motif of changelessness and divine control is applied to the widest possible range of human activities. The literary form comprises fourteen pairs of contrasts. The use of this double seven number helps to convey the idea of completeness. These contrary lines couple basic human experiences and their equally basic opposites. This device is usually called a *merism* and suggests that the poles that are stated mean to include every similar activity that occurs between them. The pair, for example, *"to be born"* and *"to die"* (3:2) embrace each major event, perhaps even each moment, in the human life cycle. The poem is wrapped in an introduction (3:1) and a conclusion (3:9).

The introduction establishes the theme of set or appointed times. *"Season"* means literally "appointed time" (NASB) as its use (Heb. *zᵉmān*) elsewhere indicates: in Nehemiah it marks the schedule for the cupbearer's journey to Jerusalem and his return (2:6); in Esther it pinpoints the calendar for the two-day feast of Purim in celebration of rescue from the genocidal plots of Haman (9:27, 31). *"Purpose"* in verse 1 means "event," "activity," or "matter" (see 8:6 which carries a thought similar to that of 3:1). The breadth of the word (Heb. *ḥēpheṣ*, which may also mean "delight" or "pleasure" in 5:4 and 12:1; see also "acceptable" in 12:10) is assured by its parallel use to *"everything"* in 3:14 and to *"work"* ("deed" or "task") in 3:17. It seems to include all the major activities in which human beings engage under the sovereign will of God.

The human component in all of this is made clear in two ways. First, the items in the catalog all involve human participation. They are not activities of the elements like earth, sun, wind, and sea in 1:4–11. Second, the conclusion (3:9) centers in the futility of all the human activity involved in life as summarized in verses 2–8.

Most of the verses are self-explanatory, but a comment or two on some may be helpful: *"To kill"* (v. 3) does not mean to commit murder. Hebrew has a special word for that, as the Ten Commandments attest (Exod. 20:13; Deut. 5:17; Heb. *rāṣaḥ*). "Kill" might involve capital punishment as prescribed in Old Testament Law or the slaughter of enemies in the battles which marked Old Testament history in virtually every era.

The meaning of *"stones"* (v. 5) may be the most puzzling question. Some Jewish tradition connected it to the *"embrace"* that follows and related the casting and gathering of *"stones"* to engaging in or refraining from sexual intercourse, *"stones"* being a metaphor for semen. But none of the other items on the list seems to be figurative, so we should probably look for a literal meaning. A more reasonable suggestion connects the casting of stones with the ancient practice of rendering a field useless to an enemy by covering it with stones—a form of scorched earth policy (2 Kings 3:19, 25). The gathering of stones is best illustrated in Isaiah's song of the vineyard (5:1–2), which describes the clearing of stony ground and the use of the stones for a watchtower and winepress. Though walls and shady shelters are not mentioned, they could well be included in the constructive use of stones.

"To gain" (lit. "to seek") and *"to lose"* (lit. "to destroy") in verse 6 probably take us into the realm of economics (see on 11:1–2) and refer to investments in goods or real estate. As I write this, the volatility of world stock and oil prices gives this interpretation a particular relevance and reminds us of how little we can do about such things.

"To tear" and *"to sew"* (v. 7) may describe the beginning and ending of a mourning period, when garments are first ripped (see Job 2:12) and then mended. More likely it speaks of the regular household activities of sewing clothes for the family and tearing them into rags when they are worn out or outgrown.

In line after line, the wise man reviewed life's most basic experiences and deepest emotions and concluded that each has its set time. From the universal experience of birth and death to the practices of harvest, from the delights and restraints of friendship to the waging of war and the pursuit of peace—the Teacher covered the normal events in human life.

His conclusion was bleak:

> What profit has the worker from that in which he labors?
> *Eccles. 3:9*

The gray conclusion helps us understand Koheleth's point. The whole range of life is beyond human control, though by nature we have to share in these activities. Our toil is basically profitless because God has so planned and controlled the events in our lives that all our efforts make almost no significant change.

This conclusion leads us back to the *guiding question* of 1:3. The answer expected is resoundingly negative—"None, none at all." The Second Demonstration brings no more encouragement than did the First with its fruitless "royal experiment." The failure of wisdom to solve life's puzzles (1:12–18), the inability of pleasure to offer ultimate meaning (2:1–11), the intrusive and arbitrary presence of death for wise and fool alike (2:12–23), the relentless fixity of times and seasons (3:1–8)—these all conspire to block our endeavors to unravel life's mysteries and reweave them in clear, bright patterns. We live according to God's determination, announced Koheleth, not ours. We live in time, conscious of it virtually every minute, but it is *God's planned time* that dictates our important activities and significant events.

November 22, 1963, is an unforgettable day for those of us old enough to remember. I was entertaining a distinguished European scholar at Fuller during the first year of my presidency. He had completed his morning lecture, and we stopped in my office on the way to lunch. Inez's face was blanched and her lips taut as she relayed the news that President John F. Kennedy had just been shot in Dallas and was on his way to Parkland Hospital. He, his family, and the entire nation were overwhelmed by an event over which no one seemed to have control. Ironically, we learned that day, the President had planned to cite the words of Ecclesiastes' poem as part of his address. That irony has etched in my mind the purpose of the poem. It was not to encourage Koheleth's students to do things at the *right* time as though they had full freedom to choose, which was probably to be Mr. Kennedy's point. The preacher's aim, to the contrary, was to warn them to accept God's *fixed* seasons and not to fight against the divine timing of the human calendar.

The point of the illustration is not to blame God for a tragic assassination but to call attention to the ever-present limits to human freedom. Daily we face the possibility of disaster, given the impact of the fall on creation, the rebellion of the human spirit, and the presence of the demonic in persons and organizations. Vigilance to do what we can and trust in God to make sense of circumstances beyond our control—these are the responses that help keep us sane in a world gone crazy.

Our frustrating restrictions were a major theme of the Preacher's argument, along with *God's planned time.* Submit to God's determination, he has counseled, and accept his plans for your times. *His* plans are what count because *our* lives are restricted by the great gulf between him and us. The reason why our toil ends so profitlessly is stressed in these words:

> 10 I have seen the God-given task with which
> the sons of men are to be occupied.
> 11 He has made everything beautiful in its time.
> Also He has put eternity in their hearts, except that
> no one can find out the work that God does from
> beginning to end.
>
> *Eccles. 3:10-11*

Our ignorance of God's ways—this is the vexing problem. God controls our times, but he has not told us how and why. We walk in the dark, merely submitting to what God has determined, blind to his purposes, lame in our efforts to cooperate.

Koheleth again describes the process by which he scrutinized and contemplates the ways of God with the human family (v. 10). The context seems to link this investigation to the events and activities described in the poem (vv. 2–8)—human interaction with divinely ordered times and seasons (v. 1). His process is familiar to us (1:13–14; 2:11, 13). He peers over the shoulders of the best people (on *"sons of men,"* see 1:13) he can find, desperate to discover a correlation between what they do and what happens to them. *"I have seen"* (3:10; Heb. *rā°āh,* see 1:14) describes the method, and *"God-given task"* its object. All these terms are familiar to us. The *"task"* (on the noun *°inyān* and its verb *°ānâh,* see at 1:13) is life's true business, described in the First Demonstration: *"to seek and search out by wisdom all that is done under heaven"* (1:13). It is not an optional human effort like shuffleboard or Scrabble. *"God-given"* describes both its possibility and necessity. (For the sovereign grace conveyed by the verb "give," see on 1:13.) Because we are made in God's image we can try to probe life's depths and have enough success at it to know we have not done it well. Lesser creatures would not be able to recognize even that, just as an ignoramus would not be able to tell whether the world was laughing with him or at him. A certain level of discernment is required to tell which. And because we are God's stewards made in God's image, we have to try. Part of our task as those commissioned to tend God's garden and fill the earth with people who will worship him (Gen. 1:28; 2:15) is to wrestle with how and why life works.

God's ways are good—*"he has made everything beautiful in its time"* (v. 11)—so proposes the Preacher. We must read this text in terms of its context. *"Everything"* (Heb. *hakkōl*) stands first in the sentence for emphasis and reaches back to *"to everything"* in the introduction to the poem (3:1); its scope is the opposites in life sketched in verses 2–8. "Beautiful" (Heb. *yāpheh*) may mean "pretty" or "handsome" (see Song of Sol. 1:15–16), but here as in Ecclesiastes 5:17 it should be translated "appropriate, proper." *"Its time"* ties back to the repetitive use of the word in 3:1–8. This means that *"everything"* speaks not of creation but of divine activities in human lives. The whole line then is a summary of the message of the poem and is remarkable evidence of Koheleth's positive attitude toward God's sovereignty.

Yet God has done something to tangle the matter: *"he has put eternity into their hearts."* This is a difficult line to interpret. What it seems to mean is that God has placed within us a sense of concern for the future. We are made to be curious over our destiny, to wonder about our fate, to concern ourselves with where life is leading. Yet we can do so little about it. That was where the frustration sharpened for Ecclesiastes. Within humankind *("their"* = *"sons of men"* in v. 10) is the urge to know the future; God has placed that urge there. But we have no capacity to satisfy that urge. It is a sharp thirst beyond our power to quench. We yearn to be free enough to contribute to our destiny; we sense that there is a destiny that needs shaping; yet we do not have the freedom to do much about it, because God is the One who determines the times of our life.

This interpretation deliberately chooses *"eternity"* as the correct understanding of Hebrew *ʿōlām*. Other readings include "world, " or "love of the world" (Gordis, pp. 221–22), and "ignorance," based on a root "to hide" (see Heb. *ʿālam*, a passive form of which occurs as *"secret thing"* in 12:14). *"Eternity"* to Old Testament people was not timelessness or *absence* of time. They knew no such realm. It was, rather, *extension* of time—as far back and as far forward as one could imagine—"time in its wholeness" (JB), "sense of time past and future" (NEB).

The tension then is twofold. On the one hand, it is a tension between the specific events that take place in the *"time"* that God has set for them and the role of these events in the larger, longer stretches of time—the *"eternity"* that gives these events their significance. On the other hand, it is a tension between our inability to *"find out"* the purposes of God and our strong sense, a facet of God's image within us, that there are purposes beyond our ken to be pursued. In verse 11 Koheleth introduces the Hebrew verb *māṣā'*, "to find, or discover"; its frequent uses in the rest of the book, e.g., 7:14, 24, 26, 27, 28; 8:17; 12:10, illustrate its importance as the key goal of wisdom—not just to "see" or "study" or "ponder in the heart" but to catch the truths about how life works. The tensions are aggravated by our hearty failures to discern these purposes at all. *"From beginning to end,"* a merism covering the whole range of knowledge, describes the completeness of this failure. Koheleth's point is not that we cannot quite catch the whole thing. No sensible person would doubt that God's grasp of life's meaning is greater than ours. The Preacher's frustration is that we cannot truly comprehend any part of it—not the *"beginning,"* not the *"end,"* not anything in between.

Where does all of this leave us? Our toil does not yield the profit we desire. Our struggle to understand the future is often empty, though we are driven to keep trying, by the sense of *"eternity."* What can we do that is useful, enjoyable, meaningful, as we submit to God's determinations?

The teacher answered these questions by pointing out *our limited possibilities:*

> 12 I know that there is nothing better for them than
> to rejoice, and to do good in their lives
> 13 and also that every man should eat and drink
> and enjoy the good of all his labor—it is the gift of God.
> *Eccles. 3:12–13*

Full freedom we do not have, the Preacher concluded. God keeps the calendar of our lives. The red book that schedules our hours and days sits on his desk and is filled out by his hand. Our task is to submit to his determinations, but we are not to do this lying down. We do have possibilities for productive effort, for contributing to our welfare, for enjoying life. We should receive life as God's gift and make the best of it. The simple delights of food and drink and work come from his hand; they are tokens of his grace.

The Second Demonstration (3:1–15), like the First (1:4–2:26), has reached an impasse. We cannot fathom life's depths nor can we quit trying. Again Koheleth seizes the opportunity to put forward his *alternative conclusion* about dealing with life (see the chart and discussion of the six conclusions at 2:24–26). However frustrating may be the complexities of *"time"* and *"eternity"* the simplicities of God's grace are available to each of us in the work station and the dinner table. Joy there will help to ease all the pain we find elsewhere.

> 14 I know that whatever God does,
>   It shall be forever.
>   Nothing can be added to it,
>   And nothing taken from it.
>   God does it, that men should fear before Him.
> 15 That which is has already been,
>   And what is to be has already been;
>   And God requires an account of what is past.
> *Eccles. 3:14–15*

These verses are a coda, playing again the themes of 3:1–11 with echoes of earlier tunes. *"Forever"* (v. 14) repeats the note of *"eternity"* in verse 11, using the same Hebrew word, *ʿôlām.* *"Nothing . . . added"* and *"nothing taken,"* recapture the strains of the fixity of creation, sounded in the poem (1:4–11) and proverb (1:15) which hold center stage as the First Demonstration begins. This fixity entails absence of all novelty or innovation (v. 15), a motif for which we have been prepared in the words of 1:9–10 in the opening poem.

Two notes are added in these verses that seem to underscore Koheleth's theme of divine sovereignty. First, the repetitive, changeless relationship of past and future is God's doing. That seems to be the gist of the difficult, painfully compact line of verse 15c. Though some translations inject the thought of final accountability or judgment (NKJV, NIV) and others find here a picture of divine compassion (JB: "yet God cares for the persecuted"), the context requests and the

Hebrew allows a description of God's relationship to the changeless-ness of life which is the dominant emphasis of the passage (3:1–15):

"And God summons each event back in its turn" (NEB).

No wonder there is nothing new! God sees to it by governing the repetitions of past events (see Fox, p. 196; Crenshaw, p. 100).

The second and clearer note is the strong statement of purpose which closes verse 14:

God does it, that men should fear before him.

"Time," with its series of events both painful and joyous, is more than a calendar of appointments. It is also a call to worship and obedience. God's unyielding sovereignty is attested in life's happenings. Our responses are to trust him with our Whys and Whens, to be thankful for the Whats that ease our pain and spark our joy, and, with the rest of creation, to say yes to his ground rules for our existence. *"Fear,"* introduced here in Koheleth, sums up these responses and becomes a dominant theme as his demonstrations and advice develop. The verb (Heb. *yārēʾ*) with *"God"* as object occurs in 5:7; 8:12–13; 9:13; 12:13; the participle or noun "fearer" with *"God"* as object crops up in 7:18 and 8:12. Koheleth's use of the word is evidence of the deep piety which underlay his probings. For Israel's sages *"fear"* was the virtual equivalent to the "love" which described the basic relationship to God commanded by Moses (Deut. 6:4–5) and Jesus (Mark 12:29–30). He had drunk heartily of the wisdom teaching on the centrality of fearing God (see Prov. 1:7; 9:10 and Communicator's Commentary, vol. 15a, chap. 14) and that draught fortified him for life.

We should read this section of Ecclesiastes with humility, but not despair. It offers at least as much of a security blanket as it does a straight jacket. If our times are in someone else's hand—and we know they are often beyond our control—whom would we choose to manage them rather than God? Our options are narrow since all human agencies—family, friends, experts, governments—are subject to most of our own limitations. We can attribute our circumstances to chance and let the numbers come up as they will, like the throw of the dice. We can blame the devil for everything bad and live in terror of his next prank or plot. Neither luck nor Satan presents credentials worthy of our trust or fear or love.

Koheleth offered us more than a measure of wisdom when he called us from fretting over life's times to loyalty to life's Sovereign. We cannot know all that God's hand is doing in the mysterious ebb and flow of our circumstances. But the daily supply of grace in the simple gifts of life tells us that his hand is a good one. And in that message we find joy and comfort.

Epilogue: The Greater Wise Man

This was not a bad conclusion that the Preacher had come to, but it was still not as bright as we would like. He sailed under gray clouds, while we long for clear, blue skies. We may not want to have full control over our futures, but we would like to know more about them. We may be willing to leave tomorrow in God's hands, yet we would like to know better the God who programs our tomorrows.

Happily, Jesus Christ has come with just that information. He has put our problem of freedom into clear perspective. He has taught us to be humble about our knowledge of the future and yet to trust God's goodness as he leads us into it.

For Ecclesiastes, what hobbled and fettered true freedom was God's mysterious control. Jesus understood our human problem at a deeper level. What made our search for freedom futile was not so much God's determinism as our rebellion. Our human lust for freedom, acted out by Adam and Eve in the Garden, brought a lifelong loss of freedom. Wanting freedom on our terms cost us true freedom on God's terms.

That was why Jesus had to do a new thing before true freedom became a reality: "Therefore if the Son makes you free, you shall be free indeed" (John 8:36). The new thing was that God's only Son had come. The rest of us are slaves, unable to free ourselves. Jesus came as the Son, the one who had ever and always been free. He—God's free one—had the power and authority to share his freedom with us.

And what freedom it is! It is *the freedom to accept life as God gives it*. Ecclesiastes said the same thing, but he said it more grimly. Jesus knew the Giver better. He knew how grandly God can be trusted. And he urged us to find freedom through trust: "Now if God so clothes the grass of the field . . . will He not much more clothe you, O you of little faith?" (Matt. 6:30). The God whom Jesus revealed can be fully trusted with the pages of our calendar. His love for us will not fail. Knowing that, we find freedom.

The darkest threats to our freedom God has defeated. The menace of judgment has been conquered by the power of forgiveness. The specter of death has been put to flight by the wonder of resurrection. In Jesus Christ, God has shown himself to be a God of loving power and powerful love.

Far from feeling cramped by his control of our lives, we have the freedom to live today and to wait for tomorrow knowing that God's agenda is always what is best for us. The hand that writes the schedule in the red calendar book is a loving hand, in fact a hand that loved so much it endured nails for our sake.

Away with arrogance, then! We do not control our future, God does. And away with anxiety! The God who steers us into his future is a God whose trustworthiness has been thoroughly proven—by Jesus Christ and by all who have truly followed him.

CHAPTER SIX

Second Demonstration: Distortion of Justice

Ecclesiastes 3:16–4:16

We want life's stories to have tidy endings. Though we enjoy happy endings, we do not insist upon them. We know that there are stories in life that do not end with the blissful couple strolling hand in hand toward the sunset. And we can accept stories with sad endings: Samson's final defeat of the Philistines costs him his own life; Romeo and Juliet die with their love unfulfilled; the king's horses and the king's men fail in their heroic efforts to reassemble Humpty Dumpty. Not all stories work out the way we would choose. But we learn to live with tinges of sadness.

What is harder to live with is injustice. We want our stories to have a tidy ending even if they do not end happily. We can cope with Cinderella's distress when the coach returns to a pumpkin at midnight. What we could not cope with would be the injustice of having the cruel stepsister rewarded rather than Cinderella. What would stun us would be to find out that the Lone Ranger was really a cattle rustler or that Dick Tracy was a disguised chief of the Mafia.

Injustice is something that makes us all somewhat edgy if not downright uncomfortable. Fairness is a virtue we all intuitively prize. We want life's stories to have tidy endings—where all accounts are paid and all offenders punished. There is something wrenching and jarring to us to have the wicked turn out winners in the end. A world where that happened regularly would be more than we could bear.

It is probably a tribute to the influence of the Bible that we feel this way. So thoroughly have the prophets' concern for justice and Jesus' teaching about rewards permeated our thinking that we expect most of life's stories to end satisfactorily, even if they do not end happily. There may be an even deeper reason why we want this to happen: it may be a reflection of God's image within us. Though that image is tarnished by our sin, it has not been destroyed. It may cause our consciences to call to account those who offend our sense of justice, and it triggers reflexes within us when we experience or witness injustice.

Judicial sentiment, Edward John Carnell, my predecessor at Fuller Seminary, used to call this feeling. It is the sense of outrage that bubbles up within us when we feel that we or others close to us have been treated unfairly.

Judicial sentiment was something that the Preacher, whose observations on life are logged in the Book of Ecclesiastes, felt keenly. He saw by his sharp and persistent investigations that some of life's stories—too many of them—ended untidily. His idea of justice, based as it was on the scriptural traditions of his people, was offended far too often. The verdict on life with which his book began—*"vanity of vanities, all is vanity"*—was confirmed by the lack of justice he observed in his society.

THE FORMS INJUSTICE TAKES

Like a many-headed monster, injustice threatened to destroy Koheleth's society and undermine all sense of right and wrong among its citizens. Oppression of the powerless (3:16–22), economic exploitation of the poor (4:1–3), jealous competition among the aggressive (4:4–6), compulsiveness on the part of the successful (4:7–12), and fickleness displayed by the populace (4:13–16) were five of the forms injustice took as it ravaged the countryside.

Oppression of the powerless often centered in the courts of law or the seats of government. It was this political oppression with which the Preacher began. The flow of 3:16–22 moves something like this:

The observation of injustice	v. 16
The declaration of judgment	v. 17
The reflections on judgment	vv. 18–21
The *alternative conclusion* on how to live with injustice	v. 22

We can understand how disheartened the wise man must have been:

> 16 Moreover I saw under the sun:
> In the place of judgment,
> Wickedness was there;
> And in the place of righteousness,
> Iniquity was there.
>
> *Eccles. 3:16*

Wherever he looked in our broken world (*"under the sun,"* see on 1:3) he *"saw"*—"observed and reflected upon"—the fact that the established courts of the land (*"place of judgment"* or *"justice,"* Heb. *mishpāṭ*) were as crooked, corrupt, and ineffective as Amos had described them so scathingly centuries earlier (5:7, 10, 24). This Hebrew term for "justice" or "judgments" has several nuances in Koheleth. It may describe divine judgment of those who revere or despise God's ways (11:9; 12:14). It may depict a canniness that knows what and when to speak if you want to stay on the good side of those who hold power over you (8:5–6). It may, as here, picture the flawed practice of human justice in the corrupt law courts and political structures (5:8). "Place of righteousness" is virtually synonymous with "place of judgment." Courts are the places where grievances should be redressed, where loyalty to the standards of the community are honored, and breaches of those standards are punished. None of this was being done, as the terms *"wickedness"* and *"iniquity"* (the same strong Heb. word *reshaᶜ*) point out.

> 17 I said in my heart,
> "God shall judge the righteous and the wicked,
> For there is a time there for every purpose
> and for every work."
>
> *Eccles. 3:17*

The teacher's initial response to the legal mayhem was a declaration to himself (*"in my heart"*; see 2:1, 15). He knows that *"God,"* not the courts, has the last word. Condemnation of the *"wicked"* or "the guilty" citizens (the same Heb. root used in v. 16) and the vindication of their *"righteous,"* that is, "innocent" countrymen, will take place in God's appointed *"time."* Here a belief in divine justice is tightly tied to the previous theme (3:1–15) of God's control of the timing of human events. On *"purpose,"* see the remarks in 3:1, where the same Hebrew word occurs. Koheleth is probably looking for God to pay accounts in this life rather than in the world beyond. Just because the court missed the boat, no one should think he or she got off scot-free. God does not always clear the docket on our timetable. The force of *"there"* (Heb. *shām*), the final word in the Hebrew of verse 17, is to reach back to the double use of *"there"* (Heb. *shammâh*) in verse 16 and to promise that the injustices (v. 16) will be righted by God in the very sphere of human activities where they took place. Judgment after death was beyond Koheleth's horizon.

The theme of judgment prompted further reflections:

> 18 I said in my heart, "Concerning the condition
> of the sons of men, God tests them, that they may see
> that they themselves are like animals."
> 19 For what happens to the sons of men also
> happens to animals; one thing befalls them: as one
> dies, so dies the other. Surely, they all have one
> breath; man has no advantage over animals, for all is
> vanity.
> 20 All go to one place: all are from the dust, and
> all return to dust.
> 21 Who knows the spirit of the sons of men,
> which goes upward, and the spirit of the animal,
> which goes down to the earth?
>
> *Eccles 3:18–21*

"I said in my heart" introduces further thoughts on the declaration of verse 17 by repeating its opening words. The thematic connection between verses 16–17 and 18–21 is not easy to catch. Thoughts of divine judgment (vv. 16–17) may have triggered further musings on death (remember 2:12–23), which was often considered a form of judgment, especially when the death was untimely.

Three observations about death seem to arise in Koheleth's heart. First, death is God's sure sign to the human family (*"sons of men,"* v. 18; see 1:13) that we are different from him. *"Tests"* is one translation of a difficult Hebrew word (*bārar*) which also means to "sort out" or "separate." By making us mortal (destined to die), God has shown (*"may see"* should be read as "has shown" or "to show," a rendering that entails the change of one vowel and is attested in both the LXX and Vulgate translations) that we are finite creatures, much more like *"animals"* than like God (v. 18). The least that this means is that we have to trust God's deeds since our own are fallible beyond words and our lives too short to see that ultimate justice is done.

The second observation is that the universality of death muddies, to our human eyes, the justice of God. How can death be a meaningful sentence for our crimes of injustice if everybody dies—human being and beast alike (v. 19)? *"Happens"* and *"befalls"* translate the Hebrew *miqreh* which we met in the earlier paragraph on death in 2:14–15. There the contrast was between the *"wise"* and the *"fool"* who though vastly different from each other in life partook together of the *"same event"*—death. Whatever Genesis may teach about human dominion over *"animals"* (Heb. *bᵉhēmāh* here stands for animals in general in contrast to birds or fish; Gen. 1:26; 2:20), Koheleth features what animals and people have in common: (1) death, (2) *"breath"* or *"spirit"* that animates the living and abandons the dead (v. 19), (3) destiny—the *"place"* where both (as *"all"* should be understood) *"return"* is the *"dust"* (v. 20) from which we were created (Gen. 2:7; 3:19).

The third item on which Koheleth reflected was the mystery of what happens at death (v. 21). Apparently the conventional interpretation, based on the clear differences between human beings and the animal world spelled out in the Genesis story, saw human death as the reversal of creation. Genesis 2:7 pictured the Lord God forming the man of dust as a potter would fashion clay and then breathing divine life into that molded matter so that the man became a living person. Death was read as dissolving that union and releasing each element to travel in the direction from which it came: *"the spirit"* (Heb. *rûaḥ*, not the Genesis term which is *nᵉshāmāh*) toward its source, while the body returns to *"dust"* as the curse on Adam and Eve promised (Gen. 3:19). But what about animals? At their death the body decomposes and disappears into the *"dust."* That is clear enough. But what about their breath or *"spirit"* (again Heb. *rûaḥ*)? Where does it go? Standard teachings must have suggested that it, in contrast with the human *"spirit,"* descended *"down"* (or "below") to the "ground," as *"earth"* must mean here. The Hebrew wording for these two directions is stronger than English can gracefully make it: "ascend above" is literally what the human spirit is supposed to do, while "descend below" describes the journey of the animal spirit. The verbs carry the note of direction themselves, and they are reinforced by adverbs which make the routes doubly clear.

As logically pat as this conventional teaching seemed, Koheleth douses its advocates in cold water. *"Who knows,"* the introduction to the rhetorical question in verse 21, means "nobody knows." The conventional theory had not met the Teacher's test of careful scrutiny. No one had experienced the ascent of the human spirit and lived to tell about it. And no one who observed a person's death could produce evidence of what actually happened. Koheleth's firm conclusion remained unshaken (v. 19): as far as ultimate destiny is concerned a human being (*"man"* in v. 18) has no provable, palpable, measurable *"advantage"* (Heb. *môthār*, a word built on the same root as *yitrôn*, "profit"; see at 1:3) over the lowly beasts that plow our fields, let down their milk, and lick our hands.

This whole subject of death as a vehicle of judgment, the teacher warns, is riddled with enigmas: *"for all is vanity"* (v. 19), that is, the whole subject of human survival after death is fraught with mysteries beyond our ken. The ways in which God may dispense justice in this life or beyond took Koheleth out of the range of his ability to observe. The easy answers of conventional wisdom (v. 21) he refused to pin his hopes on; the harder answers again, as at the close of the First Demonstration (2:26), he has branded as useless speculation and left in God's hands. His view of death afforded him no other choice. Human beings neither lived long enough nor were confident enough of eternal life to do anything else. The wisest of them, such as Koheleth, knew that.

Backed thus against the wall of death's certainty and finality, the Teacher reached for the third time to his *alternative conclusion* (v. 22; see at 2:24–26; 3:12–13).

> 22 So I perceived that there is nothing better than
> that a man should rejoice in his own works, for that is
> his heritage. For who can bring him to see what will
> happen after him?
>
> *Eccles. 3:22*

Acute investigation of the options for making sense of the how and when of God's justice in human affairs and sober reflection on our human limitations to understand or contribute to it are what is suggested in *"I perceived"* (lit. "I saw"; see on 1:14). The note of rejoicing is a constant in these conclusions. It brightens the somber outlook of the book like a red scarf on a gray dress and conveys one of Koheleth's most persistent and significant messages: life has happiness, pleasure, even fun if we go at it aright. *"His* (or her) *own works"* are the source of the person's joy. The whole range of human endeavors is in view, perhaps deliberately highlighted as a way of alerting us to the possibility of taking delight even in the round of activities embraced in the merisms of 3:2–8. God may control the timing but that does not mean that all the divine prescriptions that regulate our lives have to taste like castor oil.

Missing in this statement of the *alternative conclusion* are food and drink. It may be that the context which centers in matters of justice called for a focus not on personal survival and refreshment but on human efforts (*"his own works"*) to practice and enforce justice with the limited resources available to us. Finding joy in such community concerns, along with our other works, is part of the lot or portion (*"heritage"*; on Heb. *hēleq* see at 2:10) bequeathed to us by the God of grace. Joy *now* is the dominant note as the final clause suggests. *"For"* marks it as the motivation, the reason: no one (as in v. 21, this is the force of *"who"*) has the ability to *"bring"* us back from death to enjoy further fruit in life or garner more information about it (*"see"*). Hindsight may have 20/20 vision, but if it is not available we do well to make the best of the 20/100 vision available to us now.

Economic oppression seemed to have accompanied political injustice:

> 4:1 Then I returned and considered all the oppres-
> sion that is done under the sun:
>> And look! The tears of the oppressed,
>> But they have no comforter—
>> On the side of their oppressors there is power,
>> But they have no comforter.
>
> *Eccles. 4:1*

The description was pitiful. From his wide-ranging knowledge and richly varied experience (*"returned and considered,"* here and in 4:7, is literally "I saw again"; "saw" as a verb of perception and reflection carries out the process of 3:21 and is repeated in 4:4, 7, 15), the Preacher drew an irrefutable conclusion—oppression was rampant throughout our world (*"under the sun"* see 1:3). The oppressed had no one on their side to give them aid or comfort. The pathos of this situation is hammered home in the style and vocabulary of verse 1: (a) the form is a virtual lament (see on 2:16), sobbing with grief over a fate worse than death; (b) *"tears"* highlights the tragedy by using a term expressive of deep and sustained grief (for Heb. *dimʿâh* see Ps. 6:6; Jer. 9:1; Lam. 1:2); (c) the note of *"oppression"* is sounded three times, depicting the deed, the victims, and culprits; (d) the *"power"* of the *"oppressors"* stands in marked contrast to the *"tears of the oppressed"* on whom they readily and without hindrance worked their wicked will; and (e) like a dirge the repetition of *"But they have no comforter"* rings with the poignancy of Amos' lament over fallen Israel, *"There is no one to raise her up"* (Amos 5:2).

The age in which Ecclesiastes lived was far removed from the golden days of Israel's beginnings. The sense of concern for the poor, the widow, the alien, and the orphan had long since dimmed, outshown by the highly organized commercial structures that had been borrowed from the Phoenicians and others. Apparently this was an age when the rich continued to acquire more, while the poor toiled ever harder to make ends meet. Wages were low, hours were long, rights were few. The oppressed had no ways to express themselves except through tears, and no one to wipe those tears except other oppressed.

The Preacher's evaluation of the lot of these wretched souls, oppressed in the courts and in the markets, was bitter:

> 2 Therefore I praised the dead who were already dead,
>> More than the living who are still alive.
> 3 Yet, better than both is he who has never existed,
>> Who has not seen the evil work that is done under the sun.
>> *Eccles. 4:2–3*

What a drastic solution to the problem—to be dead or unborn was to be preferred to such oppression. *"Praised"* is a dramatic word to magnify the benefits of being *"dead."* Most translations paraphrase it to catch its force: "I salute" (JB); "I declared that the dead . . . are happier" (NIV); "I congratulated" (NASB). *"Never existed"* takes us back to *"I hated life"* (2:17) and marks the low-water line in Koheleth's appreciation of living. Even if we modulate the text a bit by allowing for exaggeration or hyperbole, the pathos is powerful and the horror of oppression is clear. What a cry of compassion from an otherwise stern observer—the sobs of the poor had fallen on sensitive ears!

Competition among the aggressive (4:4–6) was another form injustice took:

> 4 Again, I saw that for all toil and every skillful
> work a man is envied by his neighbor. This also is
> vanity and grasping for the wind.
>
> *Eccles. 4:4*

The wise man had probed the subject of work before. He had concluded that hard work did not produce the results that teachers often promised their pupils (*"toil"* is the familiar Heb. ʿāmāl; see at 1:3; *"skillful work"* is Heb. kishrôn, which is work that lends to profit or advantage and is often translated "achievement"; see at 2:21). But here he dug deeper. He exposed the hollowness of much of our motivation for hard work—envy. The NKJV suggests that the one who does the work is the object of the *"neighbor's"* envy. Most translators flip it the other way: the worker is motivated by his envy of the neighbor. Though the feelings could obviously have been mutual as some readings indicate: "rivalry" (NEB, NASB) and "mutual jealousy" (JB).

This was a painful observation. It undoubtedly unnerved his hearers as it unmasked their hypocrisy. They claimed to be toiling for all kinds of good motives—love of their family, concern for their community, service to their God. Rationalizations, the Preacher called these. At the bottom of the matter, the reason we work so hard is to keep up with or get ahead of our neighbors.

Think of the injustices to which envy may push us. We may be tempted to cheat our neighbors of their rights, to resent their accomplishments, to cut the corners of our own integrity—and all in the name of winning. The fabric of our communities gets torn into small pieces in our jealous competition. And the sense of concern for the welfare of others which is the heart of true justice becomes unraveled in the process. That was why the wise man branded so much of our toil as *"vanity,"* unfathomable mystery (see at 1:2), trying to grasp life's meaning in ways as futile as a shepherd's attempt to capture the *"wind"* and lead it into the sheepfold (see at 1:14).

When hard work caused such bitterness and strife, was it really to be as highly valued as some had taught? Ecclesiastes quoted a favorite proverb advocating hard work. It is the kind of saying with which aggressive workaholics defended their behavior.

> 5 The fool folds his hands
> And consumes his own flesh.
>
> *Eccles. 4:5*

Laziness is self-destructive, a form of cannibalism, was their point. On *"folds his hands"* as a standard gesture of the foolish sluggard, see Proverbs 6:10, and 24:33. Who wants to emulate him? The Preacher's answer came in his proverb, a counter-proverb in fact, arguing for peace and harmony rather than for toil:

> 6 Better a handful with quietness
> Than both hands full, together with toil
> and grasping for the wind.
>
> *Eccles. 4:6*

The *"better"* form of proverb points to a sharp contrast. Its aim is to dramatize the choice so that one may choose the right course in the comparison without hesitation. Here the comparisons are both qualitative and quantitative. Qualitatively, the difference is between the small amounts that can be cradled in one open palm and the much larger portion that can be clutched between two clenched fists.

The handful of ashes, grasped by Moses and Aaron and scattered to the winds, illustrates the generous amount of a substance that can be carried in two hands (Exod. 9:8; Heb. *hōphen* in the dual form is the word used in both Exodus and Ecclesiastes). Qualitatively, the contrast lies between the two ways of acquiring what is in the hands: (1) you can get enough with *"quietness"* (Heb. *nāhat*), which pictures the calm, quiet strength of the wise teachers (9:17) and the complete freedom from stress or pressure of a stillborn baby (6:5), or (2) you can gain more than twice as much with *"toil"* (Heb. *ʿāmāl*; see at 4:4; 1:3), which stresses the backbreaking efforts necessary to acquire excessive amounts of wealth. Koheleth's preference is clear: the stress-packed, frenzied labor that envy produces is not a life-style worth comparing with the simple sufficiency to be garnered by composed and moderate efforts. When the choice is quality over quantity, he will opt for quality every time. To reinforce he adds a note that likens *"toil"* to *"grasping for the wind"* (see 4:4), one of his favorite expressions for futility. On the value of peace and quiet to the wise, see Proverbs 15:16; 16:8; 17:1.

Compulsiveness on the part of the successful (4:7–12) was still another form in which injustice showed itself. To Koheleth greed was at least as sour a motive as envy. His keen eye *"saw"* it and immediately labeled it as another universal (*"under the sun,"* see 1:3) human conundrum, an instance of behavior that defies explanation (*"vanity,"* see 1:2). Note that the verdict of *"vanity"* begins and ends these verses. The illustration of the greedy workaholic lends itself to no other explanation than that in which it is wrapped—*"vanity."* On *"returned"* see 4:1; on *"grave misfortune"* see 1:13; 5:13.

The drive to achieve and to acquire has awesome force.

> 7 Then I returned, and I saw vanity under the sun:
> 8 There is one alone, without companion:
> He has neither son nor brother.
> Yet there is no end to all his labors,
> Nor is his eye satisfied with riches.
> But he never asks,
> "For whom do I toil and deprive myself of good?"
> This also is vanity and a grave misfortune.
> *Eccles. 4:7–8*

The familiar ʿāmāl (see on 1:3) pops up twice in verse 8 to describe the drive that nudges us from bed early and keeps us in the factory or office late. Long after we have enough to care for our own needs, some of us keep pushing for more. To work hard to help loved ones may be understandable, but the avaricious person in the story has *"neither son nor brother,"* no male heirs to inherit, supervise and benefit from his holdings. The son, especially the eldest would have first claim; in the absence of a *"son,"* the testator's *"brother"* would be the heir (see Deut. 21:15–17; Num. 27:1–11 for Old Testament patterns of inheritance). His unsatisfied *"eye"* (see 1:8), not the support of his family, is his basic motivation.

This compulsive drive can contribute to injustice, unless those who acquire wealth ask the question that the Preacher posed, putting himself into the skin of the wealthy person. *"For whom do I toil and deprive myself of good?"* This question has no introduction in the Hebrew text. *"But he never asks"* is supplied for clarity by NKJV. Other translations, with equal or more reason, quote him as asking the question and, thanks to his compulsiveness, giving it no answer (NIV, NEB).

Koheleth saw *"riches"* (Heb. ʿōsher) as more of a gift than an acquisition (5:19; 6:2). He goes so far as to list them with the boons that happen by *"time and chance"* (9:11). The goods God has given were not intended to make the rich richer. They were intended to serve the needs of all God's people. The drive to accumulate goods must be accompanied by an urge to share them. If not, then injustice is the sure result. Persons with ingenuity, energy, and opportunity can hoard huge resources while others go begging.

The results are damaging both ways. Those who have spend their health and peace in getting more, while depriving themselves of other experiences that are *"good,"* like quietness, leisure, and time for relationships. Those who don't have become bitter and jealous toward those who have. For both, the result is a futility that leaves life's story with an untidy ending.

In the long run the real loser is the person who suffers loneliness, loss of identity, and the fatal flaw of leaving no heir to carry on the family continuity and preserve its name. To the Hebrews, the hope for permanence lay not in eternal life or bodily resurrection but in the durability of their name, perpetuated by their sons and their sons' sons throughout the generations. No amount of wealth could compensate for that loneliness and virtual annihilation.

The teacher took pains not only to warn against greed but also to advocate fellowship and its power to combat both greed and loneliness. The wise man described this power in words that have become justly famous:

9 Two are better than one,
  Because they have a good reward for their labor.
10 For if they fall, one will lift up his companion.
  But woe to him who is alone when he falls,
  For he has no one to help him up.

11 Again, if two lie down together,
    they will keep warm;
  But how can one be warm alone?
12 Though one may be overpowered by another,
    two can withstand him.
  And a threefold cord is not quickly broken.

Eccles. 4:9–12

From the institution of marriage to the practice of collective bargaining, generations of people have tested the truth of these words. One of God's great gifts in helping us deal with problems of oppression, poverty, loneliness, and injustice is the company of others.

The introduction (v. 9) sets the theme for the paragraph, promising a *"good reward"*—blessings whether material or spiritual (see 9:5)—to those who face life's tasks (*"labor"* repeats the note of ʿamāl from v. 8). The translation obscures an even stronger connection: *"two are better than one"* (v. 9) echoes the first line of verse 8 which is literally, "There is one and not two." The contrast drawn between verses 7–8 and verses 9–12 is clear-cut. The former describes lonely greed; the latter, blessed fellowship.

The *"good reward"* is illustrated in three vignettes: (1) traveling with a *"companion"* (for Heb. ḥābēr as "comrade" or "partner" joined by covenant in a bond of fellowship, see on Song of Sol. 1:7; 8:13) is infinitely safer than venturing out alone with no one to *"help you up"* if you *"fall"* into a pit or slide off the path into a crevice (v. 10); (2) sleeping close to a family member or fellow traveler will supply enough body heat to combat the frosty evenings to which Palestine was no stranger (v. 11; see the wintry scene in Jer. 36: 22–30); (3) siding with a partner in a time of assault may be the difference between *"withstanding"* (lit. "standing in front of") an assailant and being *"overpowered"* (v. 12; Heb. tāqaph is used of God's irresistible power in 6:10 and Job 14:20).

The concluding line is probably a proverb attached here as the climax of the whole passage, with relevance to the wretched oppressed who *"have no comforter"* (4:1), to the man plagued by loneliness and greed (4:8), as well as to the trio of two-are-better-than-one illustrations (vv. 10–12). Strength in numbers is the message, with the triply braided cord as the clinching illustration. The number *"three"* builds on the "one-two" pattern featured throughout and goes it one better.

Fickleness displayed by the populace (4:13–16) is the last form of injustice described in the Second Demonstration (3:1–4:16).

> 13 Better is a poor and wise youth
>   Than an old and foolish king who
>   will be admonished no more.
> 14 For he comes out of prison to be king,
>   Although he was born poor in his kingdom.
> 15 I saw all the living who walk under the sun;
>   They were with the second youth
>   who stands in his place.
> 16 There was no end of all the people
>   over whom he was made king;
>   Yet those who come afterward will
>   not rejoice in him.
>   Surely this also is vanity and grasping
>   for the wind.
>   *Eccles. 4:13–16*

The fickleness of the citizenry described in verses 15–16 is all the more vexing because they have turned their backs on the *"wise youth"* (v. 13) who overcame vast difficulties to be their sovereign (v. 14). The overall message is that the advantages of wisdom are only relative. They help a ruler do well during his reign but assure neither stability nor acclaim, once his successor takes over. As with wisdom and wealth (2:12–23), political power may pale into insignificance at the changing of the guard.

In *structure* this passage is a *"better"* proverb whose comparison is expanded by an illustration that is virtually a parable. The force of the proverb is to highlight folly's inability to compete with wisdom, which overcomes the disadvantages of *"youth,"* imprisonment, and poverty so as to outrank both age (which was accorded great value and respect by the conventional wisdom teachers; Prov. 20:29) and station. The *"foolish king"* loses his grip on the throne when he no longer heeds advice that would keep him out of trouble. *"Be admonished"* (Heb. *nizhar*) recurs in 12:12, where the teacher warns against the making of books. It is a favorite word in Ezekiel where it describes both divine warnings, and the kinds of alarms sounded by alert watchmen (chaps. 3, 33). The senile king's foolishness lulled him to sleep at the switch, and he was too foolish to know it.

The parable tells the story of the *"wise youth's"* rise from *"prison"* and poverty to power in the *"kingdom"* of the aged monarch (who must be the *"his"* in *"his kingdom,"* v. 14). But the story that begins with the from-pauper-to-prince theme in verses 13–14 takes a bizarre turn at verses 15–16. The entire populace—*"all the living who walk* (that is, "conduct their lives") *under the sun"*—apparently abandon the *"wise youth"* to lend their support (as *"with"* seems to mean) to the next young monarch (*"second youth"*—*"second"* here may be a catchword linking their paragraph to the *"one alone"* who had no *"second,"* that is, *"companion"* in v. 8, and to the *"two are better than one"* in vv. 9, 11–12). *"Stands in his place"* (v. 15) describes this usurpation of monarchy, whether by revolution or normal succession. *"His"* in *"his place"* refers to the first young king who is pushed aside.

The final scene (v. 16) describes a vast multitude of subjects acclaiming their loyalty to the second young king who stood before them as their newest ruler. Yet the ringing cheers serve only to sober Koheleth, knowing as he does that the next generations (*"those who come afterward"*) will take no more joy in this king than his generation took in his predecessor.

It seems best to treat this story of the three monarchs—one old and foolish, one young, wise, and poor, and one described only as the second youth, whose virtues or vices did not much matter—as a parable. Links to the stories of Joseph's rise to power under Pharaoh, David's selection to replace Saul, and Daniel's ascendancy in Nebuchadnezzar's court—all rags-to-riches events—are worth noting. But we cannot be sure that Koheleth had them specifically in mind.

Fame and station are fickle and not even wisdom is powerful enough to overcome the chronic lack of memory which is a notable human foible (see on 1:11; 2:16). The enigma of why this should be so evokes another frustrated conclusion from the Preacher, as he closes his Second Demonstration of his major theme: All this is another instance of our elusive, baffling failure to draw sense from human experience. (For *"vanity,"* see on 1:2; for *"grasping of the wind,"* see on 1:17.) A desperate ending this is, choked out of a vexed spirit. Koheleth has not given us a tidy picture of the triumph of justice. Rather, he has choreographed four scenes, each driving home with increased intensity the pervasiveness of injustice in society from peasant's hovel, to law court, to palace. He has tightened down the screws of our uneasiness, and he offers as relief no sage words of advice. They would not lift us out of our pain, however much they might help us to live within it.

Epilogue: The Greater Wise Man

This low, long cry for justice that Ecclesiastes voiced was picked up and sounded more strongly and more hopefully by Jesus. The example he set shows us best how to deal with life's injustices.

Where he could, he not only lamented over what was wrong in life; he did something about it. Think of the Temple money-changers cheating the worshipers in the very place where prayer to the living God was to be offered. Lashing them with whip and tongue, Jesus went after them and turned them out. Where he could not change the situation, as in his crucifixion, he bore with the injustice, while praying for those who persecuted him.

Both acts were deeds of love. His concern for human welfare, for human salvation, prompted him to firm intervention in one case and to strong intercession in the other.

What he did not do was condone injustice or despair over it. He acted in force and in love. He recognized its wrong and tried to help both those who were inflicting it and those who were afflicted by it.

He was acting as judge in both events. And he has a right to. He is the Father's appointed judge with whom all of us reckon now and will reckon in a day yet to come (Acts 17:31).

Futility was how the older Teacher described a world fraught with injustice. He knew that the systems "under the sun" could not be depended on.

We know this, but we know more. We know that God is leading his people beyond futility to a concern for justice in every area of life. More than that, we know personally the Lord who will judge all injustice and see to it that all life's stories have the tidy endings for which we so earnestly yearn.

CHAPTER SEVEN

First Words of Advice: God, Government, Greed

Ecclesiastes 5:1–12

Critics often rub us the wrong way, but we would find it hard to get along without them. Their opinions frequently seem harsh and arbitrary, and their judgments are rendered with a sarcasm that sometimes bites.

On television we watch them with eyes that squint questioningly. We shrug off their estimates of the state of music or art with a mild skepticism that says, "How do they know what is good or bad? How can they say what the rest of us should like?"

They rub us the wrong way, yet they render us a service. By describing an attractive art exhibit, they suggest how we can spend a profitable Saturday. When they pan a senseless play or a silly book they save us the effort and expense of finding out for ourselves. Who wants to waste an evening with a soprano that sings flat or a tenor that cracks on high notes. Discerning critics often rescue us from such fates.

But they do more. When they do their work best, their discernment rubs off on us. We begin to sense the difference between great music and trite tunes, between contrived plots and compelling drama, between doggerel verse and well-crafted poetry, between the random splash of colors and distinguished art, between an entertaining adventure story and a life-molding novel. Where critics enhance our sense of beauty, invigorate our imagination or enlarge our appreciation of life, they have done us royal service. We are much the better for their work.

At times critics help even more. I have in mind not only critics of the *arts* but also critics of our *society*. Theirs is the task of analyzing social trends and highlighting our social problems. They do this in many ways. Experts in consumer affairs point to some of the flaws in our advertising and merchandising practices. Social critics call attention to our moral trends. Marriage counselors analyze our changing attitudes toward the family and the impact they may have on the stability of our nation. Political journalists scrutinize the conduct of our government officials and expose their foibles. Humorists pinpoint our foolish attitudes.

All of these critics may rub us the wrong way at times, but we can scarcely do without them. They lay bare our prejudices, spotlight our weaknesses, and warn about our dangers. Overstatement, even exaggeration, is their loud way of getting our attention. But think what life would be without them. We would deceive ourselves and be bilked by others. Despite all their wild extravagance and pompous arrogance, critics make a valuable contribution to our society.

It was just this kind of contribution—the contribution of carping yet constructive criticism—that the Preacher, Ecclesiastes, tried to make. His society needed what he had to say. They had overvalued wisdom, almost to the point of using it to control God. They had overprized pleasure, hoping by it to find life's true meaning. They had perverted justice by diminishing the rights of the poor and the oppressed. And they had overestimated their freedom to make life-shaking decisions, by ignoring the mystery of God's ways and the inevitability of death. A futile way of life was what the Preacher accused them of living. With his sharp pen he had pricked the balloons of their hollow hopes.

But he did more than that. He also offered words of practical advice. We have heard them in his *alternative conclusions*, where he urged his followers to find joy in God's simple gifts of food, drink, and work (2:24–26; 3:12–15, 22). Now we hear them in the first of the three series of proverbs—5:1–12; 7:1–8:9; 9:13–12:8—that alternate with the four sets of Demonstrations—1:4–2:26; 3:1–4:16; 5:13–6:12; 8:10–9:12.

The Words of Advice have some characteristics that mark them off from the Demonstrations. First, they feature *proverbs* in at least three typical forms: (1) *admonitions*—imperatives addressed directly to the hearers telling them what and what not to do and usually giving reasons introduced by *"for"* or *"lest"* (see 5:1, 2, 4, 6); (2) *sayings*—indicative sentences describing how life works and implying a command to behave in line with what the proverb teaches (see 5:10, 11, 12); (3) *comparisons* introduced by "better"—a dramatic form of contrast that sharpens the advantage of one form of conduct over another (see comments on 4:6 ; 6:9; 7:1, 2, 3, 5, 8). While proverbs may occasionally garnish the arguments in the Demonstrations (1:15, 18; 2:14; 4:5–6), in the Words of Advice they are the main menu.

Second, in the Words of Advice the subjects change more frequently than in the Demonstrations. For instance, in the thirty-eight verses of 7:1–8:9 eight separate issues are treated. Third, the verdict of *"vanity"* that punctuates the demonstrations is found only sparingly (see 5:10; 7:6, 15; 11:8, 10; 12:8).

Fourth, the personality of Koheleth remains in the background except for a few instances when he introduces his own observations: "I *have seen"*—7:15; "*I have proved"*—7:23; "*I have applied my heart"*—7:25; "*I find"*—7:26; "*says the Preacher"*—7:27; "*All this I have seen"*—8:9; "*This wisdom I have also seen"*—9:13; "*Then I said"*—9:16; "*I have seen"*— 10:5. These introductions or summations serve to establish continuity between the two main types of material and to remind the reader that there is one Teacher at work though he uses both advice and demonstration to make his point.

Fifth, as we noted in 2:24–26, the *alternative conclusion*, found six times in the book, does not appear in the Words of Advice but only in the Demonstrations. One way of looking at these clusters of proverbs is to see them as extended comments on the *alternative conclusion.* They flesh out the picture of a life that enjoys the simple things as divine gifts and that lives modestly, peacefully, reverently, and sensibly—a life, in other words, that walks in the fear of God (5:7; see on 3:14).

The first collection of Words of Advice (5:1–12) speaks to three topics:

prudence in worship	5:1–7
caution toward government	5:8–9
restraint of greed	5:10–12

Basic issues these are, sketching ground rules for effective living in a small cluster of sentences. Koheleth was a gifted social critic. We listen to his counsel with both pain and profit.

A PIETY GONE STALE

The religious practices of Koheleth's countrymen did not escape his keen eye. Usually the wise men left such matters as prayer, sacrifice, vows, and rituals to the priests who were in charge of the Temple. But not Ecclesiastes. Fake religion distressed him as much as proud wisdom, vain pleasure, abused justice, or hollow freedom.

Apparently the people took a mechanical attitude toward the sacrifices which God had commanded. They were offering them in huge volume and with great attention to detail. But they were missing the deeper meaning, the key purpose, of those animal offerings. *Listening to God is better than sacrifice* was the Preacher's word to them:

> 1   Walk prudently when you go to the house of
> God; and draw near to hear rather than to give the
> sacrifice of fools, for they do not know that they do evil.
> *Eccles. 5:1*

"The sacrifice of fools" was empty sacrifice, going through the ritual but missing its meaning. What was the basic purpose of the offerings that God required? It was communion with God expressed by *"hear,"* which means virtually to obey, and *"draw near,"* which frequently describes the intimacy between God and those who go to him for worship and fellowship (Deut. 5:27; Pss. 34:18; 85:9; 1 Kings 8:59). Therefore, the sacrifices dealt with the major human needs: They brought forgiveness, when accompanied by a contrite heart; they expressed thanksgiving, when the offerer was truly grateful; they fulfilled vows, when God had brought unusual blessing. The sacrifices were the means by which God's people were to declare their total dependence on God. Listening (*"hear"*)—paying attention to God—then, was an essential requirement, if the sacrifices were to have any meaning. The whole requirement of reverent obedience and humble penitence was captured in the clause, *"walk prudently,"* which is literally "watch (or guard) your feet." Here as in Proverbs *"feet"* summed up a total way of life that could lead toward or away from God:

> Ponder the path of your feet,
> And let all your ways be established.
> Do not turn to the right or the left;
> Remove your foot from evil.
> *Prov. 4:26–27*

What were the Preacher's fellow citizens doing wrong? They were treating sacrifices like magic. They thought blood and smoke were what God wanted. They forgot that spirit and heart were essential ingredients of true sacrifice. The words of the psalm had escaped their minds:

> For You do not desire sacrifice, or else I would give it;
> You do not delight in burnt offering.
> The sacrifices of God are a broken spirit,
> A broken and contrite heart—
> These, O God, You will not despise.
>
> *Ps. 51:16–17*

What Samuel had told Saul, they needed once again to hear:

> "Behold, to obey is better than sacrifice,
> And to heed than the fat of rams."
>
> *1 Sam. 15:22*

A piety gone stale needed sharp criticism, and Ecclesiastes did not hesitate to give it. For similar words of the wise, see Proverbs 15:8; 21:3, 27.

The wise man's second criticism followed closely his first. Not only is listening to God better than sacrifice, but *brevity in prayer is better than extravagance:*

> 2 Do not be rash with your mouth,
>   And let not your heart utter anything hastily
>   before God.
>   For God *is* in heaven, and you on earth;
>   Therefore let your words be few.
>
> *Eccles. 5:2*

Again, the Preacher wanted to remind his hearers of the greatness of God who could see through any extravagance in prayer. Wild promises, unguarded commitments, vain repetition were all to be avoided. Poise, control, measured speech and action were considered expressions of sound conduct by the wise. Haste, to the teachers, almost always meant waste. The verb in *"Do not be rash"* (Heb. *bahal*) is used by Koheleth in connection with a hot, short-fused, temper (7:9). The root read here as *"hastily"* (Heb. *mahar*) is a favorite term for wild, rash, mindless conduct in Proverbs: feet that "make haste to shed blood" (1:16); "feet . . . swift in running to evil" (6:18); an impulsive litigant who wants to "go hastily to court" (25:8).

The second half of the verse gives the reason (or motivation, note *"for"*) that explains the admonition against haste. Prayer was solemn conversation with a mysterious God. The vast gap between human-

132

kind and God—a gap measured by the difference between *"heaven"* and *"earth"*—demanded sobriety, not extravagance. Neither the volume, nor the eloquence, nor the frequency of prayers were what influenced him. In no way could God be manipulated into answering prayer. What he would hear were the simple, sincere, brief words of those who truly submitted to his majesty and sought his help.

Any other approach was as full of fantasy as a wild dream. The Preacher illustrated his point with a proverb:

> 3 For a dream comes through much activity,
> And a fool's voice is known by his many words.
>
> *Eccles. 5:3*

"For" connects verse 3 with the preceding command (v. 2). The saying (note the indicative, not imperative grammar) is a comparison. The point is made in the second half: you can tell a fool's voice by the multitude of words, even if you cannot catch the content. The comparison is stated in the first half. Certain things just go together: *"Much activity"* (or "business"; on Heb. *ʿinyān,* see 1:13) produces *"a dream,"* apparently as the by-product of stress and anxiety—a side glance of Koheleth at the futility of frenzied work. Likewise, foolishness prompts wordiness. Jesus and the Preacher agreed on this (Matt. 6:7). A piety gone stale permitted vain, dream-like babbling as a substitute for prayer. No wonder the Preacher took pains to point out its futility.

The Preacher's last criticism dealt with the vows that people rashly offered. This was his word: *faithfulness in keeping vows is better than fickleness.* Here is how he put it:

> 4 When you make a vow to God, do not delay to
> pay it;
> For He has no pleasure in fools.
> Pay what you have vowed—
> 5 Better not to vow than to vow and not pay.
>
> *Eccles. 5:4–5*

Vows played a prominent part in the lives of Israel's men and women. A vow was one way to show how seriously they took their need to God. In times of emergency they used vows to underline their prayer requests (1 Sam. 1:11; Ps. 22:25–26). A barren woman who longed for a son, a frightened soldier under enemy attack, an innocent person accused of serious crime—each might vow to offer a special sacrifice to God if God would deliver him or her from the predicament.

How easy it was to vow, and how hard to pay! The painful lesson of Jephthah's integrity in keeping his vow to Yahweh at incredible cost to himself and his family (Judg. 11:29–40) was long forgotten. Vowing and paying cannot be separated (Ps. 76:11). That was the tendency Ecclesiastes criticized. Apparently one way to get out of the vow was to tell the priest or the Temple representative sent to collect the pledge (called here *"the messenger"*) that it was a mistake. In stern words that threatened God's judgment, Ecclesiastes warned against this:

> 6   Do not let your mouth cause your flesh to sin,
> nor say before the messenger of God that it was an
> error. Why should God be angry at your excuse and
> destroy the work of your hands?
>
> *Eccles. 5:6*

"Flesh" here stands for the whole person viewed as a unity. No amount of rationalization could detach *"mouth"* and *"flesh"* in God's sight. He made us to be a whole creature, not segmented parts. He wanted *"heart"* and *"flesh"* together to cry out to him (Ps. 84:2).

"Error" (Heb. *shᵉgāgāh*) suggests an inadvertent or unintended mistake. It is the regular word for unintentional sin in the ritual laws (Lev. 4:2, 22, 27; Num. 15:24–29). Such excuse-making carries no weight with God but actually provokes his anger. *"Be angry"* (Heb. *qāṣaph*) is used of human wrath (like Pharaoh's in Genesis 40:2 or Moses' in Exodus 16:20) but primarily it describes divine displeasure at human disobedience in about twenty of its occurrences (such as Lev. 10:16; Deut. 1:34; Isa. 47:6; Zech. 1:2). *"Work of your hands"* probably is material wealth, perhaps garnered in some venture which the vower had asked God to bless. When the investment paid off or the crop proved bumper, the vow was gainsaid. Accordingly, God would shape the penalty to fit the crime and wipe out (*"destroy"*; Heb. *hibbēl*, an intensive form of verb) the gains as *"the little foxes . . . spoil the vines"* (Song of Sol. 2:15) or as Yahweh and *"His weapons of indignation [come] to destroy the whole land"* (Isa. 13:5).

Then, good wise man that he was, Ecclesiastes clinched his point with a summary command:

7   For in the multitude of dreams and many
words there is also vanity. But fear God.

Eccles. 5:7

The first sentence of the summary has prompted a variety of translations. Some, like NEB, have left it out! Of the options available, the one that makes best sense and leaves the Hebrew text intact follows a line proposed by R. Gordis. It makes one sentence of the whole verse: "For in the multitude of dreams, enigmas (vanities), and many words, truly fear God." Thus read, the text recapitulates the pictures of busyness, haste, verbosity, and fickleness that plagued the worship of God as Koheleth viewed it. In the midst of that confused and compromised context comes the simple, powerful command: "Truly (Heb. *kî* often translated as "but" or "for" can also be a sign of emphasis—"surely," "indeed," "certainly") *fear God*" (3:14). The imperative here as throughout 5:1–7 is singular. If the Teacher is addressing a group, he is dealing with them one by one to put responsibility for prudent piety on the shoulders of each person. "*Fear*" encapsulates the proper attitude toward prayers, sacrifices, and vows whose true meaning had been so badly mangled by foolish, half-hearted worshipers.

By now we have gotten the Preacher's message. He has been saying that God must be taken with unconditional seriousness. He was saying, further, that his neighbors had failed to do that. Yet like most critics he was better at exposing the weaknesses of his people than he was at helping them be strong. Many critics can tell when a singer like Kathleen Battle has a rare off night; none of them can sing better than she does on any night. Social analysts can chart the drift of our society much more readily than they can steer us on a safer course.

GOVERNMENT TURNED CORRUPT

Learning to live with bad governments was something the Jews had to master. After all, they had suffered the indignities of foreign domination for about four centuries by the time Koheleth began to teach. From approximately 733 B.C., part or all of the land of Israel was governed by outsiders—Assyrians for about 130 years, Babylonians for some 65 years, Persians for more than 200 years. And after the Persians, when Koheleth may have been gone, came the Seleucids who ruled the Syrian portion of Alexander's empire. Then in 63 B.C., after a century or so of Jewish freedom under the Maccabean rulers, the Romans arrived and stayed till the dissolution of their empire four centuries later when they were succeeded by the Byzantine rulers of Constantinople who exercised authority over Palestine until the rise of Islam, in the seventh century A.D.

The Preacher's counsel focused on understanding the reality of corruption and greed in government, with the assumption that such understanding would help his Jewish kin to cope with the inevitable. He describes the contemporary scene in terms that curdle the blood of any son or daughter of Israel raised on the Law, the Prophets, and the Proverbs, all of which condemn the practices Ecclesiastes described:

> 8   If you see the oppression of the poor, and the
> violent perversion of justice and righteousness in a
> province, do not marvel at the matter; for high official
> watches over high official, and higher officials are
> over them.
> 9   Moreover the profit of the land is for all; even
> the king himself is served from the field.

Eccles. 5:8–9

"Oppression" (see on 4:1–3) and *"violent perversion* (lit. "robbery," Ps. 62:10) *of justice and righteousness"* (see on 3:16) are not new themes in the book. What is new here seems to be the specific connection with the administrative structures of government. This is made clear in the Hebrew word for *"province" (meḏînāh),* which describes a judicial district with a centralized system for enforcing and adjudicating the law (see 2:8). Its most frequent use is in Esther, where nearly forty times it depicts the Persian provinces and their governmental structures by which Ahasuerus ruled the empire. *"High official,"* which translates a word meaning "lofty" or even "proud" (Heb. *gāḇōªh* ; Isa. 2:15; 5:15), confirms this bureaucratic setting.

The *"perversion of justice"* takes place not in spite of the government officials but because of them. They are supposed to be checking on each other to make sure that the law is upheld and the rights of the citizens guarded. Instead, they are protecting each other, covering up for each other, which is what *"watches"* seems to mean here. The evil has permeated the system so that each tier of the administration is free to work injustice—taking bribes, browbeating the defenseless, extorting higher taxes than called for, confiscating property and goods, demanding special favors, and commandeering people to work for them—because each official is supported in these crimes by his superior. *"Do not marvel"* suggests that this was a pattern so endemic in Jewish society under foreign domination that it could virtually be taken for granted. For comments on *"matter,"* that is the persistent presence of *"oppression"* and corrupt legal practices, see on 3:1.

Verse 8 may be seen as further commentary on 3:16 and 4:1–3. The *"wickedness"* in the *"place of judgment"* (3:16) was sparked by the administrative corruption. And the "oppressed" had *"no comforter"* (4:1) because the official who ought to have protected their rights used their political "power" against them.

Verse 9 raises the question of the king's relationship to all this. The Hebrew text is terse and cryptic and has had generations of scholars scratching their heads to probe its meaning. The major question has to do with whether verse 9 is a contrast to verse 8 or a climax. Was the king part of the problem (NIV, JB), or was he thought to make a difference in maintaining stability despite the corruption (NKJV, RSV, NEB, NASB)? The Jerusalem Bible (Reader's Edition, 1968) may give us a slight nudge toward a possible solution. It sees verse 8 to contain quotations in defense of the seamy bureaucratic practices:

> "You will hear talk of 'the common good' and 'the service of the king'."

I would adopt this suggestion but translate it a bit more literally. The bureaucratic rationalize their greed with words like those:

> "There is profit to the land in all this; after all the king has a right to the tilled field."

On *"profit"* (Heb. *yitrôn*) see 1:3. *"Land"* speaks here of a political, not a physical entity (Fox). The rights of the *"king"* to a portion of the crop can be noted in Amos' first vision which mentions the *"king's mowings"* as the first part of the harvest payable to the government as taxes (7:1). On this reading, the administrators justified their greed on the basis of the rights of the king to the produce of the land.

As offensive as all this was to Koheleth, his main point seems to be to encourage his hearers to accept this as part of life's reality, since neither he nor they could do much to change a system in which no power was available to them. At the same time there is not a hint that he would want them to emulate such behavior. He knows that greed never pays and proceeds to say so in the last three verses of his words of advice.

GREED FOUND EMPTY

From the specific form of greed that haunted government officials, the Preacher turns to the general problem of greed that plagues those who seem to have enough already. His words are not directed to the poor; he did not blame them for wanting to meet their basic needs and have a little left over. We have already heard his harsh criticism of those who exploit the poverty of others (5:8; see also 4:1–4). It is toward the persons who are richer than they are wise that his words are aimed.

> 10 He who loves silver will not be satisfied
>   with silver;
>   Nor he who loves abundance, with increase.
>   This also is vanity.
> 11 When goods increase,
>   They increase who eat them;
>   So what profit have the owners
>   Except to see them with their eyes?
> 12 The sleep of a laboring man is sweet,
>   Whether he eats little or much;
>   But the abundance of the rich will not permit
>   him to sleep.
>
> *Eccles. 5:10–12*

There is something about the drive to acquire that impels us to seek more and more. If it is insecurity that prods us to seek wealth, wealth itself will not cure that insecurity. If it is the desire for power that pushes us, money will not quell that desire. For many people the thirst for more material goods is insatiable. Long after their basic needs are met, they crave for more. Long after they have the permanent security they seek, they strive for more. Long after they have all the luxuries they covet, they itch for more. Koheleth uses a chain of proverbs (sayings as the indicative grammar shows) to get this idea across The first link (v. 10) makes the basic point: wealth cannot satisfy. The second (v. 11) and third (v. 12) links illustrate the point: wealth attracts idle hangers-on (v. 11), and wealth increases anxiety.

The first proverb uses strong language. "Loves" is not a word that the Preacher uses lightly. The other texts where the verb (Heb. ʾāhab) is found are the familiar "a time to love, and a time to hate" (3:8) and the alternative conclusion, "Live joyfully with the wife whom you love . ." (9:9). The noun (Heb. ʾahᵃbāh) occurs in contrast with "hate" (9:1, 6) in contexts that confirm how powerful are these emotions. When "love" is directed toward God, spouse, or neighbor it is holy, wholesome, and rewarding. When "silver" (Heb. keseph, see on 2:8; 7:12; 10:19; 12:6) is its target, it is sick, selfish, and especially frustrated, as "will not be satisfied" (Heb. śābaᶜ, see on 1:8; 4:8; 6:3) promises.

Vain, futile (Heb. hebel), and also puzzling—why would anyone want to live that way?—that kind of life is. All the enjoyment of what these people have is clouded by the thought of what they want next. All gratitude for present blessing is overshadowed by the fear of tomorrow's losses. All generosity may shrivel because the wealthy person is preoccupied not with how he can help others, but with what he can gain next.

"You'll never get anything from him," a friend of mine declared flatly. We had been discussing a prospective donor to Fuller Seminary. "Your only chance is to get something from his widow." I was puzzled by my friend's bluntness. "Money means power to that man," he went on to explain. "All his life he has been acquiring goods and land. Acquisition is his way of life. It is psychologically impossible for him to give any substantial amount away." Sad to say, my friend was right. That industrious and frugal man fit Ecclesiastes' words to a tee: he loved money yet never had enough to be satisfied with it.

The Preacher's second bit of evidence in his argument that seeking material goods was a frustrating way of life is presented in verse 11. It takes a lot of hired help to manage wealth, business, and property. Besides that, would-be friends and long-lost relatives appear as from nowhere when the word of wealth ("goods," Heb. ṭôbāh, includes the "silver," "abundance" or "material wealth," and "increase" or "produce" of v. 10) spreads. Even though the Preacher lived in a highly organized, complexly commercial society, the old customs of kinship and hospitality had not disappeared. Friends and relations could still lay some claim to the wealth of their loved ones. And these claims often proved burdensome to the wealthy, whose only *"profit"* or "advantage" (Heb. *kishrôn*, see 2:21; 4:4) was to look at them briefly before they vanished. And, as Koheleth has twice reminded us, the eye's appetite is insatiable (1:8; 4:8).

The wise men in Proverbs had viewed the friendly attention that wealth brings more positively:

> Many entreat the favor of the nobility [or the generous],
> And every man is a friend to one who gives gifts.
> All the brothers of the poor hate him;
> How much more do his friends go far from him!
>
> *Prov. 19:6–7*

A mixed blessing at best, Koheleth, the Preacher, called this. Friends, family, and servants gather around wealth. They may pester the rich person and dissipate what he has. How often have we read of an athlete—say, a boxer—whose golden moments found him surrounded by an entourage that gladly shared his wealth, but whose twilight days saw him both broke and abandoned. Wealth can carry its own frustration—that was the Preacher's apt observation.

The argument proceeded. Wealth not only fails to satisfy; it attracts fair-weather friends and also increases anxiety (v. 12). In a sense, this is a counter-proverb; it swims against the stream of conventional wisdom. We would expect the lot of the *"rich"* to be touted above the life of the manual worker (*"laboring man"*). But Koheleth goes to the heart of the matter. Whose *"sleep"* is *"sweet"* like honey (Judg. 14:18) or lovemaking (Song of Sol. 2:3)? Not the rich persons, but the exhausted and simply fed worker. *"Eats"* (v. 12) probably means "spends" as it does in 6:2. Its use to describe life-style, including "earnings" (5:16) and "expenses," is fitting since, for virtually all persons in antiquity and most even in the modern world, food is the largest regular expenditure, a fact hard to grasp in our American economy. Here the Preacher's point was not so much the anxiety over the responsibilities of wealth, as it was the anxiety caused by the use of wealth. *"Abundance"* is literally "satisfaction," a noun (Heb. *śābāʿ*) related to the verb used in verse 10. This is an ironic choice of words: the lavish possessions which ought to satisfy have the opposite effect. Fancy parties, rich food, high living, risky investments—none of these is conducive to relaxation. The overindulgence which wealth makes possible and the stress which fame and attention produce all work against sleep. And where *"sleep"* flees, hardly anything else in life can truly be enjoyed. Insomnia is much more likely to occur in the fancy houses on the hilltops than in the small cottages in the valley. Wealth may bring frustration in many forms. And sleeplessness is surely one of the more vexing.

Epilogue: The Greater Wise Man

Where religion has gone sour, where religious exercise has replaced true worship, more than criticism is needed. One of Jesus' most powerful words spoke to this need:

> "But the hour is coming, and now is, when the true worshipers will worship the Father in spirit and truth, for the Father is seeking such to worship Him. God is Spirit, and those who worship Him must worship in spirit and truth."
>
> *John 4:23–24*

Here Jesus came to the heart of the matter. The reason that we must take our worship seriously is that God's own nature demands it. As spirit, that is, as ultimate and infinite Person, our heavenly Father longs for communion with his people, not for hollow symbols or empty actions. False worship is as much an affront to God as obscene insults are to a wife or husband. Better to bribe a judge than to ply God with hollow words; better to slap a policeman than to seek God's influence by meaningless gestures; better to perjure yourself in court than to harry God with promises you cannot keep. The full adoration of our spirit, the true obedience of our heart—these are God's demands and God's delights.

Where government has turned corrupt, special insight is a necessity. "'Whose image and inscription is this?'" Jesus asked, holding out a Roman coin (Mark 12:16). That question and its answer give directions to us as Christians even when our government officials may let us down. The command, "'Render to Caesar the things that are Caesar's'. . . " (Mark 12:17) was not based on the righteousness of the emperor or of the underlings that manned his sprawling bureaucracy.

It was based on Christ's suggestion of the need for government in a broken world full of sinful persons. And more, it was based on the realistic judgment that almost any government is better than no government. Anarchy is the worst possible form of politics. At the same time, Jesus' call to Zacchaeus, the crooked tax collector (Luke 19:1–10), gave notice that God's demand outweighs Caesar's. Belonging to God means that corruption should be resisted by the righteous and the grievances caused by corrupt government redressed wherever possible. What Zacchaeus had swindled from others he gladly offered to repay in quadruple measure, and what he had gained by oppressive taxes he would redistribute to the poor. The experience of God's grace revealed his greed, and he saw it for the ugly thing it was. Repentance has the power to change all behavior—even that of those who abuse their political power.

Where greed has been found empty, there is offered by the Greater Wise Man the hope of "treasures in heaven, where neither moth nor rust destroys and where thieves do not break in and steal" (Matt. 6:20). And, we may add in keeping with Koheleth's proverbs, it is in heaven, where we have access to Christ's riches in glory which do satisfy, and which do not erode through the lust of fair-weather friends, and do not keep us awake. Treasure and heart are tied together in a tight human bundle. One of life's greatest experiences of masochism is to have our hearts in the wrong place. Deposit them in the bank, invest them in the stock market, wrap them in the deeds to real estate holdings, and you commit a massive act of self-torture. Put your treasury in heaven invested in love for God, deeds of kindness to others, and commitment to the advance of Christ's kingdom, and your heart will be there too.

The elderly father of a close friend of mine showed a wry smile and a twinkly eye as some of his young business colleagues talked about their yachts. My friend caught his father after the meeting and asked what had lit that quiet glow of humor. His dad smiled again. "They were taking delight in the boats they owned and sailed, and I could not help but think of the airplane that I own in Africa." The old man, one of the most generous servants of God I have ever known, had given a missionary society money to buy an airplane to serve Christ in Africa. His treasure and heart were together serving the Lord of heaven. He knew that no joy—not even of yachting on a great lake in a summer breeze—could outdo that.

CHAPTER EIGHT

Third Demonstration: Risks and Frustrations of Wealth

Ecclesiastes 5:13–6:12

I kept wondering as I watched the gold ball bounce from bumper to bumper. It was just a game on television but it sent me wondering about a basic question in life. The bouncing of the gold ball on the giant pinball machine was worth money to the contestant—$200 per bounce. I wondered as the audience screamed in sheer delight; I wondered as the player jumped and shrieked for joy.

My question was simple: Why do we find the hope of acquiring wealth so exciting? That bouncing ball was not really going to change the life of the person participating in the game. It could not heal any disease, solve any marital problems, or guarantee him security on his job. Yet his excitement suggested it could do all three. And so did the enthusiasm of the studio audience who cheered and sighed as the ball rolled from success to danger. This scene at the studio was being eyed by an audience of millions at home who daily share the emotional thrill of this or other game shows where instant wealth is the aim. Instant wealth—think of the lure it has held for human minds and hands! For it pirates attacked ships bearing precious cargo; for it prospectors slogged mountain trails behind their burros; for it conquistadors sailed the Spanish Main and massacred a host of Indians; for it gamblers flood the casinos of Las Vegas; for it a multitude of people play the weekly lotteries and enter the magazine sweepstakes.

Why? Why the lust for wealth, the almost *universal* lust for wealth? Probably because wealth is viewed as power. Some see it as the power to create more wealth. How often we greet the news of a successful investment with the response, "It takes money to make money." For others wealth means the power to get your own way. A woman in the Los Angeles ghetto was explaining why there was a violent shootout in her neighborhood where six people were killed, while no blood was shed when the newspaper heiress Patty Hearst was captured in San Francisco. Her explanation was simple: "The rich can always get things done their way."

My point is not to justify these feelings about wealth, but only to try to understand why wealth has such attraction to those who do not have it. In the world of the Bible, many viewed wealth not only as power to create more wealth or as power to get things done the way one wanted, but as a sign of God's blessing. After all, many of the prominent figures of biblical history were allowed to garner huge wealth: Abraham, Jacob, Joseph, David, Solomon, to name a few. And some proverbs taught that righteousness would lead to wealth:

> In the house of the righteous there is much treasure,
> but in the revenue of the wicked is trouble.
>
> *Prov. 15:6*

Again

> A good man leaves an inheritance to his children's children,
> but the wealth of the sinner is stored up for the righteous.
>
> *Prov. 13:22*

Undoubtedly, words like these made the people yearn for the wealth that was a sign of blessing, rather than for the righteousness that might, in God's time, lead to prosperity. It was this almost compulsive concern with material possessions that led to some of Ecclesiastes' strongest words.

They form the heart of his Third Demonstration of the inscrutability and immutability of life as God designed and sustains it. Wealth carries with it risk and frustration for those who manage to garner it. That is the gist of the section from 5:13 to 6:12. The transition from the Words of Advice (5:1–12) is marked by (1) the resumption of the first-person style—*"I have seen"* (5:13, 18; 6:1, see on 1:14), (2) the use of the catch-phrase *"under the sun"* (5:13, 18; 6:1), (3) the appearance of the *alternative conclusion* (5:18–20), and (4) the occurrence of the *vanity verdict* (6:9).

The structure of the Third Demonstration looks like this:

THE RISKS OF THE WEALTHY

The wealthy lead risky lives. That was the Preacher's first argument, and one that he labored at length. He based it on his personal observations of the way life works.

> 13 There is a severe evil which I have seen under
> the sun:
> Riches kept for their owner to his hurt.
> 14 But those riches perish through misfortune;
> When he begets a son, there is nothing in his hand.
> *Eccles. 5:13–14*

Each of us can add his or her own frustrations to this. With money, gain is usually related to risk. Fortunes have been made in oil. Huge companies have been founded, and numbers of families—from the Rockefellers to the Hunts—have acquired affluence through investments in oil. But think of the dry holes! Probably four of them have been drilled for each well that has brought in oil. As many people have lost money in oil deals as have made anything—perhaps more.

Losses like these must have been a common occurrence in Koheleth's time. *"Under the sun"* (see 1:3) points to a widespread phenomenon, not an isolated instance. The pain of the lost investment is amplified in these verses. *"Evil"* (harm, misfortune, disaster; see on Heb. *rā'âh* at 2:21) is itself a very strong word for the harsh effects of misguided conduct. Yet *"severe"* (Heb. *hôlâh,* "sick," "sore"), both here and in verse 16, pushes *"evil"* beyond its normal range and suggests a calamity of excruciating proportions—a total disaster. *"To his hurt"* (again Heb. *rā'âh*) underscores how personal and painful the damage was. Even more agonizing is the hint in *"kept* (or "guarded") *by their owner"* that he hoarded funds to invest that otherwise his family might have enjoyed, and his whole plan of frugality boomeranged.

"Misfortune" (v. 14) is literally "bad business" and rubs salt in the bankrupt person's wounds by reminding him of his responsibility for the unsound investment. No wonder Koheleth added words of advice about diversification that scatters the eggs or *"bread"* and does not put them all in one basket (11:1–2)! The final note in the tragic recitation is the harsh reality that the unfortunate investor has *"nothing in his hand"* to bequeath to a *"son"* except the empty legacy of resources painfully acquired and rashly squandered.

This note is amplified in a sorry description of emptiness, futility, darkness, and grief which are the lot of the loser pictured in these verses:

> 15 As he came from his mother's womb,
>   naked shall he return,
>   To go as he came;
>   And he shall take nothing from his labor
>   Which he may carry away in his hand.
> 16 And this also is a severe evil—
>   Just exactly as he came, so shall he go.
>   And what profit has he who has
>   labored for the wind?
> 17 All his days he also eats in darkness,
>   And he has much sorrow and sickness and anger.
>   *Eccles. 5:15–17*

Rarely will there be great return on investment without great risk. Stock market, commodity exchange, and real estate investment all demonstrate this. Wealth drives us to acquire more wealth. That was the Preacher's closing argument in his Words of Advice (5:10–12). Now pointedly he has coupled that with his story about the dangers of loss. We are pushed to make more, he has told us, yet that very push puts us in jeopardy of losing everything and of leaving our family as paupers and ourselves as embittered derelicts.

"Labor" (Heb. *ʿāmāl*, v. 15; see on 1:3) again embraces the total task of coping with life and trying to wring meaning and material sub-

stance from it. *"Severe evil"* (v. 16) repeats the lament of verse 13 (see comment there) and underscores its poignancy by decrying the utter lack of *"profit"* in work (*"labored,"* the verb *ᶜāmal,* see at 1:3) that has chased the goal of material wealth, a target elusive like the *"wind"* (see 1:14). The rhetorical question *"what profit?"* echoes the *guiding question* in the theme of the book (1:3) and tells us that no valid answer is found in wealth, any more than it was in wisdom (1:12–18), pleasure (2:1–11), or attempts to change life from the course on which God has launched it (3:1–11).

"Eats" (v. 17) stands for the daily routine of the man bereft of his riches. Dining in the golden days would have been a joyous feast—the family gathered at a table stocked high with the best foods of the land, in a room alight with scintillating conversation, the sharing of the profitable tasks of the day and the expansive hopes for the morrow. Now *"darkness"* is the mood, a shroud of doleful gloom and ominous danger—as *"darkness"* in Scripture often conveys (see on 2:13 and 12:3).

The failed circumstances rot the spirit of the broken man. The last line of verse 17 pictures his pathology. First, *"much sorrow"* (Heb. *kaᶜas;* see on 1:18; 2:33) suggests a combination of grief and anger; the man is inwardly outraged at his plight and in mourning over it. Second, *"sickness"* (Heb. *ḥᵒlî;* see 6:2) implies a failing of both body and spirit in the mysterious mix of psychosomatic illness. Third, *"anger"* (Heb. *qeseph*) speaks of fierce indignation coupled, perhaps, with incensed feelings of self-righteousness. A parallel use of the Hebrew word in Esther 1:18 attributes such feelings to the noblemen of Persia when their wives are tempted to emulate Vashti's disobedience of her husband, Ahashuerus. Such is the lot of a person whose ego is defined by material possessions. Take them away, and he loses his total reason for being.

It was not Koheleth's aim here to deal with exceptions to his formula that wealth lost is life shattered. But exceptions there are, especially among those whose hope is built on God and not wealth. Years ago one of my friends had worked for months on a deal to sell his small company for several million dollars worth of stock in the company that proposed to acquire it. The transaction came down to the wire. My friend went to New York to sign the final papers. In the course of the negotiations the stock of the parent company had moved up in price by many dollars per share. The board of the larger firm balked at the elevated cost of their purchase and reneged on the offer. A few days later I met my friend, expecting him to be devastated by the missed opportunity. He was not. His faith in God kept him strong, and his Christian common sense gave him insight: "We have had very little difficulty in our lives as a family. It's probably a good thing for our children to see that my wife and I can stay steady and love God in hard times as well as easy."

A SUGGESTION FOR THE WEALTHY

Koheleth would have understood my friend's comment. The *alternative conclusion* (see at 2:24–26) was based on similar thinking. It was a formula for keeping steady no matter how hard or in what direction life rocked your boat. This is the fourth occurrence of it in the book.

The best answer that the Preacher could give to the desperate reactions described in verse 17 was that we would enjoy what we have, whether little or much, and not try compulsively to hoard it:

> 18 Here is what I have seen: It is good and fitting
> for one to eat and drink, and to enjoy the good of all
> his labor in which he toils under the sun all the days
> of his life which God gives him; for it is his heritage.
> 19 As for every man to whom God has given
> riches and wealth, and given him power to eat of it, to
> receive his heritage and rejoice in his labor—this is
> the gift of God.
> 20 For he will not dwell unduly on the days of his
> life, because God keeps him busy with the joy of his
> heart.
>
> *Eccles. 5:18–20*

This is not bad advice. It reminds us that what we have is a gift of God, created and provided by him. Like all his creation, these gifts are good. They are not to be despised or rejected, but to be enjoyed.

Koheleth is not speculating here. The *alternative conclusion* is grounded in his careful observation and reflection ("*I have seen,*"

see 1:14) as firmly as are the observations on wealth in 5:13 and 6:_
The wise man has taken careful note of how wholesome and solid
human life can be when people follow the path charted in the *alternative conclusion*. *"Good"* and *"fitting"* (lit. "handsome" or "beautiful")
tie this kind of conduct (v. 18) to God's creative plan, as 3:10–13 point
out. At the same time the passage is worded to form a deliberate
connection and contrast with the sad observations about lost wealth
in 5:13–17. Both experiences are widespread and typical in our kind
of world, as *"under the sun"* (vv. 13, 18) shows. Both speak of *"riches"*
(vv. 13, 14, 19), but from very different angles: *"riches kept for* (or *"by"*)
their owner" and *"perish"* ("are lost," v. 14) versus *"riches"* *"given"* by
God, which last as part of an inheritance (v. 19). Both feature *"labor,"*
but in one case he takes *"nothing"* from it, no *"profit"* at all (vv. 15–16),
and in the other he is able *"to enjoy the good of all his labor"* (vv. 18–19).
Both allude to a family *"heritage"* (or "inheritance") but the shattered
man has nothing to leave his *"son"* (v. 14) while the joyful man's
stable *"heritage"* is mentioned twice (vv. 18–19). Both seem to
live long lives, though the loser spends *"all his day"* in the gloom
of his vanished fortune (v. 17) while the winner takes joy *"all the
days of his life"* in productive labor (v. 18) and is occupied with joyful
tasks (v. 20). Finally, the bereft person stews daily in the broth of his
bitterness, rehearsing, reviewing, and reliving his misfortunes (v. 17),
but the fulfilled man does not *"dwell unduly"* (lit. "remember much")
on the incidental happenings of the past, whether
weal or woe, but plunges with a *"heart"* full of *"joy"* into the opportunities of the present. Which person would you rather have as
a neighbor? Following the *alternative conclusion* makes princely
people.

Mr. Maddox is a name that presses through my boyhood memories into the present. I can picture his hands and face clear as a bell,
though it must be forty-five years since I have seen him at all. The
face is scarred with the telltale pocks of flesh deeply burned. The
hands were claws bound rigid by fistfuls of scar tissue. He had escaped with his life from a flash fire that exploded on him and had
rashly seized a metal fan to shield his face only to burn his hands
crisp on the searing metal. What I most clearly remember were not
the hands and face, frightful though they were, but the laugh. Mr.
Maddox seemed to enjoy every minute of every day. No bitterness,
no shyness, no meanness did he carry as scars from the fire. His gift

of unsullied joy, unbeatable humor, and a moment-by-
of well-being with God. He was a model of Koheleth's
ed, grateful, joyous, busy person.

THE FRUSTRATIONS OF THE WEALTHY

The Preacher capped his case with one more line of evidence,
again based on personal observation:

> 1 There is an evil which I have seen under the
> sun, and it is common among men:
> 2 A man to whom God has given riches and
> wealth and honor, so that he lacks nothing for himself
> of all he desires; yet God does not give him power to
> eat of it, but a foreigner consumes it. This is vanity,
> and it is an evil affliction.
> 3 If a man begets a hundred children and lives
> many years, so that the days of his years are many,
> but his soul is not satisfied with goodness, or indeed
> he has no burial, I say that a stillborn child is better
> than he—
> 4 for it comes in vanity and departs in darkness,
> and its name is covered with darkness.
> 5 Though it has not seen the sun or known
> anything, this has more rest than that man,
> 6 even if he lives a thousand years twice—but
> has not seen goodness. Do not all go to one place?
> 7 All the labor of man is for his mouth,
> And yet the soul is not satisfied.
> 8 For what more has the wise man than the fool?
> What does the poor man have,
> Who knows how to walk before the living?
> 9 Better is the sight of the eyes than the
> wandering of desire.
> This also is vanity and grasping for the wind.
> *Eccles. 6:1–9*

Whether it was illness, economic reversals, or fraudulence that
cheated a person of his wealth the Preacher did not say. Any of these
may block full enjoyment of what one has.

A person develops a new product and then calls in someone else to help him market it. Before long, the newcomer has taken over and the inventor has been robbed of his rights. A person toils for years to build his business and is snatched by death at the moment the business turns a comfortable profit. These are the vexations Koheleth had in mind. Solemn reminders they are of the frustrations that one faces if getting rich is the chief aim, including the frustration that *wealth can readily be taken from us*. We should remember that as we watch the ball bounce its way through the marble machines. Neither instant wealth nor long-term wealth can accomplish all they promise. Their failure to do that sharpens our frustration.

The movement of 6:1–9 may be charted like this:

Introduction to the observation	v. 1
Content of the observation	v. 2
Reflections on the observation	vv. 5–6
Proverbs confirming the observation	vv. 7–9

Koheleth introduces (v. 1) his final observation (*"I have seen"*; see 5:13, 18) by featuring the frequency—*"common"* is literally "much" or "many"—and the ubiquity—*"under the sun"* means "everywhere in our broken world" (see 1:3)—of the *"evil."* *"Evil"* here as often in the book means "painful misfortune," a "happening fraught with danger or frustration," "something that blocks life's blessing and robs it of joy." *"Men"* (Heb. *ʾādām*) stands for persons regardless of gender (see 1:3).

The sovereign hand of God (v. 2) looms large in these oft-repeated instances of financial loss. God is the source of the monetary *"riches,"* the material *"wealth"* or *"possessions,"* and the consequent status and esteem—*"glory"* (Heb. *kābôd*) of the person. They are his gifts of grace which, to Koheleth, accounts for the fact that some have much and others very little. Yet the Preacher also credits God for the untoward circumstances which robbed the *"man"* (Heb. *ʾîsh* does imply male gender) of his ability (*"power"*) to find enduring satisfaction (as *"eat"* must mean) in his wealth. The mention of *"God"* here is probably Koheleth's way of saying that the blame for the loss did not rest with the owner. Circumstances beyond his control intervened.

The *"foreigner"* or *"stranger"* may describe someone from outside the country or, more probably, someone from beyond the circle of the man's family, neighbors and close associates, someone whom he did not know and who cared nothing for him. Whether by confiscation, court order, or distress sale, the "stranger" assumes control of the wealth and proceeds to enjoy it ("*consumes*" is the same word as "*eats*" earlier in the verse) in full view of the suffering loser.

The *vanity verdict* reminds us of what plaguing mysteries such ill-fated situations are, impossible to make sense of, utterly baffling in their topsy-turviness. "*Evil affliction*" is literally "bad sickness" and harks back to 5:13, 16 where the same two Hebrew roots are used, but with "sick" as the adjective and "evil" the noun—"*severe evil.*" The word-play links together the two observations about vanished wealth. Though "*evil affliction*" obviously describes the lot of the poverty-stricken sufferer, it also is Koheleth's estimate of these oft-repeated circumstances which are fraught not with material loss but with painful confusion, uncertainty, and vexation about the ways of God.

The reflection on these matters (vv. 3–6) centers in the plight of the wretched sufferer. To put it bluntly, he is better off dead. Nothing can adequately compensate for his loss, not even a huge family ("*a hundred children*" is a symbol of abundant blessing in a painfully humorous exaggeration; see Pss. 127, 128), not a long life ("*many years*" would ordinarily be a sign of divine approval; see Prov. 4:10). The staggering blow in these reflections comes in the comparison of the man's agony with the fate of a "*stillborn child.*" Deprived of the pleasure of enjoying the fruit of God's blessing and his own labors ("*goodness*" is the blanket word for this fruit), he is worse off than the "*stillborn*" baby who is not given a normal "*burial*" ceremony. Scholars debate whose "*burial*" is in view. The NKJV and other versions refer it to the man. It seems to make more sense to connect it to the dead baby (see Crenshaw). If it refers to the man, it heightens the pathos by adding to his other vexations the note of neglect of proper care at death.

Verse 6 will return to the man's distress, but meanwhile the description of the sorry lot of the stillborn is featured to strengthen the comparison (vv. 4–5). Mystery and lack of identity are pictured as the baby's fate. "*Vanity*" describes the enigma of the whole event. Why do some babies die in the womb while others come out kicking and screaming with life? "*Darkness*" (see on 2:13–14; 5:17) speaks of the cloud of sadness and even horror that hovers over the birth scene. Used with the "*name*" or personal identity of the child, it depicts the absence of selfhood, the utter nothingness of the stillborn's existence. For the link between "*name*" and human existence, see 6:10.

Verse 5 embellishes the description by stating the total deprivation of the baby: not seeing the *"sun"* is equal to not living at all (see 7:11, where *"those who see the sun"* are those who live and make the most of it); not to have *"known anything"* is a stark expression for never having lived, experiencing nothing (Heb. *yādaᶜ*; often describes knowledge that comes from experience or acquaintance). Note Koheleth's summary proverb that places *"knowledge"* at the center of *"life"*:

> For wisdom is a defense as money is a defense,
> But the excellence of knowledge is that wisdom
>   gives life to those who have it.
>
> *Eccles. 7:12*

Despite the complete absence of identity (v. 4) and utter lack of experience of life, the stillborn (*"this,"* v. 5) has a huge advantage over the shattered man—the advantage of *"rest"* or even "pleasure" as the rabbis sometimes translated the word (Heb. *naḥat*, see at 2:24). To feel nothing, know nothing, experience nothing, Koheleth deems preferable to the vexing pain of missing out on all the things that bring satisfaction—again the word is *"goodness"* (v. 6; see v. 3). No length of life—*"a thousand years"* is a tenfold exaggeration just as were the *"hundred children"* of verse 3 (Job's ideal family numbered ten!)—can compensate for life robbed of its quality, especially when that quality was once within one's grasp. Koheleth was not alone in this preference. Job expressed it in even more powerful and poetic terms (Job 3:11–19).

The reflection concludes (v. 6) with a familiar theme: both go to *"one place."* The rhetorical question demands the answer, Yes! *"All"* refers to the man and the stillborn and should be translated "both" (see at 2:14). The leveling effect of death is a familiar theme: it happens alike to the wise and the fool (2:14), to beasts and human beings (3:19–20). As in 3:20, *"one place"* must refer to Sheol, the grave or the abode of the dead (see 9:10), omnivorous and insatiable in its appetite (Prov. 30:16).

The chain of proverbs (vv. 7–9) undergirds the lessons drawn from the tragic observation (vv. 1–2) and reflections (vv. 4–6) on ill-fated wealth. The first (v. 7) ties closely to the preceding verses. It seems deliberately ambiguous (Crenshaw). It may describe the man whose "appetite" (as *"soul,"* Heb. *nephesh*, may be read) is not appeased *("satisfied")*. Or it may continue the account of the *"one place"* to which both the man and the stillborn are going (v. 6). The interpretation depends on the *"his"* of *"his mouth."* Hebrew has no neuter gender, no way of saying "its" mouth. If *"his"* is Sheol, then the picture is of its relentless devouring of the human family in its bottomless gullet (Heb. *nephesh* may also mean "throat"), gulping down all our *"labor"* (again Heb. *ʿāmāl* to summarize our efforts to make the best of life). If the *"his"* refers to our human *"mouth,"* then the point is that all our toil which is geared to sate our appetite is in vain (Prov. 16:26 takes a more positive view). We have basic needs that food, drink, and other purchasable pleasures cannot meet.

The middle link in the chain (v. 8) is even harder to understand. Its first half clearly reaches back to the leveling impact of death on both *"the wise"* and *"the fool"* (2:13–14). *"More"* means "advantage" and speaks of the fact that the apparent differences between the two are only relative. Translating *"more"* as "absolute (or final) advantage" would bring out the meaning. This saying (v. 8) seems to have one eye at least on the allusions to Sheol in the two preceding verses. It is the ravenous appetite (v. 7) of that *"one place"* (v. 6) that levels the ultimate distinction between persons of wisdom and persons of folly.

The second half of verse 8 has caused scholars to wring their hands in frustration. Many emendations have been suggested. They are only guesswork since the ancient versions seem to support the Masoretic Text in our Hebrew Bible. One possible way to find meaning in the obscure question is to carry over "advantage" from the first half and insert it between *"what"* and *"does."* Then we may understand *"walk before the living"* as connoting something like "conduct himself properly in life." This picture would not contain a contrast parallel to the *"wise"*/*"fool"* antithesis of verse 8a. To do that would require mention of the "rich" who are not in the picture at all. What the second half as interpreted here would do is to complement the first half: "Given Sheol's appetite, neither the wise nor the fool can escape it. Furthermore, even poor people, who overcome hardship to live a productive and respectable life, cannot enjoy any ultimate advantage. They too will end in Sheol's belly."

The final proverb in the chain (v. 9) seems to call its hearers to live life now, to make the most of present circumstances—the events and things that lie in *"the sight of the eyes."* The closest English equivalent to this proverb is probably, "A bird in the hand is worth two in the bush." Be content with what you have—your work, your food, your family; do not count on what is beyond your reach. What you see with your eyes you can deal with; what you crave with your soul you may not attain.

The Preacher would surely apply this verse to all the treasures that his friends were vainly striving after. Do not spend yourself, he has warned, reaching for meaning, for wisdom, for pleasure, for freedom, for permanence, for justice, for wealth that are beyond your grasp. He might support the observation that hope springs eternal within the human breast, but he would quickly add that such hope can be futile. Life may not get better, not here on earth.

This interpretation assumes a special reading of the proverb's second line, which rendered literally says, "than the going of the soul." The special reading infers that "going" means *wandering* and that "soul" (Heb. *nephesh*) means "desire" or "appetite" (see v. 3). But "going" can more readily mean "going away," "departing," in the sense of "dying" (3:20; 5:15–16; 6:4, 6; 9:10; 12:5), and *nephesh* can mean breath, life, or spirit. So understood the comparison—the *"better . . . than"*—is between the advantage of seizing whatever is available in life and the inevitability of death which provides no opportunity for even modest forms of enjoyment. This latter interpretation would link the saying to the words about Sheol and death in verses 6–8 and provide a fitting capstone to the whole sequence of thought in 6:1–9. Furthermore, it serves as a reinforcement of the *alternative conclusion* stated in 5:18–20, urging the readers to make the most of life's simple blessings while there is time. In so doing it seems to anticipate the Words of Advice to young people that conclude the book (11:9–12:7).

The *vanity verdict*, found here in full form for the last time, brands either greedy and fantasy-filled coveting (if we assume *"the wandering of desire"* interpretation) or the certainty of death, especially ill-timed death (if "departing of the soul" is preferred), as an enigma, an unsolvable puzzle in the ways of God with the human family.

THE LIMITS OF FREEDOM

The Third Demonstration (5:13–6:12) draws to a close with what seems a set of reflections on the limits of human freedom. Though not tightly connected to what has occupied Koheleth's attention, these musings are not at all an unsuitable conclusion to a demonstration that has dealt with two vexing grievances faced by the rich—bad investments (5:13–17) and cruel confiscation whether by trickery or theft (6:1–9).

The normal response in such circumstances would be for the aggrieved person to beg for another chance, to guess what might have been done differently, or to hope for a future in which prosperity once more blossoms. As natural as these reactions feel, Koheleth deems them fruitless. Human destiny is so solidly fixed in God's hands that fretting about the past or striving to plot the future are activities on which no energy should be spent.

> 10 Whatever one is, he has been named already,
> For it is known that he is man;
> And he cannot contend with Him who is
> mightier than he.
> 11 Since there are many things that increase
> vanity,
> How is man the better?
> 12 For who knows what is good for man in life, all
> the days of his vain life which he passes like a
> shadow? Who can tell a man what will happen after
> him under the sun?
>
> *Eccles. 6:10–12*

"Man" (Heb. *ʾādām;* see 1:3) is what we human beings have *"been named."* Our character, nature, and power have been determined by that name, which itself testifies to our earthiness (*ʾādām* from *ʾᵃdāmâh,* "soil" or "dirt"). *"It is known"* by us and by God that our limitations have been set by the One who named us. We are human not divine. Therefore we lose all arguments (*"cannot contend"*) with God who is not just slightly but infinitely mightier than we. "Go with God's sovereignty" is the implied command of this verse. It echoes a theme familiar to us from the poem on the changelessness of creation (1:4–11), the problem of our inability to change the way things are (1:15), the verses on the fixity of time and our need to bend to it (3:1–9), the verdict that what God does is fixed forever, with its consequent call to fear God (3:14–15).

Verse 11 may add another word of caution to remind us of our human limits. Talking a lot (*"many things"* is more lit. "many words") is one way we try to transcend our limitations. We rationalize, apologize, overexplain, beg, and argue—only to make things worse ("; *vanity"*). Even our ability to talk gives human beings (*"man"*) ι ____ advantage (on Heb. *yôthēr*, "the better" see 6:8). Who can outargue God (v. 10), especially since he knows our hearts?

The crowning human limitation is the inability to know the future (v. 12). *"Who knows?"* and *"who can tell?"*—the double question is to be answered in the negative: No one but God knows and he is not telling (3:11). *"Vain"* and *"shadow"* suggest life without substance— life neither understandable, nor reliable, nor meaningful. The days flit by, and we fail to make an indelible mark. The future crowds in, and we cannot discern its size or shape—not in this cabined world of ours (*"under the sun"*; see at 1:3).

Epilogue: The Greater Wise Man

Thinking again about wealth and its risks requires more to be said. And all of us need to hear. By ancient standards and even by comparison to most of the people in today's world, any of us who can buy or borrow this book and has the time to read it is rich. Our diet, our transportation and mode of living, our discretionary spending— all these mark us off from the truly poor. We can look to Jesus, the wise man greater even than Solomon, to say the needful things to us rich folks. *Contentment is more satisfying than wealth* was one of Jesus' words. The truth of this word he demonstrated in his own life. Without a place to lay his head, he lived contentedly knowing that his loving Father would supply all his need. Whether treated shabbily by religious leaders or entertained lavishly by wealthy admirers, he was ready to make the most of his circumstances by practicing what he preached: "'Therefore do not worry, saying, "What shall we eat?" or "What shall we drink?" or "What shall we wear?" . . . your heav-enly Father knows that you need all these things'" (Matt. 6:31–32).

Doing God's will is more important than gaining goods. That was another word that Jesus gave to take us beyond the frustration of the quest for wealth. His story of the man who acquired vast lands and built huge barns is painfully clear. God sabotaged his plans and rebuked him for them: "'Fool! This night your soul will be required of you; then whose will those things be which you have provided?' So is he who lays up treasure for himself, and is not rich toward God" (Luke 12:20–21).

"Rich toward God"—what an apt description of the direction God wants us to head. We do not jump up and down in front of life's marble machines, or stay glued to the television for the lottery spins, greedy for instant gain. We gratefully receive what we have and then put it to God's purposes: our modest enjoyment and his faithful service.

And when we do this, Christ's third word becomes true for us: *Doing God's will brings the highest wealth of all.* On one occasion, Peter and the other disciples wondered whether their sacrifice of leaving jobs and homes to go with Jesus would be recognized.

> Jesus . . . said, "Assuredly, I say to you, there is no one who has left house or brothers or sisters or father or mother or wife or children or lands, for My sake and the gospel's, who shall not receive a hundredfold now in this time—houses and brothers and sisters and mothers and children and lands, with persecutions—and in the age to come, eternal life."
>
> *Mark 10:29–30*

Talk about investments—one hundredfold Jesus promised, and at no risk except persecution. For God himself is the Guarantor of the returns. And talk about wealth! Life's marble machines that promise instant gain are exposed as tawdry toys in the face of the profit Jesus promised—eternal life. It is his grace, not our gain, that leads us beyond the frustrations of earthly wealth to the riches that bring full satisfaction: the riches of fellowship with God now and forever.

CHAPTER NINE

More Words of Advice: Solemnity, Caution, Compromise

Ecclesiastes 7:1–8:9

They may be the grimmest words we ever hear. The surgeon comes through the swinging doors of the waiting room, her green gown patched with sweaty stains, her steps are halting, her eyes are clouded, her words are faltering: "No hope."

Or the pediatrician hovers over the incubator, his stethoscope glued to a tiny chest. The parents press their faces to the window of the cubicle in sheer dismay, as the physician slowly straightens up, drapes the stethoscope around his neck, and shakes his head with fearful finality: "No hope."

The words bombard the ears and addle the brain. They are heard daily in a hundred hospitals, but we never get used to them. Life without hope carries more trauma than the human spirit can bear.

That was one reason why the message of Ecclesiastes hit his hearers with such shock. Like a master internist he fingered humanity's wrist, listened to the chest, checked the whites of the eyes, reviewed the medical chart, and uttered the solemn pronouncement: "No hope. At least not where you're looking for it."

Koheleth's chosen method of dealing with a life where the level of hope was low was to couch his thoughts in Words of Advice, a second collection of proverbs or short clusters of sayings akin in form to those at 5:1–12. The clusters are sometimes tied together with the catchword "better," which introduces comparisons like those in 4:6, 13. Other connections between the clusters are hard to find, and commentators will differ in their dividing of this section. What follows is my suggestion for grouping and describing the various topics:

Sobriety is better than levity	7:1–7
in the face of death	vv. 1–4
in the face of injustice	vv. 5–7
Caution is better than rashness	7:8–10
Wisdom is better than folly	7:11–12
Resignation is better than indignation	7:13–14
Integrity is better than pretentiousness	7:15–22
Reflections on human limitations	7:23–8:1
Admonitions on respect for authority	8:2–9

By and large, the comparisons, sayings, and commands in this section are a somber lot. Their color is gray. Their tone is measured. Their goal is not to spark joy but to forestall false optimism. They do not promise to make life exciting; they aim to make it bearable.

SOBRIETY IS BETTER THAN LEVITY

A mysterious future dampens hope (6:10–12), but even more chilling is the certainty of death. *Death is too certain to allow for hope.* Here the Preacher returned to a familiar theme—the reality of death which darkens all human optimism, which scrambles all human plans, which shatters all human dreams (2:14–16; 3:19–21). Ecclesiastes chose a startling strategy of presentation in describing death. Death is the great reality, so it is to be preferred even to birth, which does little for us but launch us on the seas of suffering.

Here he elaborates on a tune he has previously played, when he *"praised the dead who were already dead, more than the living who are still alive"* (4:2) and when he preferred the lot of the *"stillborn . . . though it has not seen the sun or known anything"* to the life of a person whose fortune has been stripped away (6:3–4). With a chain of proverbs the wise man tied together his thoughts on death, the great enemy of hope:

1 A good name is better than precious ointment,
   And the day of death than the day of one's birth;
2 Better to go to the house of mourning
   Than to go to the house of feasting,
   For that is the end of all men;
   And the living will take it to heart.
3 Sorrow is better than laughter,

> For by a sad countenance the heart is made
> better.
> 4 The heart of the wise is in the house of mourning,
> But the heart of fools is in the house of mirth.
>
> *Eccles. 7:1–4*

Strong words, dark words! But the Preacher would have called them realistic. He had looked at the certainty of death, and it loomed so large that it dwarfed life. Death, not life, was the dominant issue to be faced. In the light of it, mirth and laughter were a luxury only fools could indulge in. The wise and the serious had to pay their full attention to death.

The relation between the two halves of verse 1 is probably a comparison: "Just as a good name is better than precious ointment, so the day of death, than the day of one's birth." Proverbs often make comparisons by sheer juxtaposition, placing thoughts to be compared side by side with no explicit words of relationship. Koheleth's artistry and irony here are remarkable. The artful opening line is just four words in Hebrew. The first and fourth are literally "good" (Heb. *ṭôb*), meaning first *"better"* and then *"precious."* *"Name"* or *"reputation"* and *"ointment"* (lit. "oil") form a pun since they sound quite alike (Heb. *shēm* and *shemen*). The ironic note is found in the contrast between the two halves of the first verse: the first half states a truth well attested in Hebrew wisdom—the value of a name well-thought-of (see Prov. 22:1 and Song of Sol. 1:3; for the opposite, a reputation so foul that it left its bearers nameless, see Job 30:8); the second half comes with stinging surprise—the superiority of *"death"* to *"birth."* And it is the second half that sets the tone for the next three verses, which focus on the topic of *"mourning."*

"House" (vv. 2, 4) speaks of the site where the events of sorrow or joy were commemorated. A "threshing floor" was the place where Jacob's sons mourned his death in a rite of lamentation that lasted seven days (Gen. 50:10). The *"feasting"* may have honored a birthday (see Job 1:4–5) or a marriage (Song of Sol. 3:11; 6:13) or a special experience of good fortune, like the return of the prodigal in Jesus' story (Luke 15:22–24). The final line of verse 2 spells out the reason for Koheleth's preference of *"mourning"* to *"feasting"*: it stimulates reflection on human destiny (*"the end"*) and helps us to be realistic as we ponder (*"take it to heart"*) mortality. His words anticipate John Donne's:

And therefore, never send to know for whom the bell tolls.
It tolls for thee.

This reflective mood is continued in verse 3. *"Sorrow"* (Heb. *kaͨas,*
see 1:18; 2:23) describes the vexation and anger that may escort grief.
It is a better schoolmaster than *"laughter,"* which can be a narcotic that
dulls the pain of reality and blocks the process of reflection and
meditation that improves our ability to think things through and make
sound choices—both thinking and choosing are tasks of the *"heart"* as
the Hebrews understood it.

The garland of funereal thoughts reaches full blossom at verse 4,
where what was implied in the work of the heart (vv. 2–3) is made
explicit. The path to the *"house of mourning"* (see v. 2) is trodden by
"wise" persons; the path to the *"house of feasting"* (see v. 2) is beaten
hard by the steps of *"fools."* Somberness in the face of life's brevity is
not just slightly better than levity. The gulf between the two is as wide
and deep as the difference between wisdom and folly.

To sing a song of hope, to whistle a tune of expectation, to let loose a
laugh of anticipation in such a climate was the height of folly. His opponents may have chided him with words like, "Come now, Koheleth,
relax, cheer up, life is not so grim as your picture of it." But the Preacher
would have none of it. Mindless festivities were fearfully misleading
in his view. They marked all who engaged in them as fools.

> 5 It is better to hear the rebuke of the wise
>   Than for a man to hear the song of fools.
> 6 For like the crackling of thorns under a pot,
>   So is the laughter of the fool.
>   This also is vanity.
> 7 Surely oppression destroys a wise man's
>   reason.
>   And a bribe debases the heart.
>
> *Eccles. 7:5–7*

No levity, the Preacher gloomily pronounced. Because death is the
end of us all, it should claim our attention and spare us the bitter
disillusionment of a hope that cannot be.

Yet even the wise, somber and realistic as they are, cannot escape
life's hazards scot-free. True, they do not waste their energies on an
empty, idle *"song"* (v. 5). They do not believe that all one has to do is,

"Pack up your troubles in your old kit bag and smile, smile, smile." A solid word of correction (*"rebuke,"* like Nathan's word to David in 2 Sam. 12:1–12) was worth a whole book of silly songs, which were an exercise in meaninglessness (*"vanity,"* v. 6). They and the *"laughter"* (see v. 3) that went with them had as little lasting value as a sprig of *"thorns"* *"crackling"* as they burned under a cooking *"pot."* A pun adds bite: *"thorns"* (Heb. *sîrîm*) and pot (Heb. *sîr*) sound alike. Moffatt and others have echoed the wordplay with "nettles under a kettle."

The cautionary note about the *"wise"* in verse 7 may be read as the climax of verses 5–7, though some scholars make it the lead verse of the cluster in 7–10. The nub of the thought in this verse seems to be that, despite the vast gap between the behavior of the wise and the fool, there are pitfalls to which even the *"wise"* may be vulnerable. These hazards seem to be "extortion" (as *"oppression"* may be translated, NIV) and its companion "bribery." The former can drive a person mad (Whybray's reading, p. 116); the latter "utterly addles one's thinking," as *"debases* (or *"destroys")* *the heart"* is to be understood.

An obvious question is whether the *"wise"* is the culprit or the victim of this financial misconduct. Experience tells us that either could be the case. Lust for money has corrupted the most sage among us. But it is more likely that the crimes here are perpetrated against, not by, the *"wise."* Their reputations—remember the first half of 7:1—may have been damaged by false witnesses bought off by bribes or may have been defrauded by crooked business partners. There is ample evidence that the wise may have been despised as well as envied by their foolish neighbors. The threat of injustice called them to sobriety along with the fact of death.

The next three clusters (vv. 8–10; 11–12; 13–14) seem to combine Koheleth's peculiar mix of conventional and nonconventional wisdom (see on 4:5–6). The traditional teachings with which they begin are countered by the more somber outlook which is characteristic of Koheleth.

CAUTION IS BETTER THAN RASHNESS

The themes in verses 8–9 have counterparts in Proverbs. Their emphases on self-control are part of the standard curriculum in which the older teacher steeped their pupils, especially the neophyte managers in Israel's budding bureaucracy.

> 8   The end of a thing is better than its beginning;
>   The patient in spirit is better than the proud in spirit.
> 9   Do not hasten in your spirit to be angry,
>   For anger rests in the bosom of fools.
> 10   Do not say,
>   "Why were the former days better than these?"
>   For you do not inquire wisely concerning this.
> *Eccles. 7:8–10*

When it comes to the human *"spirit"* or disposition, as *rûªḥ* means here (v. 8), *"patience"* (lit. "length") is a much *"better"* trait to cultivate than pride (lit. "height"). The hair-triggered temperament is dangerous to those who possess it and to anyone around them (Prov. 14:29). One way to cultivate patience is to take to heart the opening line that stresses the importance of calm perseverance that keeps an eye on the long-range goals of life *("the end")*. How easy, yet how foolish, it is to muster enthusiasm for the *"beginning"* of a task yet lack the staying power to see it through. My basement room in my grade school years was cluttered with partially finished model airplanes. As soon as I put the basic structure together, glued the balsa wood, slapped the paper on it and painted it tight with banana oil, I bought the next kit, pinned down the plans, and began the process again. It has taken me years to cultivate the art of putting the finishing touches on my work. I still have to fight the temptation to hurry the final drafts and rush the proofreading of a manuscript. I need to tape this proverb to my desk.

Verse 9 also rings with the cautions of Proverbs. Its admonition—note the imperative mood of line 1 and the motivation introduced by *"for"*—conveys the same idea as the saying in Proverbs 12:16. The words for *"angry"* and *"anger"* stem from the same root (Heb. *kaʿas*, see 1:18; 2:23; 7:3) which conveys a bundle of meanings from "vexation" to "grief" to "anger." Failure to control these reactions marks us as *"fools"* who are on intimate terms—*"bosom"*-buddies we might call ourselves—with "anger." *"Rests"* means "resides" or "constantly lurks"—a thought about as pleasant as going steady with cholera.

Koheleth gives the cluster his unique spin in verse 10. Again the form is an admonition followed by an explanatory clause. His rebuke seems to be addressed to the more conservative teachers whose words he has just cited in verses 8–9. Caution beats rashness, he seems to be saying, but this does not mean that no risks should be taken. To take no risk, to venture no new ideas, or initiate no new enterprises is to live completely in the past. He seems to be quoting their question— *"Why were the former days better than these days?"*—a question that meant, "These days are not like the good old days, are they?" Such a reactionary attitude does not reflect true *"wisdom,"* which always must leave some openness to God's surprises. (For an interpretation along these lines, see Crenshaw, following Lohfink.)

WISDOM IS BETTER THAN FOLLY

The benefit of *"wisdom"* suggested in verse 10 is expanded in the next cluster (vv. 11–12). But the thought of the two verses is obviously drawn from conventional wisdom. The exuberance over wisdom's profit and usefulness will be modulated some in the two subsequent verses (vv. 13–14), which seem to say "yes, but . . ." to this description of wisdom.

> 11 Wisdom is good with an inheritance,
>   And profitable to those who see the sun.
> 12 For wisdom is a defense as money is a defense,
>   But the excellence of knowledge is that wisdom
>   gives life to those who have it.
> *Eccles. 7:11–12*

We should note the parallel structure of these verses (Ogden). The first lines of each relate wisdom to wealth. The second lines connect wisdom with the art of living. The brief passage reaches its climax in verse 12b where wisdom is described as a giver of *"life."*

"Inheritance" (Heb. *nah*^a*lāh*, used only here in Ecclesiastes) describes possessions passed from generation to generation at the death of the father (Prov. 17:2; 19:14). They may seem reliable because they are already in the hands of the family. But without *"wisdom"* in their use, they may be squandered or embezzled, as Koheleth had already warned (5:10–17; 6:1–9). *"Profitable"* (or "advantageous," Heb. *yôtēr*) is parallel to *"good"* and adds further weight to wisdom's worth. Used here, *"profitable"* plays two roles: (1) it reaches back to the rhetorical questions in 6:8, 11, where it is read *"more"* (v. 8) and *"better"* (v. 11),

and suggests that despite the pessimism featured in them, there are some advantages of *"wisdom"* that should neither be overplayed nor overlooked; (2) it reaches back even further to the *guiding question* of 1:3—the question of what *"profit"* (*yitrôn*, 1:3, and *yôtēr*, 2:15; 6:8, 11; 7:11 are from the Heb. root) there is in our human toil, especially in our efforts to crack the code of divine mystery in life. *"Those who see the sun"* are the living (6:5; cf. Job 3:16; Pss. 49:19; 58:8; the latter two passages use *"light"* instead of *"sun"* to mean the same thing). Nothing said here seems to blow away the dark clouds of death that hangs heavy over the Preacher (2:12–23; 3:16–21; 6:1–9). *"Wisdom's"* advantage applies to the living and to them alone.

The nature of that advantage is made clear in verse 12. *"Excellence"* translates the familiar *yitrôn*, *"profit"* (see on 1:3). *"Knowledge"* (Heb. *daʿat*; see on 1:16) is used as a synonym for wisdom, and as usual connotes knowing what God wants and doing it. Combined, *"knowledge"* and *"wisdom"* give *"life"* to those who have (lit. "own") them. More is meant here than "keep alive" or "offer a livelihood," though *"wisdom"* contributes substantially to both. What *"wisdom"* does best is to help us not only to use wealth well but also to develop a quality of *"life"* not totally dependent on wealth (Luke 12:15).

This conclusion (v. 12b) seems to be designed to rebut the viewpoint of the first line of verse 12, which compares *"money"* (lit. "silver"; see on 5:10) with *"wisdom."* Both offer certain forms of protection or shelter (*"defense"* is lit. "shade," relief from the heat that life "under the sun" entails). But *"money"* is no match for *"wisdom"* when it comes to giving life to those who possess it. On the comparison between wealth and wisdom, see Proverbs 8:10–11; for *"wisdom"* as the source of *"life,"* see Proverbs 8:35.

RESIGNATION IS BETTER THAN INDIGNATION

The tone changes immediately as we move from verse 12 to verse 13. Whether Koheleth is arguing with the more conventional wisdom of the previous passage or simply offering cautionary notes on his own teaching we cannot tell for sure. Either way we run head-on into two crucial themes of the book: (1) our incompetence to change life as we would like (v. 13); (2) our inability to learn anything valuable about the future (v. 14). Whatever *"profit"* wisdom may bring in its life-sustaining and life-embracing ministry, we must never become so heady as to ignore these two stern and vexing limitations.

> 13 Consider the work of God;
>   For who can make straight what
>   He has made crooked?
> 14 In the day of prosperity be joyful,
>   But in the day of adversity consider:
>   Surely God has appointed the one
>   as well as the other,
>   So that man can find nothing that will
>   come after him.
>
> *Eccles. 7:13–14*

These words are, first, a *call for sober reflection. "Consider"* in both verses is the familiar word "see," used so frequently by the Preacher to describe the sages' task of scrutinizing with a gimlet eye and then reflecting on it with a tough mind (see on 1:14; 7:15). Second, they are a *confrontation with divine sovereignty*. In the flow of the text God's name has not appeared for more than twenty verses. Suddenly we are told to consider how *"God"* works in making life *"crooked"* and bringing *"prosperity"* (lit "good"; see 2:24) as well as *"adversity"* (lit. "evil," see on 2:21). Third, these verses are a *caution to humility*. Life at its crucial points is in higher hands than ours. See 1:15 for language close to that of 7:13 but without a specific mention of *"God."* We cannot prevent what God wants to do (v. 13); we cannot predict (*"find,"* Heb. *māṣā'*; see on 3:11) what God is going to do after we have passed from among those *"who see the sun"* (7:11). *"After him"* (see also 3:22 and 6:12) seems almost certainly to describe death, beyond whose horizons Koheleth and his fellow sages in the Old Testament had no power to see. Finally, these verses are a *caveat against indignation*. Bumping our heads against the stone wall of God's sovereignty can make us downright angry. Why can't we change what we don't like? Are we stuck with the constant problems of joyless work, ceaseless pain, endless hassles in the home, fruitless efforts to make sense of life's puzzles, pointless speculations about what tomorrow may bring? "Often we are," says the Teacher. Better it is to let God's sovereignty do its thing than spend our days flushed with anger, aglow with indignation. There is almost no malady in life which high blood pressure will cure. Anger, which we all feel at times and which great biblical figures like Jeremiah and the psalmists felt with keen intensity, will rarely improve our circumstances. It can, however, ruin our chance at any joy and can rain on the parades of everyone around us.

INTEGRITY IS BETTER THAN PRETENTIOUSNESS

These verses (7:15–22) stand on their own as counsel to integrity, but they also connect with and branch out from the assertions of God's strange but sovereign ways in 7:13–14. The chain of thought is triggered by the observation that neither the righteous *("just")* person nor the *"wicked"* always gets the appropriate reward (v. 15). This being the case it is no good pretending to be what one is not—very righteous or very wise. That way of life fools neither God nor neighbor and threatens to be self-destructive in its hypocrisy (vv. 16–18). In contrast, the *"wisdom"* that skirts both temptations carries more clout than the political influence of the whole city council (v. 19). Wise fear of God is the key to integrity since no one is or can claim to be sinless (v. 20). Part of integrity, then, is to try to do right and not worry when others badmouth you (v. 21). After all, honesty leads you to own up to the fact that you, on occasion, have badmouthed *("cursed")* others (v. 22).

15 I have seen everything in my days of vanity:
   There is a just man who perishes in his
      righteousness,
   And there is a wicked man who prolongs
      life in his wickedness.
16 Do not be overly righteous,
   Nor be overly wise:
   Why should you destroy yourself?
17 Do not be overly wicked,
   Nor be foolish:
   Why should you die before your time?
18 It is good that you grasp this,
   And also not remove your hand from the
      other;
   For he who fears God will escape them all.
19 Wisdom strengthens the wise
   More than ten rulers of the city.

20 For there is not a just man on earth who does
      good
    And does not sin.
21 Also do not take to heart everything people
      say,
    Lest you hear your servant cursing you.
22 For many times, also, your own heart has
      known
    That even you have cursed others
                                                Eccles. 7:15–22

As he does so frequently in the Demonstrations, Koheleth cites his personal experience (*"I have seen,"* v. 15, last appeared in 6:1) as the source of the truth of the chain of observations, admonitions, and sayings that comprise this passage. *"Everything"* (v. 15) should probably be read as "both" (so also in v. 18), as is sometimes the case (see on 2:14). Standing first in the Hebrew sentence it focuses attention on the two examples of what seems to be flaming injustice. *"Days of vanity"* (Heb. *hebel*) speak first of the brevity of life but also of its frustrating character, facing us as it does with puzzle upon puzzle, mystery after mystery.

"There is" (v. 15), which introduces both unsettling observations, suggests that the instances of injustice are not the norm but are frequent enough to prompt inner distress about the ways of God's governing. These exceptions to the conclusions of conventional wisdom are too common to be swept under the rug. The sages of Proverbs may be statistically right:

> The fear of the Lord prolongs days,
> But the years of the wicked will be shortened.
>   *Prov. 10:27*

But there are galling exceptions. A person may be as loyal as one can to God's ways and the neighbor's welfare (*"just"* translates the Heb. word for "righteous"; for the meaning of the root, see on 3:16; 5:8) and yet perish in that esteemed state of commendable behavior. Another person who deliberately lives in total disregard of divine claims and human decency has his days prolonged. With no show of contrition or repentance, such a one may live in fine health to ripe years steeped in *"wickedness"* every step of the way. *"Wicked"* and *"wickedness"* (see at 3:17) are stock words in Proverbs to describe the blatantly bad conduct of those who are also called fools. The Hebrew root for *"wicked"* is *rāshā͑* and is found occasionally in Koheleth (3:17; 7:15; 8:10, 13–14; 9:2). *"Wickedness"* should be literally "evil," from the root *rā͑āh*, the regular word for bad behavior and its hurtful results (see at 2:21).

From this vexing observation about what seems to be divine injustice, the Preacher moves to an admonition, as the imperative verbs indicate (vv. 16–17). At first glance he seems to be counseling moderation, but, as Whybray (pp. 120–21) has noted, the classical golden mean—"in nothing too much"—is not the point. Pretense is. Claiming to be better than we are—self-righteousness—and posing as wiser than we are—playing at wisdom—these are the deadly sins against which Ecclesiastes warns us in verse 16 (see v. 20 as comment on the impossibility of perfect righteousness). In a sense they are one sin, since *"righteous"* and *"wise"* are virtually synonymous in wisdom literature, especially Proverbs. The same may be said of *"wicked"* and *"foolish"* in verse 17.

The self-destructive nature of this conduct is made clear in a rhetorical question which serves as the motivation or argument to support the command (v. 16c): pretending is one of the sins that are bound to find us out. We brag on our prowess; then fall flat on our face in our failure to maintain the pose.

I once seized the old-fashioned knife-blade can opener at a family picnic. I went at the lid as though life depended on getting at the beans inside. My hand and wrist swung into the forward-up-down-forward rhythm I had learned as a child. *Few of us old-time craftsmen are left,* I thought to myself. *Lucky for the picnic that I showed up. No skilled mechanic like me; no beans for the party. It's just that simple.* No sooner had those insolent thoughts passed through my boastful mind, than slip, scrape, slash. My index finger had raced along the jagged edge of the almost opened can and lost the race in a bloody finish. As I write I can see the alabaster colored scar that for thirty years has silently rebuked my pride and pretense. I could cite other transgressions of Koheleth's ideas of righteousness and wisdom, but they would be too personal and painful to recount.

The second admonition (v. 17) is a counter-balance to the first. If we are called to lean away from false claims to righteousness and wisdom, an antidote is not to fall off the other side by diving into wickedness (again the root *rāshaʿ*; see v. 15) and folly. That overcorrection is almost sure to be fatal, as the motivating question (v. 17c) warns us. Some there may be who defy the odds, swim in the pools of wickedness, and avoid drowning (v. 15). There is no assurance that we shall be among them. Most of the time, even in the short run, wickedness and foolishness produce disaster. In the long run, as we know from the New Testament, that result is inevitable.

The force of the two admonitions is captured in the summation of verse 18. Its advice is that we hang on to (*"grasp"* or "seize") the first admonition with one hand while not releasing (*"not remove"*) the second admonition (*"the other"*) from the other *"hand."* Balance is the key: no pretense; no impetuousness. "Both" (as *"all"* should be read; see v. 15) temptations can be avoided (*"escape"*) by the one who sober-mindedly and humbly seeks to do things God's way (*"fears God"*; see at 3:14).

This even-handed balance is lauded in verse 19. *"Wisdom,"* which is called "life-giving" in verse 12, is also an incredible source of strength that will help the *"wise"* person avoid the pitfalls listed in verses 16–17. In this sense, *"wisdom"* is once more linked closely to the fear of God which is its beginning and source (Prov. 1:7; 9:10) as well as its summary and climax (Eccles. 12:13). The *"ten rulers"* (or city officials) are probably an exaggeration (hyperbole) for the sake of emphasis, though it is just possible that *"ten"* was a set number of city directors as *"ten"* became the fixed number (Heb. *minyān*) of men necessary to form a synagogue. The point here must not be missed: a God-directed person may make better decisions about right and wrong than the consensus of a whole flock of pragmatic politicians who do not fear God.

Verse 20 seems to reach back to verse 18 and make clear why a balanced life of God fearing is so essential, why no one who is wise dare let go of God's admonitions against pretense and impetuosity: "As for the human family, surely (as Heb. *kî, "for"* should be read here) there is no one fully righteous (see vv. 15–16) on earth, if we describe righteous (*"just"*) in terms of always doing the right thing (*"good"*) and never doing the wrong thing (*"sin"*)." Here the Teacher has picked up a common biblical theme (see 1 Kings 8:46; Ps. 143:2; Job 15:14–16; Prov. 20:9) and used it to underscore his words about integrity, which depends on not pretending to be what we are not and not brashly practicing what we should not.

In the closing verses (21–22), Koheleth makes personal his point about our flawed conduct with a two-pronged admonition. First, in integrity we should close our *"heart"* if not our ears to what other people say about us. To take seriously the words of others by mulling them over is to put ourselves at risk of being hurt or of judging others harshly. The picture of the *"servant cursing"* (or perhaps "demeaning" or "disparaging") the owner makes the situation both realistic and graphic. Second, in integrity we should face our own propensity to sin by remembering the times, whether by tongue or by thought (*"heart"*), we have spoken badly of others and heaped harsh wishes on their heads. "Judge not, that you be not judged" was Jesus' way of putting this matter (Matt. 7:1).

REFLECTIONS ON HUMAN LIMITATIONS

In this section of the Words of Advice we meet Koheleth in what may be his most puzzling presentation. Tracing the various options as to the force of this paragraph and its connections with what led up to it and what flows out of it would lead us too far afield to be profitable. One major thrust of the passage is its teaching on the limits of human wisdom. As we seek to interpret the passage we find ourselves saying "Amen" to the Preacher's observations about the remoteness and depth of wisdom (vv. 23–24). Did the Preacher puckishly illustrate his point by making his arguments hard to follow, let alone fathom?

> 23 All this I have proved by wisdom.
>   I said, "I will be wise";
>   But it was far from me.
> 24 As for that which is far off and exceedingly deep,
>   Who can find it out?
> 25 I applied my heart to know,
>   To search and seek out wisdom
>   and the reason of things.
>   To know the wickedness of folly,
>   Even of foolishness and madness.
> 26 And I find more bitter than death
>   The woman whose heart is snares and nets,
>   Whose hands are fetters.
>   He who pleases God shall escape from her,
>   But the sinner shall be trapped by her.
> 27 "Here is what I have found," says the Preacher,
>   "Adding one thing to the other to find out the
>   reason,

28 Which my soul still seeks but I cannot find:
    One man among a thousand I have found,
    But a woman among all these I have not found.
29 Truly, this only I have found:
    That God made man upright,
    But they have sought out many schemes."
8:1 Who is like a wise man?
    And who knows the interpretation of a thing?
    A man's wisdom makes his face shine,
    And the sternness of his face is changed.

Eccles. 7:23–8:1

The *tone* of the passage is personal and reflective. It is not the anonymous counsel we often find in the three collections of Words of Advice (5:1–12; 7:1–8:9; 9:13–12:8). It comes closer to the tone of the four Demonstrations (1:4–2:26; 3:1–4:16; 5:13–6:12; 8:10–9:12) with the heavy use of the first person pronoun, the citation of personal investigations and conclusions, and the insertion of the title *Koheleth* for the second and last time in the body of the text (see 1:12). All its other occurrences are in the introduction (1:1–2), and conclusion (12:8–10).

The *theme* of this section is the Teacher's test and its results. It recounts the Preacher's persistent attempts to use his *"wisdom"* as the means for putting to the "test" ("*prove,*" v. 23, should be translated as "test"; see 2:1, where the lengthy process of testing began) various theories about finding true profit and ultimate meaning in life. And it reveals the limited and negative results of that test.

The *structure* may be analyzed along these lines:

Confession of failure of the test for true wisdom	7:23–24
Summary of the intensity and breadth of the test which ranged from profound wisdom to crazy foolishness	7:25
Statement of one discovery—the dangers of a grasping woman	7:26
Elaboration on the search and its one discovery	7:27–28
Generalization on the contrast between what God created and what humankind has become	7:29
Boast of success in his vocation despite the seeming failure	8:1

The interpretative *keys* which help unlock the meaning of this passage include observations like these. First, *"all this"* (v. 23) probably looks back rather than forward. It may include Koheleth's experimental research *("test")* from 2:1 on. It certainly embraces the observations and admonitions of 7:15–22, especially the matter of unjust retribution in 7:15.

Second, the *"wisdom"* (v. 25) which the Teacher sought with such fervent intention, *"I will be wise"* (v. 23), reaches beyond all the customary understanding and insight that the best sages, including Koheleth, already possessed. After all, he had consistently exhibited an uncanny sagacity in his basic teachings on how to behave in the Words of Advice already canvassed. He was not after an ordinary teaching credential; he had already graduated *summa cum laude* or won Teacher-of-the-Year awards (see 8:1). His quest was for a wisdom beyond all that wisdom—insight into the way life worked at its profoundest levels, a grasp of the mysteries of how God rewarded and judged the human family, comprehension of the timing and purpose of divine activity.

This higher *"wisdom"* is described as *"the reason"* (vv. 25, 27), a term that translates Hebrew *ḥeshbôn* (found only in Ecclesiates), whose root meaning is "think," "devise," or "calculate." It seems to mean "the bottom line," "the sum of all things" (RSV). To get at it, Koheleth used every tool and skill available to him. The verbs *"search"* and *"seek out"* convey the ideas of depth and breadth in the investigation (see on 1:13 for Heb. *tûr* and on 3:6, 15 for *baqqēsh* which is repeated in 7:28–29: *"seeks," "sought out"*). Yet the tools were too dull and the skills too inept to plumb wisdom's depth—*"exceedingly deep"* (v. 24) is literally "deep, deep," the repetition intensifying the meaning—or to range across its breadth. *"Far from me"* (v. 23) shows the huge gap between Koheleth's aims and his achievements. And he was not alone: *"who can find it out"* invites the answer, "no one." (v. 24; see Job 28).

Lee Edward Travis was the founding dean of the Graduate School of Psychology at Fuller Seminary. His intellectual pilgrimage illustrated Koheleth's frustration. As a brilliant young psychologist, he was the first American to develop techniques of electroencephalography and study human brain waves. As he began his research he was heady with the hope of getting to the core of what it means to be human. Yet the more he worked in the lab at the University of Iowa the further away he found himself from the profound aims of his research. Later, he turned to the study of speech impediments, especially stuttering. For years he labored with students and colleagues to understand the physical and emotional causes of defective speech. He helped to found the American Speech and Hearing Association. Along the way he transferred his hope from brain-wave research to studies in speech pathology. Again his hopes were dashed. The closer he tried to approach the essence of humanity the further away it moved. Finally, when he met Christ as Lord and Savior, he uttered his "Eureka!" In that one encounter, he had found the answer both to what we human beings are and to what we need. A wise man always, yet he, in Christ, came to know the wisdom beyond wisdom.

A third key to this passage (7:23–8:1) is the listing of the broad agenda to which Solomon turned (7:25) as he pressed his pursuit for the ultimate wisdom. The specific turn in his approach is signaled in the verb *sābab* (first word in v. 25, *"applied"* in NKJV) which described the ceaseless action of the wind in 1:6 and Koheleth's painful change *("turned my heart")* of mind in 2:20. The specific shift seems to entail a new focus on the *"wickedness* (Heb. *reshaᶜ*; see on 7:15, 17) *of folly"* and *"foolishness and madness,"* better read "foolishness which is madness" (7:25, RSV). The wording here seems to point to an intensified version of the curriculum that Koheleth had set out for himself at the beginning of his quest (1:17; 2:12). *"Wickedness"* is an item added in 7:25. So is *"folly"* (Heb. *kesel* which occurs only here with this meaning; elsewhere it denotes "confidence," Prov. 3:26). As noted above, *"wickedness"* and *"folly"* may be synonymous. Indeed, a likely translation is "wickedness which is folly," in parallel to the phrase that follows, "foolishness which is madness." It is the exploration of the nature of this extreme behavior and the questions it prompts about its causes and consequences that accounts for the seemingly sharp transition from verse 25 to 26. *"Wisdom"* the Preacher could not find out (v. 24). What he was in the process of discovering (the participle form suggests ongoing research and discovery: *"I find"* = "I am finding," v. 26) was despicable human conduct (vv. 28–29).

The fourth key to the meaning of the passage is to read verse 26, beginning with, *"More bitter than death"* as a quotation from conventional wisdom. Understood thus, *"I find"* or "I keep finding" means "I keep hearing men say" and serves as introduction to the quoted proverb. The proverb itself does not refer to women in general but to the "immoral (lit. "strange," "foreign to our way of life") woman" of

Proverbs (2:16–19; 5:3ff; 6:20–29; 7:5ff.). Her ways smack of *"death"* (see Prov. 2:18; 5:5; 7:27). Dealing with her bears *"bitter"* consequences (Prov. 5:4). Her person is an arsenal of hunting equipment: *"snares"* (the verb form is *"prey"* in Prov. 6:26), *"nets"* (see the fishing imagery of Babylonian cruelty and ruthlessness in Hab. 1:15–17), *"fetters"* (like Samson's "ropes" in Judg. 15:14). She is fully equipped to lasso and hogtie her victims.

Eluding her clutches seems to be a combination of human alertness and divine providence (v. 26b). Both *"he who pleases"* (lit. "one who is good") and the *"sinner"* (lit. "one who misses the mark") are somewhat ambiguous. The words may mean "fortunate" and "unfortunate" and put the whole outcome in God's unpredictable hands or they may have a strong moral connotation depicting the behavior of the two types of persons. As in the similar passage, 2:26, the meaning probably combines the two extremes: those who do good are fortunate to have divine protection; those who do not, are not. Yet we cannot overlook the element of sovereign grace where God gives help to those who deserve it not. One scholar at least makes this sovereign grace Koheleth's main point. "This favor of God simply comes over a person or fails to come—those are the chances of life over which one has no control. . . . In other words it is not wisdom but God who determines who will go free and who will not" (Loader).

The fifth key to our passage is to read verses 27–29 as Koheleth's rejection of the conventional wisdom expressed in verse 26. While he frequently found people passing on that proverb, what he found for himself—*"Here is what I* (note that the editor added *"said the preacher"* to distinguish the quoted saying from Koheleth's opinion) *have found* (v. 27)—took quite a different turn. He was not afraid to stand on his contrary opinion because he had confidence in his meticulous method of investigation: *"adding one thing to the other* (lit. "one to one") in the course of trying to ferret out the elusive bottom line (*"reason,"* Heb. *ḥeshbôn*, see at v. 25) which, he acknowledges, his whole person (*"my soul,"* v. 28) quests after, but *"cannot find."* This inductive method of item by item, case by case, logical step after logical step has not gotten him to the goal of the higher *"wisdom."* Yet it has not been fruitless. He has learned much about human nature—its foibles and failures—along the way.

Understanding what he has learned is the sixth key to opening the meaning of this whole puzzling text. His initial findings—note the drumming repetitions of *"I have found," "I have not found"* in verses 27–29—begin with a look back at the last two lines of verse 26. They deal with the question as to whether anyone is "good" (as *"he who pleases"* should literally be rendered) enough to warrant God's providential protection from the wicked woman's wiles. That word "good" should be carried forward and used as light on the findings of verse 28: *"One* [good] *man among a thousand I have found, But a* [good] *woman among all these I have not found."* The literary mood here is hyperbole, deliberate exaggeration for emphasis. A *"thousand"* stands for a large number, though there may be a side-glance of the thousand women in Solomon's harem, who turned the king's heart away from God (1 Kings 11:3). The difference between the results of the investigation is precisely one tenth of one percent. The aim is not to put down women as a gender but to show how utterly scarce, if not nonexistent, genuinely good people are, people who would have passed muster with God to justify his deliverance of them from feminine snares or any other kind.

All of this is preparatory to the final, summary finding—well above the evasive bottom line, but important nonetheless: The whole human family (as ʾādām must mean here; see at 1:3) has deliberately (*"sought out"* translates the same verb that describes Koheleth's inquiries in v. 25) and wickedly developed *"many schemes"* to deviate from being *"upright"* (Heb. *yāshār*), a favorite word for stellar conduct in Proverbs (2:7; 3:32; 11:3, 6, 11 and more than twenty other places) and in Job, where it is defined by "feared God and shunned evil" (1:1, 8; 2:3). *"Schemes"* is a sister word in Hebrew to *"reason," "sum,"* or *"bottom line"* in verses 25, 27 *(hishshᵉbōnôth* and *heshbôn).* The two words frame a pun: what was really desired was a single, comprehensive answer to the great mysteries of God's way with humankind *(heshbôn).* Koheleth could not find it, careful though his method was. What he did find were the *"schemes" (hishshᵉbōnôth).* The "sum" would have led toward a greater understanding of God; the *"schemes"* became destructive weapons (see 2 Chron. 26:15) that devastated God's plan for the human family. One might almost think that Koheleth had the text of Genesis 3–6 before him as he wrote these words.

The final key is to see Koheleth as the wise man described in 8:1. He comes back to where he began in using wisdom to break the code of life's main mysteries (vv. 23–24). He did become wise as he had resolved in verse 23, not wise enough to figure out the purpose and pattern of God's ways but wise enough to know that they were beyond figuring. After totaling the data of life one by one (v. 27), he concluded that the better part of wisdom was not to blame God for seeming unfairness in the distribution of rewards (7:15, which sets the stage for the rest of chapter 7), but to focus on the mess that the human family, both women and men, had made of the perfect start God had given it at creation (7:29).

This double discovery—(1) ultimate wisdom is beyond reach and (2) human perverseness not divine injustice should be our focus— leads him to extol the wise man's office and, hence, himself as a prime incumbent (8:1). Parallel rhetorical questions, the second expanding on the first, are the sticks he uses to beat his drum. Together they tattoo his boastful claim: "No one else is *like a wise man*, because only he has the gifts and tools to interpret (Heb. *pesher*, *"interpretation"* is used only here in the Old Testament but is a favorite label of the men of Qumran for their commentary notes on Scripture) a word or a matter (*"thing"* translates Heb. *dābār*) beyond the grasp of ordinary mortals.

That interpretative gift, just displayed by Koheleth, is what makes a sage's *"face shine"* with the satisfaction of a job well done, like a kid aglow with an excellent report card or a surgeon agleam with the thrill of a life saved. The language may also hint at an attitude of generous compassion toward others, like that conveyed by Yahweh's shining face (Num. 6:25; Ps. 67:1). Whether the *"changed" "sternness"* (v. 1d) is a gradual or a sudden experience is hard to say. One possibility is that *"wisdom"* (v. 1c) stands for a breakthrough in wisdom, a discovery like Koheleth's double find in 7:23–29. In this case, the change *"of his face"* may depict the transformation from the stern concentration with which the investigations were pursued to the radiant joy sparked by the thrill of invention. In any case it is a relief to know that what has seemed to be a grim, gruff countenance as Koheleth conducted his Demonstrations and meted out his Words of Advice was not his only face.

ADMONITIONS ON RESPECT FOR AUTHORITY

Our attitude toward authority tends to be ambivalent. We are like the eighteen-year-old lad who joins the army to find security and learn discipline and then resents the first military haircut. He wants to have his life organized but not to the point of polishing his buttons and shining his shoes. He longs to know who he is and how he fits into life, but he would rather find this out by other ways than close order drill or double time marches.

Ambivalence toward authority—I suppose we learn it in our families almost from birth. We want the security of parents who support us and guide us as we grow, yet we chafe under their correction and squirm to escape their regulations.

Certainly part of the problem is ours. Human sin, in the first place, was a contest of authority (7:29). What God had ordered, our first parents had rejected. They pitted their will against God's word and set a pattern of rebellion that all of their descendants—with one exception—have followed.

But part of the problem with authority is that those who wield it are also rebels. Drill sergeants and parents, school teachers and bosses, playground directors and kings are all in revolt against authority—in some measure, at least.

So the ambivalence is fed from both sides. Those who exercise authority are prevented from doing it well by their own conflicts with it, and those whose lot is to follow drag their feet because they resent being pushed around by others. Yet both groups know that without authority little in life can be accomplished. When leaders will not lead or followers will not follow, something akin to chaos is the result.

Probably nobody in the Old Testament sensed the ambivalence that we feel toward authority more acutely than Ecclesiastes. With sharp insight, he had observed the ways of kings and commoners and the conflict between them caused by the use and abuse of authority. The problem of authority, he saw, as part of the mystery with which life is marked. Just as wisdom, pleasure, and wealth offer much less than they appear to, so authority as a good goal in life has that same deceptive emptiness.

The *setting* of 8:2–9 needs brief comment. By Koheleth's time Persian hegemony over Palestine (539–332 B.C.) had probably given way to that of the successors of Alexander the Great: (1) Ptolemy whose capital was in Alexandria and whose dominion was principally Egypt and North Africa; (2) Seleucus, who ruled the Asian provinces from his throne in Babylon; (3) Antigonus, who controlled Asia Minor and several of the provinces of Greece. For about twenty years, the three generals fought each other for mastery of Palestine and Syria. Finally

Ptolemy and Seleucus defeated Antigonus in 301 B.C., and Ptolemy, the stronger of the two victors, and his successors held the reins of Palestine for the next century or so.

This political background suggests that *"king"* (vv. 2–4) need not be read literally. The citizens of Judah, even the top administrators, would have had little personal contact with royalty. *"King,"* therefore, must stand for "king's representative," the person to whom the foreign ruler delegated authority. Given the slowness and uncertainty of communication, that official had to exercise virtually absolute authority under guidelines laid down by the king. Ptolemy followed in the steps of the pharaoh's and ruled like an autocrat. Whoever served in his stead in the provinces beyond Egypt must have behaved about the same way.

The text assumes that some Jews had access to this high officer in Jerusalem. While Koheleth mentions no priests, we can imagine that prestigious members of the high priest's family, elders in the city council, as well as wealthy landowners, successful merchants, and government officials whose offices were left intact from the Persian period were among those with entrée to the Ptolemaic governor.

The *structure* of the passage seems to suggest that the admonitions on court behavior (vv. 2–3) serve as an introduction to the deeper question of the way in which all human authority is outranked by death and its refusal to adhere to a predictable schedule. The sequence of thought moves along these lines:

Admonition A: obey the king in keeping with your oath of
              loyalty before God   v. 2
Admonition B: stay loyal to the government even though
              tempted to join those who foment rebellion   v. 3
      Proverb A: the king's power is absolute   v. 4
         Proverb B: a loyal and wise citizen stays away
                     from rebels unless the time and process
                     are unequivocally right   v. 5
            Proverb C: every situation has its right time and
                        process, though anxiety about disaster
                        makes it hard to wait   v. 6
      Proverb D: Even kings live in this uncertainty since, like
                  the rest of us, they cannot predict what will
                  happen and when   v. 7

Proverb E: Four statements about the inevitability and untimeli-
ness of death   v. 8
Concluding observation: power to rule can be downright
oppressive   v. 9.

Authority has its dangers. The Preacher knew them well. The authority of the king was the theme with which he chose to end this
second set of Words of Advice (7:1–8:9).

The first *danger* that he saw in authority was that it often displays *a
pompousness that seeks to intimidate.* The more powerful the authority
is, the more it may fall victim to this. Kings were especially susceptible. Here are the Preacher's thoughts concerning them:

> 2 I say, "Keep the king's commandment for the
> sake of your oath to God.
> 3 "Do not be hasty to go from his presence. Do
> not take your stand for an evil thing, for he does
> whatever pleases him."
> 4 Where the word of a king is, there is power;
> And who may say to him, "What are you
> doing?"
> 5 He who keeps his command will experience
> nothing harmful;
> And a wise man's heart discerns both time
> and judgment.
>
> *Eccles. 8:2–5*

"Commandment" (v. 2; lit. "mouth of the king," which stands for
what he speaks) refers to the royal orders in general, not any special
instruction. *"Oath to God"* is a reminder that all of our promises are
made before God and, accordingly, take on a seriousness beyond the
words with which they are uttered. On the other hand, the generally
pragmatic tone of the context keeps us from making an absolute out
of the *"oath."* Perhaps "solemn oath" is the best way to read it, since
the rest of the passage puts much more emphasis on the power of the
king to command what he wants and punish the disobedient as he
likes.

The disobedience is twice described as *"evil thing"* (vv. 3, 5; in the
latter verse NKJV obscures the repetition by translating it *"nothing
harmful"*). Recent studies have indicated that *"evil thing"* may mean an

act of rebellion or treachery against the throne. If that is the case then the first line of verse 3 does not refer to a rapid and impolite exit from the throne room but a brash change of loyalty that removes the rebel from the king's side to the conspirators'. The explanatory clause that ends verse 3 speaks not of the king's petty pique or hurt feelings but of the length to which he will go—*"whatever pleases him"*—to quash a coup.

Two proverbs (vv. 4–5) reinforce the command in the two admonitions (vv. 2–3). The first proverb underscores the absolute authority (*"power"*; Heb. *shiltôn*, see also v. 8, crops up in English as Sultan, the title of the rulers of the Ottoman empire) of the king's word, which neither courtier nor commoner has the right to question. The second proverb reiterates, in the first line, the warning (v. 3) against joining a conspiracy. The person shrewd enough to follow the king's *"command"* (Heb. *miṣwāh*, see on 12:13, where divine commands are in view)—especially the order to stay loyal—will not make common cause with the revolutionaries. He will pay no attention to them, nor acknowledge their existence—*"not know"* (Heb. *yādaʿ*, *"experiences"*) is literally how the Hebrew goes. What he will know (again Heb. *yādaʿ*, *"discerns"*), if he has a *"wise man's heart"* (*"mind,"* *"understanding"*) is *"both time and judgment."* *"Time"* (Heb. *ʿēth*) takes us back to the famous poem that spells out how God fixes times and seasons according to his sovereign plan (3:1–8). *"Judgment"* is a possible reading of Hebrew *mishpāṭ*; so is *"justice."* But here the emphasis seems to be on the orderly process for getting something done: "procedure," NIV; "way," RSV; "method for action," NEB. Considering, however, the impact of divine timing and activity on a wicked king, *"judgment"* is always standing in the wings. Koheleth views the king's power as intimidating but not absolute. The time may come when toppling the throne is the right course of action, but it will be the wise not the rabble who best discern when and how.

Given the long history of arbitrary foreign rule, including the matter of which of Alexander's political heirs would control Palestine (see above on the *setting* of this passage) and the century-long struggle of the Seleucids to wrest the territory from the Ptolemies, one can imagine the kinds of court intrigue which lie behind Koheleth's counsel about the right time and the right way.

Little is said here about statesmanship. Little is said about the welfare of the land and its people. The emphasis is on the welfare of the person courting the favor of the king. "A manual on the manipulation of governors" might be the title of this section. Do what the king wants, and he will do what you want. That is the heart of the matter. Considering the kinds of kings they worked with, the wise may not have been able to do much better than this.

Unhappily, much authority works in whimsical ways. The purposes for which it is given, the care with which it is to be exercised, the obligations which it carries—these are blurred when the ruler becomes heady with power. Overawed by a sense of glory, such persons are vulnerable to all kinds of manipulation. Whoever will feed their pompousness by telling them how good and wise they are can readily lead them to do things that are bad and stupid. Intimidation and manipulation are not mutually exclusive terms. The more the lion on the throne stands rampant to cow his subjects the more susceptible he may become to those who scratch his back like a pussycat's.

The second *danger* that Koheleth found in authority was that it sometimes demonstrates *an arrogance that rejects limitations.* The power to wield some authority can easily be confused with the right to wield all authority. We are like office boys who sit in the boss's chair after hours and swivel ourselves in a fantasy that pictures us as masters of all we survey. Scarcely anything bubbles to the head faster than power.

Yet when it comes down to it, all authority except God's must labor under severe limitations. Our arrogance seeks to override them. But they are there nevertheless, and we use our authority best when we keep them constantly in mind.

A lesson in humility was what the wise Teacher tried to give:

> 6 Because for every matter there is a time and
>   judgment,
>   Though the misery of man increases greatly.
> 7 For he does not know what will happen;
>   So who can tell him when it will occur?
> 8 No one has power over the spirit to retain the
>   spirit,
>   And no one has power in the day of death.
>   There is no release from that war,
>   And wickedness will not deliver those who
>   are given to it.
>
> *Eccles. 8:6-8*

The when *("time")* and how *("judgment"* or "process") of verse 5 are generalized in the third proverb of the series (v. 6). *"Every matter"* takes us back to the poem on *"time"* (3:1), and the comments that follow it (3:17). The advice here is toward prudence and patience. Affairs of government are not exempt from God's sovereign control. They are included in *"every matter."* The intent of the proverb is stated in the second line: knowing that God has his own timing and methods of action helps us bear the *"misery"* (lit. "evil" or "danger"; Heb. *rāʿāh*; see 2:21) which weighs heavily upon us. Just what form the *"misery"* takes we are not told. It probably has to do with tolerating high-handedness or injustice at the hands of rulers like the one described in this passage. What seems sure is that this *"misery"* is aggravated by the uncertainty of the timing and methods God will use to redress the matter.

The fourth proverb (v. 7) seems to make this connection. It also begins to focus attention not only on the courtier or administrator to whom the admonitions (vv. 2–3) were directed but on the ruler himself who is, as much as anyone, in the dark about the future. Faced with the mysteries of God's ways, king and commoner are equally frustrated.

The fifth proverb (v. 8) seems to bring the content of *"time and judgment"* (or "mode of action," see v. 5) out in the open: it is untimely death. The fourth proverb (v. 7) focused on lack of knowledge; here (v. 8) the theme is lack of power. Four evidences of this lack, each beginning with a negative "no" or "not," are listed, almost in the manner of the numerical sayings of Proverbs 30:

  (1) *No one* (lit. "man" or "person"; Heb. *ʾādām*, see 1:3) *has power* (lit. is "master"; Heb. *shallît*, as in 7:19; 10:5) *over the spirit* (Heb. *rûªḥ* may mean wind, but context calls for *"spirit"*) *to retain* (Heb. *kālāʾ*; see Hag. 1:10, "the heavens . . . withhold the dew") *the spirit,* so that the person will not die; note, "the spirit . . . goes upward" as a picture of death (Eccles. 3:21).

  (2) *No one* has *power* (Heb. *shiltôn*, "authority"; see v. 4) *in* (or "over") *the day of death,* not even the ruler, whose word carries full weight in his own land.

  (3) *No discharge* (Heb. *mishlaḥat* from a root to "send") describes God's dispatching of angels of destruction (Ps. 78:49); Koheleth uses it in the sense of sending a soldier home from the midst of battle *("in that war")* where the provisions of neither furlough nor exemption (Deut. 20:5–8; 24:5) could be applied. In *Boots,*

his famous poem on soldiering, Rudyard Kipling pictures the endless line of soldiers stomping out the rhythm of their march, as almost robot-like they trudge toward battle. Each stanza he punctuates with Koheleth's line:

"There's no discharge in the war!"

Death has that relentless military discipline to it, when its time has come.

(4) No rescue *("will not deliver")* will *wickedness* (Heb. *reshaᶜ*, see 3:16; 7:25) provide for those *"who are given to it"* (lit. "are its masters," "own it").

Let arrogance learn the limits placed on all human authority. It does not know the future and, therefore, must make its decisions humbly. It cannot stave off the day of death and, therefore, must build contingencies into its plans. It may trigger responses beyond its control, like a war, which an authority may begin but not be able to end. It may engage in wicked conduct with tragic results from which there is no recovery. Such are the pitfalls of authority when its reins are in haughty hands.

The third *danger* that Ecclesiastes noted in authority was that it often presents *a power that abuses relationships.* His summary sentence scarcely needs comment:

> 9   All this I have seen, and applied my heart to
> every work that is done under the sun: There is a time
> in which one man rules over another to his own hurt.
> *Eccles. 8:9*

This pattern of authority (condensed in *"all this"*) misused was not an isolated instance. Koheleth's experience and reflection (on *"I have seen,"* see 1:14; on *"applied my heart,"* see 1:13) down through the years, in situation after situation (*"every work"*) everywhere he looked in this broken world (*"under the sun"*; see on 1:3), add up to one inescapable conclusion: an ongoing human reality is the hurtful oppression of the subjects by their rulers. This is as broad and binding a generalization as the many other convictions which Koheleth has expressed. *"Time"* here does not mean a fixed, set time as it normally does in Ecclesiastes. *"Time in which"* = "while" and describes time in its unending march through history. *"Rules over"* is literally "lords it over," another instance of the root *shālaṭ,* whose derivatives stitch together this passage on authority (vv. 4, 8, 9). Who receives the brunt of the damage? The oppressed person seems the obvious answer: "his hurt" (Heb. *ra^c*, "harm" or "damage") is a better rendering (RSV, JB, NEB, NASB) than *"his own hurt,"* though the Hebrew allows either meaning. And in a sense, both readings are accurate: the tyrant who manhandles others almost always pays for his crime in the end. The words are tragic: "while man lords it over man to his hurt" (RSV). The authority whose purpose is to help the human family cope with its problems and achieve its goals has been thrown into reverse gear. It has worked just the opposite of what it was intended to do. Public servants have viewed themselves as masters and laid the whip of oppression to the backs of those whom they were supposed to serve.

"No hope!" Like a tight-lipped surgeon still stunned by the sounds and smells of death, the Preacher mouthed his desperate verdict: Look at life—with its mysterious future, with its certain death, with its wicked ways—look at life, and abandon hope.

The same realism that made the Teacher suspect all hope made him stress practical wisdom as a way of struggling through life. As at other points he had urged his hearers to settle for simple delights like work, food, drink, and fellowship, so here he counseled them to resist the temptations of bribery (7:7); to exercise patience, not pride (7:8); to control their anger (7:9); to abstain from a nostalgia for the good old days (7:10); to submit to the will of God which human beings do not have power to change (7:13); to avoid a compulsive commitment either to self-righteousness or wickedness (7:16–17); to fear God (7:18); and to ignore malicious comments that others may make about them (7:21–22).

In a world where one faced frustration on every hand, this was probably sane advice. At least it was the best the Teacher—given his view of life and his time in history—could do. He had lost touch with the great promises of the earlier wise men who had offered hope to the people in words like these:

> The hope of the righteous will be gladness,
> But the expectation of the wicked will perish.
> *Prov. 10:28*

To Ecclesiastes' eyes, that clear distinction between the righteous and the wicked had become blurred and his whole view of hope was clouded as a result. More than that, he was tone-deaf to the songs of the prophets that rang with hope about the latter days when God's glory and righteousness would be revealed to Israel and the world.

No full-blown hope, just some sage counsel was the best he could do. It was certainly a useful assortment of wise words. But all of us need more than that.

Epilogue: The Greater Wise Man

One reason why Jesus' message blew through the ancient world like a gust of fresh air was that it carried new hope, great hope. It shed brilliant light on a future that for Koheleth and his students was shrouded with gloom.

With considerable wisdom and with abundant candor, Ecclesiastes had shown the weaknesses in human views of hope. He had taught his followers in what not to hope; but it took Jesus to show the human family where high hope could be found. The Preacher's motto was "look at life and scale back your hopes." Jesus' word was better: "Trust me and find hope."

Ecclesiastes' conclusion was buttressed by three lines of argument. Jesus answered each of them. That the future is too mysterious to encourage hope was the Preacher's opinion. Jesus' answer was *the hope of a glorious coming,* bright with power and righteousness. Many times he described it in phrases like these:

> "and they will see the Son of man coming on the clouds of heaven with power and great glory; and He will send out his angels with a great sound of a trumpet, and they will gather together His elect from the four winds, from one end of heaven to the other."
>
> *Matt. 24:30–31*

What a climax to history! What a destiny for God's people! We are not only spectators, but full participants in the fulfillment of God's great plan to make his name known across the earth! Who can cry "no hope" in the light of that stupendous event?

That death is too certain to allow for hope was Koheleth's judgment. Jesus' answer was *the promise of resurrection and eternal life:*

> "for the hour is coming in which all who are in the graves will hear His voice and come forth—those who have done good, to

187

the resurrection of life, and those who have done evil, to the resurrection of condemnation."

John 5:28–29

Death's lease on human life has been broken, even when death seems untimely. Since Christ's resurrection the human family has been under new ownership. Resurrection is the destination of us all. But only those who truly trust Jesus as God's full truth can really hope in resurrection.

For them death is no longer a nemesis which tramples plans and mocks achievements. It is a portal of hope—death is—leading to resurrection and eternal friendship with God. Who can whisper "no hope" in the face of that resurrection?

That humankind, with all its schemes to thwart God's will, is too sinful to have reason for hope was Ecclesiastes' conclusion. Jesus' shattered it with the *offer of full forgiveness.* It was to those who recognize their sinfulness that Jesus came. They are the lost sheep which the Shepherd carries home from the wilderness; they are the lost coins that the woman joyfully finds; they are the prodigal children whom the Father enthusiastically welcomes (Luke 15). Who can mutter "no hope" in the sight of that welcome?

When the physicians of this world's problems have exhausted their skill in social reform, economic theory, educational philosophy, and political strategy, they will shake their heads and sigh, "no hope." But theirs is not the last word. Jesus came to do God's full work—the full work of the God of hope (Rom. 15:13).

CHAPTER TEN

Fourth Demonstration: Mystery and Mortality

Ecclesiastes 8:10–9:12

It was one of Alfred Hitchcock's best. Ruth and I saw it twenty years ago or more and can still recall virtually every scene. The half-hour television drama on the old black-and-white set began with a couple chatting cordially as they drove through a country town. Their peaceful drive was interrupted by the shriek of a siren and the flashing of lights behind them. As they slowed their car in response, the police vehicle lurched past them and then cut in front of them forcing their car into a low concrete wall at the edge of the road.

In shock they climbed out and discovered the bump had broken their right front wheel. They turned to protest the matter to the policemen who were now at their side, when one of the burly cops slugged the bewildered man in the face. "You saw him start to swing at me, didn't you?" he growled at his partner, whose surly response was, "I sure did!"

Ruth and I could feel our outrage heat to the boiling point and beyond as we watched the next scene unfold. The tow truck came along and hauled the car to the garage where an unearthly fee was quoted for the towing and repairs. The incensed couple was dragged to the office of the Justice of the Peace where all their protests fell on deaf ears and an exorbitant fine was levied for their alleged speeding and attempted assault. It was obvious that the whole crew—police, truck driver, mechanic, and judge—were in cahoots. We watched in disbelief as the shattered couple, demeaned, defrauded, and downcast, climbed into the car to make their way out of that wicked town. Everything in us cried out, "That's not fair. Life ought not to be that way. Is there no justice to be found?"

Despair and hopelessness hung over us like the winter fog over San Francisco Bay. Then as the couple eased their way out of town, the man asked the woman, "Did you get all that?" She opened her purse, pulled out a compact tape recorder, and began to replay the entire scenario. The winds of relief began to disperse the fog. The sunlight of comprehension began to shine. The question about justice was answered with a banging "yes." The couple were government agents investigating reports of speed-trap rackets in the small town. They had their hard evidence. Vindication was on the way.

For the first time in the whole thirty minutes Ruth and I took deep breaths. We felt safe to go outside and face the world. Justice had not been banished from the land.

We had experienced what Edward John Carnell, my teacher and predecessor as president of Fuller, called *judicial sentiment*, the feeling of utter vexation that roils within us when someone does something unfair and seems to get away with it. It is the inner disturbance we experience when we read Cinderella's story and watch the cruel behavior of her stepsisters.

Koheleth was no stranger to such *judicial sentiment*. With obvious pain he pointed to injustice in the courts, marketplaces, and palaces of the land (3:16; 4:1; 5:8–9). With even more pain he wrestled with what seemed to be inconsistencies in God's justice. This theme has dominated much of his thought from 6:1 on, though it was introduced as early as 2:26.

This unity of theme makes the distinction between Demonstration and Words of Advice more difficult to draw here than elsewhere in the book. I have labeled this segment (8:10–9:12) as Demonstration Four because the amount of *reflection* on it outweighs the bits of instruction. The reflective tone is signaled in a host of familiar clues:

> "Then I saw" (v. 10)
> "Yet I surely know" (v. 12)
> "I said that this also is vanity" (v. 14)
> "So I commended enjoyment" (v. 15)
> "When I applied my heart" (v. 16)
> "Then I saw" (v. 17)
> "For I considered all this in my heart" (9:1)
> "I returned and saw under the sun" (9:11).

Like the other three Demonstrations, this one is marked also by repetitions of the *vanity verdict* (8:10, 14; 9:9), the *under the sun* rubric

(8:15, 17; 9:3, 6, 9, 11), and the *alternative conclusion* (8:15; 9:7–10). We may track the flow of thought somewhat like this:

Reflections on the mysteries of divine justice   8:10–14
Alternative conclusion on joyous living   8:15
Reflections on the mysteries of all divine activity   8:16–17
Reflections on the universality of death   9:1–6
    Illustration: proverb on the importance of life   9:4b
    Illustration: poem on the importance of life   9:5–6
Alternative conclusion on joyous living   9:7–10
Reflections on the mysteries of divine providence   9:11–12

The whole passage is a masterpiece of melody and counterpoint. The melody and its variations ponder the seeming inappropriateness of God's response to our human activity. The counter-theme (8:15; 9:7–10) muses on our proper human response to God's unfathomable ways.

INCONSISTENCY: THE MYSTERIES OF DIVINE JUSTICE

The first set of reflections explores the pattern of rewards that prevails in human experience. The wicked seem sometimes to be honored for their hypocrisy, while the righteous are forgotten despite their piety (v. 10); divine judgment often lingers so long that fear of it ceases to be a corrective to society's proneness to do wrong (v. 11); in short, the system of rewards on occasion, at least, works backwards—righteous people get what is due the wicked and vice versa (v. 14).

The thoughts (vv. 12–13) sandwiched between these criticisms of divine justice show clearly that Koheleth was suggesting that the apparent inconsistencies in God's dealing with the human family were the exceptions not the rule: in the great bulk of situations those who *"fear God"* will receive blessing *("good")*, while the *"sinner"* and the *"wicked"* person will ultimately perish even though the *"sentence"* (v. 11) may seem frightfully slow in coming.

> 10 Then I saw the wicked buried, who had come
> and gone from the place of holiness, and they were
> forgotten in the city where they had done so. This also
> is vanity.

11 Because the sentence against an evil work is
not executed speedily, therefore the heart of the sons
of men is fully set in them to do evil.

12 Though a sinner does evil a hundred times,
and his days are prolonged, yet I surely know that it
will be well with those who fear God, who fear before
Him.

13 But it will not be well with the wicked; nor will
he prolong his days, which are as a shadow, because
he does not fear before God.

14 There is a vanity which occurs on earth, that
there are just men to whom it happens according to
the work of the wicked; again, there are wicked men
to whom it happens according to the work of the
righteous. I said that this also is vanity.

Eccles. 8:10–14

To support the overall interpretation of these verses given above,
some specific comments are needed. Verse 10 is not without problems in text and translation. As it reads in NKJV and other English
versions, it is hard to see why it would conclude with the *vanity verdict* (see on 1:2). After all, for the wicked to be *"buried"* and *"forgotten"*
is precisely the lot they deserved. Why call it *"vanity"*? Among the
several suggestions for emendation offered by commentators I prefer
that of Whybray. It calls for three main changes: (1) the last two Hebrew consonants of *"buried"* should be reversed to mean "approach,"
"draw near" (Heb. *qᵉbūrîm* to *qᵉrēbîm*), describing their frequent access
to the Temple, as "place of holiness" should be understood (see on
5:1); (2) the word "righteous ones" (Heb. *ṣaddîqîm*) should be inserted
as the subject of *"were forgotten"* as counter-balance to the *"wicked
ones"* of the first line (that such a word may drop out is indicated by
the loss of "to the wicked" in 9:2; see comments there); (3) the word
"so" or "thus" (Heb. *kēn*) near the end of the sentence may be read as
"right"—it is the modern Hebrew word for "yes." These changes,
each of them reasonable enough in light of the Hebrew text, result in
the kind of contrast between the lots of the wicked and the righteous
that the context calls for:

Then I saw the wicked approaching and entering the place of holiness and doing so frequently, while the righteous were forgotten in
the very city where they did the right things. This also is vanity.

192

The sham piety of the wicked grabbed the headlines on earth and seemingly in heaven while the true obedience of the righteous was totally ignored and hence unrewarded.

Next (v. 11) we hear what is both a comment on verse 10 and a description of another instance of divine inconsistency. Note that nothing is said here about human responsibility to execute sentences. From this silence, and indeed the whole context, especially the emphasis on the fear of God (vv. 12–13), it seems safe to say that the One who does not work *"speedily"* enough is God. Lack of a timely *"sentence"* (Heb. *pithgām,* used only here and in Esther 1:20) triggered dangerous by-products: (1) confusion about the dependability of divine justice, and (2) lack of decisiveness in human law enforcement. When God seems to let people get away with wrongdoing, government sanctions and strictures may also go slack. Divine and human law, in biblical thought, are much more closely connected than most of our current theorists of law believe. Indeed, as my lawyer friends tell me, the study of jurisprudence—the foundation, rationale, and intention of law in human society—is gathering cobwebs in the classrooms of our law schools. Part of the universally acknowledged justification for punishment is deterrence. The greater was the time-gap between crime, sentence, and punishment, the more occasion was given for the *"heart"* of people (*"sons of men,"* see at 1:3) to *"be fully set"* to do more *"evil"* (Heb. *raʿ*; see on 2:21).

Attention now turns (v. 12) to the lot of those whose lives are steeped in the fear of God. The repetition in *"those who fear God, who fear before Him"* (see on 3:14) shows how imbued their lives are with reverence for God's person and obedience to God's will. "Good" (*"well"* is Heb. *ṭôb*; see 2:24) speaks of God's protection and blessing. The intent of the verse is to quell the confusion about God's seeming inconsistencies. It does so by deliberate exaggeration or hyperbole: *"a hundred times"* shows how endemic and regular is the evil conduct of the *"sinner"* (see 2:26; 7:26; 9:2, 18); he is of the worst sort conceivable. *"His days are prolonged"* should be revised to read "God is postponing his sentence": (1) *"days"* does not appear in Hebrew until the next verse; (2) the participle is active not passive, literally "making long"; (3) the participle calls for a subject and *"God,"* whose name appears in verses 12–13, is the logical choice of subject as the One who stands behind the whole process of reward and punishment; (4) *"sentence"* should be supplied from verse 11 as the needed object. In sum then the verse attests the fact that divine slowness in punishing the wicked should not dampen the hopes of the faithful for their own just and joyful reward.

Indeed, verse 13 dashes any tendency toward envy among the God-fearers. As "good" ("well") was the key promise above (v. 12), so "not . . . good" ("well") is the chief threat here (v. 13). No matter how long their sentence may be postponed, the "days" of the wicked will fade "as a shadow" in the dark night of their judgment. (For "shadow" see on 6:12; 7:12; I have not found it necessary to accept the recent suggestion of M. O. Wise (Journal of Bibilical Literature 109:249–57), that "shadow" in its three occurrences is a misreading of a phrase borrowed from Aramaic, to be translated "because.")

The reflection of verse 14 drags us back to the nagging fact that justice at times seems topsy-turvy. "There is" (Heb. yēsh) seems to make this the exceptional situation, not the normal one described in verses 12–13. It is as though the Preacher gestured to an odd series of events on the margin of the scene that could readily be overlooked, had he not pointed us to something that "there is" over there. "According to the work" in both occurrences means "according to the way we should expect their work to be rewarded." It is as though the dunce cap and the "best of class" medal were wrapped alike for the school assembly and given to wrong recipients. The verse has vanity fore and aft, like book ends. "Puzzling this is, to the point of frustration," was the Preacher's summary of the matter. Inconsistency there may be in human justice. That is bad enough. Even one town like Hitchcock's speed-trap (see above) is too many. But when the unchanging, all-sovereign God of justice seems to work erratically, even once in a while, life defies explanation.

ENJOYMENT: LIVING IN THE MIDST OF MYSTERY

Koheleth ventures no solution as to the mysteries of divine justice. As has been his tack in each of the previous Demonstrations (2:24–25; 3:12–13, 22; 5:18–20), he now ventures a strategy for coping with, not a formula for cracking open, the mysteries of God.

> 15 So I commended enjoyment, because a man
> has nothing better under the sun than to eat, drink,

> and be merry; for this will remain with him in his
> labor all the days of his life which God gives him
> under the sun.
>
> *Eccles. 8:15*

The simple graces from God's hand are the daily staff of life. We should lean on them particularly hard just at those points where bafflement bodes spiritual defeat. *"Commended"* is literally "praised" (Heb. *shābaḥ*), the same word with which the Preacher saluted death in 4:2. When the mystery of justice or any other mystery looms overwhelmingly before us, what better distraction, what sounder reorientation can we gain than to fix our hearts on the certainty of what we understand: food, drink, and rejoicing. *"Labor"* (see on 1:3) there will be—both the *"labor"* to gain sustenance and the *"labor"* to gain understanding. But we have a "stand-by" (to adapt one translation of *"remain"*, JB) to see us through *"the days of (our) lives"* that *"God gives."* That stand-by is *joy.* (For a larger discussion on the forms, uses, and meanings of these *alternative conclusions,* see on 2:24–25).

INACCESSIBILITY: THE MYSTERIES OF DIVINE ACTIVITY

As crucial as the *conclusion* (v. 15) is to Koheleth's strategy, he lingers with it only for a moment. He turns next to what throughout the book has been the heart of his search. He tells how he sought to clutch once more at that will-o'-the-wisp that has flitted just beyond his fingertips each time he has come close—the wisdom beyond the wisdom, the wisdom that will take him further into the mysteries of divine activity than any sage has yet had access.

> 16 When I applied my heart to know wisdom and
> to see the business that is done on earth, even though
> one sees no sleep day or night,
> 17 then I saw all the work of God, that a man
> cannot find out the work that is done under the sun.
> For though a man labors to discover it, yet he will not
> find it; moreover, though a wise man attempts to
> know it, he will not be able to find it.
>
> *Eccles. 8:16–17*

As for wisdom, Koheleth here has reached his limits in the search for it. His concluding line *"he will not be able to find it"* recalls the despair of 7:23–25, but with even greater intensity and finality. In 11:5 he will remind his students of the limits of their wisdom, but after 8:16–17 he says nothing more of his own quest.

We may chart briefly the stages in that quest. It began at 1:13. *"I set my heart"* in that verse and *"I applied my heart"* (8:16) translate the same Hebrew clause: his dedication and concentration are the point. *"Seek and search"* (1:13) are matched by and *"know"* and *"see"* (8:16): profound knowledge is the aim. *"All that is done under heaven"* (1:13) corresponds to *"the business* (Heb. ʿinyān, see "task" in 1:13) *that is done on earth"* (8:16): the curriculum is vast in scope, so vast that it is called *"grievous"* (lit. "evil" in 1:13) and sleep-defying (8:16). The first stage ends with the double conclusion that human wisdom is incapable of making fundamental changes in the way life works (1:14–15) and that whatever wisdom may be acquired sharpens rather than eases the anguish of the wise (1:18).

The second stage celebrated the superiority of wisdom over folly, but only for a fleeting instant (2:13–14a). Death *("the same event")* rained on the celebration and caused its cancellation (2:15–16).

The third stage follows the meditation on *"time"* (3:1–8). It reflects on the fitness of God's way of doing things (3:11). But more than that, it depicts the frustration caused by the basic human conflict: the gulf between our God-given realization that life has dimensions to it that we ought to grasp *("eternity,"* 3:11) and our human inability to probe the depths of God's work.

The fourth stage finds Koheleth's frustration sharpened by the remoteness and depth of a wisdom beyond our reach (7:23–25). *"Who can find it out?"* is his anguished exclamation. Then he settles for an important conclusion that many of the less wise had missed: the whole human family has rejected God's plan of uprightness and tried to scheme its way through life instead (7:29).

The final stage is dominated by the repetition of the failure of the quest: *"a man* (person) *cannot find"*; *"he will not find it"*; however resolved a wise person may be in the intention *("attempts")* to lay hold of the divine mystery, *"he will not be able to find it"* (8:17). The finality of this conclusion informs us that the problem defies solution. More time, greater intelligence, better methods, a new team of researchers—none of these is the answer. The problem lies in the difference between divine and human, between God and even the best of God's creatures.

The eager beginning of the quest at 1:13 and its unsa[t]sion at 8:17 form a bracket within the book that fe billboards its essential message: we are called to live as well as we can within the limits imposed on us by the fundamental differences between us and God. To seek to exceed those limits is both arrogant and dangerous. Where the boundaries lie, how they are marked, and why we want to live within their constraints are what the Words of Advice deal with. No wonder Koheleth reserves the longest set of them (9:13–12:7) for the close of his book.

CERTAINTY: THE UNIVERSALITY OF DEATH

Before he brings his thoughts to an end, however, he returns to the topic that has given him so much pain along the way: death (2:14–23; 3:18–21). What baffle most are two things: (1) the lack of correlation between the *timing* of death and the nature of human conduct—the wicked may live long and the righteous die young; (2) the inescapable fact of death—neither man nor beast, wise nor fool can stave it off.

How and when death works may be a mystery (9:1). That death works and works in everyone is a certainty (9:2):

> 9:1 For I considered all this in my heart, so that I
> could declare it all: that the righteous and the wise
> and their works are in the hand of God. People know
> neither love nor hatred by anything they see before
> them.
> 2 All things come alike to all:
> One event happens to the righteous and the
> wicked;
> To the good, the clean, and the unclean;
> To him who sacrifices and him who does not
> sacrifice.
> As is the good, so is the sinner;
> He who takes an oath as he who fears an oath.
> 3 This is an evil in all that is done under the sun:
> that one thing happens to all. Truly the hearts of the

> sons of men are full of evil; madness is in their hearts
> while they live, and after that they go to the dead.
>   4 But for him who is joined to all the living there
> is hope, for a living dog is better than a dead lion.
>   5 For the living know that they will die;
>   But the dead know nothing,
>   And they have no more reward,
>   For the memory of them is forgotten.
>   6 Also their love, their hatred, and their envy
>   have now perished;
>   Nevermore will they have a share
>   In anything done under the sun.
>
> *Eccles. 9:1–6*

The key line is *"All things come alike to all"* (v. 2). The *"all things"* is the *"one event"* (see on 2:14–15; 3:19), which is death. Two consequences are drawn from this announcement of death's certainty: (1) the time or kind of death tells us nothing about a person's standing with God (9:1–2); (2) almost any kind of life is preferable to death (9:4–6).

Coming to these conclusions took considerable pondering (*"in my heart"*) and "sorting out" (v. 1) which may be a better translation than *"declare"* (on Heb. *bārar*, see at 3:18). *"For"* (Heb. *kî*) may mean "surely" and underscore the intensity of the deliberation. The outcome of the deliberation is the opinion that not even the *"righteous"* and *"wise"* control their own destinies.

Deciding the results of their efforts (*"works"* includes both the labor and its outcome) rests in God's power (*"hand"*). There is no universal principle of cause and effort that can be discerned and applied as a general rule. Here, as often, Koheleth's outlook flew in the teeth of the conventional wisdom that made a consistent connection between conduct and reward. *"Love"* and *"hatred"* describe God's disposition, not human attitudes: we cannot look at what happens to us in the ups and downs of life and tell from them how God feels toward us. If we are to know that, we have to have clearer information than what comes from our personal circumstances, or even the kind of death we die. Some versions (RSV, JB, NEB) read *"anything"* as "vanity" or its equivalent (*hakkōl* and *hebel* look quite alike in their consonantal form in Heb.), though NKJV has probably made the better choice.

The principle of God's mysterious sovereignty in the matter of death is amplified and illustrated in the poem of verse 2. The pairs of words are deliberately chosen to cover the range of moral, social, and religious life. The word *evil* (or "bad," Heb. *ra^c*) is usually added to the third line as the called-for opposite of *"good"* (NIV, RSV, JB, NEB). The attention to religious duty is noteworthy: *"clean"* and *"unclean"* refer to ritual purity in keeping with the laws of the priests; *"sacrifices"* speaks of religious obligation as does the *"oath,"* which here, where the positive word regularly precedes the negative one, must be a commendable act like making a vow before God, not a violation of the Third Commandment. This list of duties recalls the advice on temple conduct featured in 5:1–7 and again shows Koheleth's regard for Jewish religious practices. But no keeping or violating of this checklist seems to have any impact on the death of its adherents or opponents.

The total unpleasantness *("evil")* of all this is summarized in verse 3. It is inescapable *("under the sun,"* see 1:3) and unrelenting. For as long as we live, its dark reality haunts human *"hearts"* to the point of distraction and incoherence *("madness,"* see on 1:17). Its terror is unrelieved until we join the company of the *"dead."* And that is no party, as the grim and barren picture of Sheol *("the grave")* in 9:10 reminds us. The double use of *"evil"* in verse 3 is not intended to brand either God or human beings as wicked. This verse is neither an act of blasphemy nor a tract on original sin. It is a bleak and painful reminder of the toll that fear of death takes on human happiness.

However meager, feeble, or painful is our lot in life, it is still better than death (vv. 4–6). The *"living dog"/"dead lion"* comparison makes that clear. As in many *"better"* proverbs, the contrast gives the saying its bite: dogs were at the low end of the social scale among animals (witness David's Philistine enemy, 1 Sam. 17:43; Abner's angry outburst, 2 Sam. 3:8; Hazael's sharp question, 2 Kings 8:13); lions were at the high end (note Judah's status, Gen. 49:9; and Dan's, Deut. 33:22; David's ability to chill even the lion-hearted, 2 Sam. 17:10). Yet the difference between *"living"* and *"dead"* tipped the scale completely in the other direction.

The difference is spelled out in a short list of arguments: (1) the one still alive *("joined to all the living"* requires a switch of consonants in Heb: *y^{e}buhar*, chosen, needs to be read as *yehubbar*, "joined" or "linked") has *"hope"* (v. 42; lit. "confidence," see Isa. 36:4) not hopelessness; (2) the living are yet capable of the gift of knowledge, even if only of the knowledge that they will die (v. 5); however depressing knowledge of death may be, it still outranks the total absence of knowledge which is Koheleth's picture of the realm of the dead; (3) the living may be encouraged and rewarded by the reputation *("memory")* they have gained in life (v. 5); as for the dead, all that is *"forgotten"* (Heb. *shākah,* see 2:16) as though it had never existed; (4) the living yet cling to the feelings and affections that are so central to human existence—*"love," hatred,"* and *"envy"* or "jealousy" is the summary list here—while the dead are consigned to a fate without pain, pathos, or passion, indeed without relationships of any kind; (5) the summary is as harsh as it is sweeping—no *"share"* (Heb. *ḥeleq,* "lot," "portion," see 2:10, 21; 3:22; 9:9), no sense of owning or being owned is left to the dead, while the living, if only by the fingernails, can still cling to what God has given them.

If we read these verses at face value and not as *irony,* then we need to comment on other things that Koheleth has said. His gist here is that life is better than death; yet elsewhere he has said the opposite:

> Therefore I praised the dead who were already dead,
> More than the living who are still alive.
>
> *Eccles. 4:2*

Add to this the verdict that *"a stillborn child is better than"* a man whose fortunes have turned against him (6:1–6) and the proverbs that prefer the *"day of death"* to the *"day of one's birth"* (7:1) and *"the house of mourning"* to *"the house of feasting"* (7:2).

What shall we say about the seeming contradiction between 9:1–6 and the other passages? First, for Koheleth there is no great sin in saying contradictory things, especially when each side of the contradiction is appropriate to the point being made. We have heard him both laud and lambast wisdom. Second, exaggeration was a regular component of Hebrew, as of modern American, speech. At times the Preacher deliberately overstated his point to keep it so sharp that it would penetrate the dull ears and hard hearts of his countrymen. And of course, the proverbial form flourishes on overgeneralizations. Third, if we have to take a choice we should read the words on the preference for life as the more literal ones and the passages that exalt death as hyperbolic expressions to underscore the grimness of life.

Fourth, the context of 9:1–6, where the longest, brightest form of the *alternative conclusion* follows (9:7–10), reinforces the view that 9:1–6 is to be read positively not ironically.

ENJOYMENT: LIVING IN THE MIDST OF MYSTERY

7 Go, eat your bread with joy,
   And drink your wine with a merry heart;
   For God has already accepted your works.
8 Let your garments always be white,
   And let your head lack no oil.
9 Live joyfully with the wife whom you love all the days of your vain life which He has given you under the sun, all your days of vanity; for that is your portion in life, and in the labor which you perform under the sun.
10 Whatever your hand finds to do, do it with your might; for there is no work or device or knowledge or wisdom in the grave where you are going.

Eccles. 9:7–10

The mood shifts dramatically in verses 7–10, the first cluster of commands we have heard since 8:2–3. The multiple use of imperatives is one contrast:

> *"Go," "eat," "drink"   v. 7*
> *"Let your garments . . . be white,"*
> *"let your head lack no oil"   v. 8*
> *"Live joyfully with the wife"   v. 9*
> *"Do it with your might"   v. 10.*

Another contrast is the difference between the utter isolation from life described in 9:5–6 and the total engagement in life pictured in 9:7–10. Yet the contrasts do not obscure the connection between the thrust of Demonstration Four and the *alternative conclusion*: life is called brief, puzzlingly brief (*"vain," "vanity,"* v. 9; Heb. *hebel,* see 1:2); its limitations are not wished away—*"under the sun"* (v. 9; see 1:3); it is still laden with *labor* (Heb. *ʿāmāl,* v. 9; see 1:3); the *"grave"* still yawns to gulp us down its maw (v. 10, Heb. *sheʾol*). Joy experienced in circumstances like those is not escapist, not self-deceiving, not hedonistic euphoria. It is seeing life whole, real, valuable, and graceful.

The text is alive with grace notes: (1) our efforts to serve and please God in our labors ("*your works,*" v. 7) have been "*accepted*" by God as pleasing (Heb. *rāṣāh*) sacrifices, as Esau was pleased with Jacob at their reconciliation (Gen. 33:10), as the Lord would be pleased with repentant Israel and their offerings and firstfruits (Ezek. 20:40); (2) that acceptance has turned life into a wedding feast, better than either the "*house of mourning*" or "*the house of feasting*" (7:2)," a wedding feast where "*garments*" gleam, free from the dust and ashes of sorrow, and the "*head*" glistens, anointed with oil as from the hand of the great Shepherd-Host (v. 8; see Ps. 23:5); (3) even the "*days*" which sometimes seem brief and empty are tinged with the touch of the gracious Giver, who knows what "*portion*" (Heb. *ḥēleq,* v. 9 is the word translated "*share*" in the bleak picture of Sheol, v. 6) you need in order to avoid despair and can handle without arrogance.

This is the final occurrence of the *alternative conclusion* (see on 2:24–25). We shall not meet it again in the text. Appropriately it is the longest and most comprehensive form. It captures what has been included in the five earlier versions and adds some peculiar yet central insights of its own:

> The celebrative garb and oil   v. 6
> The joyful relationship with the wife   v. 9
> The admonition to enthusiastic work   v. 10

In the very face of death, expansive joy is not only possible but demanded. Only God's grace can make it so. A time there is for everything (3:1), and now, whatever and wherever our "now" is, is a time for enjoyment.

Koheleth's closing reason for these commands is the *motivation* introduced by "*for*" in the last lines of verse 10. They reach back to all the things of which death deprives us in verses 4–6 and add some of their own: "*no work*" cancels the joy of what God has already accepted (v. 7); no "*device*" (Heb. *heshbôn*) harks back to Koheleth's attempts to sum up the wisdom beyond wisdom which makes sense of all of life—the "*reason*" (see 7:25, 27); no "*knowledge*" and no "*wisdom*" mean that the major quest of Koheleth's life and of ours, as he saw it, remains forever unfinished.

UNPREDICTABILITY: THE MYSTERIES OF DIVINE PROVIDENCE

Koheleth does not close Demonstration Four without another venture into an area of divine mystery. Input does not determine outcomes, says the Preacher. Life is not a predictable computer. God's providence has many ways of intervening. As in matters of justice in 8:10–14, we may assume that in this final reflection he is dealing with exceptions to the expected. The expected needs no explanation. Much of the time the outcome of a *"race,"* "battle," system of reward, or contest for promotion is predictable. Accounting for when it is not is the Preacher's task here.

> 11 I returned and saw under the sun that—
> The race is not to the swift,
> Nor the battle to the strong,
> Nor bread to the wise,
> Nor riches to men of understanding,
> Nor favor to men of skill;
> But time and chance happen to them all.
> 12 For man also does not know his time:
> Like fish taken in a cruel net,
> Like birds caught in a snare,
> So the sons of men are snared in an evil time,
> When it falls suddenly upon them.
> *Eccles. 9:11–12*

Here again Ecclesiastes was challenging the opinions of the other wise men. Basic to their teaching was the conclusion that good conduct brought good results. Fundamental to their authority over their students was their ability to predict what would happen as the result of any course of conduct. Good causes work good effects. Speed does win the race, and strength, the battle. Diligence and intelligence do result in security and wealth. Not so, argued Koheleth. God's patterns are not predictable. Chance often has as much influence on our well-being as human behavior.

"Returned" (v. 11, see 4:1, 7) suggests a connection between this topic and those recently treated in this section. Mystery in God's dealings with the human family and divine control over how things happen are the common thread. The image of the runner *("swift")* according to Crenshaw applies to a courier racing to carry a message more than to an Olympic-like contest. *"Bread"* as frequently in the Bible means "living," "livelihood" (Amos 7:12). *"Favor"* (Heb. *ḥēn*, lit. "grace") refers to the good reputation, the acclaimed status, of people who have *"skill,"* literally "those who know how to do things well."

This set of supreme virtues is not always enough. Timing (*"time,"* see on 3:1) may upset the best of plans and the keenest of abilities. *"Chance"* is the unavoidable and unforeseen circumstance (Heb. *pegaʿ* is found also in 1 Kings 5:4 [v. 20 in the MT] with the adjective "evil" to describe a "bad accident" or "harmful occurrence") that upsets the whole enterprise: a hole in the path that sprains the courier's ankle, a flawed piece of iron that weakens the warrior's sword, an element of teaching that alienates the wise person's pupils, a ship that sinks and wastes the investment of the understanding person, an earthquake that undoes the work of the skilled craftsman. Given enough time with a sufficient variety of challenges, says Koheleth, unpredictable, untoward consequences will come the way of *"them all."*

Far from being foolproof, unflappable, and immune to failure, the most talented among us can be vulnerable to mishap on occasion (v. 12). And we have no way of predicting when this may happen—a human being (*"man,"* Heb. *ʾādām*, see 1:3) *"does not know"* his or her *"time."* (3:1). The apt illustration is drawn from hunting and fishing (see on 7:26, where *"snares,"* *"nets,"* and *"fetters"* describe the wiles of certain women). *"Evil time"* suggests the unforeseen accident, as in 1 Kings 5:4. *"Falls suddenly"* carries on the snaring imagery and shows that *"evil time"* here has no reference to a wicked era but to an unexpected mishap that catches any person (*"sons of men"*) off guard and devastates well-laid plans.

Epilogue: The Greater Wise Man

Divine mystery and human mortality are not artifacts of the past like the Venus de Milo or the temple at Baalbek. These realities are our daily companions. We do not know why death comes early or late, why athletes keel over in their prime and victims of accidents live for decades without opening their eyes.

What we do learn from the life and words of Jesus is that we have a heavenly Father whom we can know. This personal acquaintance comes not from painful search or patient contemplation like Koheleth's but from the revelation of the Son of God:

> "All things have been delivered to Me by My Father, and no one knows the Son except the Father. Nor does anyone know the Father except the Son, and the one to whom the Son wills to reveal him."
>
> *Matt. 11:27*

The gulf of mystery that Koheleth and the rest of us could not bridge has been spanned from the further side by Christ's revelation of the Father and by the gracious invitation to *"learn of me"* those things that not only make for wisdom but encourage rest (Matt. 11:29).

More specifically the puzzles over injustice and death find their key in what Jesus says and does. Length of life is no more a gauge of quality of life. *Eternal life* has come into the picture and has, among other things, provided the context for all loyalty toward God to be rewarded and all rebellion against God to be punished. Koheleth knew no such scenario as Jesus gave us in the parable of talents. The old sage had no real inkling of the ultimate judgment that offered, "well done, good and faithful servant. . . . Enter into the joy of your Lord," and "You wicked and lazy servant," your destiny is "outer darkness" with "weeping and gnashing of teeth" (Matt. 25:21, 26, 30). If we look for all wrongs to be righted in this life the questions of justice will swamp us. The good news of life after death is that fellowship with God continues and total vindication of divine justice becomes possible.

The bleak picture of Sheol from which all good things are barred—knowledge, memory, passion (Eccles. 9:5–6)—is replaced by Jesus' architectural sketch of "my Father's house" with its "many mansions" prepared for us by the Savior whose presence will accompany his people throughout eternity (John 14:2–3). Koheleth rightly dreaded the sting of death and resented every victory achieved by the grave. Given what he knew, he could do no other. The Greater Wise Man is "the way, the truth, and the life"; we can follow him into eternity with untroubled hearts (John 14:1–6).

Finally, Jesus gave the ultimate answer to Koheleth's desperate declaration: "People know neither love nor hatred by anything they see before them," (Eccles. 9:1). In words of love (John 3:16), in deeds of love (John 13:1), and in the final sacrifice of love (John 19:17–30), Jesus made unmistakably clear the disposition of the Father who sent him and his own willing participation in that consummate gift of love. We are not left guessing about the divine mood toward the human family. *"God is love"* (1 John 4:8) is shouted at us from every page of Jesus' story.

As in Hitchcock's irritating picture of injustice, the final word does not go to the cheaters, liars, and oppressors. In the end their mouths will be stopped and their guilt exposed. Koheleth taught his students to cope with life's mysteries and their mortality by finding joy in their daily round of ordinary activities. Jesus teaches his disciples to do the same. But he teaches more. His life, death, and resurrection point to an inheritance incorruptible undefiled, and unfading and to a joy that flows not from what we see but from what we believe—*"a joy inexpressible and full of glory"* (1 Pet. 1:3–9).

CHAPTER ELEVEN

Closing Words of Advice: Guidelines to Practicality

Ecclesiastes 9:13–10:20

You can hear it frequently in offices and factories around the nation. Usually it is expressed with some degree of fervor—or even anger. The context is often an occasion where a junior manager comes to his boss with a question about a difficult situation where the boss's advice is needed.

Wise supervisors resist the temptation to give advice in such circumstances. Instead they reply to the question with a statement like this: "Don't bring me problems; bring me solutions!" The point is well taken—and for several reasons, even though the spirit in which it is voiced is less gentle than it should be. The people nearest the problem usually can develop the best solutions because they know the facts intimately. Furthermore, they, not their bosses, have to carry out the suggestions. They can do this better if they have had a strong part in formulating them. Beyond that, if the supervisor has to do their thinking for them, they are not fulfilling their responsibility to her or him. Finally, it is obvious that pointing out a problem is normally ten times easier than discovering a solution. Identifying what is wrong in life is only a small step toward setting it straight.

Koheleth, the Preacher, was wise enough to know this. The management maxim—solutions, not just problems—was familiar to him.

Though he is best known for the sharp way in which he pointed out the false values to which his countrymen had dedicated themselves, he should also be remembered for the practical solutions that he gave to many human problems.

These practical suggestions comprise the balance of the book. The four sets of Demonstrations (1:4–2:26; 3:1–4:16; 5:13–6:12; 8:10–9:12) have been completed. At 9:13 Koheleth begins his third and final collection of Words of Advice (the prior two were found in 5:1–12; 7:1–8:9). This collection is his longest section of the book. It divides into three parts:

Guidelines to practical living	9:13–10:20
Principles of financial investment	11:1–8
Ground rules for the young	11:9–12:8

The initial section on practical living is the subject of this chapter. Its overall theme is the virtue and fragility of wisdom. In its contrasts of wise and foolish conduct in government and society it resembles the Book of Proverbs more than does any other section of Ecclesiastes. Commentators and translators do not see eye to eye on the number and length of the subdivisions within the section— 9:13–10:20. My outline coincides substantially with that of Fox and runs like this:

Reflection on wisdom's virtue and fragility	9:13–18
Introduction to the story	9:13
Story of wisdom's effectiveness and the oblivion to which it was consigned	9:14–15
Koheleth's reaction to the story	9:16
Proverbs praising wisdom yet warning of its limits	9:17–18
Sayings on the dangers of folly	10:1–3
Metaphor on the theme of 9:18	10:1
Literal descriptions of foolish behavior	10:2–3
Sayings on kings and citizens	10:4–7
Admonition to calmness in court	10:4
Observations on royal folly	10:5–7
Sayings on the consequences of carelessness	10:8–11
Sayings on the consequences of unguarded speech	10:12–15
Sayings on the foibles of the ruling class	10:16–20
A woe to a land with an unfit ruler	10:16
A beatitude to a land with disciplined leaders	10:17
Saying on the dangers of laziness	10:18
Saying on the risks of excessive festivity	10:19
Admonition on the danger of demeaning the nobility	10:20

WISDOM—EMPLOYED AND FORGOTTEN

The reflective style—"*I have also seen under the sun*" (v. 13), "*Then I said*" (v. 16)—marks a transition from Demonstration Four to these Words of Advice. It will slip in again at 10:5, 7—"*I have seen under the sun,*" "*I have seen*"—and then fade for the rest of the book as the sayings and admonitions of proverbial language dominate the closing pages.

13 This wisdom I have also seen under the sun,
and it seemed great to me:
14 There was a little city with few men in it; and a
great king came against it, besieged it, and built great
snares around it.
15 Now there was found in it a poor wise man,
and he by his wisdom delivered the city. Yet no one
remembered that same poor man.
16 Then I said:
"Wisdom is better than strength.
Nevertheless the poor man's wisdom is
despised,
And his words are not heard.
17 Words of the wise, spoken quietly, should be
heard
Rather than the shout of a ruler of fools.
18 Wisdom is better than weapons of war;
But one sinner destroys much good."
Eccles. 9:13–18

"*Wisdom*" here (v. 13) means something like "a true discovery of how wisdom works and is treated." "*Great*" signals how important ("notable," NEB) he deems the discovery to be, while "*under the sun*" shows that the story he is about to tell can happen anywhere. It describes a pattern, not an isolated incident.

As for the story (vv. 14–15), its closest parallel in form and content is the account of the fickleness of the citizenry narrated in 4:13–16. Here not fickleness but forgetfulness is the point—forgetfulness just when "*wisdom*" had worked a surprising victory. The details are designed to highlight wisdom's prowess: (1) The odds against the "*little city,*" (we would call it a "town") were long—its population was meager *("few men")* and its enemy formidable *("great king")*; (2) the siege left the town in dire straits—*"besieged"* is literally "surrounded," and *"great snares"* likely refer to earthen siegeworks or ramparts built around the town to enable the enemy warriors to throw spears, shoot arrows, and ultimately storm the town despite its defenses:

> "They deride every stronghold,
> For they heap up earthen mounds and seize it"

is Habakkuk's description (1:10) of such assault techniques; (3) the solution to the plight came from the least likely source—not the military or political leaders but a *"poor* (Heb. *miskēn,* see 4:13 in the parallel story mentioned above) *wise man,"* who held no office and whose voice would not readily have been heard, given the fact that conventional opinion would not have correlated poverty with wisdom but probably with folly; (4) the rescue (*"delivered,"* Heb. *mālaṭ* in an intensive form) was as thorough as it was dramatic; note Koheleth's other uses of the verb, "escape" in 7:26, "deliver" in 8:8.

Given the drama of the story, the climax is a frightful letdown. We would expect the *"poor"* man to receive all the accolades the town could muster and to be promoted to a place of authority and honor. Instead, *"no one remembered"* him (v. 15). Koheleth has made his point: *"Wisdom"* is invaluable; it can accomplish incredible feats; yet it can also be tossed on the scrap heap of oblivion, even by those who have benefited richly from it. Nothing is said about how the victory was accomplished only about who did it and wisdom's stellar role. All unnecessary details are omitted to spotlight how indispensable is wisdom and how readily it can be shelved when the battle is over.

The three summary sayings (vv. 16–18) underscore these messages. The first (v. 16) reflects on the irony that wisdom outranks strength—Koheleth has already informed us, *"Nor is the battle to the strong"* (9:11)—and yet if the person who possesses wisdom is not duly respected, the words fall on deaf ears. The second (v. 17) makes the positive point that the *"words of the wise"* (even if their speaker is a *"poor"* man) ought to carry their own authority—neither the volume of the voice (*"quietly"* vs. *"shout"*) nor the office of the speaker (*"wise"* vs. *"ruler of fools"*) should be the test of accuracy. The third saying (v. 18) affirms that, as the story has proved, *"wisdom"* outfights

210

weaponry (see Prov. 21:22, 31), yet a real fool (as *"sinner"* seems to mean here; see 2:26; 7:20, 26: 8:12; 9:2) can undo the positive results (*"good,"* Heb. *ṭôb*) accomplished by wisdom. Suppose a traitor had betrayed the town which the poor man's wisdom was trying to rescue, or a watchman asleep at the switch had failed to sound a warning of enemy attack. No plan can work well unless those who execute it are faithful to their assignments. Remember the battle that was lost for want of a horseshoe nail! Catch the contrast in verse 18 between *"one"* and *"much."*

FOLLY—CORRUPT AND CORRUPTING

In an early speech, the Preacher warned us not to bank on wisdom as life's highest good:

> For in much wisdom is much grief,
> And he who increases knowledge increases sorrow.
> *Eccles. 1:18*

He was speaking to extremists, to those who touted wisdom as the key to life's problems, as the pearl of great price for which everything else should be sold. He warned those who praised wisdom to the heavens that it would produce at least as much bane as blessing.

He made his misgivings clear about those who overvalue wisdom. Yet nowhere did he celebrate foolishness. With all its problems, wisdom was to be heartily preferred to folly. Do not let wisdom be your god, but let it be your guide, was his advice.

Foolishness has its dangers, and in three sayings the Teacher warned his pupils against them:

> 10:1 Dead flies putrefy the perfumer's ointment,
> And cause it to give off a foul odor;
> So does a little folly to one respected for wisdom
> and honor.
> 2 A wise man's heart is at his right hand,
> But a fool's heart at his left.
> 3 Even when a fool walks along the way,
> He lacks wisdom,
> And he shows everyone that he is a fo
> *Eccles. .*

Folly has dangers and wisdom has limits—those twin points are made in the first proverb. Folly is so powerful that a little of it—like a bad smell—can overwhelm large amounts of wisdom. This saying seems to use the "fly in the ointment" metaphor to reinforce the idea of 9:18. The *"flies"* do the same thing to expensive perfume as the *"sinner"* does to the things *"wisdom"* is trying to achieve. This is a reminder that the effectiveness of the wise is not measured in batting averages where three hits in ten tries is superb baseball, but in fielding averages where one error in thirty chances is too many. The story is told of a German scholar whose years of impeccable scholarship were disgraced by his use of the wrong Hebrew word for "kill" in an offhand note on the Decalogue's command against murder. Harsh treatment that was for a learned person, but it serves as a warning against taking lightly either wisdom or the role in teaching it.

Folly is also dangerous because it heads us in the wrong direction; so says verse 2. With apologies to left-handed people, we must note that *"left,"* here, is synonymous with evil. Recall how the Latin word for "left hand," *sinister,* has brought its negative connotation into English. *"Right hand"* here means doing correct things and especially making good choices, as *"heart"* implies. The antithetical parallelism highlights the contrast normally present between the sound judgment of the *"wise man"* and the poor judgment of the *"fool."*

This poor judgment is not a well-kept secret. The very *"way"* a *"fool walks"* announces that he *"lacks"* (for the negative force of this, see 4:8, *"deprive,"* and 9:8, *"lack"*) *"wisdom"* (lit. "heart," or "good sense"). *"Walk"* and *"way"* probably signify "conduct," or "direction of life" here as they do so often in Proverbs and in Psalm 1:6. The fool's actions speak for themselves. *"Shows"* is literally "says." By poor decisions he announces his status as *"fool."*

POWER—USED AND ABUSED

Wisdom is a guide in *governmental affairs.* That was a point that Koheleth returned to frequently. Like all wise men he recognized that human life is basically political. Whether we thrive or chafe will in large measure depend on how we are governed. All of us—from tribal aborigines to urban intellectuals—live under governments.

Knowing how to deal with those who order and regulate our lives is an essential part of our education.

> 4 If the spirit of the ruler rises against you,
>   Do not leave your post;
>   For conciliation pacifies great offenses.
> 5 There is an evil I have seen under the sun,
>   As an error proceeding from the ruler:
> 6 Folly is set in great dignity,
>   While the rich sit in a lowly place.
> 7 I have seen servants on horses,
>   While princes walk on the ground like servants.
>
> *Eccles. 10:4–7*

The Preacher's advice was practical—almost shrewd: "stay on good terms with the powerful." Use your power of self-control to offset the abuse of power displayed in the temper tantrum of your superior (v. 4). The admonition is too sparse for us to reconstruct the exact situation. The dangers of a *"spirit"* out of control in a person were warned about in 7:8–9. The latter verse implies that the *"ruler"* here (10:4) was behaving like a fool. But that does not, argues Koheleth, give an administrator or courtier the license to behave in kind. *"Do not leave* (Heb. *tannaḥ*; see 7:18, *"remove")* *your post"* (lit. "your place") may mean merely, "Don't walk out in the middle of a tirade." More likely, in the light of 8:3, it means, "Don't desert the ruler and join ranks with the rebels who are out to unseat him." *"Conciliation"* is literally "healings," a word that the Bible applies to strained relationships (Judg. 8:3; Prov. 12:18) as well as physical ailments. *"Pacifies"* is really "puts at rest" (Heb. *nûªḥ*; see *"permit to sleep"* at 5:12), while *"great offenses"* or *"sins"* describes the outrageous conduct of an ill-tempered leader. The lesson is that the self-controlled person who has less rank is really more powerful than the out-of-control supposed superior.

"Be aware of life's injustices" was another part of the Preacher's practical advice. His sharp eye had seen rulers make tragic mistakes. They had often put the wrong people in power (vv. 5–7). The warning is a good one. Inequities do arise in life, especially in government. But the Preacher did not tell us what to do about them. Are we to correct such abuses (*"error,"* v. 5; see 5:6 for the other use in

Ecclesiastes of the Heb. *sh^egāgāh* which means "a flat-out mistake" for which there can be no valid excuse) or merely to be warned against them? In his kind of society, there may not have been much choice. Still, Koheleth cannot be encouraging his students to be complacent about something so harmful (*"evil,"* v. 5; see 2:21) to and pervasive (*"under the sun,"* see 1:3) in society. At least he is saying, "Be watchful when others do it"; at most, "Whenever it is in your power to prevent such arbitrary mismanagement, make sure you do so." *"Dignity"* is literally "high and elevated places." *"Folly"* and those who practice it ought to be kept away from seats of power both for the bad example that sets and for the havoc they have almost unlimited capacity to wreak on their communities. If the *"rich"* make better officials, as Koheleth suggests, it is because they usually have more experience of managing large enterprises and their potential for success has already been tested. And to the practitioners of conventional wisdom, wealth would have been viewed as a sign of divine blessing. The Preacher knew that such was not always the case, but he also knew that very few fools stayed wealthy for long, so great was their aptitude for squandering what they had.

The harmful outworkings of foolish political decisions are pictured in the closing observation of this section (v. 7). *"Servants"* are out of place on *"horses"* because they rarely have the experience and talent to lead armies to battle. *"Horse"* in biblical parlance is almost always a military animal (Prov. 21:31; Hos. 14:3; Rev. 19:11). For *"servants"* to lead the cavalry while the *"princes"* (Heb. *śārîm* often describes military commanders; Hos. 7:16; 13:10) slogged along with the foot soldiers is a ridiculous waste of talent. Again the issue is not class per se but competence, which in some situations, unfortunately, comes only with class.

WORK—CARELESS AND CAUTIOUS

Koheleth links together four pictorial sayings centered in the realm of work (10:8–11). It is tempting to find in them the well-known pattern of retribution that the sages stressed with their students. In that case, "love your neighbor as yourself" would be the theme. And "do no harm to others lest you hurt yourself" would be the unifying lesson. But that does not seem to be the case.

The sayings should be read more literally and seen as warnings of the hazards of the workaday world. Accidents do happen and with enough regularity to cause governments, corporations, and labor unions to plaster the walls of the workplace with suggestions for safety and notices of penalties where the suggestions are not heeded. Work is wisdom's world as well as home, palace, marketplace, and city gate.

> 8 He who digs a pit will fall into it,
>   And whoever breaks through a wall will be
>   bitten by a serpent.
> 9 He who quarries stones may be hurt by them,
>   And he who splits wood may be endangered by
>   it.
> 10 If the axe is dull,
>   And one does not sharpen the edge,
>   Then he must use more strength;
>   But wisdom brings success.
> 11 A serpent may bite when it is not charmed;
>   The babbler is no different.
>
> *Eccles. 10:8–11*

The key to the passage may be, *"But wisdom brings success"* (lit. "profit," "advantage," Heb. *yitrôn,* see 1:3). Wisdom, with its cautious common sense, coaches its adherents to be careful and thereby cut down the possibility of accidents in otherwise hazardous work.

The verbs of verse 8 should be read as possibilities not predictions: *"may fall"* not *"will fall"; "may be bitten"* not *"will be bitten."* The NKJV has already made that adjustment in verses 9 and 11. The *"wall"* (v. 8) is probably mud brick if a house is in mind, or dry, mortarless stone if it surrounds a garden or field. The threat of accidental snake bite is clearly documented in Amos' picture of the Day of the Lord (5:19). Quarrying *"stones"* or splitting *"wood"* were important if relatively scarce occupations (v. 9). *"Stones"* would have been reserved for public buildings or the homes of the wealthy; commoners used mud-brick, not unlike California adobe from the period of the Spanish missions; *"wood"* was also valuable since Palestine would have lost most of its stands of timber well before Koheleth's day, and logs from Lebanon would have been very expensive as the prophets noted in their denunciations of the luxury of wood-paneled palaces or homes (Jer. 22:13–15; Hag. 1:4).

The final sayings in the chain (vv. 10–11) make even more clear the virtues of wisdom: "An ounce of prevention is worth a pound of cure" would probably be our English equivalent, or "a stitch in time saves nine." Wisdom helps us save energy—like the wisdom to sharpen the axe ahead of time. The axe blade would have been iron in Koheleth's time and the sharpening would have involved rubbing on other iron, as the saying in Proverbs 27:17 reveals. Wisdom prevents accidents—like the foresight to charm the snake *before* it bites. Simple, practical wisdom to keep our folly from showing itself and hurting us—that was the wise Teacher's aim in this chapter. Biblical pictures of snake charming are available in Psalm 58:4–5 and Jeremiah 8:17. They, with Amos 5:19, seem to assume that the reptiles were poisonous though most of the serpents in ancient and modern Palestine were not. Psalm 58:4–5 puts emphasis on the charmer's *voice*. This thought is implicit in the literal description of Koheleth's *"charmer"* as *"master of the tongue."* The NKJV mistranslates this as *"babbler"* and seeks to make a comparison with the snake bite. Other translations capture the force of the line: "there is no profit for the charmer" (NIV); "the snake charmer loses his fee" (NEB). Lack of caution proves costly is the point.

WORDS—GRACEFUL AND CALLING

Three proverbs (vv. 12–13, 14, 15) center in the gift of speech and its impact on its hearers. Koheleth, like the wise teachers of Proverbs, knew that his students were headed for positions of responsibility, whether in government service or business. As persons of prominence they had to watch their language. Success or failure would be determined, in some measure at least, by the winsomeness, accuracy, and frugality of their speech. Like the snake charmer (v. 11), they had to be "masters of the tongue." The exposition of Proverbs in this Communicator's Commentary series discusses the importance of speech in chapters 2, 15, 18, and 26 as well as in many places elsewhere in the book. Koheleth makes his point here with the clarity and brevity which he admires and commends.

12 The words of a wise man's mouth are gracious,
But the lips of a fool shall swallow him up;
13 The words of his mouth begin with foolishness,
And the end of his talk is raving madness.
14 A fool also multiplies words.
No man knows what is to be;
Who can tell him what will be after him?
15 The labor of fools wearies them,
For they do not even know how to go to the city!
Eccles. 10:12–15

The description (v. 12) of the wise person's *"words"* is both terse and telling: *"gracious."* The Hebrew term *(ḥēn)* is even shorter, but it embraces both the affect such speech has on the hearer—"pleasant," "winsome"—and the admiration it engenders for the speaker—"favor" (see *"favor"* to men of skill in 9:11). None of this needs further comment nor illustration from the Preacher.

He does, however, feel the need to expand the other side of the topic—the dreadfully negative outcome of fool's talk. First, it is self-destructive (v. 12). Fools' *"lips,"* meaning what comes out of them, are suicide-weapons: *"swallow"* is to "gulp down," "devour," "destroy" (see 2 Sam. 20:19–20 for a military use of Heb. *bālaᶜ* and Prov. 19:28 for the insatiable appetite it describes). We think it bad enough to have to "eat our words." How much worse it is when our words eat us! There could scarcely be a more dramatic description of the dangers of ill-chosen speech. The follow-on lines in verse 13 describe the process of this self-destruction: It begins with *"foolishness."* How else would a fool begin? Then from there everything is down hill till it hits bottom (*"the end,"* lit. "afterward"). The bottom point is grim: *"raving madness"* is an accurate paraphrase of the literal "evil madness" which describes both the seriousness and the harmfulness of the results. For *"madness,"* see on 2:12. The more fools speak the worse their talk and state of mind become.

The second saying (v. 14) brands the whole activity futile. The volume and length of a fool's harangue adds nothing to its quality. The reason is clear: the fool is tempted to speculate on the future, to voice opinions about unforeseen events that neither he nor anyone else can discern—whether in the fool's lifetime (*"what is to be"*) or after his death (*"what will be after him"*).

The final saying (v. 15) sums up both the fate and competence of *fools*. First, their endless efforts at talking—so *"labor"* (Heb. *ʿāmāl*; 1:3) must mean here—accomplish nothing more than the exhaustion of their energies—a bane to them and a boon to their audience. Second, their lack of wisdom is glaringly exposed: *"they do not even know how to go to the city!"* is probably a stock saying like "They can't even find their way home," or "They don't know enough to come in out of the rain."

Rulers—Decadent and Disciplined

These Words of Advice began with reflections on the need of wisdom in places of power and the quickness with which the work of a wise person was forgotten once the crisis had passed. The final cluster of teachings returns to the palace and alerts us to the peculiar temptations to be found in its precincts (see also 8:1–9).

> 16 Woe to you, O land, when your king is a child,
>   And your princes feast in the morning!
> 17 Blessed are you, O land, when your king is the
>   son of nobles,
>   And your princes feast at the proper time—
>   For strength and not for drunkenness!
> 18 Because of laziness the building decays,
>   And through idleness of hands the house leaks.
> 19 A feast is made for laughter,
>   And wine makes merry;
>   But money answers everything.
> 20 Do not curse the king, even in your thought;
>   Do not curse the rich, even in your bedroom;
>   For a bird of the air may carry your voice,
>   And a bird in flight may tell the matter.
> > *Eccles. 10:16–20*

The dark and the bright side of political life are contrasted in the antithetic sayings of verses 16–17. But in my understanding of the movement of the verses, the *beatitude* (v. 17) is the only glimmer of light in a gloomy scene. It pictures the way the court functions if the body politic is to maintain its health: (1) the *"king"* is born and bred to the manner (for *"nobles"* or *"free men,"* Heb. *hōrîm,* see Neh. 2:16; 4:14, 19; 5:7; 7:5; 13:17) and therefore trained to cope with the high demand and wide range of royal responsibilities; (2) the political and military leaders (see *"princes"* at 10:7) engage in their festivities *"at the proper time"* (in the evening not the *"morning,"* v. 16) and for the right reason—*"strength"* (Heb. *gᵉbûrāh* frequently has martial overtones, "strength to fight," 9:16) not carousing (*"drunkenness"* is lit. "drinking" whose aim is not merely to slake thirst). This beatitude (v. 17) contrasts with the rest of the passage in the same way that verse 12a sounds the only positive note in 10:12–15.

The *woe-cry* (v. 16) not the *beatitude* sets the tone of these remarks on the hazards that misguided rulers inflict on their land. *"Woe"* (v. 16) and *"blessed"* (v. 17) mark poles of experience; the first is to be avoided ("trouble to you" is one way of reading it); the other is to be treasured ("happy are you"; see JB, NEB). Jesus employs the same contrast in the form of his beatitudes preserved in Luke:

> "Blessed are you poor,
>   For yours is the kingdom of God. . . .
> "But woe to you who are rich,
>   For you have received your consolation."
>   *Luke 6:20, 24*

The cause of the trouble noted by Koheleth was an unfit *"king"* (v. 16). *"Child"* (Heb. *naᶜar,* "youth," "lad") may also mean "servant," one unsuited to wield authority because of lack of training and experience. If so, this passage resumes the theme of 10:4–7 which specifically pictures *"servants"* misplaced as leaders while *"princes"* are forced to take more menial positions.

Chaos was the result of the undisciplined regime that stemmed from ill-prepared leadership. It showed itself in the physical neglect of public buildings (v. 18), where the picture of collapsed roof beams (*"building decays"*) and the water-soaked *"house"* may be a metaphor of the damage done to the kingdom by the lazy, pleasure-loving leaders (on *ᶜāṣēl,* lazy, sluggish, see Prov. 6:6, 9). It showed itself further in the waste of *"money"* (v. 19, lit. "silver"; see 2:8) that was a public crime, adding to the shame of the carousals described in verse 16 and repeated here. The lavish, riotous, and cruel banquet in Esther (chap. 1), may remind us of the potential degradation of royal drinking bouts.

The final result of the political chaos that seems to dominate this passage is the embargo that is placed on all criticism of dissent (v. 20). *"Curse"* here is probably not an invoking of judgment on the *"king"* (who may also be the one called *"rich"* in the parallel clause), but a voicing of disparaging comments ("revile," NIV; "speak ill," NEB; see on 7:21–22). *"Rich"* seems to connect this verse with verse 19 and suggest that the reviling thoughts and words were triggered by the whole program of carousing (v. 16), laziness (v. 18), and profligacy (v. 19) that tarred the reputation of the court. The *"bird"* (v. 20) must be both *hyperbole* to show how carefully a would-be critic had to control tongue and mind, and *metaphor* to show how comprehensive and controlled was the king's network of informers. We use the same metaphor today, "A little bird told me." The admonition called for a pragmatic prudence on the courtier's part. That such restraint was necessary gave a pathetic ring to the whole regime.

It is only fair to say that the unified interpretation of this list of sayings (vv. 16–20) is not shared by all commentators. Some would see the last three verses as detached pieces of advice added to close the whole section that began at 9:13. Moreover, many would give verse 19 a neutral or positive interpretation about the joys of festal living when one has money to afford them. In that reading, the verse would be an expansion of the thought conveyed in the *alternative conclusion* of 9:7. In verse 19, *"answers"* is related to the participle that is read *"keeps him busy"* (Heb. root ʿānāh) in 5:20. "Provides" or "supports" is probably the gist in verse 19, where *"everything"* (lit. "all") means *"both"*: *"but money provides both (bread [feast] and wine)."*

Our society is indeed fortunate. Most of us have the power not only to rejoice in good government but to change bad government or governors where necessary. Drunkenness and folly in high places are not usually what we have to put up with. We can best show our respect for governmental authority by insisting that it keep its contracts and fulfill its responsibilities with efficiency and integrity.

With verse 20, the first section of the closing Words of Advice comes to an end. In chapter 11 the subject and style change sharply. Koheleth has said his last words about court protocol, caution in work, wise speech, and wisdom's virtue and vulnerability. He has done his best to equip his students to handle life as it comes with prudence and poise. He knew these problems as well as anyone in Scripture. But he did not allow himself or his students to wallow in them. Apt solutions were part of his curriculum. And for them, his students who were his contemporaries must have expressed their thanks. We his modern students can add our Amen.

Epilogue: The Greater Wise Man

Jesus, too, believed that God's people should have the wisdom to deal with life's problems. When he commissioned his disciples, he gave them this advice: "'Behold, I send you out as sheep in the midst of wolves. Therefore be wise as serpents and harmless as doves'" (Matt. 10:16). That is about as practical as one can get—counseling persons to guard against persecution without becoming bitter or hostile.

In what ways did Jesus lead his people beyond the shrewd advice of Koheleth? How did he show himself as the Greater Wise Man? He gave us *a firmer confidence in God*. Ecclesiastes set out patterns for his pupils to follow; Jesus introduced us to the person of his Father. The older wise man wanted his students to understand how life worked; the greater Wise Man called his followers to know the One who makes life work. Practicality at its best—this knowledge.

Jesus also brought to us *a clearer awareness of God's kingdom*. This active, personal rule of God among the human family was a major theme of his ministry. To his disciples he issued these orders: "And as you go, preach, saying, 'The kingdom of heaven is at hand.' Heal the sick, cleanse the lepers, raise the dead, cast out demons. Freely you have received, freely give" (Matt. 10:7–8). "The kingdom of heaven is at hand"—what practical words these are! God is at work in our world, in our history, in our society, in our lives. His power to save and to heal, to comfort and to convict is at hand. His demands become our guide, and his provisions, our resources. What an older wise man could only *encourage* us to do, the power of God's Spirit *enables* the citizens of the kingdom to carry out.

This awareness of God's kingdom also taught us how to deal with human government—a theme to which Ecclesiastes gave more than passing attention. God's kingdom requires us to be citizens responsible to our earthly governments while it also insists that our first loyalty is to the Lord who created us and redeemed us. We respect our governors but we do not fear them. They, too, with all their pomp and power, are subject to God's authority. They govern best when they govern according to God's will; we serve our governments best when we encourage them to do this.

Finally, Jesus took his pupils beyond the wisdom of the older Preacher when he instilled in them *a stronger sense of the power of love.* So much of what Ecclesiastes said dealt with shrewd conduct. Jesus knew that getting along in life was more a matter of concern than cunning. He spurred his disciples to pray for their enemies and to do good to those who mistreated them. Make love your aim—not just success. Make love your aim because love *is* success—by God's measurements. Those were Jesus' exhortations. He knew God's ways perfectly because he himself was God, and he knew that God's ways are the ways of love.

The wisest, most practical solution of all was what Jesus brought. As we remember all the pain caused when we are clever but not compassionate, when we are shrewd but not generous, when we are sharp but not sensitive, we can vouch for the practicality of love. Solutions, not problems, are what we need. Like no one else in history, Jesus met that need.

CHAPTER TWELVE

Closing Words of Advice: Principles of Financial Investment

Ecclesiastes 11:1–8

Ours may be the first generation in civilized times that has not raised its young on proverbs. From the beginnings of recorded history in Egypt and Sumeria, concise sayings which describe the benefit of good conduct or the harm of bad have been used to teach children how to behave.

From the islands of the sea to China, from the Bedouin of the Arabian peninsula to the Eskimos of Alaska, proverbs have been a standard way of summarizing life's experiences. In our own country both the biblical proverbs of Solomon and the Anglo-Saxon wisdom collected in *Poor Richard's Almanac* by Benjamin Franklin have helped generations of parents coach their offspring in the art of successful living.

Because proverbs are based on experience, they work best in situations where change is nonexistent or gradual. Settled, rural societies where the pattern of life has remained much the same for centuries find proverbs a congenial way to package and pass on their wisdom. Tribal life, with its uniformly accepted values and its stable social relationships, usually employs a rich stock of proverbs.

Our generation—for the most part—has abandoned the use of proverbs, although one still finds them on locker room walls. There loud signs exhort athletes to do their best with slogans like "When the going gets tough, the tough get going," or "What matters is not the win nor loss but how you play the game." Proverbs have seemed too preachy for many of our young people. They have sought to discover their own values rather than to conserve the values of the past. Change has been such a constant companion in their lives that they have discarded yesterday's wisdom in a frantic effort to cope with a future that seems so different from the past.

But perhaps the old saying is proving true, "The more things change, the more they stay the same." Proverbs seem to be coming back into vogue. From bumper stickers to wall posters, from embroidered hangings to desk mottoes, we see wisdom placarding its advice. Once again we may begin to raise our youngsters with warnings to caution like, "Look before you leap," or to decisiveness like "She who hesitates is lost." When they chafe under our advice, we may remind them of these words:

> Poverty and disgrace will come to him who disdains correction,
> But he who regards a rebuke will be honored.
>
> *Prov. 13:18*

A world burned and scarred by new values that proved false, or a world confused and bitter at the absence of values much needed, may well turn to proverbs to regain its sense of direction. Proverbs—wise sayings which capture the lessons of experience and bring some order to the chaos of living—are one of the means that men and women have used to deal with a life that seems to be drained of meaning.

Even Ecclesiastes, who spoke so much to life's futility when people tried to make profit or pleasure or prestige or permanence their aim, used proverbs to help students make their way beyond the futility, beyond the vanity, he so forcefully described. How to be fruitful in a world where so many lives are barren was one question that he handled with proverbs.

Fruitfulness, as the Preacher defined it, meant both prosperity and joy. Having things was not enough, if a person could not enjoy what she had. Life is lived on a double path as Koheleth charted it. We walk a middle line with one foot on the side marked *the path to prosperity,* and the other foot on the side labeled *the road to joy.* As he saw it, without the one we have no chance for the other. Err to either side, and you pursue only half a life.

The interpretation of 11:1–8 depends some on how the chapter is divided. Many commentaries and translations make a major break at 11:6 and treat 11:7–8 either as a separate section or as introduction to

11:9ff. Good reasons may be found for their decisions. Here, however, I have chosen (with Zimmerli, Michel, NKJV and others) to treat verses 7–8 as conclusion to 11:1–6, underscoring the joy to be found in working while there is yet opportunity.

> 11:1 Cast your bread upon the waters,
>   For you will find it after many days.
>   2 Give a serving to seven, and also to eight,
>   For you do not know what evil will be on the
>   earth.
>   3 If the clouds are full of rain,
>   They empty themselves upon the earth;
>   And if a tree falls to the south or the north,
>   In the place where the tree falls, there it shall lie.
>   4 He who observes the wind will not sow,
>   And he who regards the clouds will not reap.
>   5 As you do not know what is the way of the
>   wind,
>   Or how the bones grow in the womb of her who
>   is with child,
>   So you do not know the works of God who
>   makes everything.
>   6 In the morning sow your seed,
>   And in the evening do not withhold your hand;
>   For you do not know which will prosper,
>   Either this or that,
>   Or whether both alike will be good.
>   7 Truly the light is sweet,
>   And it is pleasant for the eyes to behold the sun;
>   8 But if a man lives many years
>   And rejoices in them all,
>   Yet let him remember the days of darkness,
>   For they will be many.
>   All that is coming is vanity.
>   *Eccles. 11:1–8*

Put in a nutshell the *theme* of the passage is this: we should use wisdom boldly and carefully, cannily yet humbly, taking joy from life while remembering that our days of joy are limited by the certainty of death.

The structure and movement of the text can be analyzed as follows:

Make the most of what you have, counseled the wise man, and you will find *the path to prosperity*. His first proverb that illustrated this is familiar yet often misunderstood:

> Cast your bread upon the waters,
> For you will find it after many days.
> *Eccles. 11:1*

The misunderstanding is that we usually take this casting of bread as a picture of charity. "Do good deeds and you will be rewarded" is a customary interpretation.

But the Preacher's practical shrewdness and the context within the book suggest something else—namely, advice not about charity but about wise investment. Where did one gain the highest return on one's money? In investments overseas: in the rich export and import business of the Mediterranean ports like Tyre and Sidon. *"Bread upon the waters"* that you will *"find"* *"after many days"* was Ecclesiastes' way of describing investment in those lucrative mercantile enterprises where fortunes were to be made.

There was risk involved, of course. And in the second admonition, the Teacher urged his students to diversify their investments to hedge against such risk:

> Give a serving to seven, and also to eight,
> For you do not know what evil will be on the earth.
>
> *Eccles. 11:2*

Misfortune and calamity (here as usual in Ecclesiastes called *"evil"*; see on 2:21) are part of life. Who knows what crop will fail, what ship will be seized by coastal pirates, what merchant will abscond with the profits? Spread your investments (*"serving"* is lit. "lot" or "portion"; Heb. *ḥēleq*, see at 2:10) widely—to seven or eight places—so that no one or two tragedies can wipe you out. That advice was crucial to the path to prosperity.

"Seven or eight" is a Hebrew numerical formula called X, X + 1. It occurs frequently in Proverbs (chaps. 6, 30) and in the first two chapters of Amos. Here it is not to be taken literally but means "plenty and more than plenty," "the widest possible diversification within the guidelines of prudence. . . ." Seven means "plenty," and eight means, "Go a bit beyond that."

Close observation as well as wise investment was what the Preacher prescribed as part of his formula for fruitfulness (vv. 3–4). Although some of his countrymen may have been paying too much attention to the actions of the *"wind"* and the *"clouds"*—not as observers of the weather, but as practitioners of magic, Koheleth believed that certain observable trends in the patterns of wind and rain had to be right for them to do their work successfully, especially their sowing and reaping (v. 4).

Learn to watch the weather, Koheleth commanded. It is God's work. He will do his work on schedule, and you must seek to understand it.

> If the clouds are full of rain,
> They empty themselves on the earth;
> And if a tree falls to the south or to the north,
> In the place where the tree falls, there it shall lie.
>
> *Eccles. 11:3*

The processes of creation go on without your worry, and you could not change them if you tried. So keep your eye on those processes and get on with your work, Ecclesiastes urged.

Contemplation of the right time or the suitable season will result in hedging against costly mistakes that come when one harvests (*"reaps"*) or *"sows"* at the wrong time.

> He who observes the wind will not sow;
> And he who regards the clouds will not reap.
>
> *Eccles. 11:4*

The wrong *"wind"* will blow away the seed; misgauging the possibility of rain *("clouds")* can either make us hurry the harvest prematurely or tarry to the point where we miss its peak. *Rain* is the key here as in other semidesert parts of the world. Its importance in these verses is signaled by the fact that *"clouds"* are mentioned at the beginning and end. The passage is literally enveloped in *"clouds"* (vv. 3–4).

As much as wisdom drawn from observation helped them learn important things, there were other things that wisdom could not tell them. These limits were drummed home in the triple beat of *"you do not know"* (vv. 5–6). Koheleth warned his pupils not to try to guess at *all* of God's ways, just because patterns in creation taught them *some*. They are as mysterious as the act of conception:

> As you do not know what is the way of the wind
> Or how the bones grow in the womb of her who is with child,
> So you do not know the works of God who makes everything.
>
> *Eccles. 11:5*

The chief question here is whether Koheleth was listing two or just one unknowable reality. The two (so NKJV, NIV, JB, NASB) are the *"way of the wind"*—what causes it, why it blows sometimes and not others, and what determines its force and direction—and *"how the bones grow in the womb"* of a pregnant woman (*"bones"* stand for embryo, the unborn child; see Isa. 66:14 and Prov. 14:30 where *"bones"* describe the whole person). If just one unknowable reality is in view, it would be the question of how the "life-spirit" (so Crenshaw and Fox) "comes to the bones in the womb of a woman with child" (RSV). To choose between the two options is almost impossible. If the double-mystery interpretation is adopted, *"everything"* should probably be read *"both,"* as frequently in Koheleth (see 2:14). The combined mystery of wind (or spirit; Heb. *rûªh* can mean either) anticipates Jesus' word to Nicodemus:

> "The wind blows where it wishes, and you hear the sound of it,
> but cannot tell where it comes from and where it goes. So is ev
> eryone who is born of the Spirit."
>
> *John 3:8*

Let God take care of his mysteries and you take care of your work, was the Preacher's conclusion:

> In the morning sow your seed,
> And in the evening do not withhold your hand;
> For you do not know which will prosper,
> Either this or that,
> Or whether both alike will be good.
>
> *Eccles. 11:6*

"Morning" and *"evening"* seem to be a *merism,* embracing the whole day. *"Sow your seed"* diligently and abundantly is the gist of this admonition. The reason for the diligence (*"for"*) is that the mystery of which seed grows and how it does (*"prospers"*; Heb. *kāshēr,* see 10:10; Esther 8:5, means lit. to be right or proper and is the root of the familiar Jewish word *kōsher*) is in God's hands and cannot be known to us. The limits of our wisdom are a catalyst to industry not despair. Verse 6 is the counterpart to verses 1–2: both speak of hedging against the ups and downs of life that we *"do not know"* about and cannot control. The sphere of activity in the beginning verses seems to be mercantile investment in export and import overseas; the final verse uses the language of agriculture. We cannot be certain of the literalness of either. The points are boldness, diversification, and hard work—a common sense that applies to almost every field of endeavor.

So alongside the path to prosperity, the wise Preacher lined out *the road to joy.* Find the beauty in every day, was his simple advice in the conclusion to this remarkable passage:

> Truly the light is sweet,
> And it is pleasant for the eyes to behold the sun.
>
> *Eccles. 11:7*

Reminded of life's fragility and the limits of our understanding of it, he encouraged his friends to celebrate every hour of daylight. *"Sweet"* is a strong word picturing the exquisite joy that each new day can bring: joy like the taste of honey (Judg. 14:18), like a kiss (Song of Sol. 2:3), or like the attraction of God's word (Ps. 19:10). *"Pleasant"* (lit. "good") depicts the blessings that the gift of each day of sunlight offers.

There is an urgency to this celebration, noted the wise Professor, because *death is coming* and lasts so long:

> But if a man lives many years,
> And rejoices in them all,
> Yet let him remember the days of darkness,
> For they will be many.
> All that is coming is vanity.
>
> *Eccles. 11:8*

Enjoy the tasks at hand; savor each bit of food and drink; share your joys with the wife of your youth. Make the most of what you have, Ecclesiastes has urged, because the *"days of darkness"* are coming when your enjoyment will cease. Death will pull the blinds and black out the light of life.

These words on prudent investment, dedicated labor, and daily joy reprise the final alternative conclusion of 9:7–10, where the closing admonition urges its hearers to give themselves wholeheartedly to life's varied labors: "Whatever your hand finds to do, do it with your might" (9:10). The reason for the command is the one given in 11:8: the rate of unemployment in the grave is precisely 100 percent.

Epilogue: The Greater Wise Man

Most of this Old Testament advice has been affirmed by the New Testament's Greater Wise Man. He, too, believed that we should make the most of what we have. This was part of what he had in mind in his parable of the talents. Who can forget his stinging words:

"So you ought to have deposited my money with the bankers,
and at my coming I would have received back my own with interest. Therefore take the talent from him, and give it to him who
has ten talents. For to everyone who has, more will be given, and
he will have abundance; but from him who does not have, even
what he has will be taken away."

Matt. 25:27–29

Abilities, goods, wealth, opportunities—all these are divine gifts of
which we are stewards. One of the things that Jesus will do when he
comes again is to judge how well we have used his gifts.

Part of our commitment to Jesus as Lord is our commitment to invest our money, our time, our energy in endeavors that will pay
dividends. Ecclesiastes was right. But he did not tell the whole story.
He did not know that the coming of our Lord Jesus is the event toward which all our living and giving and saving and spending point.
If God-fearing men and women in Old Testament days felt that wisdom demanded sound investment of what they had, how much more
should we, as Christ's return approaches?

And part of our commitment to Jesus as Lord is to rejoice in God's
good gifts. In the heart of the prayer that the Master taught his followers is the plea for daily bread. What Jesus urged us to plead for,
God has promised to supply. Though we do not live on bread alone,
we do need bread for the sustenance and refreshment of life. Our
Savior made wine at a wedding and celebrated in advance that great
Wedding yet to come, by eating and drinking with crooked tax collectors and known sinners.

In so doing this he taught us a greater enjoyment, a higher prosperity, than Koheleth's friends could imagine. Jesus taught us to eat
and drink in enjoyment of God's provision; but more than that he
taught us to eat and drink in anticipation of God's victory. The day is
coming when all of God's people will sit at history's finest banquet
and will feast to the full in fellowship with each other and with the
Savior, who is our Bridegroom. Every Christian meal, every Christian party, every gathering in Christian fellowship should be
enlivened with the hope of the Banquet yet to come.

Jesus wants us to make the most of what we have in the use of our
goods and the enjoyment of his gifts. But beyond that, he wants us to
be the best at what we are. What are we basically? Investors? Yes,

and preferably wise ones. What are we? Enjoyers? Yes, and preferably grateful ones.

Yet we are more. We are *lovers,* meant to adore God's person and to serve our neighbor's needs. These are the human realities, the spiritual yearnings, that Ecclesiastes saw only dimly.

In Jesus they come clear. What he says to us takes us beyond all futility to full fruitfulness: "I am the vine, you are the branches. He who abides in Me, and I in him, bears much fruit . . ." (John 15:5).

Love is the fruit on which Jesus focused: "This is My commandment, that you love one another as I have loved you" (John 15:12). To many, proverbs and slogans may seem an obsolete method of teaching the way to success. This command can never be obsolete. It is rooted in the very nature of God; it flowered in the sacrifice of Jesus Christ; it is the true source of human fruitfulness. Where love is at work, there is no room for futility, for "love never fails" (1 Cor. 13:8).

CHAPTER THIRTEEN

Closing Words of Advice: Ground Rules for the Young

Ecclesiastes 11:9–12:8

He was a theologian, a teacher, and a mountain climber. I knew that, but I was still not ready for his words: "I would like to get another crack at the Alps or at least a chance to tackle the Tetons." His eyes were steely as he spoke, and they flashed with hopes about the future.

Speechless in amazement, I looked at his lithe, tall frame, trim as a javelin, erect as a lance. My amazement was not based on any doubts about his prowess. His climbing feats were known to a wide circle of his acquaintances. What surprised me about his hopeful words of scaling the Alps or the Tetons was the fact that he was over ninety years of age.

He knew what it was to grow older without letting either the thought or the reality of aging destroy his spirit. In so doing he had learned one of life's most needed lessons. He had learned to mature while he aged. His spirit had enlarged and ripened even while his body felt the taxing toll of time. Joy and hope were strong even where muscles and sinews had begun to weaken.

Coping with the futility that some feel in old age was a skill he had developed well. His vitality was evidence that he had heeded the urgings of Koheleth in his final words to his students. "Make the most of your youth, for ahead lie the difficult days of old age and the certainty of death."

My friend had extended his youth not only into middle life but far beyond. He knew full well the force of the key commands with which the Preacher closed his Words of Advice: *"rejoice"* (11:9) and *"remember"* (12:1)—*"rejoice in your youth"* and *"remember your Creator."*

9 Rejoice, O young man, in your youth,
  And let your heart cheer you in the days of
    your youth;
  Walk in the ways of your heart,
  And in the sight of your eyes,
  But know that for all these
  God will bring you into judgment.
10 Therefore remove sorrow from your heart,
  And put away evil from your flesh,
  For childhood and youth are vanity.
12:1 Remember now your Creator in the days of
    your youth,
  Before the difficult days come,
  And the years draw near when you say,
  "I have no pleasure in them":
2 While the sun and the light,
  The moon and the stars,
  Are not darkened,
  And the clouds do not return after the rain;
3 In the day when the keepers of the house
    tremble,
  And the strong men bow down;
  When the grinders cease because they are few,
  And those that look through the windows grow
    dim;
4 When the doors are shut in the streets,
  And the sound of grinding is low;
  When one rises up at the sound of a bird,
  And all the daughters of music are brought
    low;
5 Also they are afraid of height,
  And of terrors in the way;
  When the almond tree blossoms,
  The grasshopper is a burden,
  And desire fails.
  For man goes to his eternal home,
  And the mourners go about the streets.
6 Remember your Creator before the silver cord
    is loosed,
  Or the golden bowl is broken,
  Or the pitcher shattered at the fountain,
  Or the wheel broken at the well.

7 Then the dust will return to the earth as it was,
   And the spirit will return to God who gave it.
8 "Vanity of vanities," says the Preacher,
   "All is vanity."

Eccles. 11:9–12:8

Ecclesiastes' last words were inked with anxiety over a foreboding future. Do you suppose it was his own aging that he dreaded? Like the rest of us preachers, were his sharpest words directed at himself? Was he raising the volume of his voice to calm his fears?

We do not know for sure. Koheleth was prone to observe what went on, then offer his comments and issue his commands. Yet he was not afraid to vent his own feelings at times, especially hatred of life and labor, when they seemed to be nullified by the fact of death, over whose timing and circumstances he had so little control (2:17–23).

Anger, despair, sorrow—all these feelings he must have experienced. Occasionally, his steely-eyed way of looking at things and his vise-like mental grasp of them let go a little and released a trickle of his own emotions for us to feel. Such an instance may be traced in the urgency of the commands (11:9–12:1) and the poignancy of his word pictures (12:2–7) which shape the *structure* of this section:

Admonitions to joy	11:9–10
Live the life of joy	9a–b
Motivation: God will judge	9c
Avoid the life of pain	10a–b
Motivation: youth is brief	10c
Admonition to be faithful to God	12:1a
Motivation: death is certain	1b–7
Literal description of old age	1b
Figurative description of old age	2
Dramatic description of a funeral	3–5
Figurative description of death	6
Literal description of death	7
Summary of Book: Sweeping Conclusion	8

The outline suggests that *death* is Koheleth's crowning topic—death and how we get ready for it. Some interpretations read 12:3–5 as an allegory on *aging* (Crenshaw, Eaton), while others find in it an

235

account of a decaying mansion or manor house which serves as a parable for the gradual deterioration of human physical powers (Gordis, Whybray). An allegorical approach founders on a couple of sharp rocks: (1) The details of the word-pictures are sometimes hard to interpret with even moderate assurance, especially verses 4c–d and 5; (2) some parts of the passage seem much more literal than others, for example, the final lines of verse 5.

The focus on death (see Fox, Ogden) rather than aging is encouraged by a number of considerations in the text. First, it fits more compatibly with Koheleth's oft-repeated emphasis on the certainty of death and the unpredictability of its timing. Second, *death* is the theme of the verses that immediately precede our section (11:7–8), verses that act as a bridge to 11:9–12:8 from the commands to wise, diversified, and diligent use of wealth, time, and energy (11:1–6): their emphasis on *"light"* and *"darkness"* anticipates 12:2, while their theme words, *"rejoice"* and *"remember"* set the tone for the crucial admonitions of 11:9 and 12:1. Third, *death* is clearly the dominant reality described literally in 12:5, figuratively in 12:6, and literally again in 12:7. Finally, the time-frame of the passage is bound together as one unit by the catch-word *"before"* (12:1b, 2—*"while"* should be read "before," RSV, NIV—12:6, each of which uses the Heb. phrase, ʿ*ad* ʾᵃ*sher lōʾ*, lit. "until when not"). Within that time-frame is embraced a second time element *"in the day when"* (vv. 3–5). The force of all this is to suggest that the events described from 12:2 to 12:7 are not a sequence of actions but a collection of activities that surround the death and burial of a person. Only verse 1b seems to note old age as the setting of death.

"Enjoy life now, for God is judging how well you celebrate his gifts." That is the first of Koheleth's ground rules for the young.

> Rejoice, O young man, in your youth,
> And let your heart cheer you in the days of your youth;
> Walk in the ways of your heart
> And in the sight of your eyes.
> But know that for all these
> God will bring you into judgment.
> Therefore remove sorrow from your heart,
> And put away evil from your flesh,
> For childhood and youth are vanity.
>
> *Eccles. 11:9–10*

"Vanity" here means "fleeting," "brief." Like a bubble the days of our *"youth"* soon burst, so we have to clutch them while we can.

The Preacher pounded home the importance of making the most of our youthful years in several ways. First, he employs three different Hebrew roots: *bāḥar,* "to choose," lends its sense of being fit, in the prime of life, ready for military service if necessary, to two words, (v. 9)—*"young man"* and *"youth"* in the phrase *"days of your youth"; yeled,* "child," lies behind the twice-used noun translated *"in your youth"* (v. 9) and *"childhood"* (v. 9), both indicating the period of life before one enters full adult responsibilities in family and community; *shāḥōr,* "black" is the base of *"youth"* at the end of verse 10; scholars differ in the derivations of this meaning—some connect it with the black hair of youth, others tie it to the word for "dawn" with its dark beginning of the day (RSV, "the dawn of life" instead of *"youth").*

Second, Koheleth uses both a positive and a negative approach in the two admonitions. *"Rejoice," "let your heart cheer you"* (lit. "do good to you"), *"walk in the ways of your heart"* are strong positive commands that open wide the gate to joy and urge the young student to rush through it. To do that, however, the second set of admonitions must be honored: *"Remove sorrow* (or "vexation"; Heb. *kaʿas;* see 1:18; 2:23), *"put away evil"* ("harm," "danger," "pain," RSV).

Third, the motivation of each admonition gives a powerful incentive to obey it. Divine *"judgment"* here (v. 9) centers in the issue of whether the young person responded actively to the call to joy. The means of joy were divine blessings as the six *alternative conclusions* have avowed, especially the fullest of them in 9:7–10. To shun such grace was a capital act of disobedience. The second motivation (v. 10) quietly points to the theme of *death* in labeling the period of *"youth"* as frustratingly brief and temporary *("vanity").* "Make the most of a time that is all too short" is its message.

Obviously the wise man was not counseling a rebellious or wild style of life when he told his students to *"walk in the ways of your heart."* Lawlessness, wickedness, lewdness were as much out of bounds for him as for any of Israel's teachers. Take your fill of life; do your best at what you do; live each day to the hilt in work, in love, and in the enjoyment of God's good gifts. All of these are tangible, visible displays *("and in the sight of your eyes")* of God's grace; God will judge us as to whether we have made the most of them.

The second ground rule makes God even more the center of attention:

> Remember now your Creator in the days of your
>   youth,
> Before the difficult days come,
> And the years draw near when you will say,
> "I have no pleasure in them":
>
> *Eccles. 12:1*

This verse was not a command to piety so much as to *"pleasure."* The Hebrew word *ḥēpheṣ* (see also 5:4 and 12:10) can have that sense as well as the meaning "affair," "activity," "matter" (see 3:1, 12; 5:8, 8:6). The Preacher was not begging his pupils to get right with God in terms of obedience in their worship (5:1–7) but of enjoyment in everyday life. Bad days are coming in which pleasure will be impossible, was his warning. In light of the aging process, take life's pleasure now. "Difficult (lit. *"evil,"* see 2:21) days" he has called them, days fraught with misfortune or even disaster, bereft of all experience of pleasure. *"Remember now your Creator"*—remember that God has given you his gifts for your pleasure. Make the most of them while you have the energy and the vitality, was his admonition. Some interpreters have rejected the reading *"Creator"* and seen the word "pit" or "cistern" here instead. "Cistern" they have viewed as imagery of a wife (Prov. 5:15–19) and "pit" as a description of the grave.

In the first interpretation, the admonition would be an encouragement to sexual activity (9:9), in the second, it would urge the young to keep in mind the fact of death (11:8). Some find in *"Creator"* also a warning of death in light of the view that at death the *"Creator"* takes back the human *"spirit"* which he originally *"gave"* (12:7). The details of the aging process do not seem to be Koheleth's main concern. The fact of old age he highlights because it is a harbinger of death. And death is what he goes on to describe with three unforgettable word pictures.

Death is like the *coming of winter*, was his first and most gentle comparison:

> Remember now your creator . . . before the sun and the light and
> the moon and the stars are darkened and the clouds return after the
> rain.
>
> *Eccles. 12:1–2 (paraphrase)*

Most of the year in the Bible lands the sun could be counted on every day. But in winter, after the autumn rains, cloudy, colder days would come. These were the days when nature was dormant—the days between the rich, fall harvest of fruit and grapes and the appearance of the almond blossoms as the messengers of spring. Leafless trees, songless birds, fruitless vines, clouded skies—these were the signs of winter. And they were also symbols of the dark, unknowing, unfeeling state of death. The darkening of the *"light,"* God's first act of creation, and of the "lights of the firmament," *"sun,"* *"moon," "stars"* (Gen. 1:3–4, 14–16) suggests that, for Koheleth, death removes us from all the good things of God's creation (see 11:7–8).

The second graphic picture of death features a *funeral scene* and the impact death has on the community:

> In the day when the keepers of the house tremble,
> And the strong men bow down;
> When the grinders cease because they are few,
> And those that look through the windows grow dim;
> When the doors are shut in the streets,
> And the sound of grinding is low;
> When one rises up at the sound of a bird,
> And all the daughters of music are brought low.
> Also they are afraid of height,
> And of terrors in the way;
> When the almond tree blossoms,
> The grasshopper is a burden,
> And desire fails.
> For man goes to his eternal home,
> And the mourners go about the streets.
>   *Eccles. 12:3–5*

This passage has baffled interpreters as much as any in the book: Crenshaw reads it as an imaginative picture of aging, an approach I also used in earlier comments on Koheleth; Ogden sees it as pictorial language for the complete cessation of activity that death entails; Fox has developed most fully the funeral setting which I follow here.

"In the day" ties the timing of these verses to the *"before"* of verse 2, which in turn links the entire passage (12:1–7) to the controlling command *"remember."* This means that we are dealing with one long sentence headed by an imperative verb, *"remember,"* followed by

three *"before"* clauses (1:1b, 2, 6), the second of which is expanded by the *"in the day when"* clauses of verses 3–5. The darkness of death (v. 2) is the context for the *"in the day when"* of verse 3.

The *"day when"* is the day of a funeral, indeed of "your" funeral, since it continues the address to the young person who is the implied subject of *"remember"* (12:1). With consummate artistry (though not as much clarity as we would wish), Koheleth escorts his students to the scene of their own funerals.

The scene begins at a *"house"* (v. 3), presumably the *"house"* of the deceased. It is rocked from top to bottom by the loss of one of its inhabitants: (1) the servants (*"keepers"*; see 2 Sam. 20:3 where some of David's concubines are left to *"keep the house"*) *"tremble"* (Heb. zûᶜ; see Esther 5:9) in fear and grief; (2) the *"strong men"* (ḥayil suggests either skilled or influential; Gen. 47:6, *"competent"*; Prov. 31:10, "noble character," NIV) are twisted or contorted (*"bow down"*; Heb. ᶜāwat means *"made crooked"* in 7:13) in gestures of grief and mourning; (3) the maid-servants who grind the grain for cereal and bread (*"grinders"* in Heb. is a feminine participle which suggests the ongoing occupation of the women) dwindle down to a *"few,"* apparently because most of them have left with the funeral cortege (v. 5); (4) the women who *"look* (again a feminine participle) *through the windows"* (Heb. ᵃrubbôth are window openings which allowed air in and smoke out; they may have been partly shaded by latticework; Gen. 7:11; 8:2; Hos. 13:3) turn dark with sorrow (*"grow dim"*; Heb. ḥāshak was read *"darkened"* in 12:2 and describes the dark appearance of the disheartened Nazarites in Lam. 4:8); (5) the *"doors"* of the house are *"shut"* (v. 4) so that no one in the *"streets"* or "marketsquare" (Heb. shûq is the equivalent of Arabic suq, "bazaar," "open market") can enter; (6) the *"sound"* (lit. "voice") of the *"grinding"* stones has hushed to an almost inaudible level (*"low"*), since so few maid-servants are left, and they probably have no heart for their work.

The scene changes in the middle of verse 4. The center of attention has shifted from the house to the *funeral procession,* one like the cortege that Jesus broke up when he revived the son of the widow of Nain: "And when He came near the gate of the city [on the way to the cemetery outside the gate], behold, a dead man was being carried out. . . . And a large crowd from the city was with her" (Luke 7:12). The key to this interpretation of verses 4c–5 is found in the final lines of verse 5. The literal words here shed light on the more veiled lines above: (1) *"the man goes to his eternal home"* describes the procession that bears him to the cemetery and grave; (2) the *"mourners go about"*—the Hebrew verb describes the circuitous turnings of the wind in 1:6—*the streets* (or "open marketplace"; see on v. 4).

The section from the second half of verse 4 to the final two lines of verse 5, seems to contain two sharp contrasts between the women who lead the lamenting—*"daughters of music"* (v. 4)—and the ongoing life of nature that surrounds them as they chant, bow, and whirl their way to the cemetery. The vitality of God's creation is dramatically present in the face of human death: (1) A bird begins to sing a song that injects a startlingly cheery note in a scene where the lamenting women are *"bowing low"* in a posture of grief (v. 4); sad chant and happy tune vie for attention at a time when life stops and yet goes on; (2) the mystery of death grips with terror the hearts of the mourners so that fear of the unknown and unseen—whether high up (*"height"*) or beneath their feet (*"way"* or "road")—puts them in a panic that separates them dramatically from the burgeoning of life visible in the *flora* that surrounds them, where the *"almond tree blossoms"* white with new life, the lily-laden sea-onion bush is loaded (*"burden"*) with pods, and the caper shrubs are sprouting their tasty berries.

So read, this contrast is a detailed picture of the constancy of created activity first celebrated in the opening poem (1:4–11). It seems to comment on the lead verse of that poem:

> One generation passes away,
>   and another generation comes;
> But the earth abides forever.
>   *Eccles. 1:4*

The slow-step march to the funeral, depicted literally in the final lines of verse 5, illustrates the coming and going of the *"generations"* (or life cycles); the budding shrubbery signals the reassurance of an abiding *"earth."*

A few sentences of comment are necessary to suggest how one may arrive at the reading just sketched, which at a couple of places is so markedly different from standard translations. First, it is an attempt to let the more literal statements about *death* at the end of verse 5 provide the clue for understanding what leads up to that. Second, it tries

241

to be consistent in depicting how the *"house"* (v. 3) and the *"streets"* (vv. 4, 5; v. 5 also mentions *"path"*) looked and sounded during the funeral procession. No shifting back and forth from more literal to more allegorical interpretation has been employed. Third, in the middle three lines of verse 5 the rendering has taken its cue from the *flora* that are mentioned: (1) *"almond tree blossoms"* is the clearest clause of the three; (2) both the Greek and Latin versions have "caper bush" not *"desire"* in the third clause (Lat. *capparis* transliterates the Greek word which rightly understood the Heb. ʾ*abiyyônāh* as a plant not a term for sexual appetite), though my reading (following Fox and some earlier commentators) emends the verb *"fails"* to "buds" (Heb. *pārar* to *pārah*, see Song of Sol. 7:12); (3) the presence of trees or bushes in these two clauses raises questions about the *"grasshopper"* in the middle clause; the Hebrew term occurs in a dietary list as an edible flying insect (Lev. 11:22) and as an image of human frailty in Isaiah 40:22; if *"grasshopper"* is intended in 12:5 the verb *"is a burden"* (Heb. *sābel*, "carry" or "bear") should be read "is getting fat" (lit. "is loading itself up")—a picture of a ravenous insect gorging itself on the verdure of new growth; finding the *"grasshopper"* as an unwanted intruder in a text that pictures greenery, some commentaries (Ginsberg and Fox) have emended it to a word for "squill" or "sea-onion," a word familiar to the rabbis in postbiblical times (Heb. *ḥāgāb* to *ḥāṣāb*. The "squill" or "sea-onion" is a member of the lily family whose bulb was used medicinally in the Mediterranean world.

If the botany and philology of this interpretation seem tedious, we should recall that there is relatively little consensus among the commentators about a more imaginative and less literal rendering. Understanding this section of Koheleth is no smooth picnic. The direction one takes in interpreting it depends on which set of ants one prefers to party with.

In verses 6–7, the theme of *death,* sounded so clearly in the introduction to (v. 2) and conclusion of the funeral scene (v. 5f-g), becomes even more prominent. *"Before"* (v. 6) harks back to its earlier occurrences (vv. 1b, 2) and like them depends on the command *"remember,"* which accounts for the repetition of that verb in the NKJV. In Hebrew the verse begins with *"before."* Verse 6, the third graphic picture of death, is a cluster of images which convey the idea that life, precious (*"silver," "gold"*) as it is, is utterly destroyed at death. The act of death itself is likened to a *"cord"* that is *"loosed"* (or "broken" if we adopt the suggestion that Heb. *yĕrāḥēq*, "be removed," be emended to *yinnātēq* which Koheleth used in 4:12), letting drop and break to smithereens the precious vessel of life that it suspends. There is nothing gentle about this picture of death. The verbs *"broken"* and *"shattered"* are strong words for destruction: (1) Hebrew *rāṣaṣ* found twice in 12:6 is used in crushing acts of oppression in Hosea 5:11 and Amos 4:1; (2) *shābar* describes the shattered, useless cisterns from which Judah could no longer drink (Jer. 2:13). Three vessels are mentioned: *"golden bowl"* like the kind used to hold lamp oil (Zech. 4:2–3), *"pitcher,"* a large clay container like the one Rebekah brought to the well (Gen. 24:14–20), and "jug" (*"wheel"* is a possible translation, though we do not possess much evidence that wheels or pulleys were used on well ropes in biblical days), another round jar of some kind, as the Hebrew root suggests. The triple illustration speaks of the certainty and finality of death. *"Well,"* the site of the smashing of at least the third vessel, is probably a wordplay on "grave" and includes a glance at the burial scene. Hebrew *bôr* means pit, cistern, or well, but it can also be the place of death and burial, as shown in the *"pit"* where the brothers dumped Joseph (Gen. 37:20–29) and the *"pit"* which the psalmist thought would be his grave (Ps. 28:1).

Burial is certainly in view—and in literal language—in verse 7, where the *"dust"* of the buried body returns *"to the earth."* Koheleth had previously argued that the stock formula for *death* could not be proven:

> Who knows the spirit of the sons of men, which goes upward,
> and the spirit of the animal, which goes down to the earth?
> *Eccles. 3:21*

It is tempting but not necessary to find a contradiction of this in 12:7. Koheleth has no thought of afterlife in his picture of death in 12:1–7. The talk of darkness (v. 2) and the grave (vv. 5–7) rule that out. Actually each of the two passages has its own purpose. The point of the first is to argue that one cannot prove, at least on Koheleth's terms, that the death of a beast differs in kind from the death of a person. The second passage aims to recount a dissolution of the human personhood as a reversal—*"return"* does not hint at a new status—of the creative process of Genesis 2:7. The body, without which the Hebrews could not imagine full humanity, crumbles to dust, and God withdraws the life-spirit which he had given to energize the body into a *"living being."* We should not infer, from the Preacher's words, any conclusions about what happened after the spirit or "breath" (Gen. 2:7) and the body were sundered. Part of hearing Koheleth in his own time and setting is to resist the temptation to read back New Testament teaching into his texts.

The *sweeping conclusion* of 1:2 is repeated almost verbatim in 12:8. The only difference is that this final summary drops the second occurrence of *"vanity of vanities"* which gave additional punch to the theme in 1:2. The reason for the omission may be that the persistent note of how empty life often is, given the fact that human beings cannot plumb the unfathomable depths of God's design, has been sounded in virtually every chapter.

The repetition of the conclusion forms an envelope that wraps the whole text in the sackcloth of enigma. With very little exaggeration, Fox (p. 309) labels this packaging "the most prominent and powerful inclusion in the Bible." What this structural device tells us is that all efforts to pierce the mystery of God's ways within the book have come up short, far short. The six *alternative conclusions* (see on 2:24–25) and the three collections of *Words of Advice* (5:1–12; 7:1–8:9; 9:13–12:7) have not lifted us above the mystery but given us insights to live within it. When, why, and how God works in our world is as baffling a matter in the end as it was in the beginning. Yet getting to know that and learning to live with these sharp limitations is a lesson well worth all the efforts—Koheleth's and ours.

Epilogue: The Greater Wise Man

The Christian gospel has better news to offer than the somber analysis of the old Preacher. And it has a better prescription for our geriatric problems. "Take life's pleasure now" was a maxim that the early Christians would have understood, though they would have added other ingredients to Ecclesiastes' recipe—ingredients like enjoying Christ's fellowship and witnessing to his kingdom. But "take life's pleasure now" cannot be the only advice the gospel gives, if it is to be good news. What good will it do us to seize *today* if we dread *tomorrow* with its creeping senility and its looming death.

The better prescription that Jesus Christ offered was this: "Look forward to your destiny." What Koheleth had said was to live all you can while you can, because the time was coming when such exuberant life would be impossible. What Jesus said was to live fully all your life, even in old age—and beyond.

Doing God's will was part of what Jesus ordered as a way of maturing and not just aging. *Aging* is a negative process. It speaks of wrinkles and tremors, of frosted vision and spotty hearing. *Maturing* is a positive experience. It points to greater wisdom and increased patience, to stronger love and enriched understanding.

One great purpose of the Christian gospel is to help us grow as persons into a maturity patterned after Christ's. *Doing the will of God* is central to this growth. It is the heart of our relationship with God, a relationship that refines and mellows us, that strengthens and perfects—in spite of the limitations of aging. Is this not what Jesus meant when he pointed to his disciples and said, "'Here are My mother and My brothers! For whoever does the will of My Father in heaven is My brother and sister and mother'" (Matt. 12:49–50)?

Doing God's will means living in his love and centering on his purposes. It brings us into line with him and with ourselves. It keeps us alert and hopeful because it presents us with fresh possibilities. At times we may be almost paralyzed by the thought of death, but opportunities for love are ever present, and strength to love is not totally dependent on physical vitality. The aged are good at loving, especially when they have matured for decades in the knowledge that God loves them. Remember your Creator, and start early to learn of God's love.

Facing death with confidence was another part of Jesus' prescription for maturity. The specter of death is part of what makes old age a wintry season. Jesus urged his followers not to fear it even when it came in violent forms. Their attention was to be given to God, not to those who might bring about their death: "And do not fear those who kill the body but cannot kill the soul. But rather fear Him who is able to destroy both soul and body in hell" (Matt. 10:28). The God who notes the fall of the sparrow cares much about his own children. He will see us through the door of death and beyond. Beyond the door where the lamp has been broken and the pitcher has been smashed is brighter light and sweeter water. Our dying is God's business; God's will is our business. The aged are good at trusting, especially when they have matured for decades in their confidence that God cares. Remember your Creator, and start to trust God's will.

Moving in history's direction was a third part of Jesus' pattern for maturity. Time marches on, but not by itself. God is moving it as part of his program that began at creation and will consummate with Christ's coming. The passing of the years is not a scourge but a sacrament. It is God's way of heading history in his direction. If time seems to be taking its toll, remember that Jesus pointed his life toward that *hour* when he would glorify God and rescue us by his death. We can let time do its work, even though it sometimes seems cruel, with the hope that time's work is God's work. It is heading not so much toward death as toward life. The aged are good at hoping, especially when they have matured for decades in the truth of the promises of God. Remember your Creator, and start early to hope in God's victory.

Look forward to your destiny. It may not be climbing the Alps or the Grand Tetons in your nineties; it may be something far grander and more adventuresome—like doing God's will in love and trust, facing death with courage and confidence, and moving in history's direction with hope and anticipation. Aging may have its futile sides, but its futility is no match for the maturity that Christ provides.

CHAPTER FOURTEEN

Conclusion: The Teacher's Discipline—The Student's Duty

Ecclesiastes 12:9–14

The words that close Koheleth's book seem not to have come from the Preacher's hand. The two places where he is mentioned (12:9–10) speak of him in the third person. Beyond that, they describe his work in a degree of detail and a tone of appreciation that appear to be the words of someone else—an editor who may have been Koheleth's student. The epilogue (12:9–14) is usually divided into two parts on the basis of form and content.

Structurally the clue that divides the passage is the repetition of the introductory phrase translated *"moreover"* (v. 9) and *"further"* (v. 12; Heb. *yôthēr* means "a remainder" or an "additional thing"; related to *yitrôn*, "profit" or "advantage," it occurs also in 2:15; 6:8, 11; 7:11, 16). The first half (vv. 9–11) is in the indicative mood grammatically and describes Koheleth's activities as a sage (vv. 9–10) along with the stimulating and motivating role that the teachings of the wise played in the lives of their students (v. 11). The second half (vv. 12–14) is dominated by imperatives alerting students to the perils and advantages of their study.

The teacher's discipline and *the student's duty* are the rubrics we use to describe the contents of the two halves of the epilogue. The tone of the two halves is sufficiently different to have prompted some scholars (Loader, for example) to suggest a separate author or editor for each half. His chief argument is his interpretation of the second half as a criticism of the thought of the book, while the first half is openly appreciative of Ecclesiastes' work. Would the same person have written both? Our answer to that question will be offered in the comments on the text.

Another viewpoint of the epilogue's composition should be mentioned here. Michael V. Fox has ventured the idea that the author of the epilogue is also the author of the whole book. "Qoheleth," as Fox sees him, is not an actual person but a *persona*, a dramatic mask, donned by the author and made to speak the author's radical thoughts while not jeopardizing the author's status in the circles of the wise. After the *sweeping conclusion* of 12:8, the author drops the mask and uses his own voice to express appreciation for the work of Qoheleth and in fact to defend it from critics who would brand it as beyond the pale of orthodox wisdom teaching (vv. 9–11). At the same time the editor, as Fox reads him, takes the liberty of adding a conclusion (vv. 12–14) which ranges beyond what Koheleth taught and leans more heavily on divine revelation than did the Preacher.

These various theories of the composition, authorship, and purpose of the epilogue warn us that even when we arrive at the last six verses of the book, we are not yet through with the tough sledding. Yet here, as elsewhere in the twelve chapters, there are useful lessons to be learned about the task of garnering and applying wisdom and how good teachers and good students go about their work of understanding the wonders and mysteries of God's dealings with the human family.

The Teacher's Discipline

The epilogue's first paragraph makes three main points. First, it identifies Koheleth's chief task as a wise man occupied with teaching the *"people." "Wise"* (v. 9) probably is used in at least a semiofficial sense. Koheleth is described as more than an intellectual who had some other occupation. The text makes it sound as though he were a member of a circle of sages—called *"scholars"* in verse 11—whose main work was devoted to composition and instruction of wisdom not only for an elite cadre of students but for the population at large. Second, it describes the methods and goals of Koheleth's ministry (vv. 9–10): careful, winsome, and upright teachings. Third, it witnesses to the pain inflicted by the teaching, designed as it was to correct bad behavior and prod its hearers toward the good path (10:2).

9 And moreover, because the Preacher was wise,
he still taught the people knowledge; yes, he pondered
and sought out and set in order many proverbs.

10 The Preacher sought to find acceptable words;
and what was written was upright—words of truth.

11 The words of the wise are like goads, and the
words of scholars are like well-driven nails, given by
one Shepherd.

Eccles. 12:9–11

The sage's subject kept him busy "continually" as "*still*" can also
be translated (v. 9). And well it did, because that subject was "*knowledge*" (see on 1:16, 17, 18; 2:21, 26; 7:12; 9:10). As always in wisdom
literature (see Prov. 1:4, 7), "*knowledge*" is much more than information. It involves the "know-how" of understanding and applying
God's will in everyday life, and even more it entails the "know-
whom" of a relationship of fear, obedience, and loyalty toward God.
What a curriculum for God's "*people*" (Heb. *hāʿām*, Jews, covenant
people) to master!

The scholar's preparation for this task included three key activities:
"*he pondered*" (the derivation of the Heb. word is debated; it may
mean "weighed" or perhaps even better, "listened," since the consonants match those of the word for ear—ʾizzēn/ʾōzen); he "*sought out*"
or "searched thoroughly for" (Heb. *hāqar* is the familiar verb "search
me" in Ps. 139:1); he "*set in order*," or "composed" (Heb. *tiqqēn* is read
"*make straight*" in 1:15; 7:13). "*Many proverbs*" is the object of all this.
To catch the scope of the task, we need to grasp the range of materials
called "*proverbs*." Hebrew *mᵉshālîm* (singular *māshāl*) embraced a
cluster of forms like these: (1) taunt or mocking words (Deut. 28:37;
Isa. 14:4); (2) discourse (Job 27:1; 29:1); (3) instruction or lecture (Prov.
1:8–19; 2:1–22); (4) wisdom speech (Prov. 8:1–36); (5) brief sayings on
notes of instruction or warning which are drawn from experience (1
Kings 4:32; Ezek. 12:22–23; Prov. 10:1; 25:1). Two explanations of the
meaning of *māshāl* vie for scholarly support. It apparently derives
from a root that means either "to rule" or "to compare," both senses
are found in the Semitic consonants *mshl*. The common thread that
ties the various uses of *māshāl* together in the Old Testament seems to
be "instruction," "lesson."

If diligence in the study and composition are the theme of verse 9,
elegance and truthfulness are highlighted in verse 10. "*Acceptable*" is

the same word (Heb. *ḥēpheṣ*) translated *"pleasure"* or "delight" in 12:1. Here it apparently describes the compelling, artful, memorable, and catchy ways in which Koheleth sought to express himself. *"What was written"* is usually changed by translators and commentators to "and he wrote" by a slight alteration of the spelling (Heb. *wᵉkātûb*, a passive participle becomes *wᵉkātôb*, an active infinitive) suggested in some Hebrew manuscripts and in the Syriac and Latin versions. *"Upright"* means "most honest," an apt description of Koheleth's skill at seeing life as it is, not as we would like it to be.

The horizons of wisdom scholarship are widened in verse 11. Not just Koheleth's technique is in view but that of wise teachers in general. *"Words of the wise"* reminds us of the headings of the two collections of sayings in Proverbs 22:17 and 24:23. Both this title and *"many proverbs"* (v. 10) point to some continuity between the work of Koheleth and his colleagues and the canonical Book of Proverbs. Even where the later sages took issue with parts of the Solomonic collection, they still saw themselves as members of the same enterprise, trying to discern orderly patterns in life that could help their hearers make sense of God's ways in order to live successfully within them. Parallel to *"words of the wise"* are *"words of scholars"*—*"scholars"* is literally "masters of the collection," the group of sages who belonged to the guild responsible for gathering and transmitting wisdom teachings.

Their sayings are described in pointed terms: (1) *"goads"* seem to be cattle-prods like those mentioned in the old account of the tools that the Philistines sharpened for the Israelites in the days when Israel's technical capabilities were more primitive than their neighbors' (1 Sam. 13:21); (2) *"nails,"* like those used to prop up idols which the prophets mocked (Isa. 41:7; Jer. 10:4), were apparently "imbedded" or "implanted" (as *"well-driven"* may be translated) into sticks that could be used as prods. Together these terms describe the stinging pain that students endured in the course of learning how to forsake folly and follow wisdom.

The final clause of verse 11 has sparked considerable discussion. One question deals with what is *"given."* Is it the *"words"* or the *"nails"*? If it is the *"words"* then *"one Shepherd"* is often understood as God for whom the title (Ps. 23:1) is highly appropriate (so NIV, RSV, NASB) or else as a "teacher," whom some would identify as Solomon, the patron of Israel's wisdom literature. If *"given,"* however, refers to the *"nails"* then a literal shepherd is in view: "a shepherd uses these (nails or pegs) for the good of his flocks" (JB). The *"shep* clause, on this reading, is simply a description of the kind of individual being described and says nothing about the source of the *"words."* Grammatically the choice is a toss-up, since *"one"* can also serve as an indefinite article: *"a" "shepherd"* or *"some" "shepherd."* The larger question is whether the epilogue is pointing to a divine source for wisdom. Some scholars (Fox has written most emphatically on this) would make a clear distinction between wisdom writings and divine revelation. Others, among whom I count myself, would find it a highly appropriate claim for Jewish wisdom teachers to recognize the God of creation and history to be the ultimate source of what they learn and teach.

THE STUDENT'S DUTY

The subject shifts sharply at verse 12. It is directed to a specific student—*"my son,"* an address not used in the text of Koheleth but found frequently in Proverbs (1:8; 2:1; 3:1, etc.). The *"son"* is probably representative of all the individuals and even groups who will benefit from the text. The aim of 12:12–14 is to spell out the double obligation laid upon students who want to take wisdom teachings seriously and apply them in their own lives: (1) they are to follow the sage's advice (*"be admonished"*) to stick with the wisdom writings described in 12:9–11, including Koheleth's work and that of the other wise men whose collected sayings are in view (v. 11) and resist the temptation either to add to their inventory or to be distracted by the writings of others, presumably outside the circle; (2) they are to short-cut the labyrinth of opinion and center their lives in the fear of God, which they demonstrate by obedience to God's commandments, fully aware that God holds them accountable for all their conduct, even deeds that no one sees.

> 12 And further, my son, be admonished by these.
> Of making many books there is no end, and much
> study is wearisome to the flesh.
> 13 Let us hear the conclusion of the whole matter:
> Fear God and keep His commandments,
> For this is man's all.

> 14 For God will bring every work into judgment,
>   Including every secret thing,
>   Whether good or evil.
>
> *Eccles. 12:12–14*

The first command, *"be admonished"* or *"be warned"* (JB) echoes a word (Heb. *zāhar*) used in the description of a king so deprived of his senses by senility that he takes no one's advice, especially if that advice is a warning (4:13). The editor-teacher of the epilogue does not want the young students to fall in that trap. *"By these"* should probably be read as "more than these," where *"these"* refers to the sayings and collections of the wise in verse 11. The reason for the warning is stated in the second half of verse 12, which serves as the motive clause for the imperative verb. *"No end"* means "no purpose" not "no completion," while *"study"* is probably "meditation" or "pondering" (Heb. *lahag* seems to be a shortened form of *lahagôt* an infinitive of *hāgāh*, to "meditate aloud," Ps. 1:2, with the preposition *la* attached). *"To the flesh"* states the physical toll taken by too much intellectual endeavor, especially when it entails unreasonable complexities and subtleties.

The *"conclusion"* (lit. "end") is what the editor begs the students to give attention to (v. 13). After all, his aim like that of all wisdom teachers is to lead the young people to effective and successful paths in life. This aim he encapsulates in the admonition and motive clause with which the book concludes (vv. 13b–14). It is an impressive attempt to give them an all-embracing key to life. Its scope can be demonstrated by the repetition of the Hebrew *kōl*, in its various meanings, whether *"all," "whole,"* or *"every"*:

(1) The *"whole matter"*—everything pertaining to the topic is embraced in the conclusion;

(2) The *"whole duty of man"* should be retranslated *"the duty of every person"*—universal are the claims of the Creator; no one is exempt ("this applies to every person," NASB);

(3) *"every work"*—all human deeds face divine judgment;

(4) *"every secret thing"*—it may escape the eyes of others and be "hidden" (see 3:11; 8:17) even from those who do these works, but God will guarantee its just reward in his process of *"judgment"*; *"good"* and *"evil"* cover the whole range of human

conduct and remind us that *"judgment"* can have a brightly positive (Matt. 25:34–40) as well as a grimly negative side to it (Matt. 25:41–46).

A central question about the second half of the epilogue (vv. 12–14) is this: Is it a concise summary of Koheleth's teaching, as Jerome the great Latin commentator and translator found it to be? Or is it an expanded conclusion that embraces more than Koheleth had in mind and includes fidelity to the commands of the Torah (Pentateuch) along with the teachings of the wise.

"Fear God" can readily serve as an expression of the essence of Koheleth's words on human duty (3:14; 5:7; 7:18; 8:13). *"Keep His commandments,"* which helps interpret *"fear God,"* has no clear parallel in Koheleth. Rather, to many scholars it sounds like a call to give priority to the precepts of Moses and second place, only, to the words of the wise.

To be dogmatic on this question is not the course of prudence. But a couple of suggestions may be order. First, if we read *"proverbs"* (v. 9) and *"words of the wise"* or of *"scholars"* (v. 11) as including the teachings in the canonical Book of Proverbs, which in turn seem to have been influenced by the *"commandments"* of Deuteronomy (compare Deut. 4:40/Prov. 4:4; Deut. 4:1/Prov. 7:1–2), then *"commandments"* may apply to both law and wisdom (see Gerald Wilson's article in bibliography).

Second, and this is the approach toward which I lean, the commands that lace together the three sections of *Words of Advice* along with the implied and expressed commands of the *alternative conclusion* (2:24–26; 3:12–13, 22; 5:18–20; 8:15; 9:7–10) may define what the epilogue's editor understands by *"commandments,"* though Koheleth does not use the word (Heb. *miṣwôt*) in this sense.

Fearing God and keeping his commandments, then, may be understood in the light of what the Preacher has been saying throughout the book. God's will, he has told us, is that we not build our lives on wisdom, wealth, prestige, or lust. Rather, we should accept life as it is with its problems and mysteries and savor its modest pleasures as we can. To do this is to fear God and obey him. Grasping after more, or chafing because we have less, is futile. God reserves to himself the right to determine our lot; our response is to make the best of it. That is why Koheleth's theme from beginning to end is "take life's simple pleasures now."

The motive clause with its promise of fair and sweeping *"judgment"* is hard to reconcile with all Koheleth's reflections on the seeming arbitrariness of divine judgment (2:26; 3:17; 6:2; 7:15; 8:14; 9:2-3). At the same time, we should remember, as Ogden has pointed out, that Koheleth's own attitude toward judgment is ambivalent, not cut and dried. As puzzling to him as divine justice is, he is by no means ready to abandon the hope of it (8:12; 11:9). That drastic solution would have cut him loose from any moorings of trust in the God whose acts of grace make life livable for him.

The editor's terse words probably account for the seeming difference in outlook. The reflection form which is the backbone of Qoheleth's musings on the mysteries of justice lends itself to the weighing of issues. But the editor's aim was to furnish a brief and unforgettable slogan by which his students could live. Hence, he short-cut the ambivalence and moved with dispatch to the sum of the matter, as the brief imperatives enabled him to do. If in doing so, he rode roughshod over Koheleth's troubled musings, so be it! The Preacher had one aim in mind; the editor, another. One wrestled with exceptions; the other nailed down the rule. One raised questions that merited pondering; the other proposed a guideline for living. Even Koheleth himself could never have closed his book with the counsel, "Let justice be hanged!" If the editor, for the sake of clarity and brevity, had to come down on one side or the other, he came down on the right side. It is hard to believe that he would not have had Koheleth's support in this decision.

Epilogue: The Greater Wise Man

By now we have grasped the Preacher's and the editor's confirmation of it: most of what we lean on to bring meaning and dignity to our lives will burst like a bubble under our weight. We have to make the best of an awkward situation in which things cannot be depended on, and God seems not always available. What God gives we are to use, without expecting any more than the simple gifts of work to do, food to eat, and friends to love.

These creations of God offer more profit than all the more promising lures which compete for our attention. Two millennia and more have not proved the wise man wrong. Our modern quest to make sense of life has the same frenetic foolishness to it that the Preacher censured. The options which he discarded, we are still pursuing. His words about their vanity, their futility, are timely.

We need to heed them—and more. We need to hear the Master Sage, the Wiser than Solomon, sent by the Father with the keys to life in his hands. All interim solutions can be set aside. The fullness of truth has stood in our midst, given the lie to our errors, and pronounced passé all temporary solutions.

We have noted the editor's warning about *"many books"* and *"much study"* (12:12). Perhaps we would have heeded that alarm, if something else had not happened. Not another book, but a final Word. A Word that called all of us to find in study not weariness but rest: "... learn from Me, for I am gentle and lowly in heart, and you will find rest for your souls" (Matt. 11:29). His students, his disciples, numbering now in the hundreds of millions, have learned to live with joy in the midst of mystery and to face life's uncertainties with quiet confidence.

Introduction to
the Song of Solomon

"Do you understand what you are reading?" (Acts 8:30). Philip's question to the Ethiopian was posed in the context of Isaiah. It is also relevant to anyone who encounters the Song of Solomon. Who is speaking? What is the situation? How many persons are involved? Why is Solomon mentioned? What was the original purpose of the book? How did it find its way into the Bible? What does it mean to us today? How do we use it in our ministries? These and a host of other questions hover over our reading of the Song. Some introductory remarks about background, interpretation, and use will get us started on these queries, and the commentary itself will seek to add to our understanding.[1]

Background

The ways in which the rabbis discussed the Song suggest that its acceptance in the Jewish canon was not a routine matter. When Rabbi Akiba called the Song of Songs "the holy of holies," he was undoubtedly overstating the importance of the book to counter the opinions of other rabbis who were put off by its erotic frankness. One conclusion to be drawn from this discussion is that literal (or natural) interpretations of the Song were well-known in early Jewish tradition, prior, say, to A.D. 100. It is possible that the celebrative use of the Song in Jewish life helps to account for its place in Scripture. Marriage, with its full range of sexual activities, was heartily sponsored by the rabbis and commended, often in very specific detail, in the Talmud, the major collection of Jewish teaching on all activities of life.[2] Where rabbis had misgivings about the sacred character of the Song, it is likely that its connections with Solomon's name and its use as an allegory of God's love for Israel were reasons more than sufficient to encourage its inclusion among the holy writings. Its importance to Jewish worship is attested in its use as the scroll assigned for reading in the synagogues at Passover.

Date and *authorship* are questions that need not detain us long, chiefly because we have no solid information. Like Proverbs, the Song is a *collection*. Its love lyrics and wedding songs, many of which may date to Solomon's time (about 930 B.C.), have been transmitted through several centuries and modified by many influences. They were living songs used in the culture, as their Mesopotamian and Egyptian parallels demonstrate.[3] That very use preserved them, added to them, and altered them, as innovative persons improvised on their lines. Those improvisations were in turn applauded and passed along. The dates of the individual segments, then, may range over almost the entire length of Israel's history. Who knows how old the oldest may be? Love songs and weddings feasts certainly antedate the history of writing and were in use in the early centuries of civilization.

The collection conserved for us in the Song, lovingly and skillfully assembled and edited, dates, perhaps, from about the time of the Jewish Exile (about 550 B.C.) or a century or so later. For the significance of Solomon's name in the Song, see chapter 1. As is frequently the case with editors or collectors of Old Testament works, we have no clue as to the identity of the scribe responsible for setting out these songs in their final form and order. As part of the Hebrew and Christian canon, the book has been received as a portion of the "all scripture" whose inspiration, authority, and profit we affirm (2 Tim. 3:16–7), though we may not be able to describe the process by which the Spirit brought the book into being.

Interpretation

The tack followed in the commentary is to treat the Song of Solomon (sometimes called Canticles, from its Latin name) as a series of six major poems (see Outline) put together in a sequence that builds from anticipation (Poems I–II) to consummation (Poem III) to aftermath (Poems IV–VI). The nuptial festivities themselves seem to center in Poems III and V, with Poems I–II serving as introduction, Poem VI as conclusion, and Poem IV as interlude. No true plot is discernible, only a sense of movement or direction. The characters seem to remain constant: 1) a woman who begins and ends the Song and is cherished as *bride* in the middle of it; 2) a man, probably a shepherd, who first is longed for and then is present to respond to the call for love; 3) a group of companions, sometimes nameless and other times labeled *daughters of Jerusalem,* to whom are credited brief comments or questions that intimate their support of the love relationship and their participation in the marriage celebrations.

This reading of the Song shies away from any *allegorical* handling of the text, since it contains no clue as to hidden or spiritual meanings of its various characters, components, or details. Even a *typological* approach that sees the Song as an expression of divine love for Israel or for the church without trying to find deep mysteries in the language goes beyond what the book itself warrants; the New Testament, which does not quote or refer to it, gives no support to attempts to spiritualize the book.[4] *Dramatic* theories are ruled out both because of the shadowy nature of the plot, if there really is one, and because the most prevalent of these theories complicates the situation unreasonably by adding a third figure, Solomon, and imposing on the poems a triangular shape that has the two men (shepherd and king) vying for the woman's hand. Attempts to connect the poetry with pagan *liturgical rites,* fairly common in the ancient Middle East, where the marital union of god and goddess are featured in mythological literature, seem to be refuted by the Israelite abhorrence of the fertility cult and its rituals. A recent explanation of the poems as descriptive of *funeral feasts* in which drinking and lovemaking were featured as a way of affirming life's continuity and joy in the face of death seems to be forced on the Song rather than derived from it. Any one of these approaches may shed light on a passage or two, but none of them can offer a reading of the book as consistent, sustained, and direct as the one we have followed, which has to support it an increasing consensus of both European and American scholars, though, of course, there is a great deal of variety as to the meanings of words and the understanding of details.

The best clues as to the message and movement of the book are the *types of songs* of which it is comprised. The recognition of the literary form has largely determined the outline of each of the six poems as I have understood them. Their use and significance is dealt with throughout the commentary. A brief listing of them here may be helpful.

- *Descriptive Songs* (he describes her: 4:1–7; 6:4–7; she describes him: 5:10–16; daughters of Jerusalem describe her: 7:1–5) portray the beauty and strength of the partners as part of the stimulation for the lovemaking of marriage.
- *Self-descriptions* were used by the woman (1) to disclaim her worthiness and in turn call attention to the fact that her lover had chosen her (1:5–6; 2:1); (2) to boast in her chastity and maturity (8:10).
- *Songs of admiration* focus on the loved one's dress, ornamentation, or general attractiveness rather than on the physical attributes (1:9–11, 12–17; 2:1–3; 4:9–11).
- *Songs of yearning* express one lover's ardent desire for the other, both when they are apart (1:2–4; 2:5–6; 8:13) and when they are together (7:6–9a; 8:1–3, 6–7).
- *Songs of invitation* voice a strong request for the loved one to come and join the partner in intimacy (he: 4:8; she: 2:17; 4:16; 8:14).
- *Formula of mutual possession* is used by the woman to indicate the depth and commitment of the relationship in which each belongs to the other (2:16; 6:3; 7:10).
- *Search narratives* describe what may be dreams, in which the woman leaves her room to seek her lover in the streets, once with success (3:1–4), once with failure (5:2–7).
- *Calls to oath* pledge the daughters of Jerusalem to do the urgent bidding of the woman, whether in refusing to stimulate love before the occasion is right (2:7; 3:5; 8:4) or in telling the absent husband of his bride's lovesickness (5:8).
- *Teasing songs* catch the banter between the lovers as they express their eagerness to be together (1:7–8; 2:15) and add notes of playfulness to the relationship.
- *Boasting songs* convey the pride that the lover has in his partner (6:9–10; 8:11–12) or that she has in her purity, maturity, and influence (8:10).

The combining, placing, and repeating of these elements give the song its power, meaning, and unity. The various poems and narratives are stitched together with an artistry that has provided inspiration to poets and stimulation to lovers through the centuries. For an illustration of this artistry, look at the *game* played between the woman and the daughters of Jerusalem in Poem IV (5:2–6:3), which seems to form an interlude to the nuptial feast.

The *literary images*, though sometimes strange to western ears, are another essential contributor to the Song's effectiveness. Tested by time and refined by centuries of use in thousands of festive occasions, they distill the essence of the lovers' admiration for each other and infuse the Song with a grace and beauty worthy of the passion and commitment that God desires to be part of every marriage. Finally, in our efforts to capture the force and intent of the Song, we should be alert to the use of *catch-phrases* and *catch-words*. The final composition was achieved by some one with an eye and ear to repetition delicately used. The pet names of the lovers, *my beloved* and *my love* (or darling), the uses of *garden, vineyard, fruit, wine, pomegranates, Lebanon, mountains, tower,* names of various *spices,* verbs like *catch* (seize, hold) and *awaken*—these are recurring terms whose repeated use binds the book together in a remarkable unity of mood and message. They also trigger reminders of their previous appearances, with the force of a signal or code that conveys a depth of connotation gathered from the previous contexts and imparted to each new occurrence.

Use

Preaching on the Song in most congregational settings is difficult. The language is so frank and the theme so specialized that the messages would probably not minister effectively to the entire church. Younger children, persons recently divorced, older men and women who are single may find the love motifs either puzzling, embarrassing, or painful. An obvious exception to this observation would be the use of portions of the Song, for example the *formula of mutual possession* (2:16; 6:3; 7:10) or the *song of yearning* in 8:6–7, as texts for wedding homilies.

Teaching the book to target audiences is another matter. Couples' classes or retreats, groups of collegians, high school clubs—these all provide occasion to treat human sexuality and marital love with a candor appropriate to the participants and the occasion. Our sexuality is related to our creation in God's image as male and female. It lies at the heart of what we are—boys and girls, women and men. It has been so broken by the fall of Adam and Eve that, since then, each of us has had difficulty sorting out clearly what it means to be a sexual as well as an intellectual and spiritual being. My personal experience, growing up in a devout, actively Christian home where the implications of my sexuality were not part of the curriculum, has made me sensitive to the church's need to deal with this crucial issue. Contact through the years with scores of churches, hundreds of pastors, and thousands of students has only confirmed this sensitivity. Communicators of biblical faith will do well to review their own performance in this matter. The Song is at hand to help.

Counseling offers abundant opportunity for the use of the pictures of wholesome sexuality displayed in the Song of Solomon. Mixed-up teenagers, eager engaged couples, anxious married persons, people hung-up on their sexuality or too "hang-loose" about it—these all can do with grounding in the fundamental realities of why God made us as sexual beings, why our sexuality fouls up so readily, and what we can do about it. The insights of the Song are indispensable to our approaches to the personal needs of the people who look to us for help.

Sexual promiscuity, sexual abuse, sexual confusion, and sexually transmitted diseases have reached epidemic proportions. The cry for sex education, beginning at an early age, is voiced ever louder and in ever more influential circles. The church must hear and be part of the answer. At stake is the true meaning of our humanity. For that, Christ is the only adequate answer. Part of Christ's answer will come to his people through the Song of Songs.[5]

Its *themes* provide balance and insight in an area where we are unsteady of foot and dull of eye. Among the many that may be singled out, these four have been useful to me and will appear more than once in the discussion of the title and six poems of the Song.

Love is mutual. The book features two people with equal commitment to the pursuit of its fullness. The woman's eagerness is matched by the man's delight. Without openly saying so, the partners have imbibed of the nectar of Genesis 1–2: sex is for enjoyment, for covenant, and for procreation. None of those God-given purposes is truly achieved without mutuality. Neither spouse does bargaining or contracting with the other. Halfway for each is not commitment enough. Both parties look for ways to say yes to each other's needs and desires. Both own the responsibility to support the other. In so doing, both demonstrate the truth of the divine covenant that yokes God to his people, Christ to his church.

Love is exclusive. Marital love is what the Song celebrates. The ceremonial settings of Poems III and V should be proof enough of this. We are not dealing with extramarital dalliance, which would not evoke the cheers of the daughters of Jerusalem and the other companions. Nor are we viewing premarital experimentation, against which the culture would have closely guarded, as the final chapter of the book testifies. No effort is spared, no literary device is left idle in making clear that the partners are pledged fully to each other and only to each other. *Metaphors* of exclusiveness (4:12–5:1; 4:4; 7:5), *vows* of exclusiveness (2:16; 6:3; 7:10), a *game* of exclusiveness (5:2–6:3), a *test* of exclusiveness (8:8–9), *yearning* for exclusiveness (8:6–7), *boasts* of exclusiveness (she: 8:10; he: 8:11–2)—these combine to form a theme so dominant that it can rightly be called the main melody of the poems. When we hear this melody sung in the context of the entire Bible we know that the tune was learned from the God of the covenant who bound himself not to leave or forsake his people. Fragments of that love song are found in Hosea 14:4–7, where Israel's Husband promises love, shelter, fruit, and healing to his bride in phrases akin to snatches of Solomon's Song. Whether on divine lips or human, it is the music of covenant loyalty, and its prominent theme is faithfulness.

Love is total. Marriage is to a person, not to a body or a brain, not to a cook or a breadwinner, not to a bank account or a security blanket. Love needs to remain bright even when affection, admiration, and approval grow temporarily dim. If love is misdirected to a physical attribute or a behavioral pattern, it finds excuse to wane when these things change. It is total when it is fixed on the whole person of the partner. The Song sings of a *total regard* that each has for the other. The relationship goes far beyond their mutual attraction. They long for each other's voices as well as bodies. They are firm friends as well as passionate lovers. They have made to each other a *total commitment* that fire cannot melt, that bribery cannot dissolve. They find their completion (Heb. *shālôm,* peace) in each other. Compared to this, all other commitments are not total but partial, except our commitment to God. But even that commitment is expressed most consistently and clearly in our covenant with each other.

Love is beautiful. It deserves to be expressed in graceful language. It has the poise to center in the beauty of the other person, not in one's own. It has eyes to see inner beauty even where outward beauty is lacking or fading. It thrives in lovely settings where the environment mirrors the quality of the love. It behaves attractively and hence imitates the beauty of God, which is the "beauty of holiness," the unique beauty of One who cares about his own and always expresses that care in righteousness and goodness.

But enough of these program notes! It is time for the concert to begin. We are ready to hear the melodies and harmonies of the best of songs. Let them sing for themselves.

NOTES

1. For further information on the background and interpretation of the Song, see W. S. LaSor, D. A. Hubbard, and F. W. Bush, *Old Testament Survey* (Grand Rapids: Eerdmans, 1982), 601–610. The best recent commentaries are these: R. Gordis, *The Song of Songs;* H. J. Schonfield, *The Song of Songs;* M. Pope, *The Song of Songs;* G. L. Carr, *The Song of Solomon;* Michael V. Fox, *The Song of Songs and the Ancient Egyptian Love Songs;* and Roland E. Murphy. *The Song of Songs.* See the Bibliography.

2. Background information on the marital and sexual patterns of the Middle East, of Judaism, and of the Bible is found in the following: R. Patai, *Sex and Family in the Bible and the Middle East* (Garden City, N.Y.: Doubleday, 1959; R. Gordis, *Sex and the Family in the Jewish Tradition* (New York: Burning Bush Press, 1967); W. G. Cole, *Sex and Love in the Bible* (New York: Association Press, 1959).

3. Roland Murphy (see note 1 above) offers a very useful summary of the parallels between the Song and ancient Middle Eastern love lyrics, pp. 41–57. The Song's Egyptian counterparts receive generous attention in Michael V. Fox's book (note 1 above).

4. A recent commentary by Raymond Jacques Tournay, *Word of God, Song of Love: A Commentary on the Song of Songs,* trans., J. Edward Crowley (Mahwah, N.J.: Paulist Press, 1988), uses the principle of "double meaning" to find in the Song both a picture of Solomon's marriage to Pharaoh's daughter and a lyrical longing for the Messiah whose love is the hope of Jerusalem and the community restored from exile. E. Ann Matter, *The Voice of My Beloved: The Song of Songs in Western Medieval Christianity* (Philadelphia: University of Pennsylvania Press, 1990), gives a superb summary of the allegorical interpretation that flourished in the Middle Ages.

5. Help in the application of the Song to pastoral ministry may be found in S. C. Glickman, *A Song for Lovers,* and J. C. Dillow, *Solomon on Sex;* see the Bibliography.

An Outline of the Song of Solomon

Title: The Royal Relationship: 1:1
Poem I. Longing and Discovery: 1:2–2:7
    A. Song of Yearning for the Absent Lover (Beloved): 1:2–4
    B. Self–description of Modesty (Beloved): 1:5–6
    C. Teasing Dialogue Imaginatively Seeking an Encounter (Beloved; Lover): 1:7–8
    D. Song Admiring Her Worth and Beauty (Lover): 1:9–11
    E. Song of Admiration in Reply (Beloved): 1:12–14
    F. Song of Admiration in Dialogue (Lover; Beloved; Lover; Beloved): 1:15–2:4
    G. Song of Yearning for Intimacy (Beloved): 2:5–6
    H. Call for Patience with Love's Course (Beloved): 2:7
Poem II. Invitation, Suspense, Response: 2:8–3:5
    A. Description of the Lover's Approach and Invitation (Beloved): 2:8–14
    B. Teasing Response Turned Serious by Affirmation of Mutual Possession (Beloved): 2:15–16
    C. Invitation to Intimacy (Beloved): 2:17
    D. Description of Frustration and Fulfillment (Beloved): 3:1–4
    E. Call for Patience with Love's Course (Beloved): 3:5
Poem III. Ceremony and Satisfaction: 3:6–5:1
    A. Dramatic and Admiring Description of the Groom's Arrival (Beloved): 3:6–11
    B. Description of the Bride's Beauty: (Lover): 4:1–7
    C. Invitation Song to Bride (Lover): 4:8
    D. Admiration Song to Bride (Lover): 4:9–15
    E. Invitation Song to Groom (Beloved): 4:16
    F. Song of Eager Response (Lover): 5:1a
    G. Song of Encouragement (Daughters of Jerusalem): 5:1b
Poem IV. Frustration and Delight: 5:2–6:3
    A. Report of a Vexing Dream (Beloved): 5:2–7
    B. Call for Urgent Help (Beloved): 5:8

C. Teasing Question (Daughters of Jerusalem): 5:9
D. Description of Lover's Beauty (Beloved): 5:10–16
E. Teasing Question (Daughters of Jerusalem): 6:1
F. Response of Delight and Commitment (Beloved): 6:2–3

Poem V. Pomp and Celebration: 6:4–8:4

A. A Descriptive Song with Touches of a Boast (Lover): 6:4–10
B. A Fantasy Experience of Separation (Beloved): 6:11–12
C. A Plea to Return (Daughters of Jerusalem): 6:13a
D. A Teasing Reply in Question Form (Beloved): 6:13b
E. A Description of the Dancing Woman (Daughters of Jerusalem): 7:1–5
F. A Yearning Song for Intimacy (Lover): 7:6–9
G. An Invitation to Fulfillment (Beloved): 7:10–8:3
H. A Call for Patience with Love's Course (Beloved): 8:4

Poem VI. Passion and Commitment: 8:5–14

A. A Question Signaling the Couples' Return (Daughters of Jerusalem): 8:5a
B. A Seductive Reminder of Love's Continuity (Beloved): 8:5b
C. A Yearning Song of Chastity (Beloved): 8:6–7
D. A Test of Chastity (Beloved, speaking for her brothers, vv. 8–9): 8:8–10
E. A Boast of Chastity (Beloved): 8:11–12
F. A Yearning Song to Hear Her Voice (Lover): 8:13
G. An Invitation Song to Take His Fill of Love (Beloved): 8:14

CHAPTER ONE

Title: The Royal Relationship

Song of Solomon 1:1

The Bible is about marriage. At the beginning it pictures the union of the first woman and the first man. It was a union accompanied by shouts of delight: *"This is now bone of my bones and flesh of my flesh"* (Gen. 2:23). It was a union solemnized with a binding command: *"Therefore a man shall leave his father and his mother and be joined to his wife, and they shall become one flesh"* (Gen. 2:24). It was a union marked by attractive innocence: *"And they were both naked, the man and his wife, and were not ashamed"* (Gen. 2:25).

The Bible is about marriage. At the end it depicts the consummation of all that God intended, as he guided the course of history with a redeeming hand, in terms of a marriage celebration:

> Let us be glad and rejoice and give Him glory, for the marriage of the Lamb has come, and His wife has made herself ready.
>
> And to her it was granted to be arrayed in fine linen, clean and bright, for the fine linen is the righteous acts of the saints.
>
> Then he said to me, "Write: 'Blessed are those who are called to the marriage supper of the Lamb.'"
>
> *Rev. 19:7–9*

The Bible is about marriage. Throughout its movement from beginning to end, it highlights its central themes with metaphors of marriage. Israel is Yahweh's spouse, bound to him as he is to her in covenant commitment, as Hosea's profound and painful experience helps us to understand. Isaiah (62:4) looks to a day when Judah and Jerusalem, called Forsaken and Desolate in judgment, will be renamed My Delight is in her (Heb. *Hepzibah*) and Married (Heb. *Beulah*) to signal their salvation. Jesus' presence as the Bridegroom fills the pages of the New Testament with ribbons and rice, as he encourages his friends to enjoy the party while he is yet with them (Matt. 9:14–15; 25:1–13; John 3:29). The apostle Paul saw our human marriages as demonstrations of *the* marriage of Christ to the church (Eph. 5:21–33).

The Bible is about marriage. And at its heart the Spirit of God has placed a collection of wedding songs. They contain no liturgy of worship, no statutes or commandments, no hymn of a psalmist, no oracle of a prophet, no vision of a seer. The are love songs pure and simple, bursting with passion, bright with desire, explosive with longing for physical love. As such, they are different from any other part of the Old Testament. From Genesis 4 and 10 to the end of Malachi, sex is for begetting. Procreation is its aim, and the perpetuation of Abraham's seed in fulfillment of God's promise is its goal. We are led to laugh and weep with Sarah as she waits month by month for Isaac's conception. We "amen" barren Hannah's stammering prayers in Shiloh's shrine as she pleads for a son to surrender to the Lord's service. In those stories we find no clues of the quality of the relationship between husband and wife; we ask no questions about romantic feelings, erotic delights.

But the Song of Songs is different. Here sex is for joy, for union, for relationship, for celebration. Its lyrics contain no aspirations to pregnancy, no anticipations of parenthood. The focus is not on progeny to assure the continuity of the line but on passion to express the commitment to covenant between husband and wife. "Eros without shame" was how Karl Barth described the tone of the Song. He saw it as a poetic commentary on the wide-eyed wonder with which the first man and woman admired each other as they stood face to face, naked and unashamed (Gen. 2:25).

That relationship in Eden was a royal one. That first pair came untarnished from the hand of God, humanity as it ought to be. And they shared the Creator's hegemony over the rest of creation. The man named the animals as a symbol of his regency. Made in the divine image, male and female, that pair enjoyed dominion over the garden in which they had been planted. Their communion with their Maker and with each other modeled what human life should look like. All of that is found in the first two chapters of Genesis. Then came chapter 3, with the vile serpent, the rebellious eating of the fruit, the guilty hiding from God, the blaming of each other, and the shameful clutching at leaves to cover their nakedness. From that hour to this, the human family has struggled to cope with its sexuality. Brokenness not wholeness has been our lot. And the forms of that brokenness have been legion: priggishness or prudishness that shuns sexuality at worst and tolerates it at best; perversion or exploitation that takes pleasure in the pain of others and treats sexual relationships as contests to be won or territory to be conquered.

The Bible, which cares so much about sexuality and marriage, amply documents how bad the situation became after Eve and Adam violated their God-mandated responsibilities and, in the process, corrupted the meaning of their sexuality. Their very maleness and femaleness in some sense reflected their relationship to God. They were made in his image, male and female (Gen. 1:27). Their capacity for strong interpersonal bonding with each other was a reflection of their union and communion with God. When by disobedience they violated that heavenly union with their Lord, they became disoriented and confused in their earthly relationships to each other. And they passed that confusion on to all their offspring.

The tragedies at Sodom and Gomorrah (Gen. 18:16–19:29) or at Gibeah (Judg. 19) document the depths to which broken sexuality can sink. The command against adultery built into the heart of the Decalogue is a reminder both of the sanctity of the marriage covenant and our human proneness to play fast and loose with it. The royal relationship, established by divine blessing at the beginning, was capable of almost infinite forms of degradation once its primary purpose to mirror God's eternal love for his people was obscured by lust and license.

The Bible is about marriage—not only marriage that is pure and joyful at the beginning and ending of the story but marriage that needs redeeming along the way. No part of Scripture sheds more light on what redeemed marital love can mean than the Song of Songs. Its very title lifts it above the lurid, the lustful, even the romantic and sets it apart from all other lyrics in the Old Testament, which contains a magnificent collection of poetic artistry.

> 1:1 The song of songs, which is Solomon's.
>
> *Song of Sol. 1:1*

The Bible is about *singing* as well as marriage. Biblical faith is personal. It calls for our engagement in it as persons; it grips our lives at their center and evokes a response from the depth of our beings. There is no way better for us to voice that total response, that full commitment to the truth of who God is and what he has done, than by singing. The great historical breakthroughs in the salvation of Israel were celebrated in song. Just listen to Moses and Miriam at the edge of the Red Sea (Exod. 15). Hear the Lord's triumphs sounded by Deborah and Barak at the defeat of the Canaanites (Judg. 5). Give ear to the epic praise of David on the heels of his rescue from the hands of his enemies, including Saul (2 Sam. 22). Great songs all! Personal and powerful.

Biblical faith is imaginative as well as personal. Our imaginations are gifts of God, the result of our creation in his image. Through our imaginations we unlock the mysteries of God's ways as we contemplate the word-pictures God has given us of himself—parent, judge, husband, farmer, shepherd. As God's Spirit activates our imaginations, corrects their foolish or wicked tendencies, strips them of their dullness, heals their blindness, we begin to grasp the reality of God's person and activities through the poetry in which he has described himself in Scripture and in which others have described God in the hymnody of our Christian faith.

Singing opens our eyes and ears to what we have not earlier understood. It draws out of us responses of which we have been previously incapable. It heads us into the heart of wonders and mysteries which only poetry is capable of capturing. The author of the Song of Songs knew this and deliberately called the attention of his people to it by naming his collection of love lyrics *"The Song of Songs."* The title is superlative like king of kings (Dan. 2:37). It means the best of songs, the outstanding song.

A haughty title that seems to be, in a book that specializes in magnificent poetry. The Targum, which translated and interpreted the Old Testament into Aramaic, took seriously this claim to superiority, listed ten great songs, from Adam's thanksgiving for pardon to the song of the exiles returned to their land, and concluded: "Ten songs were uttered in this world. This song was the best of them all."[1]

THE BEST SINGERS

The Song of Songs has an outstanding cast: a woman, usually called the *beloved;* a man, referred to as the *lover;* a group of women friends known as the *daughters of Jerusalem.* The entire scenario can be understood as the words of these two persons and the accompanying group. More complicated lists of *dramatis personae* are sometimes suggested by translators and commentators, but the text itself can best be handled by assigning its words to this three-part cast, although there are a few places where it is not easy to tell whether the man or the woman is speaking. We shall note these places along the way.

The singers are remarkable. Their literary flair, shaped in part by the conventions of a culture which valued love and gave attention to preserving and transmitting expressions of it in elegant, vivid, and sonorous language, would be sufficient to warrant the superlative title of the Song. They are fine singers.

But beyond that, they are fine persons who do the singing. The woman is honest and forthright in her declarations of love. Her yearnings and frustrations she relates to her friends, along with her joys and anticipations. Her modest, even self-effacing descriptions of her person (1:5–6; 2:1) actually enhance her attractiveness and help to evoke the florid and graphic language with which the lover extols her beauty (4:1–7; 6:4–9; 7:1–9). He, in turn, is kind, considerate, encouraging, affirming, and responsive, with no trace of machismo or need to dominate. The daughters of Jerusalem are persons we would all enjoy as friends. They are supportive of the lovers, cheering them on as they enter the delights of total intimacy (5:1). They are trustworthy in their commitment to protect the leisure and privacy which lovemaking deserves (2:7; 3:5; 8:4). They are full of ready humor as they gently tease their eager friend about the merits of her lover (5:9–6:1). The best of songs merits its name; it has the best of singers.

THE BEST SUBJECT

In the Song, *love* is mapped out as the road to royalty. The whole Solomonic motif seems to have as its point the celebration of the elegance, the dignity, the nobility of love. It is the regal virtue. Those who practice it are engaged in a royal relationship.

The final phrase of the Title sets the tone for the book: *"which is Solomon's."* The Hebrew wording is capable of several meanings: *authorship*—written by Solomon (see Introduction); *dedication*—belonging to or written for Solomon; *character*—composed in the manner or

271

style of Solomon; *subject*—dealing with Solomon. The approach of this Commentary leans toward the last two interpretations of the phrase. The Solomonic tone and the references to royal and palatial settings ought not to be taken literally, as though Solomon, David's son and king of Israel, were a chief character in the book. To see him as such almost inevitably calls for a triangular plot in which a shepherd–lover competes with Solomon for the affections of the beloved. The weaknesses of this theory are listed in the Introduction.

The royal language with which the Song is laced plays two main roles. First, it glorifies the lovers and their love by treating them as though they were kings and queens, basking in the elegance of each other and of their noble life together: the beloved calls her man the king (1:4, 12; 3:9, 11) and he echoes that language of himself (7:6); the woman's strength and beauty call for regal language as the only argot adequate to depict them—*"my filly among Pharaoh's chariots"* (1:9), *"your neck is like the tower of David"* (4:4), *"beautiful as Tirzah* (the ancient capital of the Northern Kingdom), *lovely as Jerusalem"* (6:4), *"queens and concubines* (saw her) *and they praised her"* (6:9), *"O prince's daughter"* (7:1); the beloved's name Shulamite (6:13) may refer to her hometown or may be a play on Solomon's name— *Solomoness*, a coy way of featuring her queenliness. Second, the use of Solomon's name sets up a contrast between the complexity, affluence, and polygamous character of his life as described in 1 Kings 1–11 and the simplicity, rusticity, and monogamy of the couple's lifestyle in the Song (6:8–9; 8:11–12). Their persistent and singular commitment to each other was truly more royal than a king's opulent profligacy.

The regal character of marital love was not just an ancient idea. It has persisted through the centuries and is reflected in our contemporary marriage customs. On the morning of the wedding day a modern bride may make her nuptial preparation clad in sweat shirt and cut–off jeans and crowned with curlers as elaborate as a television antenna. But at wedding time, there she is with flowing gown, graceful veil and train, delicate tiara. Every one rises as she enters the church to be greeted by a groom immaculate in tails and white tie. The next day, the sweat shirts and cut-offs reappear, but for those shining moments as they basked in the admiration and goodwill of family and friends, they were royalty. Biblical lovers know that and aim to make those moments last a lifetime. The best of songs is rightly named; its subject is the royal relationship—love strong as death and too fiery for any stream to quench (8:6–7).

THE BEST SETTING

The Song is superb because the best of singers, two lovers and their friends, celebrate the best of subjects, love, in the best of settings, a joyful covenant of mutual commitment to the lasting welfare of each other. The formula of mutual possession

My beloved is mine, and I am his.
2:16; 6:3; 7:10

signals the binding nature of the relationship to which each partner is permanently pledged. The context breathes no hint of momentary dalliances, of fleeting liaisons, of fickle self-indulgences. Neither the beloved nor the lover has a roving eye. Whether together in full enjoyment or apart in fervent longing, their thoughts are fixed on the beauty, the character, and the passion of the other.

Indeed, the setting of the Song is so sacred that Rabbi Akiba (c. A.D. 100) honored it in extravagant language: "for all the Writings are holy, but the Song of Songs are the Holy of Holies."[2] Though the Rabbi's original intent was to suppress all the arguments raised against its presence in the Hebrew Canon, his intuition was sound. A document that elevates the beauty and purity of marital love is surely charged with holiness. So idyllic is the mood of the Song that it sounds like a return to Eden. Nothing foul, vile, filthy, nor selfish tarnishes the scene. The fall that triggered such lust and fear and perversion in our human attitudes to sexuality seems suspended. Sin appears to be excluded. What once was, what again can be, in the pure desire of one partner for another, is described.

God's name is absent from the entire setting. But who would deny that his presence is strongly felt? From whom come such purity and passion? Whose creative touch can ignite hearts and bodies with such a capacity to bring unsullied delight to another? Who kindled the senses that savor every sight, touch, scent, taste, and sound of a loved one? Whose very character is comprised of the love that is the central subject of the Song? None of this is to allegorize either the minute details or the main sense of the book. It is about *human* love at its best. But behind it, above it, and through it, the Song, as part of the divinely ordered repertoire of Scripture, is a paean of praise to the Lord of creation who makes possible such exquisite love and to the Lord of redemption who demonstrated love's fullness on a cross.

Lovers have always known that song was the only adequate expression for feelings so strong, delight so high, commitment so deep. Only poetry with its combination of excess and austerity, of release and discipline can capture the aspirations and frustrations of love. Overwhelmed by our desire to give ourselves away for the sake of another and to receive from that other more than we dare ask, we do not derive a formula, concoct a recipe, recite a ritual, draw a map, lay out a graph. We sing a song. In the Song treasured in Holy Writ, we sing the best song possible.

NOTES

1. For translation, see M. Pope, *Song of Songs*, p. 296 (see Bibliography for full publishing information).

2. Cited by R. Gordis, *The Song of Songs*, p. 1 (see Bibliogaphy). The original quotation was from the Mishnah, Yad. 3:5.

CHAPTER TWO

Poem I: Longing and Discovery

Song of Solomon 1:2–2:7

The *woman* is the star of the Song. While the title, 1:1, features Solomon in a way that we have hesitantly tried to identify, the poems themselves, beginning with this one, make clear that something like two-thirds of the singing is done by the *woman*. Here, as frequently, she takes the initiative in expressing her desires for her lover's companionship and the discoveries she will enjoy when longing becomes fulfillment. In my reading, which differs somewhat from the NKJV by not giving as much prominence to the daughters of Jerusalem, seventeen of the verses in Poem I are uttered by her, and six by her lover.

She speaks of and to him in verses 2–4, and even more directly in verse 7, where she prompts his answer in verse 8 and his song of admiration in verses 9–11. And she quickly recounts her own admiration with symbols and imagery that intensify the erotic mood (vv. 12–14). His brief lines of passionate response (v. 15) are followed by her echo which pictures not only his beauty but the opulent setting of their wooded trysting place (vv. 16–17).

Her modest, even deprecating, description of herself (2:1) sparks a compliment from her lover that singles her out as a beauty unique among other young women (2:2) and sets the stage for a parallel complement from her (2:3) that leads to her strongest words of desire, as she imagines herself in intimate, private, fellowship with him, overshadowed by his lovemaking (2:4), desperate for food to enhance her pleasure (2:5), and enwrapped in his embrace (2:6).

Silently present in my reading of this Poem have been the *daughters of Jerusalem,* friends of the bride who also admire her lover but support and protect the couple with the ardor and tenacity of true friendship. They do this with a humor that lifts the situation above the maudlin. To them, toward the beginning (vv. 5–6), the woman describes herself as lacking the unscorched beauty which city girls, reared inside shady walls, might exhibit. Her rusticity does not destroy her comeliness. It reflects, rather, her rural upbringing which contrasts sharply with that of her urbane friends, whose title bears the name of Judah's proud capital. And at the end the love-sick woman trusts their friendship so much that she puts them under oath to treasure and guard the intimate encounter which she so eagerly anticipates (2:7). Their time to speak will come later (cf. 5:1, 9; 6:1, 10, 13; 8:5). For now it is enough that the poem introduce them for the vital role that they play in addressing the woman and being addressed by her (1:5; 2:7; 3:5, 8, 11; 5:16; 8:4). The royal relationship of total love is not just a matter of two people committed to that bond. It must have as well a circle of confidants who believe in the covenant that is being planned and consummated. The daughters of Jerusalem are those confidants in the Song.

Poem I, then, introduces the *dramatis personae,* the key players, and highlights the beautiful outspokenness, the passionate intensity of the *woman.* It also introduces the strong but soft-spoken *man* who is quite willing to yield center stage, for now, in order to spotlight his beloved's warmth and beauty and succinctly to assure her that her love is more than reciprocated. And it undergirds the whole encounter with the support of friends whose well wishing is displayed by their silent, smiling presence.

Whether the conversations between the lovers are actual or imagined in this poem makes little difference. Each is giving vent to strong yearning and binding troth. One of the beauties of covenant love is that it thrives and grows in the absence of the loved one as much as in the presence. The love encounter in this poem seems to be fantasy more than reality. The proposed setting for it is remote (1:7–8) and rustic (1:16–17). Yet the daughters of Jerusalem are on hand at the poem's end to promote and protect the rendezvous (2:7).

Yearning for the Absent Lover

2 Let him kiss me with the kisses of his mouth—
3 For your love is better than wine.

> Because of the fragrance of your good oint-
> ments,
> Your name is ointment poured forth;
> Therefore the virgins love you.
> 4 Draw me away!
> We will run after you.
> The king has brought me into his chambers.
> We will be glad and rejoice in you.
> We will remember your love more than wine.
> Rightly do they love you.
>
> *Song of Sol. 1:2–4*

The *woman*, who may also be called the Shulammite (6:13), begins the poem with her *song of yearning*. Three characteristics of the yearning shine through the text.

First, it is specific in its object. It is not a longing for a lover in general nor for a random experience of love to lift boredom and furnish thrills. It is a deep and glad cry for the one to whom she is committed, whom she mentions at first as *"him,"* a clue that he is absent and unavailable, and then addresses as *you,* a sign that she imagines him to be present or rehearses what she would say if he were. Her imagination peaks when she pictures herself already in the lover's chamber (v. 4), where she expresses her unbridled joy in him and his lovemaking.

Second, her yearning is passionate in its quality. It craves expression in *"kisses"* (cf. 8:1). Proverbs 27:6 provides a sharp contrast to the sincerity of the woman's wish in 1:2: "but the kisses of an enemy are deceitful." This lover had no fear of such deceit. His beloved treasured everything about him as her exuberant language signaled. His company left her more heady than *"wine"* (1:2, 4; cf. 2:4; 4:10; 5:1; 7:10; 8:2), which, when not abused (cf. the warnings in Prov. 23:29–35; 31:4–5), enhanced and enriched both public celebrations and intimate trysts (Prov. 9:2, 5), and more exhilarated than the *"fragrance of your good ointments"* (lit. "oils"). This phrase possibly refers to the use of expensive perfumed oils or lotion (Amos 6:6), especially welcome in the hot climate of Palestine, but may be an even more erotic reference to the scent of his body aroused for love. The latter interpretation may find some support in *"your name"* (v. 3), meaning here "your entire person" (cf. 1 Sam. 25:25), which is compared to some rare perfume (Heb. *tûraq* is more apt to be a noun or adjective describing

277

the ointment than a verbal form, *"poured forth"*) whose precise nature remains unknown. A hint of the royal motif may be found in the word-play of *shemen* ("oil") and *shēm* (*"name,"* "person") which not only sound somewhat alike but may also have reminded the hearers of *shᵉlōmōh*, the Hebrew form of Solomon. Such a pun would prepare for the reference to the lover as king (v. 4).

Even more ardent expressions of passion are found in the commands and exhortations issued by the woman to the man in verse 4. She wants him to take her away with him, and proposes that they *"run"* not walk to their place of solitude. *"We will run"* should be "let us (i.e., the lover and the beloved) run" and read as the eager words of the woman not of the daughters of Jerusalem. Nothing captures the passionate mood more than the uses of the word *"love"* (Heb. *dôdîm*) in verses 2, 4. The plural form suggests "acts of love;" therefore, caresses, embraces, or sexual intercourse. There is nothing abstract about the *"love"* that outranks *"wine."* It is physical, intense, and exquisitely rewarding.

Third, the woman's yearning is encouraged by her friends. Her lover has the affection and admiration of the other maidens (*"virgins,"* v. 3) in their community. That same group is the antecedent of *"they"* in the final phrase (of v. 4), reinforced by the adverb *"rightly"* (a somewhat troublesome Heb. word that NKJV has probably read correctly, though it might be a word for "virility" or "masculinity" or possibly a rare synonym for *"wine,"* as would fit the poetic parallelism. The *"love"* which the maidens share for the beloved is a different word (Heb. *ʾāhab* not *dôdîm*) from the more expressly physical activity that the beloved longs for. The repetition of *"they love you"* (vv. 3, 4) serves as a refrain to justify the woman's yearning. Peer acceptance of those we love has always played an important part in human romance. Many a dormitory conversation has been spiced by the crucial question, "Do you like him?" And many an ardent spark has been doused by the cynical response, usually picked up second hand, "I can't imagine what she sees in him."

The use of the plural *"we"* in the second half of verse 4 is not easy to explain. It should probably not be credited to the daughters of Jerusalem, who are not introduced until verse 5. The switch from the singular *"me"* to *"we"* does not spotlight a change in speakers. The woman, consistently addressing the man as *"you"* (*"your"*), has the floor throughout this segment. Rather it must represent some kind of

278

ancient Middle Eastern pattern of speech. Whether for purposes of modesty or of identification with the lover as in *"let us run"* (v. 4), we do not know. Parallels in a Sumerian wedding song suggest that the pattern is neither unique nor erroneous.[1] *"Be glad"* and *"rejoice"* add a festive mood to the whole scene (cf. Ps. 118:24) and may also help to account for the plural, as the woman anticipates the love-banquet with enough enthusiasm to suit a whole entourage.

APOLOGIZING FOR HER SWARTHY COMPLEXION

5 I am dark, but lovely,
   O daughters of Jerusalem,
   Like the tents of Kedar,
   Like the curtains of Solomon.
6 Do not look upon me, because I am dark,
   Because the sun has tanned me.
   My mother's sons were angry with me;
   They made me the keeper of the vineyards,
   But my own vineyard I have not kept.

Song of Sol. 1:5–6

The whole focus changes. The woman no longer sings of her passionate expectations but of her own shortcomings. Her song of self-description points to her modesty at best—"who am I to deserve such an attractive and admirable man?"—and her self-deprecation at worst—"I am so unworthy of him that I don't want you, my Jerusalemite friends, to remind me of it." This is one of the passages where we long to hear the tone of voice. Is there a touch of playfulness in this humble banter? The note of teasing that sounds through verses 7–8 may hint at an affirmative answer.

In the flow of Poem I (1:2–2:7), these two verses seem to contribute two important insights that heighten the picture of longing. One reason that her lover means so much to her is that he has chosen her despite the fact that she does not consider herself a textbook beauty. Alongside the *"daughters of Jerusalem,"* shielded from the baking sun by their shady towers and sheltered streets, she appears *"dark of skin"* and rough of texture like the Bedouin's crude tents. *"Curtains"* is literally "tent fabric" made of goat hair (Exod. 26:7). Both *"Kedar"* (Gen. 25:13) and *"Salmah,"* which should probably be read in place of

"*Solomon*" in Hebrew, describe Arabian tribes well-known in biblical and rabbinic literature. "*Lovely*" suggests that in form and figure (for the Heb. word, see 2:14; 4:3; 6:4) she enjoyed a comeliness that may have been compromised but not canceled by her farmer's tan.

The second reason for her desire to be with her lover is that her home environment does not seem congenial. Her brothers ("*mother's sons*"), perhaps fearful of her pubescent precocity (see her quotation of their words, 8:8–9), behaved hostilely toward her and gave her an assignment that they themselves might ordinarily assume—"*keeper of the vineyard*" (cf. 1:14; 7:12; 8:11–12), a chore that resulted in the neglect of her own personal attractiveness: "*my own vineyard I have not kept*," (or "guarded"). The major task such keeping entailed was to protect the plants, blossoms, and fruit from the ravages of greedy birds and marauding animals (Hos. 2:12; Ps. 80:8–13).

In themes and catch-words verses 5–6 sound initial notes that echo in other parts of the Song and provide clues to its basic unity. The motif of humble self-description pops up in 2:1: "*I am the rose of Sharon*." "*Mother*" appears in 3:4; 6:9; 8:2, though father is nowhere mentioned in the Song. "Brother" is alluded to in 8:1, where she wishes her lover were a blood relative so that she could display her affection for him in public. In what seems to be a quotation of a vow that her brothers took to encourage her to remain a virgin until marriage, the woman recalls her brothers' concern and her passing of their test (8:8–10). And most significantly, the lover reprises the "*vineyard*" theme at the close of the Song (8:11–12) and delights in his exclusive relationship to his vineyard, his beloved, while in no way envying the vast estates of Solomon let out to share-croppers for lucrative fees. The lover's final delight in the one he has chosen matches the woman's initial delight in being desired by him, despite her swarthy complexion. The joy of being cherished sparks an inner beauty which no cosmetic can imitate. That joy lends radiance to both persons in the Song.

PROPOSING AN ENCOUNTER

7 Tell me, O you whom I love,
　　Where you feed your flock,
　　Where you make it rest at noon.

> For why should I be as one who veils herself
> By the flocks of your companions?
> 8 If you do not know, O fairest among women,
> Follow in the footsteps of the flock,
> And feed your little goats
> Beside the shepherds' tents.
> *Song of Sol. 1:7–8*

The woman's attention shifts from the daughters of Jerusalem, to whom she had explained her sun-scorched complexion in verses 5–7, back to her lover from whom she begs information as to his whereabouts as she envisages their joyous reunion. A *teasing dialogue* is the form this snatch of poetry seems to take, as he playfully answers (v. 8) her mock-sarcastic question (v. 7).

"Whom I love" picks up the refrain of verses 3–4, where the maidens are the subject of the love, and personalizes it: she plainly and intensely (the pronoun *"I"* translates the Heb. "my soul," "my whole person") declares her affection for him and her desire to express that affection in fond fellowship. The pastoral setting not only reflects the man's occupation but intimates a privacy, far from the prying eyes of the townspeople, that will allow full enjoyment of their encounter. *"Rest at noon"* underscores the erotic mood. Midday is siesta time; the shepherd will let the flock stretch out in any shade available (Ps. 23:2) and will enjoy a quiet nap himself, unless his sweetheart joins him. Humorously, if we catch the sense correctly, she states her desire for specific directions: she does not want to traipse from flock to flock asking his *"companions"* (fellow shepherds) for information (Gen. 37:16); the veil that protects her from the noon-time sun might mark her in their eyes as a prostitute (compare Tamar's story; Gen. 38:14).

The lover's answer (v. 8) is both affectionate and humorous. *"Fairest among women"* (cf. 5:9; 6:1, where the daughters of Jerusalem so address her) consciously counters her self put-down in verses 5–6. In his eyes her swarthiness tarnished her beauty not at all. The commands to *"follow in the footsteps of the flocks"* and *"feed your little goats"* are best understood as a reply to her fear of being mistaken as a prostitute. If she poses as a shepherdess she can make her trek right up to the *"tents"* (or huts) of the other shepherds and be safe both in reality and in reputation. *"Little goats"* may be a cute erotic allusion, whose precise meaning is lost on us (but see the use of a *"kid from the flock"* in the account of Jacob's encounter with Tamar; Gen. 38:17).

ADMIRING HER WORTH AND BEAUTY

9 I have compared you, my love,
   To my filly among Pharaoh's chariots.
10 Your cheeks are lovely with ornaments,
   Your neck with chains of gold.
11 We will make you ornaments of gold
   With studs of silver.

Song of Sol. 1:9–11

The man continues with his only prolonged contribution to Poem I: *an admiration song* in the form of a sustained metaphor denoted in *"I have compared"* or "I have contrived a similitude, an apt literary comparison" (for the Heb. *dāmāh,* see Hos. 12:10 where the root is translated "parables"). *"My love"* ("my darling") introduces the third term for *love* in Poem I: *dôdîm,* acts of love (1:2, 4); *ʾāhab* "be attracted to," "have affection for" (1:3, 4, 7); *raʿyāh,* "darling," "sweetheart" (1:9, 15; 2:2, 10, 13; 4:7; 5:2; 6:4), the man's favorite form of address for his beloved.

The Hebrew highlights the metaphor by placing *"my filly"* at the head of the sentence. To catch the full force of the imagery we need to retranslate the Hebrew: "to a mare among Pharaoh's cavalry (lit. horses) I have compared you, my darling." The point of comparison is the attractiveness of the woman to other men, among whom her appearance sparks an arousal akin to that of stallions when a mare is let loose in their corral. His metaphor is the counterpoint to her refrain about the maiden's attraction to him (vv. 3, 4), and serves further to refute her humble self-assessment (vv. 5–6): she is not only alluring to him but to many of his companions (cf. vv. 7–8) as well.

The picture of regal beauty is reinforced by the mention of (1) *"Pharaoh,"* whose wealth and station warranted the finest horses, (2) the *"ornaments"* with which ceremonial horses were garbed (the precise nature of the ornaments eludes us; *"chains of gold"* probably is better rendered "strings of beads"), (3) the promise of additional jewelry and trappings of precious metal; here *"gold"* is ranked first and hence was probably more valuable than silver; other texts sometimes reverse the order, perhaps referring to a time when silver was scarcer and therefore more expensive than gold (cf. Hos. 2:8). *"We"* (v. 11) presents us with the same question faced in verse 4. It may be either the man himself using the plural in a formula of solemn promise or the man and his admiring comrades, implied in the figure of Pharaoh's stallions. The woman's value is affirmed not only in the artistry and expense of the ornaments that garnished the mare's tack, but in the careful style of the poetry itself, a sensitive and thoughtful *gift of words* which caring lovers in all generations have learned to bestow and receive.

ADMIRING HIS EROTIC IMPACT

12 While the king is at his table,
   My spikenard sends forth its fragrance.
13 A bundle of myrrh is my beloved to me,
   That lies all night between my breasts.
14 My beloved is to me a cluster of henna blooms
   In the vineyards of En Gedi.
Song of Sol. 1:12–14

The woman's *admiration song* becomes even more intense and specific than that of her lover. It also continues the use of royal language, *"the king,"* as a way of parading his importance. *Intimacy* is the keynote of the passage. For the first time she uses her favorite descriptor *"my beloved"* (Heb. *dôdî*) of the man and by it speaks both of their binding relationship and his value (vv. 13, 14; cf. 1:16; 2:3, 8, 9, 10, 16, 17; 4:16; 5:2, 4, 5, 6, 8, 9, 10, 16; 6:1, 2, 3; 7:9, 10, 11, 13; 8:5, 14). *"His table"* should be understood as "his festive couch"; whatever banqueting is depicted goes on in a reclining position, which stimulates her *"fragrance,"* called *"spikenard,"* an aromatic substance derived from a Himalayan herb (cf. 4:13–14). The intimacy allows her to savor her lover who stimulates her senses with *"myrrh,"* a scent-exuding gum from a shrub native to south Arabia and Ethiopia, valued as an instrument of international commerce (note the list of presents brought to Solomon; 1 Kings 10:25), and *"henna,"* a bush with orange-colored blossoms used both for perfume and hairdye (4:13; 7:12), still valued by some Arab women as an underarm deodorant.

Fragrance certainly adds to the beauty of a sexual embrace (how carefully Esther was groomed for her night with the king; Esther 2:12–13), but that embrace also produces its own special fragrance (see comments on v. 3). And it is the savoring of the intimacy, not merely the perfumes, that is featured here: the beloved *"lies all night between my breasts"* like *"a bundle of myrrh"* and is in as close touch with her as are the *"henna"* shrubs with the vines among which they crop up in the *"vineyards"* (remember the personal, intimate use of *"vineyard"* in 1:6 and 8:11–12) of *"En Gedi,"* an oasis of notable fertility on the west shore of the Dead Sea (cf. Jos. 15:62; Sirach 24:14). It may have been one of Palestine's centers for the perfume industry.[2] Again beautiful, graphic, and elegant language is used to extol the importance of the loved one—a ready remedy for any relationship dulled by the taking of each other for granted.

SHARING THEIR MUTUAL ADMIRATION

15 Behold, you are fair, my love!
   Behold, you are fair!
   You have dove's eyes.
16 Behold, you are handsome, my beloved!
   Yes, pleasant!
   Also our bed is green.
17 The beams of our houses are cedar,
   And our rafters of fir.
2:1 I am the rose of Sharon,
   And the lily of the valleys.
 2 Like a lily among thorns,
   So is my love among the daughters.
 3 Like an apple tree among the trees of the woods,
   So is my beloved among the sons.
   I sat down in his shade with great delight,
   And his fruit was sweet to my taste.
 4 He brought me to the banqueting house,
   And his banner over me was love.
                                   Song of Sol. 1:15–2:4

A brief but fervent interchange follows in which the *song of admiration* becomes an antiphonal duet. The man's verse (v. 15) is deliberately repetitive and almost prosaic, as though his poetic sense were stunned into silence by the passion of her singing in verses 12–14. Overwhelmed by the picture of pending intimacy, he can only exclaim *"Behold, you are fair."* A learned friend of mine once suggested that the Hebrew word for "behold" ought sometimes to be translated "Wow!" Verses 15–16 may be such instances. *"Fair"* or *"beautiful"* crops up regularly, particularly, as here, to describe the woman (cf. 4:1, 7; 6:4, 10; 7:6). It is the lover's most characteristic nonmetaphorical way to depict her winsomeness. The rote repetition indicates both the intensity of his admiration and his inability at the moment to produce the customary artistic variation of Hebrew parallelism. His one attempt at metaphor is to compare her *"eyes"* with the gray, luminescent delicacy of a *"dove."* The comparison is not to the dove's eyes (contrary to NKJV) but to the dove itself (cf. 4:1; 5:12).

Her response (v. 16) echoes his song. *"Handsome"* is the masculine form of *fair* (v. 15). In contrast to his plain repetition, she manages an appropriate synonym, *"pleasant"* ("agreeable," "lovely," applied to God in Ps. 135:3 and the root of Naomi's name in the Book of Ruth). *"Behold"* and *"yes"* reinforce her notes of admiration.

The next three lines pick up the tones of passion from verses 12–14 but look at the *setting* rather than the fragrance of lovemaking. The trysting place is rustic, yet elegant. *"Green"* (cf. 1 Kings 14:23) refers more to the bounty of the verdure than to its color. The forest's outdoor canopy lends a palatial ambience to the scene. Timber for construction was scarce in Palestine. The best wood had to be hauled south from Lebanon. Only the wealthy could afford sturdy *"beams"* and *"rafters"* (or paneling; cf. Jer. 22:14–15; Hag. 1:4). Who speaks these lines? We cannot be sure. The first seems to complete the woman's words of admiration. The second and third (v. 17) may be the man's eager and playful response. In any case, the point is that love is such a royal experience, it merits a majestic setting (note: king's chambers, v. 4; king's couch, v. 12; banqueting house, 2:4). How tragically has the coinage of love been debased by being first exchanged in the back seat of a car or on a shaky cot in a cheap motel!

The woman again (2:1; cf. 1:5–6) describes herself as plain, commonplace, unexceptionable. Despite the use of *"rose of Sharon"* and *"lily of the valleys"* in Christian poetry and hymnody, the woman's intent is to depict herself as average. *"Rose"* (cultured only later and transplanted from Persia and Armenia) is probably the asphodel (cf. Isa. 35:1), crocus, or daffodil. While *lily* (whose Hebrew gives us names like Susanna and Susan) is probably lotus. *"Sharon,"* always used with a definite article in Hebrew, means the plain that sloped west to the Mediterranean and reached from Jaffa north almost to Mt. Carmel. *"Valleys"* may describe any number of old and relatively flat declivities that annually spawned wild flowers, including the well-known valley of Jezreel (Hos. 1:5). No rare-bloom is she, no delicate hothouse specimen, but a plain, everyday blossom, readily plucked, sniffed, and tossed aside by an idle shepherd.

Not so, the lover counters (2:2). Compared with you all other young women *("daughters")* are brambles or thorn bushes. Again, as in 1:16, she plays off his cue and makes her own comparison: he is as much more beautiful and fruitful than other young men *("sons")* as is the *"apple tree"* than the ordinary trees of the woods. *"Shade," "fruit," "apple tree"* are all ancient erotic symbols, and erotic suggestions are what she has in mind (2:3–4). In her song, admiration segues to imagination, which experiences the fulness and freshness of love, beginning at 2:3b. The intimacy is all-encompassing. *"Sat down"* can mean *"dwell"* or *"remain."* *"Shade"* speaks of closeness. And the whole experience is described as *"sweet"* and full of *"delight,"* worth craving after.

The *"fruit"* and "wine" *("banqueting house"* is literally house of *"wine")* symbolize the ecstasy of lovemaking, as verses 4–7 imply (cf. 4:10–11, 16; 7:8–9; 8:2). For *"he brought me,"* see 1:4. Her imagination again pictures the consummation of her longing. The final line of verse 4 seems to be a military metaphor, *"his banner"* (waving) *"over me,"* a figure hard to picture in this tender and intimate scene. The suggestion that Hebrew *dgl (*"banner"* or *"emblem")* should be connected with an Akkadian (Babylonian or Assyrian) word meaning "desire" or "intent" may enhance our understanding of the passage: "his intent toward me was lovemaking."[3] The literal line helps us interpret the imagery which precedes it in verse 3 and follows it in verse 5.

YEARNING FOR INTIMACY

5 Sustain me with cakes of raisins,
   Refresh me with apples,
   For I am lovesick.
6 His left hand *is* under my head,
   And his right hand embraces me.

Song of Sol. 2:5–6

In the final verse of Poem I, the songs of yearning and fulfillment have blended. The woman begs for the stimulation of love or perhaps even the stimulants that will enhance and encourage the act of love. *"Sustain"* and *"refresh"* are plural imperatives, addressed either to the man, to the daughters of Jerusalem who appear on the scene again at 2:7 (cf. 1:5–6), or to anybody in general. The urgency of her commands reveals the depth of her passion. *"Cakes of raisins"* (cf. Jer. 7:18; 44:19; Hos. 3:1) seem to reflect some sort of religious ritual, perhaps a fertility rite in which the cakes were molded in the form of a female goddess. Thus, with *"apples,"* they came to be viewed as an aphrodisiac. So burning was her desire *("lovesick")* that she sought all possible fuel to keep it flaming. *"Lovesick"* may also mean "worn out from lovemaking"; hence her call for refreshment to renew the activities in which her fantasies captured her. Either way, she pictures herself nestled side by side with him in full and satisfying embrace (v. 6).

SWEARING HER FRIENDS TO PATIENCE

> 7 I charge you, O daughters of Jerusalem,
>   By the gazelles or by the does of the field,
>   Do not stir up nor awaken love
>   Until it pleases.
>
> *Song of Sol. 2:7*

Nothing she has said expresses more forcefully the exquisite passion with which the beloved longs for union with her man than these words which exact an oath *("I charge you")* from her female companions (cf. 1:5–6). It is as though she said "cross your heart and hope to die" as she extracts their pledge in a pattern to be repeated in the Song (3:5; 5:8; 8:4). *"Gazelles"* and *"does"* by whom the oath is sealed seem to be further symbols of passionate affection. In the subsequent poem she invites her lover to be *"like a gazelle"* (2:17; cf. 8:14) and enjoy her mountain-like contours, while he compares her breasts to fawns, twins of a gazelle in 4:5 and 7:3. The precise nature of her solemn demand on the daughters of Jerusalem is not easy to grasp, here nor in 3:5 and 8:4. Is the text a "do not disturb" sign to be hung on the door of their rendezvous? Are the daughters of Jerusalem being adjured to protect the privacy of the lovers? This understanding fits the context well but has trouble with the first verb which has to be stretched too far to mean "disturb" or "interrupt." "*Stir up*" is its more normal sense. The alternate and preferable meaning is that the experience of lovemaking *("love")* is too powerful, too all-consuming to be lightly aroused, unless the couple have the commitment, the desire, and the right opportunity to enjoy it.

The full implications of a loving union have been explored in Poem I. The couple's unique attraction for and commitment to each other have been described in songs of yearning, admiration, and fulfillment. The woman's imagination has had full play. She has fantasized both the power, the beauty, and the pleasure of sexual encounter. The stage is set for Poem II in which she pictures her lover's approach to make the longings of Poem I come true.

NOTES

1. M. Pope, *Song of Songs*, p. 304.
2. Ibid., p. 354.
3. Ibid., p. 376. See also G. L. Carr, *The Song of Solomon*, p. 91 (cf. Bibliography).

CHAPTER THREE

Poem II: Invitation, Suspense, Response

Song of Solomon 2:8–3:5

This poem builds on the mood of admiration and yearning which dominated Poem I and adds to it a strong note of *invitation* (2:10, 13, 15, 17). The narrator is clearly the woman, but we are made party to a lengthy speech attributed to the man and relayed to us by the woman (2:10–14). Like Poem I, this section of the Song seems to be an account of imaginative anticipation rather than a description of actual experience. The two halves of Poem II can be readily distinguished: part one is a fantasy of the lover's appearance and call to the beloved (2:10–14) and her responsive invitation to him (2:15–17); part two is a dream-narrative in which she describes her frustration in ardently seeking her lover and her satisfaction in finally finding him (3:5).

The players in the cast remain the same as in Poem I: the woman, the man, the daughters of Jerusalem (3:5). And the level of ardor is at least as high. The flow of the poem is punctuated by *rhythms of romance.* She is utterly thrilled by his approach, charmed by his voice, entranced by his invitations (2:8–13), yet her first response seems to be coyness and teasing. She hides her face and maintains a crafty silence (2:14). When she speaks it is to tease him with a cryptic, fable-like, song, about foxes and vineyards (2:15). Then coyness yields to readiness in a description of their mutual commitment (2:16), followed by a passionately poetic invitation (2:17). But, as the rhythm proceeds, her readiness is answered by his remoteness in the frustration segment of her dream (3:1–3). Finally after the teasings and the delay, the closing scene of the dream finds her together with her lover in her mother's chamber (3:4). So heady is she with the anticipation of sexual union that again she puts the daughters of Jerusalem under oath

289

not to incite such passion by any artificial means, so totally exhilarating and exhausting is it when it occurs at its own time and pace (3:5).

A *balance of intensity* is expressed in the mutuality, the reciprocity, of this poem. Whereas in Poem I the *woman's* ardor is featured. Here the interest is pictured as mutual. The text begins with his advances to her; in the first half he pursues and she responds (2:8–17); in the second half, their roles are reversed (3:1–5). The assertiveness, then, is mutual. Neither is regularly passive, shyly waiting for the advances of the other. No stereotypes of sexual roles find support in the words and deeds of these two lovers. He is no chauvinist; she is no amazon. Each feels free to take the lead, and each to be the willing follower. Partnership not hierarchy shapes their relationship. Their possession of each other is also mutual. The formula, "My beloved is mine, and I am his" (2:16) documents this. Equally committed, equally dependent, equally responsible, equally ardent, the two partners chart their course together in the remarkable duets that comprise the Song. How good of God to record it for our hearing!

DESCRIPTION OF THE LOVER'S APPROACH AND INVITATION

8 The voice of my beloved!
Behold, he comes
Leaping upon the mountains,
Skipping upon the hills.
9 My beloved is like a gazelle or a young stag.
Behold, he stands behind our wall;
He is looking through the windows,
Gazing through the lattice.
10 My beloved spoke, and said to me:
"Rise up, my love, my fair one,
And come away.
11 For lo, the winter is past,
The rain is over and gone.
12 The flowers appear on the earth;
The time of singing has come,
And the voice of the turtledove
Is heard in our land.
13 The fig tree puts forth her green figs,
And the vines with the tender grapes

Give a good smell.
Rise up, my love, my fair one,
And come away!
14 "O my dove, in the clefts of the rock,
In the secret places of the cliff,
Let me see your face,
Let me hear your voice;
For your voice is sweet,
And your countenance is lovely."

Song of Sol. 2:8–14

The woman is speaking. In fancy, she hears a welcome voice and sees an exciting figure, moving eagerly, vitally, toward her home. The *"gazelle"*-like *"leaping"* and *"skipping"* captures the mood of the lover's eagerness (vv. 8–9a). At the same time it betrays her own erotic arousal, since it recalls the vivid love–language in her charge to her friends (2:7), anticipates her graphic invitation to love in 2:17, and prepares for the repetition of the charge in 3:5. The *"gazelle"* metaphor, in fact, is a three-pronged bracket (or set of antlers!) on which hang the artistry and unity of Poem II.

The silent scene of verse 9b elevates the eagerness and tightens the suspense. She knows he is there *"behind our wall"* that marked off the property of the mother's house (3:4) from that of the neighbors. And he knows she knows. The *"windows,"* the openings in the wall of the house, were cross-hatched with *"lattice"* which guaranteed privacy and provided ventilation. No panes would have been used in that setting.

He deliberately pauses, both to heighten the drama and to compose himself, before he speaks. Then his words are direct—*"rise up,"* *"come away"* (note the repetition in v. 13)—affectionate—*"my love,"* *"my fair one"* (remember 1:15)—and poetic—folded between the two calls of invitation is a magnificent description of springtime, the season when a young man's fancy turns to thoughts of love (vv. 11–13a). The *"rain is over"* (Palestine's rainy seasons tend to be October–November and March–April), and a dry and balmy setting awaits them. Beyond such practicality, a manifold beauty will enliven their encounter: wild *"flowers"* (literally "blossoms") adorn the *"earth"* (perhaps "countryside" is the better reading here and in v. 12); *"pruning"* (as the word for *"singing"* should probably be translated) is beginning to take place in the vineyards, with the suckers and wild shoots cut back to allow all nutrients to flow to the developing grape clusters (see the clear description of this horticultural process in Isa. 18:5); the *"voice of the turtledove,"* who returned in April from its winter migration and was present in numbers sufficient to provide the prescribed animal sacrifices for the poor (Lev. 1:14; 5:7, 11; 14:22, 30; 15:14; cf. Luke 2:24), filled the scene with sound, as the *"vines"* in bloom (*"tender grapes"* here in v. 15 seems to be a paraphrase; NKJV is more accurate in 7:12, *"grape blossoms"*) permeate the air with fragrance (*"good smell";* cf. the same Heb. word in 1:3, 12).

Throughout this romantic invitation (2:10–13), the woman has apparently remained silently out of sight, like a *"dove"* (cf. on 1:15) hidden in *"clefts"* or crevices on rocky faces that jut out from the craggy terrain of parts of Palestine. The lover concludes his invitation with a call for her to set aside her shyness and let her radiant presence be known in the sight and sound which he so relishes (v. 1:4). The very word order enhances the note of beauty by forming an envelope: *"countenance," "voice," "voice," "countenance."* The emphasis seems to be on her face, the first and last item mentioned. *"Lovely"* (1:5; 2:14; 4:3; 6:4) carries the sense of fitting and suitable (Ps. 33:1; Prov. 26:1), while *"sweet"* has a range of uses from the comfort of carefree sleep (Prov. 3:24; Jer. 31:26), through praised-filled meditations (Ps. 104:34), to sacrifices pleasing to the Lord (Hos. 9:4; Jer. 6:20). It seems to connote deep-seated satisfaction.

HER TEASING RESPONSE

> 15 Catch us the foxes,
>   The little foxes that spoil the vines,
>   For our vines have tender grapes.
>   *Song of Sol. 2:15*

Who speaks these cryptic clauses that sound like a farmer's ditty deliberately veiled in the imagery of animals and horticulture? I assume the woman does, as her tongue-in-cheek way both of breaking the silence and responding, though obliquely, to the invitations of her lover. Even more important, how do we get at the verse's meaning? The best clue seems to come from the repeated word *"vines"* (or vineyards). We met the Hebrew word in singular form when the woman described the chore that resulted in her sullied complexion (1:5–6); we shall meet it again at the Song's end (8:11–12). In both places *"vineyard"* seems to suggest the precious beauty of the person, which wants cherishing and guarding, lest in some way it be ravaged. The ravagers in verse 15 are the *"foxes"* (or jackals) that love grapes and can work havoc (*"spoil,"* ruin) in a vineyard, even without the kind of help Samson gave them in his famous act of arson in the wheat fields, vineyards, and olive groves of the Philistines (Judg. 15:4–5). *"Foxes,"* as the woman sees them, seem not to be sexual attack or defloration as is sometimes suggested, but the ravages of the aging process that can sap the beauty and vitality of persons (the *"vines"* or vineyards). Read this way, the song is a positive answer to the invitation: the time is ripe (the *"tender grapes"* or "blossoms"; see at 2:13 and 7:12) for love; the freshness of youth is at its prime *("vines")*; let us give full expression to our love before aging *("the foxes")* takes its toll on our beauty and vigor *("spoil the vines")*.[1] The Preacher in Ecclesiastes was equally anxious about the aging process (12:1–7) but for a different reason.

The interplay between the rural and the urban settings of the Song can be accounted for on the basis of ancient sociology. Families tended to cluster together in towns and cities for protection, communication, and commerce. Their fields surrounded these towns and day by day they ventured out to work their crops or follow their flocks. The isolated farm house as we know it was not part of their environment. Their lives, then, flowed from town to country and back again. The changing scenery of the Song reflects that flow.

HER AFFIRMATION AND INVITATION

16 My beloved is mine, and I am his.
   He feeds his flock among the lilies.
17 Until the day breaks
   And the shadows flee away,
   Turn, my beloved,
   And be like a gazelle
   Or a young stag
   Upon the mountains of Bether.
                                    Song of Sol. 2:16–17

293

The woman's coyness gives way to openness. Her opaque response in the song of the foxes is brightly interpreted in the call to the gazelle. The formula of *mutual possession* (v. 16; cf. 6:3; 7:10) appears at strategic places in the Song to underscore the exclusiveness of the lovers' commitment to each other and the wholehearted, unreserved character of their covenant. The formula seems to entail on the human level what the familiar prophetic pattern conveys on the divine:

> "Then I will say to those who were not
>   My people,
> 'You are My people!'
> And they shall say, 'You are my God!'"
>
> *Hos. 2:23*

For the lovers, the covenant pledge carries erotic overtones: they belong to each other and intend to enjoy each other. Each use of the formula of mutual possession displays that intention. Here and in 6:3 the formula is capped with a clause that pictures the lover as *"he feeds* (his flock?) *among the lilies." "Lilies"* (or lotuses; cf. 2:1–2) in the Song not only describe the comeliness of the beloved but are also figures for the man's lips (5:13) and the upper portion of the woman's body, surrounding her breasts (4:5). Since the latter phrase in Hebrew is virtually identical to the text in 2:16 and 6:3, we should probably omit *"his flock"* which is not in the Hebrew text and has been supplied in the NKJV on the basis of the shepherd passages like 1:7–8. In the present context, however the lover is feeding himself, not the flock, in the amorous kissing and caressing of his beloved.

And she, as her imagination sketches the scene in vivid detail, is enjoying every moment of it. She wants it to last until the morning breezes signal *"day break,"* and the *"shadows"* of night *"flee away"* (2:17; cf. 4:6), when their privacy would be disturbed and their daily duties begin. *"Turn"* probably means "turn to me" in the full attention that love warrants. This part of Poem II closes by recalling the approach-scene at the beginning. There the beloved fancied her lover running toward her over the *"mountains"* like a *"gazelle."* Here she fancies him enjoying her *"mountains,"* the curvaceous contours of her body (cf. his similar description in 4:6). *"Bether"* should probably not be treated as a proper name (NKJV) but as a noun like "ruggedness" or "cleftness" emphasizing the woman's strength and shapeliness.

FRUSTRATION AND FULFILLMENT

3:1 By night on my bed I sought the one I love;
   I sought him, but I did not find him.
  2 "I will rise now," I said,
   "And go about the city;
   In the streets and in the squares
   I will seek the one I love."
   I sought him, but I did not find him.
  3 The watchmen who go about the city found me;
     I said,
   "Have you seen the one I love?"
  4 Scarcely had I passed by them,
   When I found the one I love.
   I held him and would not let him go,
   Until I had brought him to the house of my
     mother,
   And into the chamber of her who conceived
     me.
  5 I charge you, O daughters of Jerusalem,
   By the gazelles or by the does of the field,
   Do not stir up nor awaken love
   Until it pleases.

Song of Sol. 3:1–5

The scene changes abruptly in the second part of Poem II. The woman recounts what seems to have been a dream (cf. 5:2–8). As she does, she wears her heart on her sleeve, repeatedly referring to the man as *"the one I love"* (vv. 1, 2, 3, 4). The Hebrew is literally "whom my soul (my very self, my whole person; cf. on 1:7) loves." This part of Poem II complements the first part: (1) there he sought her and she kept out of sight, refusing to speak until desperately he begged her to make herself known (2:14); when she did appear she complied with his wishes readily; (2) here she seeks him, and he eludes her until her frustration is almost at the breaking point; when at last she finds him, he gladly yields to her advances.

On the basis of the LXX of 3:1 and the Hebrew text of 5:6, some versions add here "I called him, but he gave no answer" (RSV, NEB). The text as NKJV has it is to be preferred; the Song frequently varies the forms of passages that have identical components (e.g., 2:17; 8:14,

295

where the latter verse omits the opening clauses and repeats the closing ones). The woman's quest is urgent. She risks the dangers and abuses of the streets of her darkened town in her midnight search (3:2; cf. 5:7, where she is stripped and pummeled by the guards). The *"watchmen"* (or city guards) had as their main duty not the control of crime within the town but the protection of it from marauding groups of outsiders, bedouin bands, or gangs of highwaymen (cf. Prov. 1:10–19; Hos. 6:9). Nothing is said of the watchmen's conduct in this passage. They seem to have given her question (v. 3) a shrug, as she hurried by them in her pursuit.

"I held him" describes the complete relief she felt just as her despair built to a peak. The verb *"held"* is identical to *"catch"* in the song about the foxes (2:15). The word-play may be intentional: time is fleeting; she wastes no minute of opportunity to enjoy the affections of her lover. That urgency may help to account for the mention of *"my mother's house."* No time is to be spared for a tryst in the woods (cf. 1:7–8, 16–17) to enjoy the balmy beauty of a spring evening (2:11–13). She is in town and takes her loved one directly to her own home. *"Chamber"* must mean bedroom and with *"who conceived me"* may reinforce the voluptuous desires portrayed in the dream. She delights to think of making love in the very room where she was conceived (8:2). Her frustration eased, her quest satisfied, her fantasy completed, she closes Poem II as she had closed Poem I, by putting her friends under oath to recognize that love like hers was too hot to handle except under the right circumstances and was not to be artificially or prematurely kindled (v. 5).

One great lesson of the Song thus far is the *joy of anticipation.* Our interpretation suggests that the encounters pictured have been imagined, not physically experienced. That is yet to come. Part of the delight of courting is its three dimensional character. In the *present* we enjoy the conversations, the closeness, the sense of belonging during each moment we are together. And we continue to savor those times when they have joined the *past* tense. We recall the touch, rehearse the words, relive the emotions. But it is the *future* that consumes our thoughts and defines our desires. The closer we come to the event of marriage the more our hearts taste it in advance. The ultimate intimacy, the complete embrace, is all the more wonderful when we have contemplated its coming and are able to celebrate it in the fullness of covenant commitment and the freedom from fear and guilt that marriage bestows. Pity the persons, and their number today seems legion, who are robbed of the exquisite joy of anticipation by engaging in physical acts of intercourse with persons whom they barely know. Our fast-food style of life may sustain us physically. Its sexual counterpart diminishes our true humanity virtually beyond recognition.

NOTES

1. For this interpretation, see H. J. Schonfield, *The Song of Songs*, p. 85 (cf. Bibliography).

Poem III: Ceremony and Satisfaction

Song of Solomon 3:6–5:1

It is time for the wedding. The anticipation that bubbled high in the first two poems has reached the boiling point. But before the passion of each partner in the Song is given full play, the ceremonial setting has to be established (3:6–11), and the lover needs opportunity to picture the beauty of his loved one and his admiration of her (4:1–15). Chapter 4 of the Song is his day to court, his opportunity to make clear the brightness of his desire and the depth of his commitment. In a coda to the two-part poem, she, thoroughly aroused by his love lyrics, responds with her invitation for him to enjoy himself to the full (4:16). His answer, in the past tense, pictures the enthusiasm of his reaction and the richness of his satisfaction (5:1a). Poem III fitly concludes with the good wishes of the couple's friends (5:1b), probably the daughters of Jerusalem (1:5; 2:7; 3:5), who are destined to play a prominent role in Poem IV (5:2–6:3).

Three important themes are braided together in this section. Each contributes to our understanding of a biblical approach to marriage. The *splendor* of matrimony is revealed in the magnificent processional first descried at a distance, awesome and mysterious, then viewed close at hand, overpoweringly impressive in the majesty of its military precision and the exquisite details of its accoutrements. The entire scene embodies all the elements of royalty that ought to be accorded to a wedding and the couple at its center (see chapter 1). The seriousness and joy of the occasion warrant such careful attention. The transaction to be witnessed is of ultimate significance to the partners, their families, the communities in which they live, and to the

Lord, who, as our wedding ceremonies remind us, ordained marriage as the key social institution and is witness to and participant in each instance of it. Neither lavishness, which can be gauche, nor expense, which can be wasteful, is the point of the splendor. We cannot and need not do things on a Solomonic scale. Seriousness, however, is what counts. And essential is an eye to the significance of the festivities that calls for a splendor of detailed planning and careful implementation and that treats the couple as the most important people in the world for those hours.

The *esteem* of each partner for the other is a second essential. In this poem, since the woman has already had ample opportunity to disclose her craving for her lover and the regard in which she holds him (1:2–3, 12–14, 16; 2:3–6, 9, 16–17; 3:1–4), her admiration is noted only briefly (3:11). He, in contrast, has ample and uninterrupted opportunity to display his feelings toward her. Whatever male reticence may lurk within him he sets aside and boldly describes her beauty and worth. Such public disclosure to her and reverence of her are necessary components if the act of marriage is to have its proper meaning. Nothing less than whole-hearted esteem, especially on the part of us males who can be plagued by insecure arrogance and fickle wanderlust, is a steady foundation on which to build a permanent relationship. I have always appreciated the fact that the traditional wedding rites call for the man to pledge his troth before the woman pledges hers. His affection and his commitment frame the context for hers. So it is in Poem III.

The *exclusiveness* of the relationship is the last and, perhaps, most crucial strand in marriage. The woman has eyes only for her "Solomon" (3:11), despite the possible distraction of sixty hand-picked warriors (3:7–8). The man's heart beats for her alone (4:9). He ties her as close to him as the nearest blood relative, a sister (4:9, 10, 12; 5:1a), and he treasures the uniqueness of their bond: she is accessible to no one else; she is a garden which only his key can unlock (4:12). She puts it simply and best, "My garden is his garden" (4:16). "Forsaking all others, will you keep yourself only unto her . . . , only unto him?" That is the central question of the wedding ceremony. It is to be asked and answered at the beginning of the union and every day thereafter. Answering it with a fervent Yes will not guarantee untarnished happiness. But it will provide the only context within which true happiness becomes a possibility.

HER DESCRIPTION OF THE GROOM'S ARRIVAL

6 Who is this coming out of the wilderness
   Like pillars of smoke,
   Perfumed with myrrh and frankincense,
   With all the merchant's fragrant powders?
7 Behold, it is Solomon's couch,
   With sixty valiant men around it,
   Of the valiant of Israel.
8 They all hold swords,
   Being expert in war.
   Every man has his sword on his thigh
   Because of fear in the night.
9 Of the wood of Lebanon
   Solomon the King
   Made himself a palanquin:
10 He made its pillars of silver,
   Its support of gold,
   Its seat of purple,
   Its interior paved with love
   By the daughters of Jerusalem.
11 Go forth, O daughters of Zion,
   And see King Solomon with the crown
   With which his mother crowned him
   On the day of his wedding,
   The day of the gladness of his heart.

Song of Sol. 3:6–11

The break in subject and style between 3:5 and 3:6 is one of the sharpest in the book. The quiet, intimate scene of the beloved and the lover in her mother's bedroom is eclipsed by the dazzle and decorum of a vast processional. It approaches the city, presumably Jerusalem, from the southeastern *"wilderness,"* uncultivated terrain whose wild grass provides grazing fodder for flocks and herds. The bleak austerity of the landscape is a fitting stage to show off the splendor of the entourage. The dust raised by the marching feet and the *"smoke"* of the burning perfume are sculpted by the wind into *"pillars"* or columns that convey an ominous foreboding, like the lowering skies that signal a divine appearance, a theophany (Joel 2:30). The haunting fragrances of burning *"myrrh"* (see on 1:13), *"frankincense,"* a white dust-coated gum exuded from trees native to India and the coasts of southern Arabia and northeast Africa (cf. also 4:6, 14), and other *"powders"* hawked by traveling peddlers, added to the majesty (myrrh and frankincense were gifts fit for a king, Matt. 2:11) and mystery of the scene.

The mystery is solved at verse 7 when the narrator answers the question with which verse 6 began. At the heart of the procession is *"Solomon's couch"* or portable lounging bed, later called *"palanquin,"* which may picture a sedan chair (v. 9), although the Hebrew word is too rare to be defined with precision. Described in detail are the armed guard of crack troops (*"valiant men"*) that escort the train (vv. 7–8) to protect it. *"Night"* may have demonic connotations, since some Jewish traditions reveal a deep-seated dread (*"fear"*) of demonic disruptions of the wedding night. More likely, the terror had to do with vandalism or, in Solomon's case, possible assassination. Living in the era of electricity has made it hard for us to grasp the intensity with which the ancients feared the night. No wonder one of John's bright revelations about the life to come promises, "There shall be no night there" (Rev. 22:5).

The *"couch"* itself is depicted as carefully as is the guard (vv. 9–10). Expensive elegance is conveyed in every phrase. *"Wood of Lebanon"* means the best kind of wood, available at great effort and cost from the forests that draped the Lebanese mountains. (For *Lebanon's* prominent role in the Song, see 4:8, 11, 15; 5:15; 7:4; it almost always carries a superlative force: finest, tallest, strongest, best.) *"Silver,"* *"gold,"* and *"purple"* cloth, probably of wool, all add to the picture of opulent beauty. The cloth was dyed with liquid pressed from the Mediterranean shellfish called *murex.* A student of mine once calculated the number of shellfish required for the dyers to collect one ounce of the fluid—over ten thousand. *"Made,"* describing Solomon's role, must mean "ordered it made" as he had done for the temple and his own palace. We have no evidence that he himself was a crafts-man. *"Its interior paved* (or "fitted out") *with love"* (or lovemaking) may hint that the couch was set up as the site of the nuptial embrace and given the special tender touches of the *"daughters of Jerusalem,"* whose supportive role in the Song is already well documented (1:5; 2:7; 3:5). Again, the interior decor of the couch may have been adorned with carved inlays of erotic scenes such as have come to light among the furniture of Ugarit, the ancient kingdom in northwest Syria, whose literature and archeology have contributed so much to our knowledge of the Old Testament.[1]

Not until verse 11 do we find the key needed to unlock the sense of the entire passage. The command to the *"daughters of Zion"* (cf. Isa. 3:16–17; 4:4; here used as synonymous to *"daughters of Jerusalem"*), *"Go forth,"* must be issued by the beloved; she alone addresses them in the Song. It is likely then that *she* is the narrator of the entire scene. If so, Solomon, not she, is the probable occupant of the ceremonial litter. His *"crown"* (or wreath) bestowed by *"his mother"* (Bathsheba, 1 Kings 1:11) would symbolize joyful celebration, as for a wedding, not political and spiritual authority, which would have been bestowed by the chief priest (cf. 2 Kings 11: 4–20, which also described an armed military escort, as in Song of Sol. 3:7–8).

The Solomonic pageantry is part of the Song's regal motif, an elegant way of highlighting the importance of marriage and the eminence to be accorded to its participants. This interpretation assumes (1) that Solomon is a kind of code name for the lover as Shulamite (i.e., "Solomoness") is for the beloved (6:13); (2) that the picture of the processional with its entourage and trappings is hyperbolic, deliberately exaggerated to heighten the significance of the event; (3) that behind this poem may lie a royal wedding song from Solomon's time which helped to shape its extravagant descriptions of regal largesse expended in the services of love (cf. Ps. 45 for an example of a royal wedding hymn).

HIS DESCRIPTION OF THE BRIDE'S BEAUTY

4:1 Behold, you are fair, my love!
Behold, you are fair!
You have dove's eyes behind your veil.
Your hair is like a flock of goats,
Going down from Mount Gilead.
2 Your teeth are like a flock of shorn sheep
Which have come up from the washing,
Every one of which bears twins,
And none is barren among them.
3 Your lips are like a strand of scarlet,
And your mouth is lovely.

> Your temples behind your veil
> Are like a piece of pomegranate.
> 4 Your neck is like the tower of David,
> Built for an armory,
> On which hang a thousand bucklers,
> All shields of mighty men.
> 5 Your two breasts are like two fawns,
> Twins of a gazelle,
> Which feed among the lilies.
> 6 Until the day breaks
> And the shadows flee away,
> I will go my way to the mountain of myrrh
> And to the hill of frankincense.
> 7 You are all fair, my love,
> And there is no spot in you.
>
> *Song of Sol. 4:1–7*

The ceremonial scene becomes much more personal as it continues. She has urged her friends to admire her lover, decked out for the wedding service. He, in turn, is pictured as having eyes for her only, publicly describing her beauty (vv. 1–7), extending his invitation (v. 8), and declaring his admiration (vv. 9–15). Such wedding practices were observed in Syrian villages well into the nineteenth century. The closing toast of the daughters of Jerusalem (5:1b) is a clue that the songs of chapter 4, like the processional march of 3:6–11, are to be heard not as tender whispers but as public affirmations, enjoyed by the bride and witnessed by her family and friends.

The poem begins and ends, literally, with the declaration *"you are fair,"* heard first in 1:15 and to be heard again in 7:6. *"Behind your veil"* both embellishes the *"dove"* metaphor (v. 1; cf. 1:15) and reflects the wedding setting where the *"veil"* is appropriate (cf. 4:3), in contrast to 1:7 where it would be misconstrued as the garb of a prostitute. The close of this section (v. 7) deliberately repeats but also intensifies the description of verse 1. It adds *"all"* to *"you are fair"* and concludes with an absolute affirmation of her spotless perfection: she is without any blemishing feature whatsoever and has the same kind of unmarred wholeness that God expects of the sacrifices made to him (Lev. 22:20, 21).

Once the *"eyes like doves"* are mentioned, the song becomes eloquently figurative. Her head and upper torso are described with the

303

intimacy of detail and flair for artistry of an impressionistic sculptor molding a bust of his model. The *"hair"* (cf. 6:5) falls in undulating waves over her ears, neck, and shoulders with the quiet grace with which a *"flock"* of sheep, seen from a distance, seem to caress a hillside with gentle movement. *"Gilead,"* situated east of the Jordan Valley between the Arnon and the Yarmuk rivers, is singled out both for its hilly contours and its reputation for fertile pasture lands. The *"teeth"* (cf. 6:6) are clean and perfectly matched; *"none"* is missing (*"barren"*), an achievement indeed, considering the absence of dentistry and the meager knowledge of oral hygiene. The *"lips"* are flushed with color and well defined (like Rahab's scarlet rope in Josh. 2:18). *"Mouth"* is literally "speech" or "speaking," rightly read in this physical description as "instrument of speech," therefore *"mouth."* *"Lovely"* recalls 2:14. *"Temples"* (cf. Judg. 4:21–22) describe more generally the side of the face and are usually interpreted *"cheeks"* because of the comparison with the rosy, roundness of *"pomegranate"* halves (cf. 6:7). *"Behind your veil"* mirrors the phrase in verse 1 and helps to complete the picture of head and face and to mark a transition to the description of the beloved's neck and chest.

"Neck" is likened to military architecture, suggesting strength, erectness, perhaps even aloofness. Her head will not easily be turned by the blandishments of other men. The portrait of strong beauty is embellished by the comparison of her tiered or layered necklaces to *"bucklers"* (usually a small, round shield) and *"shields"* (here a virtual synonym for buckler) hung there by their warriors (*"mighty men"* is the same Heb. word as *"valiant"* in 3:7 and is a further clue to the link between the processional and this part of the ceremony). A clear picture of how strikingly shields were used to adorn citadels (*"armory,"* which literally describes a building built of stone courses or layers) comes from Ezekiel's taunt against Tyre (27:10–11). The *"breasts"* are depicted with a delicacy that contrasts dramatically to the military simile of the neck. *"Two"* (used twice) and *"twins"* speak of balance and symmetry. *"Fawns"* (cf. 7:4; the same word is translated *"young stag"* in 2:9, 17; 8:14) calls up thoughts of gentle beauty, of an intimate attractiveness that invites petting, affectionate touching. The erotic overtones of *"gazelle"* and *"young stag"* have already been noted above (2:9), as have the innuendoes present in *"feed among the lilies"* (2:16; 6:3).

A note of *yearning* (v. 6) is inserted in the poem before its literalistic summary (v. 7; see above). The first two lines are identical to those of

2:17 and with the *deer*-language help to tie Poem III to Poem II. *"Myrrh"* and *"frankincense"* recall the picture of the processional (3:6) but here refer to the fragrance of the woman's body (see on 1:3, 12–14) as *"mountain"* and *"hill"* (see on 2:8, 17) reveal. His eagerness is virtually unbearable, and his words of desire seem almost to distract him from his song of description, though he does compose himself to finish it in proper fashion (v. 7), repeating and strengthening the declaration of her beauty with which he began.

The purpose of this *song of description* (vv. 1–7) is not evaluation, as though the lover were judging a beauty contest. Its purpose is a public celebration of her worth to him and his consequent commitment to her. By carefully detailing that worth in images compellingly attractive to the ancient, Middle Eastern eye, he is underscoring how much he loves her, how deeply he wants her, how firmly he intends to stay with her. What she may have looked like to others is irrelevant. Her beauty is in the eye and heart of the one who beholds her. By the song of description he singles her out, praises her to the sky, and pledges himself to her till death do them part. It is not to compare her to other women but to exclude all other women that he sings this song.

His Invitation to the Bride

> 8 Come with me from Lebanon, my spouse,
> With me from Lebanon.
> Look from the top of Amana,
> From the top of Senir and Hermon,
> From the lions' dens,
> From the mountains of the leopards.
> *Song of Sol. 4:8*

The commitment implied in the description-song (vv. 1–7) is made explicit here in these unmistakable words of invitation. By his address to her, *"my spouse,"* the bond is sealed. The Hebrew word suggests permanent incorporation of the woman into the man's family and can be translated either "bride" as here (cf. 4:9–12; 5:1) or "daughter-in-law" as in Ruth's case (Ruth 1:6–8, 22; 2:20, 22; 4:15). Since *"spouse"* is used only in Poem III of the Song, it adds weight to the argument that this section of the book describes the actual wedding events.

The references to *"Lebanon"* and its trio of northern mountain peaks are hard to take literally[2]: *"Amana"* (probably the mountain, whose modern name is Jebel Zebedani, standing at the source of the Amana or Abana River northwest of Damascus; cf. 2 Kings 5:12), *"Senir"* (said to be the Amorite name of Mt. Hermon; Deut. 3:9; the fact that Senir and Hermon are mentioned together in 1 Chron. 5:23 may suggest that Senir denotes part of the Hermon range, possibly the southern section), *"Hermon"* (the dominant peak of Palestine, 9100 feet above sea level, whose snowy slopes are the sources of the Jordan). There is no other hint in the text that the woman is *in* Lebanon, so a literal rendering would need to translate the Hebrew for *"from"* as *in.*[3] Read thus, the call to *"come"* and "journey" (a better translation than *"look"*; cf. Isa. 57:9) would be to a peaceful, remote honeymoon, perhaps with some animal-watching thrown in. *"Lions"* and *leopards* were a regular part of Palestine's ecology well into the Christian era (cf. Hos. 13:7) and, though thought extinct, leopards have again been sighted during the past dozen years or so. The beasts may add to the erotic mood, since Canaanite mythology records accounts of the goddess of love likened to a lion.[4] Even the prospect of a honeymoon journey seems strange in a text that moves immediately to the prospect of nuptial intercourse. Better, then, it may be to hear verse 8 as a snatch of a northern love-song used here to underscore the lover's desire to be alone with and close to his bride. After all, neither "Red River Valley" nor "Springtime in the Rockies" is really about geography![5]

His Admiration of the Bride

9 You have ravished my heart,
My sister, my spouse;
You have ravished my heart
With one look of your eyes,
With one link of your necklace.
10 How fair is your love,
My sister, my spouse!

> How much better than wine is your love,
> And the scent of your perfumes
> Than all spices!
> 11 Your lips, O my spouse,
> Drip as the honeycomb;
> Honey and milk are under your tongue;
> And the fragrance of your garments
> Is like the fragrance of Lebanon.
> 12 A garden enclosed
> Is my sister, my spouse,
> A spring shut up,
> A fountain sealed.
> 13 Your plants are an orchard of pomegranates
> With pleasant fruits,
> Fragrant henna with spikenard,
> 14 Spikenard and saffron,
> Calamus and cinnamon,
> With all trees of frankincense,
> Myrrh and aloes,
> With all the chief spices—
> 15 A fountain of gardens,
> A well of living waters,
> And streams from Lebanon.
>
> *Song of Sol. 4:9–15*

If verses 1–7 detailed the beautiful features of the bride, verses 9–15 spell out the impact of those features on the groom. It is a *song of admiration,* admiration that results in arousal. Her appearance and his description of it have *"ravished my heart,"* as he puts it twice for emphasis. Other middle eastern poetry uses *"heart"* as a description of the male sexual organ whose excitement readies the husband for intercourse. The picture may well be that graphic here.[6] The feelings of belonging are conveyed not only by *"spouse"* (see on v. 8) but by its reinforcement in *"sister"* (cf. v. 12; 5:11), a term of exquisite endearment that promises the beloved a place in her husband's life as close as that of a blood relative; the two view themselves virtually as one person.

A friend of mine from India would understand this passage. He once expressed dismay when I told him I viewed my brothers as other persons. His view of family ties bound together all family members into one personality. *"Sister,"* so understood, conveys no intimation of incest. *"Eyes"* have always played a featured role in interpersonal communication. The bride's "come hither" gaze though just a brief glance *("one look")* has added to her lover's stimulation (cf. 1:15; 4:1; 6:5; 7:4). *"Link of your necklace"* seems a little out of place in a passage which focuses on the bride's person more than her adornments, though *"garments"* are in view (v. 11). "One throb of your throat" is a possible translation that offers a more powerful parallel to "one look of your eyes."[7]

At verse 10, talk has led to touch. The caressing that the beloved yearned for (1:2, 12–14; 2:3–6, 15–17; 3:4) has begun. *"Your love"* means "your acts of loving," which were being extolled and experienced simultaneously. For *"wine"* as a figure of love's exhilaration, see 1:2, 4; 2:4. *"Scent of your perfume"* captures the natural fragrance of her body aglow with her response to his touch and with her anticipation of their total union. *"All spices"* is a superlative, embracing the whole catalog of odoriferous substances already noted: ointments, 1:3; spikenard, myrrh, henna, 1:12–14; frankincense, fragrant powders, 3:6; yet to come (v. 14) are saffron, calamus, cinnamon, and aloes. Her body alone outdoes them all, even imparting to her *"garments"* (v. 11) a *"fragrance"* worthy of *"Lebanon"* (for *"Lebanon"* as "the best," see on 3:9). Kissing (v. 11) arouses them both (note her initial wish, 1:2). Whereas in 4:3 he praised how her *"lips"* and mouth looked, here he lauds their taste: *"honeycomb"* (5:1; cf. Ps. 19:11; Prov. 5:3), a favorite biblical metaphor of sweetness; *"honey and milk,"* whose combination made the promised land of Canaan attractive to Israel's wilderness wanderers (Num. 13:27). *"Tongue"* points to the depth and fullness of the kissing.

Like any wise lover, he has not rushed the pace. It is union and communion, not relief or release, that he seeks. He gives praise and pleasure at each stage. He turns now (vv. 12–15) to contemplate the final step, his entry into the inmost chamber of her personhood, the most precious expression of her femininity, which he describes in a cluster of terms that signal beauty, privacy, refreshment, and exclusiveness: *"Garden* (4:12, 15–16; 5:1; 6:2) *enclosed,"* protected from the ravages of marauders and the prying eyes of the curious, open only to him who has its key; *"spring shut up"* (the Heb. word is the same for "enclosed" and "shut up"; its basic meaning is "locked" or "fastened"), its precious liquid reserved for private use; *"fountain sealed,"* a phrase virtually synonymous with the preceding;

perhaps we should picture the spring or fountain as enclosed in the garden and responsible for its remarkable fertility and fragrance (vv. 13–14); *"your plants"* seems to refer specifically to the beloved's pubic area but suggestions vary as to how—the Hebrew word may mean tunnel, canal, or watercourse (Joel 2:8; Neh. 3:15) or also "branches" or "limbs" and could refer to her legs, as one recent paraphrase implies,

> "Stretching your limbs you open—
> A field of pomegranates blooms."[8]

"Orchard of pomegranates" seems to depict the beauty and colortone of her vulva which abounds in delights to his senses, especially his delight in her exotic fragrance to which subject he returns (note vv. 10–11) with increased zeal (v. 14). New in the list of zestful and treasured scents are *"saffron,"* a yellow powder crushed from the blossoms of a variety of the crocus family, expensive because some four thousand flowers furnish only an ounce[9]; *"calamus,"* derived from a sweet reed or cane that smells like ginger; *"cinnamon,"* bark or oil from a tree of southeast Asia; its ritual use is featured in Exodus 30:23–29, and its erotic use, in Proverbs 7:17; *"aloes,"* probably a spicy drug drawn from the leaves of a shrub native to Socotra, an island at the southern end of the Red Sea; embalmers used it (John 19:38–42) as well as lovers (Prov. 7:17); *"chief spices"* serves to summarize the list of the "choicest" or finest fragrances and to make room for any other favorites not mentioned. Valuable beyond price, rare beyond measure, delightful beyond telling is the intimate relationship he is about to enjoy. No wonder his Hebrew word for *"orchard"* (v. 13) is related to our term "paradise."

His closing words (v. 15) distill the essence of her superlativeness: *"fountain of gardens"* speaks of the abundance of her ability to provide refreshment; the plural *"gardens"* (cf. the singular in v. 12, 16; 5:1) connotes either a multitude of gardens or perhaps better, "the best of gardens"; *"well of living* (running) *waters"* is artesian, fed by an inexhaustible underground supply; *"streams from Lebanon"* carries this picture of bounty a step further; the snow packs on the high mountains guarantee a spate of water unmatched in Israel's seasonal streams that fill and empty according to the rhythms of the rainfall. One inference of this picture of abundant moisture is that her body is prepared by its own secretions for the long-awaited consummation. *"Lebanon,"* with which this part of Poem III has begun and ended (vv. 8, 15), intimates that she is the finest possible person, even more poetically and powerfully than did his declaration of her beauty *("you are fair")* at the opening and closing of the song in 4:1–7.

HER INVITATION TO THE GROOM

> 16 Awake, O north wind,
> And come, O south!
> Blow upon my garden,
> That its spices may flow out.
> Let my beloved come to his garden
> And eat its pleasant fruits.
>
> *Song of Sol. 4:16*

The beloved can remain silent no longer. The songs and embraces of her lover are begging for her response. It comes in the form of a personal *("my beloved,"* her favorite name for him; see at 1:13) invitation, issued subtly and poignantly through the *"wind,"* whether blowing from *"north"* or *"south"*; the directions are not so much specific geography as a comprehensive wish that *"wind"* from anywhere would waft her fragrant scents of readiness to him. See Ecclesiastes 1:6 for movements of the wind. *"Awake"* translates the same Hebrew verb used in the oath formula imposed on the daughters of Jerusalem (2:7; 3:5; 8:4), where it is read *"stir up."* Her song is carefully crafted to match and encapsulate his: *"my garden," "his garden"* echo 4:12, 15; *"spices"* recall 4:10, 13–14; *"pleasant fruits"* hark back to 4:13; *"come"* answers his call to her in 4:8, and may carry an added sexual nuance, since the Hebrew word (literally, "enter" or "come in") is used frequently of sexual penetration (Gen. 16:2); *"flow out"* repeats the Hebrew root translated *"streams"* in 4:15 and seals the connection between the abundance of moisture pictured there and her heightened physical preparation for love.

HIS SONG OF CONSUMMATION

> 5:1a I have come to my garden, my sister, my spouse;
> I have gathered my myrrh with my spice;

> I have eaten my honeycomb with my honey;
> I have drunk my wine with my milk.
>
> *Song of Sol. 5:1a*

The past tenses are a clear clue to what has happened. The invitation has been responded to in every detail and more. The fullness of covenant-love (*"my sister, my spouse;"* see at 4:8–9) has been experienced. The true marriage feast—the verbs focus on gathering (or plucking to eat), eating, and drinking—has been completed. Language applied to kissing and caressing in 4:10–11 is here employed to picture the delights of the total caress, the ultimate kiss. It is better *"wine,"* even more fragrant *"myrrh,"* the sweetest *"honey"* imaginable. Satiety is the result, according to the man. The woman's Amen to this song of satisfaction is yet to be heard in Poem IV.

A Toast to the Bride and Groom

> 1b Eat, O friends!
> Drink, yes, drink deeply,
> O beloved ones!
>
> *Song of Sol. 5:1b*

There is no reason for any of this to end. It is a banquet to be savored hour after hour and time after time. And so a nameless group of friends, probably the daughters of Jerusalem, lend their encouragement by toasting the intoxicating delights of love. *"Drink deeply"* is literally "get drunk" and the final words are probably not a direct address but a further reference to embraces of affection (cf. 1:2, 4; 4:10; 7:12). The toast, then, concludes, "Go on drinking and don't stop until you get drunk from your lovemaking." The poem that commenced with the public spectacle of a wedding processional concludes with the public affirmation of the lovers' private joy. Marital acts go on best behind closed doors, but their health, welfare, and delight have incalculable consequences for friends and family. Would that every couple had this kind of cheering section the night they first became intimate! Would that every cheering section had a couple as committed, as covenanted, as hungrily passionate, as this one to whom to offer its toast!

NOTES

1. G. L. Carr, *The Song of Solomon*. TOTC, pp. 112–13.

2. On the geography of this passage, see M. Pope, *Song of Songs*, pp. 474–75; see also, *The Macmillan Bible Atlas*, map 8.

3. G. L. Carr, p. 119.

4. M. Pope, p. 477.

5. R. Gordis, *The Song of Songs*, p. 85: "This verse may be a fragment of a song emanating from the mountain ranges lying to the north of Israel."

6. Pope, pp. 479–80.

7. H. J. Schonfield, *The Song of Songs*, p. 91.

8. Marcia Falk, *The Song of Songs*, p. 18 (cf. Bibliography).

9. G. L. Carr, p. 125.

CHAPTER FIVE

Poem IV: Frustration and Delight

Song of Solomon 5:2–6:3

The wedding is over. The dust and clamor of the pomp and ceremony that dominated Poem III have settled. No hint is given of the passing of time between the two poems. Is it days, weeks, months? No matter. What is clear is that passion still runs high, but that satisfaction of that passion may be delayed by the lovers' differences in schedule, energy, health, or personal circumstances. If Poem III pictured the uninterrupted revelries of the wedding night, Poem IV portrays the realisms of married life with its rhythm of frustration and delight. The two partners are not always ready for lovemaking at the same time or one partner may not even be available when the other is eager. Such frustrations are painful and can stretch the covenant bond. In turn, they can engender greater anticipation, more fiery ardor, and make the union all the richer when it finally does take place. And a sense of humor can keep frustration from souring into bitterness, as this poem reminds us.

The scene is set by a *dream* sequence (5:2–7) akin to that of 3:1–5. It is longer than the previous one, contains stronger elements of conflict—the lover, merely absent from the first dream, here knocks, calls, and then disappears, and the watchmen, who stood silent as she rushed by them with a quick inquiry of her lover's whereabouts, here take physical advantage of her—and ends in frustration: she seeks and does not find. Indeed, she not he is found by the watchmen and subjected to shame. Again, the dream is followed by an *oath* imposed on the daughters of Jerusalem (5:8), not that they let love run its course (3:5), but that they tell her lover, should they see him, that she grows faint with love.

Their response (5:9) deliberately eases the tension and heightens the mood of the dream-report. It is obviously a *tease* as both its content and form betray. The repetition of the question makes a game of the conversation and purposely delays its answer. The content of the question with its reminder of her call on them to make a vow is a humorous way of saying, can anyone possibly be handsome enough for you to exact such a binding, almost legal, commitment from us?

Their tease is like bait to her and she snaps it up—hook, line, and sinker (5:10–16). In a chain of bright metaphors and similes she describes his physical attributes from head to feet in language so brilliant that the daughters of Jerusalem are not only convinced of his stellar qualities but teasingly volunteer to go with her to enjoy them for themselves (6:1). The playful sequence is brought to a winsome close by her declaration that the quest is ended. She knows where her lover is or soon will be—in her arms feasting on the delights of her love, as the two renew and express their pledge of loyalty to each other (6:2–3).

The road to true love is not always straight or smooth. Disappointments, delays, frustrations there will be. Accepted as part of life within the deathless covenant pledge, they can be enhancements to marital joy. Better are those bumps and bends with a lifelong partner than a marble pathway with anyone else.

REPORT OF A VEXING DREAM

2 I sleep, but my heart is awake;
It is the voice of my beloved!
He knocks, saying,
"Open for me, my sister, my love,
My dove, my perfect one;
For my head is covered with dew,
My locks with the drops of the night."
3 I have taken off my robe;
How can I put it on again?
I have washed my feet;
How can I defile them?
4 My beloved put his hand
By the latch of the door,
And my heart yearned for him.
5 I arose to open for my beloved,

And my hands dripped with myrrh,
My fingers with liquid myrrh,
On the handles of the lock.
6 I opened for my beloved,
But my beloved had turned away and was gone.
My heart leaped up when he spoke.
I sought him, but I could not find him;
I called him, but he gave me no answer.
7 The watchmen who went about the city found me.
They struck me, they wounded me;
The keepers of the walls
Took my veil away from me.

Song of Sol. 5:2–7

A dream seems the most likely setting for this episode. *"I sleep but my heart* (here the seat of the thinking and choosing in which she engages; therefore, "mind" in English) *is awake"* suggests either a dream or a twilight zone between sleep and wakefulness when the imagination plays tricks on our understanding of reality. A modification of the twilight zone approach finds in the narrative evidence of a difference in intensity between the lover's ardor (v. 2) and the beloved's reluctance to inconvenience herself and respond to his overture (v. 3). It is, on this view, the difference in erotic temperature between the two of them that prompts the tension.[1] The lover's eagerness is highlighted in the lure of his *"voice"* (see on 2:8, 14; 5:16; 8:13), in the urgent manner in which he *"knocks"* (almost beats or bangs at the door; cf. Judg. 19:22), in his begging her, *"open for me,"* in the quartet of endearing names *"my sister"* (see on 4:9), *"my love"* (see on 1:9), *"my dove"* (see on 2:14), *"my perfect one"* (the positive way of saying "without blemish" as he did in 4:7; cf. 6:9 for the other occurrence of *"my perfect one,"* i.e., the one which is complete in every imaginable way; the masculine form was applied to Job, *"blameless"*; 1:1, 8; 2:3), and in his description of his *"head"* and *"locks"* dampened with the dewy night air. This last reference sets the stage for her elaborate description of his *"head and hair"* in verse 11. His absence at bedtime and his disheveled condition are best explained by some agricultural task—tending sick animals or helping ewes drop their lambs—that kept him in the fields till early morning.

Whatever hesitation is voiced in verse 3 seems to have vanished by verses 4–5. The sound of his hand *"by the latch"* (or better in the keyhole, a much larger aperture than we are used to, given the simple technology of ancient locks) had stirred her. Her *"heart,"* now thoroughly alert, was aroused to the point of murmuring or churning (*"yearned"*) *"for him."* As she grasped the *"handles"* of the door bolt (*"lock"*; but see the use of the word for gate-bolts in Neh. 3:3, 6, 13–15), she felt *"myrrh"* (see on 1:13) on her *"fingers"* in such abundance that it dripped. Where did it come from? Had he anointed the bolt with it as he slipped his hand through the key opening? Had she squeezed the *"liquid"* from the bag between her breasts (1:13)? Either answer is possible. So is another: the myrrh signaled her readiness for love. Her "mountain of myrrh" (4:6) had secreted a fragrant invitation to her husband for whose embraces she was totally prepared.

The frustration hit her with full force the moment she *"opened"* the door (v. 6), only to find *"my beloved had turned away and was gone."* His voice (*"when he spoke"*; cf. v. 2) had aroused her beyond control and she was willing to take any risk to be with him. That risk as a measure of her passion and commitment is accented in the cruel conduct of the *"watchmen"* (see on 3:3), who *"struck"* (pummeled or beat) her, *"wounded"* (or bruised) her, and stripped away the light *"veil"* or shawl which she had quickly thrown over her head and upper body for cover from prying eyes and moist night air (v. 7). No mention here is made of the *"robe"* or heavy outer tunic which she laid aside when she went to bed (v. 3). The *"watchmen"* are further defined as *"keepers of the walls"* (v. 7), a phrase which may carry sexual overtones in light of the bride's description of herself as a *"wall"* with *"breasts like towers"* (8:10). Having snatched away her protective covering, what "wall" were the watchmen guarding? The lewd acts of the watchmen are recorded to intensify the picture of the woman's passion and her single-hearted desire to find her lover, even in circumstances that left her vulnerable to terror. The fact that she pauses neither to give vent to her feelings of shame nor to call for their punishment seems to pinpoint the sharpness of her focus. Her shrouded head and midnight wandering may have marked her in their eyes as a prostitute to whom they felt no obligation to show common decency. Such an understanding would be a reason but not an excuse for such behavior. When police become muggers, life is precarious for everyone.

Whether there are sexual word-plays involved elsewhere in this report we can only guess. Twice the word *"open"* is used without door in Hebrew as object (5:2, 6). *"Latch"* is literally aperture or hole, while *"feet"* (v. 3) or *"hand"* (v. 4) can be a euphemism for genitals. Double meanings have played a part in love poetry both ancient and modern and are certainly not absent from the Song. Note *"door"* as a figure of sexual availability in 8:9.

CALL FOR URGENT HELP

> 8 I charge you, O daughters of Jerusalem,
>   If you find my beloved,
>   That you tell him I am lovesick!
>   *Song of Sol. 5:8*

The setting for this verse must come at the end of the dream sequence, if it is still in progress, or early the next morning when the woman recounted to them the whole story. Intensity of passion is still the dominate theme, passion turned pathetic by its failure to find release and fulfillment. *"Lovesick"* here seems to describe frustration from sexual abstinence rather than exhaustion from sexual activity (cf. on 2:5).

TEASING QUESTION

> 9 What is your beloved
>   More than another beloved,
>   O fairest among women?
>   What is your beloved
>   More than another beloved,
>   That you so charge us?
>   *Song of Sol. 5:9*

The daughters of Jerusalem lighten the mood with their playful query. The rapid switches in scene and tone are easily explained if the whole context is a dream. Dreams do things like that. In our reading of the Song this is only the second time that they have spoken (see 5:1b for the first). Their role here is obviously to tee up the ball for the woman to take a big swing at in her description of the lover that follows (5:10–16). Their fourfold use of *"beloved"* echoes the woman's favorite name for the man (see on 1:14). They may be mimicking the frequency with which she used it (five times in 5:2–8). *"O fairest among women"* (cf. 6:1) may be an effort to reassure her that no one so attractive will be neglected for long by her husband, but it has also a poetic role: it serves as a suspense-building line that postpones the final, punch-like, clause of the question. The repetition of the first two lines in lines four and five adds to that effect. *"That you so charge us"* takes us back to verse 8 and asks what is so all-consumingly excellent about your lover that you go to the extravagance of binding us by an oath to tell him how desperate is your love.

DESCRIPTION OF LOVER'S BEAUTY

10 My beloved is white and ruddy,
   Chief among ten thousand.
11 His head is like the finest gold;
   His locks are wavy,
   And black as a raven.
12 His eyes are like doves
   By the rivers of waters,
   Washed with milk,
   And fitly set.
13 His cheeks are like a bed of spices,
   Like banks of scented herbs.
   His lips are lilies,
   Dripping liquid myrrh.
14 His hands are rods of gold
   Set with beryl.
   His body is carved ivory
   Inlaid with sapphires.
15 His legs are pillars of marble
   Set on bases of fine gold.
   His countenance is like Lebanon,
   Excellent as the cedars.
16 His mouth is most sweet,
   Yes, he is altogether lovely.
   This is my beloved,
   And this is my friend,
   O daughters of Jerusalem!

Song of Sol. 5:10–16

In literary form the beloved's *song of description* matches what he sang to her in 4:1–7 and will sing again in 6:4–9. Like her attributes, his are praised in terms that stress strength, sensitivity, beauty, rarity, and value. The poem (like 4:1–7) begins and ends with a general introduction and a general summation, both of which are more literal than figurative. This style is designed to make plain beyond any doubt what the similes intend to convey.

"White" (v. 10) speaks of dazzling or shimmering radiance; the Hebrew word may describe plain, clear talk without stammering (Isa. 32:4). *"Ruddy"* may picture a healthy complexion not overscorched by the sun (cf. on 1:5–6) but a sound, vibrant earth tone or possibly a reddish cosmetic coloring. *"Chief"* means "conspicuous" like a flag or banner held aloft and visible from a great distance. No assembly of any size (*"ten thousand"* stands for an uncountable number, "myriads") would be so large as to lose him in the pack.

"Finest gold" (v. 11) combines two Hebrew words for gold to suggest polished luster, well-molded features, and an overall cast of excellence to *"his head."* *"Wavy"* pictures *"his locks"* (cf. 5:2) heaped up in luxuriant curls like clusters of dates or date blossoms on a palm tree. The *"raven"* color is not only black without a tinge of gray, but carries an iridescent sheen that glistens in the sunlight like the wings and body of the great black bird. The *"dove"* simile for *"eyes"* (v. 12) has graced the Song before (1:15; 4:1). Here, applied to the man, it is embellished to describe their setting. *"Doves"* seems to describe the iris, perhaps dark gray in color. *"Rivers of water"* captures the vitality and freshness of the eye, well-lubricated by its natural moisture. *"Washed with milk"* speaks of the whites of the eyes whose clarity and purity provide the apt contrast to the grayness of the iris. *"Fitly set"* is a possible reading of a difficult Hebrew phrase, but most commentators and some versions (e.g., JB, NEB) continue the figure of washing by picturing the dove-like irises "sitting by brimming (the Hebrew word looks to be related to a root meaning "full") pools."

Delicacy and fragrance characterize the *"cheeks"* (v. 13). *"Bed of spices"* (or spice-shrubs) may also suggest a graceful youthful beard, parallel to the *"bed of spices"* which may point to pubic hair in the woman's description of herself in 6:2. *"Banks* (or towers) *of scented herbs"* (a Hebrew word used only here) reinforces the aromatic note, which becomes even clearer if we change the vowels in the Hebrew word *"banks"* to a participial form, "raising" or "exuding" the aroma of *"scented herbs"* (cf. LXX, RSV, NIV). The line would then be appropriately parallel to *"dripping liquid myrrh"* (v. 13b). *"Lilies"* as a simile for *"his lips"* conveys the notion of sweet kisses (note the *"liquid myrrh"*; cf. 2:16; 4:5) and radiant, healthy color like that of a red or purple lotus or anemone.[3] The description returns to that *"most sweet* (cf. 2:3 for the same Heb. root) *mouth"* (or palate) in the summary conclusion at verse 16. In it center the tender displays of affection and the quiet grace of speech that make him so *"altogether lovely"* (or *"desirable"*) to her (v. 16).

Strength and value are the themes portrayed in the inventory of his physical attributes (vv. 14–15). *"Hands"* seems to include arms, as *"rods"* suggests. *"Beryl"* may be a more precise name for the gems that studded his arms than the Hebrew warrants, since *tarshish* usually is a place name applied to locations in the western Mediterranean like Sardinia or Spain (hence "Spanish jewels"; Carr). *"His body"* (or torso) is compared to slabs or plates of (better than *"carved"*) *"ivory"* in its sturdiness, smoothness, and rarity. The *"inlaid sapphires"* which encrust his trunk brighten the picture of wealth and splendor. *"His legs"* (or thighs) complete the anatomical overview in noble fashion with their *"marble"* columns and *"fine gold"* (see v. 11, for the same Heb. word) pedestals (*"bases"*). The summation of the picture may begin in verse 15b, where *"countenance"* stands for "entire appearance," *"Lebanon"* means "best" or "finest" (cf. on 3:9), and *"excellent* (or "choice") *as the cedars"* captures the grandeur and quality of his entire stature and bearing.

No statue of an emperor could warrant higher acclaim. Her final words signify that she has fully answered—in minute detail and grand hyperbole—the teasing question of her friends (v. 9). No wonder she risked her reputation to seek him! No wonder she subpoenaed her friends to inform him of her passion! No wonder she is pledged to him for life! He is not only her *"beloved,"* bound to her with ties as strong as those of kinship, but he is also her *"friend"* (the masculine counterpart to his pet name for her in 1:9, 15; 2:2, 10, 13; 4:1, 7; 5:2; 6:4), a companion chosen for congenial comradeship even more than for sexual attraction.

6:1   Where has your beloved gone,
         O fairest among women?
         Where has your beloved turned aside,
         That we may seek him with you?
                                               Song of Sol. 6:1

The response, in the form of a second playful question (cf. 5:9), shows how convinced were the daughters of Jerusalem by the woman's elaborate description of her husband. They are not only willing to relay her message of lovesickness to him; they are also eager to find out where he has *"gone"* or *"turned aside"* in order to help her find him. The poetic structure helps frame the tease (cf. on 5:9). The punch line *"that we may seek him with you"* is deliberately delayed by the repetition of the question and the insertion of the address, *"O fairest among women."*

RESPONSE OF DELIGHT AND COMMITMENT

2   My beloved has gone to his garden,
      To the beds of spices,
      To feed his flock in the gardens,
      And to gather lilies.
3   I am my beloved's,
      And my beloved is mine.
      He feeds his flock among the lilies.
                                               Song of Sol. 6:2–3

The precise mood of these verses is not easy to catch. If only we could hear the woman's tone of voice! Is it remorseful, as though she regrets her slow response to the lover's knock (5:2)? Reflective, as though she reminisces on their previous trysts? Baffled, as though he has gone where she cannot reach him? Hopeful, as she anticipates his return and savors its delights while waiting? I vote for the last. She seems to be making two major points: (1) she will not share her beloved with anyone, not even the daughters of Jerusalem; the two of them are bound together by the *formula of mutual possession* (cf. on

2:16; 7:10); (2) she will not accept frustration as her final lot—she knows full well how much she is loved and counts on that love to bring her lover back.

That confidence is displayed in the way she fancies his whereabouts. *"Garden"* stands for her person and its most intimate parts (4:12, 15). *"Beds of spices"* (or spice-shrubs) both connect with her song about him (5:13) and recall the scent of spicy substances that sweetened the air on their wedding night (4:13–14). *"Feed"* and *"lilies"* repeat 2:16; *"flock"* does not occur in either text in Hebrew. *"Gather"* is the only new word here and serves both to keep the passage from rote repetition of standard motifs and to add another metaphor for loving intimacy, "plucking" or "gleaning" (cf. Ruth 2:8). That the woman's hope was well-founded becomes plain in Poem V when the husband again extols her beauty. Not by smoothness but by constancy is the path of true love characterized.

NOTES

1. For the *dream* approach, see Gordis, *The Song of Songs*, p. 62, and Schonfield, *The Song of Songs*, p. 93. For the half asleep-half awake reading, see Pope, *Song of Songs*, p. 511; for the casual reception picture, see S. C. Glickman, *A Song for Lovers*, pp. 62–65 (cf. Bibliography) and Carr, *The Song of Solomon*, pp. 130–31.

2. So Gordis, *The Song of Songs*, p. 63; Pope, *Song of Songs*, p. 502; M. Falk, *The Song of Songs*, p. 19 (cf. Bibliography).

3. Pope, *The Song of Songs*, p. 541.

CHAPTER SIX

Poem V: Pomp and Celebration

Song of Solomon 6:4–8:4

This poem seems to be a counterpart to Poem III in its combination of public spectacle and private encounter. It is dominated by the man's songs of description (6:4–10) and yearning (6:11–12; 7:6–9), with a central contribution from a company of friends, presumably the daughters of Jerusalem (6:13a; 7:1–5). Not surprisingly, the woman, whose first contribution is a brief and teasing question (6:13b), has the final words in her song of invitation with its joyfully positive response to her lover's overtures (7:10–8:4). The balance and symmetry of the poem are noteworthy: it begins with the man's words of total commitment and wholehearted appreciation; it ends with the woman's attestation of her total commitment and wholehearted anticipation; in between, the daughters of Jerusalem confirm the entire arrangement by joining in the celebration of the woman's beauty and the man's good judgment in pledging himself to her.

In our reading, then, Poem IV (5:2–6:3) is an interlude in the wedding festivities designed to call attention to the rhythm of frustration and satisfaction to which all covenant couples can vouch. Hence, it beautifies and intensifies both the public and private expressions of love which grace Poem V. The specific points of comparison between Poem III (3:6–5:1) and Poem V will become apparent in the course of the commentary. Here we need note only that the woman is the awe-inspiring center of Poem V, comparable in beauty to two famous cities of Israel (6:4), more desirable than the scores of women who cluster in the royal harem (6:8), and as impressively radiant as the luminaries of the heavens (6:10). These ceremonial pronouncements coupled with the pictures of her flashing dances (6:13–7:5) make it clear that the nuptial feasts, which often last for days in the Middle East, were still running at full tilt.

323

If humility is a prerequisite of any technical study of the Song, it is called for in huge doses in this poem. There seem to be more questions per inch about the meaning of words, the identity of the speakers, and the connections between the subsections than in any other segment of the book. Since detailed lists and examinations of the options are available elsewhere, I shall try only to flag the troublesome places and state my best judgment of their meanings. Happily, the overall mood and emphasis of the poem are within our grasp. And it, like all the other major songs, will confirm the judgment of the Song's title that this song of love and of lovers and of the friends of lovers is indeed the best of songs.

A CAPITAL DESCRIPTION OF THE BELOVED

4 O my love, you are as beautiful as Tirzah,
   Lovely as Jerusalem,
   Awesome as an army with banners!
5 Turn your eyes away from me,
   For they have overcome me.
   Your hair is like a flock of goats
   Going down from Gilead.
6 Your teeth are like a flock of sheep
   Which have come up from the washing;
   Every one bears twins,
   And none is barren among them.
7 Like a piece of pomegranate
   Are your temples behind your veil.
8 There are sixty queens
   And eighty concubines,
   And virgins without number.
9 My dove, my perfect one,
   Is the only one,
   The only one of her mother,
   The favorite of the one who bore her.
   The daughters saw her
   And called her blessed,
   The queens and the concubines,
   And they praised her.
10 Who is she who looks forth as the morning,
   Fair as the moon,

> Clear as the sun,
> Awesome as an army with banners?
>
> *Song of Sol. 6:4–10*

Whatever form the frustration took (5:2–7) and whatever may have been its cause—a dream, a nocturnal anxiety attack, a turn of coolness on the woman's part—this passage assures us that the husband has lost none of his ardor. To the contrary, in power, imagery, and praise, his *song of description* surpasses all that we have yet heard from him. The intoxicating hours of the wedding night (5:1) have given his eye a keenness, his heart a warmth, and his tongue an eloquence that lift his singing to new heights. Eager anticipation (4:1–15) has matured to all-encompassing satisfaction. In the earlier songs, he looked and longed to taste. Now he has tasted and knows intimately what he had looked at. With all five senses in full play, he witnesses to the singularity, the uniqueness, the incomparability of his loved one.

In the flow of the song, the familiar is wrapped in the novel. The descriptions (vv. 5–7) of *"hair," "teeth,"* and *"cheeks" ("temples")* are repeated almost verbatim from his first song (4:1–3). He uses them here because they were standard descriptive formulae, expected by beloved and audience alike in these litanies of praise. They serve also as links to the prenuptial song and by their familiarity help to spotlight the new elements which are the core of this passage.

The first of these is the comparison with *"Tirzah"* and *"Jerusalem"* (v. 4). These are startling similes in that they liken the person of the woman to two notable cities, without singling out any specific feature either of hers or of the local architecture. Hence, they contrast with the other instances of massive imagery: *"your neck is like the tower of David"* (4:4); *"your nose is like a tower of Lebanon"* (7:4); *"your head crowns you like Carmel"* (7:5). In 6:4 the picture is all encompassing. The woman's total beauty is as impressive as that of *"Jerusalem"* (cf. Lam. 2:15) or of *"Tirzah,"* an ancient town first captured by Joshua (12:24) and later named capital of the Northern Kingdom (1 Kings 14:17; 16:8–9, 15), a privilege it enjoyed for about half a century until Omri replaced it with Samaria (1 Kings 16:24). If the site assigned to Tirzah by several archaeologists is correct, then it was situated a few miles northeast of Shechem in a well-watered area prolific in its gardens and orchards. Tirzah's very name contains a pun, since it is built on the Hebrew root "to please" or "to delight" (found in *"until it pleases,"*

2:7; 3:5; 8:4). The mention of *"Tirzah,"* which fell into obscurity in Israel's later history, suggests that the language of this song is ancient and may have been passed down through the centuries from Tirzah's heyday (about 900 B.C.), as part of traditional wedding poetry.

The second point of innovation is the summary line that wraps this song at top and bottom like an envelope: *"Awesome as an army with banners"* (vv. 4, 10). We found reason to question the military language in 2:4; we find even more reason to question it here. *"Army"* does not appear in the Hebrew text but is an attempt to describe what is "embannered" or "looked upon because of its splendor," as the Hebrew participle may literally be rendered. In both verses the word is feminine in gender, plural in number, and passive in voice. In verse 4 it seems to describe the two capitals and in verse 10, the *"morning"* (literally "dawning"), the *"moon"* (literally the "white object") and the *"sun"* (literally "the hot thing"). Renditions like "splendid to look upon"[2] or, more dramatically, "awe-inspiring as the great sights"[3] deal fairly with the Hebrew and have the advantage of intensifying the chief images—the impressive cities (v. 4), the dominant luminaries (v. 10)—without topping them with another point of comparison.

The third touch of innovation is the plea, *"Turn your eyes away from me for they have overcome me"* (v. 5). Up till now, he has been delighted to gaze into those eyes (1:15; 4:1), to look her full in the face (2:14). But he has, on the wedding night, experienced the ultimate *tête-a-tête*. He knows the power such eyes wield, the promise such eyes proffer. One gaze had sent his heart (and all his manly desires) leaping (4:9). The prolonged embrace of eye-to-eye lovemaking had imparted to her eyes the magic to provoke him to uncontrollable excitement. The rest of her face he can describe with the standard phrases (vv. 5b–7). Her eyes have to be avoided like the noonday sun.

The fourth note of innovation is the contrast between the size of a royal harem and the uniqueness of the bride (vv. 8–9). Kings were wont to measure their power, wealth, international prestige, and virility by the count of their *"queens"* (the women who held highest rank in the court and whose children comprised the noble youth of the kingdom), their *"concubines"* (a group of women who performed both sexual and social functions and were held in higher esteem than the rest of the royal entourage except the queens), and their *"virgins"* (the young women of the kingdom who, not committed to other men, might be commandeered for the amusement of the king). The increasing size of each group, *"sixty"* (note the parallel to *"sixty valiant men,"* 3:7), *"eighty,"* and *"without number"* documented the extent of the pool of valuable and beautiful women available to royalty (on the power of a king to accumulate a vast harem, note Solomon's "seven hundred wives, princesses, and three hundred concubines," 1 Kings 11:3, and Ahasuerus' edict to replace his deposed queen by recruiting candidates, among whom was Esther).

In the scales by which the lover weighed such matters, all those women were more than overbalanced by his darling, whose singularity is featured in a cluster of phrases (v. 9): *"my dove"* (5:2), *"my perfect one"* (5:2) *"the only one," "favorite"* of her mother. The capstone of the comparison comes when the women, led by *"the daughters"* (of Jerusalem?), far from miffed by the accolades accorded the bride, join their voices in calling her happy *("blessed")* and in chanting her praises. Jealousy does not wear well at a wedding. The husband has every right to feel like a king and to view his bride as a combination of Helen of Troy, Joan of Arc, Florence Nightingale, and Sophia Loren.

The final bit of innovation comes in the closing comparison (v. 10), designed to balance and outshine the picture of the capitals in verse 4. The question form *"who is she"* repeats in Hebrew the phrase which introduced "Solomon's" processional in 3:6 (cf. 8:5), thus linking the beginning and the closing scenes of the wedding festivities. It also points to the majesty and mystery embodied in the woman. Her awesomeness is so impressive that it masks her identity and raises the question, *"who is she?"* Radiance seems to be her most notable attribute as the three key nouns tell us: *"morning"* (or dawn) speaks of the gradual brightening of the day and dispersing of the night, as daylight takes command and *"looks forth"* (or bends down) to watch the activities of earthlings; *"moon"* is a figure of beauty *("fair")* with its creamy alabaster sails scudding through the indigo sky; *"sun"* portrays bright warmth and as the dominant middle-eastern element of creation is as *"clear"* ("choice" or "outstanding") as the woman is to her mother (the same Heb. word is read *"favorite"* in v 9).

It would be hard to give any relationship a better start than this. To view a partner as incomparable, as awe-inspiring, as unique, as more important than legions of others is the stuff of which permanent covenants are fashioned.

AN ACCOUNT OF MATCHLESS INTIMACY

11 I went down to the garden of nuts
To see the verdure of the valley,
To see whether the vine had budded
And the pomegranates had bloomed.
12 Before I was even aware,
My soul had made me
As the chariots of my noble people.

Song of Sol. 6:11–12

The grammar gives us no clue as to who is speaking. And the commentaries and translations are divided on the matter. My vote for the man as narrator is based on the following considerations: (a) he has clearly been the singer in 6:4–10; (b) verses 11–12 are a coda to 6:4–10 more than an introduction to verse 13, since the song of the daughters (v. 13a) is not a call for the woman to *"return"* but for her to *"turn," "whirl,"* or *"leap"* in dancing, as the context in 6:13b–7:5 indicates; (c) descriptive songs like 6:4–10 are frequently followed by songs of yearning for physical intimacy (4:6; 7:6–9) or by actual descriptions of that intimacy, as we seem to find in 6:11–12 (cf. 5:1); (d) the terms *"garden"* (cf. 4:12, 15–17; 5:1; 8:13), *"vine"* (cf. 2:13; 7:8, 12; for vineyard, see 1:6; 7:12; 8:12), and *"pomegranates"* all occur most frequently in sections where the man is speaking. He uses them to paint poetic pictures of the woman's erogenous zones, to describe the secluded and fertile settings that will shelter and enhance their lovemaking, or to do both. The Song's penchant to double meanings suggests that the last option is the most probable one here. The lavish praise of the woman's beauty had so stimulated the man that he had sought a garden spot, more especially a walnut *("nuts")* grove, in a verdant *"valley,"* decked with grape vines and pomegranate trees, as the place to enjoy the companionship of his loved one.

If we understand the basic intent of verse 12, probably the most puzzling passage in the entire book, the results of that tryst had left him ecstatic. All sense of time and place suspended *("before I was even aware")* "my passionate desire, (a possible understanding of Hebrew *nephesh, "soul"),* had mounted me on a bed like a prince." We should note the steps by which we get to this reading from the quite different translation of the NKJV: (1) "had mounted me" is literally "had placed

328

me" which NKJV reads *"had made me"*; (2) "on a bed" is a paraphrase of *"chariots,"* which were certainly not war chariots in this context but may resemble the "bed" or "palanquin" of 3:7, 9; a word very similar in root and construction is *"seat"* in 3:10; whether "bed" in 6:12 is the woman on whom the man reclined or the litter that cradled them both we cannot tell; the plural form of the word may display its elegance or majesty; (3) "like" is a possible rendering of "with" (cf. Job 9:26; 37:18; 40:15), which should be read instead of *"my . . . people,"* both words containing the same consonants in Hebrew; (4) "prince" translates the Hebrew word as a noun not an adjective, "noble." The advantages of a translation something like this are that it follows closely the Hebrew text and entails no changes of consonants, that it is compatible both with its context and with similar patterns in the Song, and that it injects no jarring element of cryptic novelty as do the readings that treat the final words as a proper name of an otherwise unknown person (LXX, Vulg., KJV). Moreover, it provides, with its feelings of princely satisfaction, a fit close to the passage that compared the beloved's stately beauty to Tirzah and Jerusalem. She is the two splendid capitals. His possession of her grants him princely rank.

A TEASING REQUEST TO DANCE

> 13a   Return, return, O Shulamite;
>   Return, return, that we may look upon you!
> *Song of Sol. 6:13a*

This call to dance (*"return"* can mean simply "turn" or, if derived from a different root found in Arabic, "leap") introduces a new event in the wedding festivities and marks the major division in Poem V. The Hebrew text noted this by beginning chapter 7 with this verse. The fourfold repetition makes a game out of it with teasing suspense and increasing intensity. The poetic form is parallel to the earlier teases uttered by the daughters of Jerusalem in 5:9; 6:1. The completion of the sentence is delayed by an address to the woman—here *"O Shulamite"* (best understood not as a reference to her hometown which has been identified with Shunem [Jos. 19:18; 1 Kings 1:3, 15] nor as an echo of a pagan deity, Shelem, but as a feminine form of Solomon and, therefore, part of the royal motif which threads through the Song; see chapter 1)—and by the repetition of the calls to dance. Only after these delays are we told the reason for the urgent commands: *"that we may look* (better, "gaze," "feast our eyes") *upon you!"* Thus far the descriptions of the woman have presented her as immobile, standing still. Now the appreciation of her attributes and the attendant mood of eroticism are enhanced by the cry for her to move, to turn about, to set her body free to display its suppleness, symmetry, and grace.

A TEASING OFFER TO DANCE

> 13b   What would you see in the Shulamite–
> As it were, the dance of the two camps?
> *Song of Sol. 6:13b*

The woman's brief answer is almost impossibly baffling, and scholarly discussions of it are voluminous. The question *"what would you see in the Shulamite?"* (also "how" or "why would you gaze at the Shulamite?") seems to be a set-up, a prelude, to introduce the affirmations of her beauty in 7:1–5. *"As it were"* (could also be "anything like") *"the dance of the two camps"*: the force of that final clause cannot be discovered with any certainty. *"Dance"* suggests whirling, writhing motions like the gyrations of the famous dervishes. *"Two camps"* (*"or double camp"*) probably signals some set line-up in which dancers, musicians, and other participants are divided into two parties for antiphonal singing and chanting. Perhaps the bride is called to do her solo in full view and to the rhythm of these two groups. In keeping with her earlier responses (cf. 1:5–6; 2:1), her question which is actually her answer—she certainly does intend to dance, as 7:1–5 proves—combines modesty and pride. She is not sure that she really deserves to be singled out for exhibition, but she is certainly not going to decline the invitation. After all her lover has chosen her above all the women of the court put together (6:8–9). She must have features worthy of public display.

A SONG FOR A DANCING WOMAN

> 7:1   How beautiful are your feet in sandals,
> O prince's daughter!

> The curves of your thighs are like jewels,
> The work of the hands of a skillful workman.
> 2 Your navel is a rounded goblet;
> It lacks no blended beverage.
> Your waist is a heap of wheat
> Set about with lilies.
> 3 Your two breasts are like two fawns,
> Twins of a gazelle.
> 4 Your neck is like an ivory tower,
> Your eyes like the pools in Heshbon
> By the gate of Bath Rabbim.
> Your nose is like the tower of Lebanon
> Which looks toward Damascus.
> 5 Your head crowns you like Mount Carmel,
> And the hair of your head is like purple;
> The king is held captive by its tresses.
> *Song of Sol. 7:1–5*

The dancing has begun. The daughters of Jerusalem had urged the bride to it (6:13a); now they sing their *description song* as they watch her whirling movements. Like a camera fascinated by swiftly stepping limbs, their eyes fix on her *"feet"* (or "steps") and move gradually upward as they trace the contours of her form. Her royal bearing is so apparent to them they call to her, *"O prince's daughter!"* (v. 1) *"Prince"* serves as a catch-link between the groom's ecstatic experience in the garden (6:11–12) and this next stage of the wedding feast. The name is not a record of her pedigree but a tribute to her elegance. The *"thighs"* (or "buttocks") are well-turned (*"curves"*) and bear the grace and symmetry of precious ornaments (*"jewels"*) crafted with care and precision by a *"skillful* (that is, "thoroughly reliable") *workman."*

The focus shifts upward to the pubic area (v. 2). The description of what is usually translated *"navel"* may be more appropriate to the vulva, given the size of the receptacle depicted as a *"rounded goblet"* (or better, "banquet bowl," cf. Exod. 24:6; Isa. 22:24) capable of holding *"blended beverage"* (wine punch mixed with spices). *"Which lacks"* is really a command, probably with a playful tone of voice: "let it never lack spiced wine!" The language of verse 2a parallels both the wish of the woman (4:16) that the spices of her garden may flow out and also the toast of their friends that the couple may drink their fill of love (5:1b). *"Waist"* (or belly), *"heap of wheat"* (cf. Hag. 2:16), and *"lilies"* that border *("set about")* the wheat all point to the pubic hair that guards and graces the vulval area.

The portions of her body depicted in verses 1–2 have played no part in the earlier descriptions which began with the eyes and hair and reached only the upper torso (4:1–5) or the face (6:4–7). Here the dance scene becomes the occasion for a full-length description which gains the freedom to portray the most intimate parts of her anatomy, both because the marriage has been consummated, an act to which those parts are essential, and because the describers are women whose familiarity with the female body allows such frankness.

As the eyes of the joyful singers pan upward, their song combines the conventional descriptions (v. 3 cf. 4:5) with the novel. The *"neck"* itself is featured for its smoothness, fairness, and strength like a *"tower"* covered with slabs or carvings of *"ivory"* (v. 4a). Nothing is said about jewelry or ornamentation (cf. 4:4). The *"eyes"* (v. 4b) are likened not to doves (4:1) but to *"pools"* of water (cf. 2 Sam. 2:13; Eccles. 2:6; note the motif of water and washing in her description of his eyes, 5:12) which reflected the face of those who gaze in them and promised refreshment to the parched. *"Heshbon,"* a town in Moab about fifty miles due east of Jerusalem, apparently possessed a famous *"gate"* (v. 4c) called *"Bath Rabbim"* (daughter of a multitude) that featured a display of pools, perhaps stocked with fish. *"Tower of Lebanon"* (v. 4d) seems to denote the mountains that face (literally "watch the face of") *"Damascus,"* rather than any single architectural structure. *"Lebanon,"* as usually in the Song (cf. 3:9), carries a superlative force. The emphasis is on the strength and placement of the nose not on its size, although middle eastern physiognomy often has proportions that differ from European standards of beauty. The woman in the Song may resemble Barbara Streisand more than the typical cheerleader in a Kansas high school.

"Carmel" speaks of grandeur and majesty (cf. Amos 1:2; 9:3), presiding as it does in regal splendor over both the plains that sweep up to it and the bay of Haifa that nestles in its shadow (v. 5). *"Hair* (literally, "locks" or "curls") *like purple"* sustains the note of royal luxury (see on 3:10) and contrasts sharply with the agrarian images of the goats of Gilead in 4:1; 6:5, which also use the more common word for hair. *"Tresses,"* yet another Hebrew word, pictures curly, flowing locks admirably suited for ensnaring her *"king,"* her lover, as noble in her eyes and the eyes of her friends as any monarch.

Clothes may make the person, according to playwrights and fashion designers. But clothes contribute nothing to this whirling figure and her dazzling beauty. Once the *"sandals"* are noted to cue the beginning of the dance, not one further word about raiment is uttered. It is the appearance of the *"prince's daughter,"* not her apparel, that counts. Even the *veil* (4:1) goes unnoticed. How or whether she was clad as she executed her leaping turns we cannot know. It was a wedding feast not a fashion show that Jerusalem's daughters depicted.

A YEARNING FOR INTIMACY

6 How fair and how pleasant you are,
   O love, with your delights!
7 This stature of yours is like a palm tree,
   And your breasts like its clusters.
8 I said, "I will go up to the palm tree,
   I will take hold of its branches."
   Let now your breasts be like clusters of the vine,
   The fragrance of your breath like apples,
9a And the roof of your mouth like the best wine.
Song of Sol. 7:6–9a

The lover has watched and listened long enough. His heart is bursting with song—with a *song of yearning.* He begins, however, by adding his note of approval to the song of description voiced so graphically by the daughters of Jerusalem. *"Fair"* (cf. 1:8, 15; 2:10, 13; 4:1, 7, 10; 5:9; 6:1, 4, 10; 7:1, 6) and *"pleasant"* (cf. 1:16) are stock terms used in the literal descriptions of beauty. His address, *"O love,"* is here unique to the Song. The Hebrew (*ʾahᵃbāh*) word occurs frequently, but always to describe the fact of love or the act of love, not the persons loved. *"Delights"* is the new term found in the Song only here. It is used as a summary word, an all-embracing descriptor of the woman's grace and charm (cf. Eccles. 2:8 for its role in a summation of Solomonic pleasures).

The daughters had detailed the attributes of the woman's whole person, toe to head. The man has been captured not only by the woman's *"tresses"* (7:5) but by her entire *"stature"* as he has heard and witnessed it (v. 7). *"Palm tree"* becomes his figure to picture her figure. Stateliness and fruitfulness are his themes. His initial interest is her *"breasts"* which he likens first to *"clusters"* of dates and then (v. 8) to *"clusters of the vine,"* that is grapes. Aroused by their sensuous movements in the dance, he wants to caress and hold them. *"I will go up to* (i.e., climb) *the palm tree"* (v. 8) expresses his desire for intercourse with the same passion and intensity as *"I will go my way to the mountain of myrrh"* (4:6). *"Branches"* are the fruit stalks of the date palm and probably another metaphor for breasts. *"Take hold"* is the same Hebrew verb we met in *"catch us the foxes"* (2:15) and *"I held him"* (3:4) in Poem II. *"Your breath"* (literally "nose" or "mouth") may be best understood from its uses in Ugaritic or Akkadian, where it can mean either the breast's nipple or an "opening," hence, perhaps here, the vulva which would certainly harmonize with the words *"fragrance"* and *"apples"* which have highly erotic meanings (4:10; 2:3, 5).[4] *"Roof of the mouth"* (i.e., "palate"; cf. 2:3; 5:16) and *"wine"* (cf. 1:2, 4; 2:4; 4:10; 5:1; 7:9; 8:2) complete the account of the full embrace in which all the erogenous zones from genitals to breasts to mouth are paired by the passionate partners.

AN INVITATION TO FULFILLMENT

9b   The wine goes down smoothly for my beloved,
Moving gently the lips of sleepers.

10   I am my beloved's,
And his desire is toward me.

11   Come, my beloved,
Let us go forth to the field;
Let us lodge in the villages.

12   Let us get up early to the vineyards;
Let us see if the vine has budded,
Whether the grape blossoms are open,
And the pomegranates are in bloom.
There I will give you my love.

13   The mandrakes give off a fragrance,
And at our gates are pleasant fruits,
All manner, new and old,
Which I have laid up for you, my beloved.

8:1   Oh, that you were like my brother,
Who nursed at my mother's breasts!
If I should find you outside,
I would kiss you;
I would not be despised.

2 I would lead you and bring you
Into the house of my mother,
She who used to instruct me.
I would cause you to drink of spiced wine,
Of the juice of my pomegranate.
3 His left hand is under my head,
And his right hand embraces me.

Song of Sol. 7:9b–8:3

"My beloved," which seems to intrude in this context, is a strong clue that the woman interrupts the man in midsentence and blends her sense of yearning with his. Alternative readings all must emend the text, since *"my beloved"* is masculine and is the bride's pet name for her husband (see on 1:13–14). Only she is privy to the effect of her kisses on him, as their wine-like exhilaration is imbibed *"smoothly"* (literally, "rightly" or "correctly"; see on 1:4) even by lovers who are exhausted by sleep and yet continue their gentle contact. A number of versions (LXX, Vulg., RSV, NIV, NEB) read "teeth" for *"sleepers"* and picture the *"wine"* gliding over lips and teeth. The two words are spelled nearly alike in Hebrew, but there is no reason not to follow the MT as NKJV has done. In a version of the *formula of mutual possession* (see on 2:16; 6:3), modified to suit the context which has featured the husband's *"desire"* for her (note that another key occurrence of *"desire"* predicts the woman's desire for the man in Gen. 3:16), she affirms her total commitment to him.

Her *song of invitation* (7:11–8:3) virtually announces the close of the public festivities. The processionals, the open songs of admiration, description, and yearning, the toasts of their friends, the teasing and gaming that added spice to the party, the provocative dancing—all these have done their part to celebrate the union, to articulate its covenant pledges, and to assure the couple of the good wishes and blessings of their friends and family. Now she seems to say, it is time for sustained solitude and unhurried love. Her first words of invitation are literal (v. 11) and prepare us to understand the horticultural language that follows (vv. 12–13). *"Field"* (or "countryside") suggests the pastoral isolation that she fantasized first in 1:7–8 and again in the words she placed in her lover's mouth in 2:10–14. *"Villages"* seems not to be the right locale to serve as synonym to *"field"* and as a quiet place to *"lodge"* (or "pass the night"). They would be observed and disturbed in any village, where they would be branded intruders. Other possible meanings of the Hebrew word for village are "henna-bushes" (NEB; see on 1:14) or "cypress" (Pope, p. 594). Either of them suits the context by underscoring the pastoral setting, though "henna-bushes" which grow among grapevines (1:14) may provide the better link to the vintner's setting of verse 12.

The artful and suggestive use of double meanings comes into play as her invitation is embellished (vv. 12–13). *"Vineyards"* (cf. 1:6; 8:12), *"vine"* that *"has budded"* (cf. 2:13, 15; 6:11; 7:8), *"grape blossoms"* (cf. 2:13, 15; 7:8), *"open"* (cf. 5:2, 5), *"pomegranates"* (cf. 4:3, 13; 6:2, 11; 8:2), *"bloom"* (cf. 2:12; 6:11), *"fragrance"*—all these terms are capable of a literal, horticultural meaning; yet each is used in the Song as an image with erotic implications. In other words the context for making love and the facets of that lovemaking are both implied in her seductive song. The erotic note is heightened by (1) *"mandrakes"* (v. 13), which are herbs that grow stemlessly and perennially in untilled fields (cf. Gen. 30:14–16). Their plum-like berry and meaty root were treasured as an aid to fertility; apparently, their fragrance was more stimulating to Middle Eastern senses than to westerners;[5] (2) *"pleasant fruits"* (v. 13) recall the vivid "garden" passages of the wedding night (cf. 4:13, 16); (3) *"gates"* (v. 13) are literally "doors" or "openings," a further re-minder of the *double entendre* which seems to be present in 5:2–5 and a delicate intimation that her garden is no longer locked (4:12).

Not that we are left to guess at the bride's intent. Indeed her plain words shed light on her double meanings. *"There I will give you my love"* (i.e., "my acts of love;" cf. on 1:2) could not be any more direct (v. 12). And only slightly more subtle is the description of all the *"pleasant fruits"* (the noun is supplied on the basis of 4:13, 16) as *"new and old."* Her devoted heart and impassioned instincts have a veritable trea-sure-trove of caresses, gestures, and postures of love *"laid up"* for him. Some of them will kindle his memory; others will stretch his imagi-nation.

Her inflamed affection vents itself in a wish: *"Oh, that ..."* (8:1). She has just issued a prolonged description of a retreat to intimacy and she can scarcely wait. If he were *"like my brother"* then she could *"kiss"* him (cf. 1:2) in public *("outside")* without being shamed, ridiculed, or robbed of reputation *("despised")*. *"Nursed at my mother's breast"* may suggest a foster brother relationship, where her mother wet-nursed and reared a near relative who was not a uterine brother to the bride. Her fantasy of an amorous adventure without seeking the seclusion of the countryside (cf. 7:11) recalls the satisfaction dream of 3:1–4 where she did envisage the two of them *in the house of her mother* (8:2). In 3:4 the label for her mother was *who conceived me*; here it is *who used to instruct me.* The change in verb seems deliberate, as it reflects the rearing that both she and her foster brother would have received (the whole scene is imaginative and hypothetical) at the mother's hands. It is not necessary to emend the text to "who bore (or "conceived," RSV) me," even though "bear" and "instruct" have certain consonants in common in Hebrew. An equally acceptable translation is "you would teach me," an obvious invitation for the lover to initiate her further into the delights of love.

The blandishments the woman promises, were such public affection feasible, echo familiar metaphors: *spiced wine* is a variation of mixed wine (*blended beverage,* 7:2); *juice of my* (note the personal pronoun!) *pomegranate* repeats and enhances the delights available in her garden (4:13). *I would cause you to drink* caps the string of verbs which feature her initiative in the whole encounter and restores to her the prominent place she has enjoyed in most of the poems: *I would find you,* *I would kiss you* (v. 1), *I would lead you* (or even "drive you"), *I would bring you* (v. 2). Her imagination plays out the scene to its vivid climax in the total embrace of love (v. 3; cf. 2:6), which she recounts not so much to him (the pronouns are third person—*his*") as to the daughters of Jerusalem, standing by as ever to share her admiration of the husband and support her affection.

A CALL FOR PATIENCE WITH LOVE'S COURSE

4 I charge you, O daughters of Jerusalem,
  Do not stir up nor awaken love
  Until it pleases.

Song of Sol. 8:4

Again this *adjuration* signals that the woman has reached the peak of anticipation (cf. 2:7; 3:5). Everything within her calls for fresh adventures in the consummation of love with her husband. The way in which the Hebrew puts the oath (*māh* not *ʾim*) suggests a tone different from the previous instances. Having already soared to the zenith of excitement, she now chides her friends to go on record publicly as to why they have contributed to her present arousal. More than that, she is demanding that they pledge not to do it again.[6] Feelings like hers are not to be toyed with, so great their explosive power, so painful their consequences if the marriage covenant is not their context. The form of this charge is the most urgent of all: no words or energies are diverted to the *"gazelles or the does of the field"* (cf. 2:7; 3:5), as the instruments of the oath. Her own passionate, personal, poignant plea is enough.

NOTES

1. See J. A. Thompson, "Tirzah," *The Illustrated Bible Dictionary* (Leicester, England: Inter–Varsity Press, 1980), pp. 1571–72.

2. Carr, *The Song of Solomon*, p. 147.

3. Gordis, *The Song of Songs*, p. 65.

4. On this interpretation of v. 8 and the possible Ugaritic and Akkadian background of its vocabulary, see Pope, *Song of Songs*, pp. 636–37.

5. J. C. Trevor, "Mandrakes," *Interpreter's Dictionary of the Bible*, III, pp. 256–57.

6. For this interpretation of the adjuration in 8:4, see Carr, *The Song of Solomon*, p. 168.

CHAPTER SEVEN

Poem VI: Passion and Commitment

Song of Solomon 8:5–14

The honeymoon has ended. The quiet days and nights in the countryside among the henna blossoms have come and gone (7:11). The couple is pictured returning to the fellowship of friends and family (8:5). The return carries the note of majesty and mystery that has sounded throughout the wedding rites from 3:6 to 8:4. The first clause of Poem VI is identical to the beginning of Poem III (3:6). The parallel is deliberate to mark the opening and closing of the wedding festivities. Beyond that, it elevates the importance of marital commitment by suggesting that a lone couple, returning to their city refreshed by their honeymoon, is a sight as important and impressive as the Solomonic entourage depicted in Poem III.

Exclusiveness, which was featured so effectively in the central songs that portrayed the actual wedding night (4:1–5:2), is again the major theme. Its significance was even better apprehended after the honeymoon than before. Wedding vows are vows of chastity; sealed by intercourse, they become even more binding and freeing for the couple. *Binding* they are, because the ultimate human relationship has been experienced and two persons have become *one flesh*—one social, spiritual, physical entity, to be put asunder by no power short of death (Gen. 2:24; Matt. 19:6). *Freeing* they are, because such vows deliver us from the weighing of other options, from the inflicting and bearing of the pains of promiscuity, from the degradation of human dignity experienced by those who separate sexual activity from covenant commitment.

The poem features (1) *a yearning for chastity* in the bride's impassioned plea to be stamped as exclusively and permanently on her husband as is his signet ring on all he possesses (8:6–7); (2) *a testing of chastity* in which she rehearses the concerns for her sexual purity expressed by her brothers and how she met those concerns with her own discipline and integrity (8:8–10); (3) *a boasting about chastity* in which the lover forswears any envy of Solomon's wealth or profligacy and delights in the precious person who dwells permanently by his side (8:11–12).

Such exclusiveness is both nurtured in the past and affirmed in the present by friends and family. We should not miss the notes of *nostalgia* and *comradery* present in this final poem. Right to the end, friends are present peering toward the desert to discern the wedding couple on their homeward trek (8:5a) and then craning their necks to hear again the bride's words of love for her man (8:13). Comradery is found here at its most persistent best, as loyal as the home crowd waiting in the stands at the close of the game for one more opportunity to cheer for their winning team!

Past remembrances loom large alongside present congratulations. The memory of his mother's birth-pangs gave special meaning to the apple tree where the couple's romance had first ripened (8:5b). There is a nostalgia about *love's continuity*, about the fertile affection that perpetuates the family line. The memory of her brothers' valuing of her virginity gave the bride grounds for gratitude and permission for pride all in one (8:8–10). There is a nostalgia about *love's protection*, about the keen concern to shelter a tender member of the clan from the pain and shame of exploitation or promiscuity.

The Song finds none of this stifling. Not the tethers of the wedding vows, not the tutoring of mothers and brothers, not the watchful expectations of friends. Affection, romance, and passion keep the covenant in place, as a commitment of joyful chastity, of exuberant exclusiveness. Hear the bride's final call (8:14), and you will know what I mean. And the covenant, publicly inaugurated, divinely defined and demonstrated, physically sealed and ratified, will, in turn, keep affection, romance, and passion in place, reserved for the unique partner and experienced at every possible opportunity.

ANNOUNCEMENT OF THE RETURN

5a Who is this coming up from the wilderness,
   Leaning upon her beloved?

Song of Sol. 8:5a

The first clause consciously mimics the beginning of Poem III, the line that signaled the start of the wedding festivities (3:6; see also Isaiah 63:1). The repetition aims to thrust the importance of the couple, sated with love yet ready for more, into bold relief. The two of them clinging together form their own processional as full of mystery and majesty as any royal parade. The speakers, whether the daughters of Jerusalem or a larger group of *"companions"* (see v. 13), use the question form as an artifact, a literary technique, as it was in 6:10, where the same two Hebrew words introduced it—*"who is she"* (literally, "this"). Everyone present knew the bride's identity in 6:10. But the question cast an aura about her which gave the opportunity to describe her in otherworldly terms: dawn, moon, sun. Here the question shines the spotlight on the couple and most brightly on the bride, whose commitment to the groom has dominated the Song from the beginning. *"Leaning"* (a Hebrew word used here only) may hint at her fatigue from the exertions of the honeymoon and travel. More likely, it calls attention to the sense of mutual dependence that their intimacy has engendered.

MEMORY OF THE BEGINNING

5b I awakened you under the apple tree.
    There your mother brought you forth;
    There she who bore you brought you forth.
                                              Song of Sol. 8:5b

The lovers behave as if they were alone. Perhaps we are allowed to eavesdrop on their conversation as they approached the city. *"The apple tree"* (see on 2:3, 5; 7:8) seems to catch the bride's attention and remind her of the beginnings of their love. *"Awakened"* is the key word used in her calls to Jerusalem's daughters to put themselves under oath (2:7; 3:5; 8:4); it links Poem VI to the earlier parts of the book and especially to Poem V which shows us how vigorously their love had been aroused. Again (see on 8:1–2), she is the initiator of the relationship—*"I awakened you"* (the second person pronoun is masculine in Heb.).

"The apple tree" seemed to have some significance in the man's family history. Whether literally as a place of courting or even birth,

or figuratively as an erotic symbol thought to enhance potency and fertility, we cannot know. But the theme of continuity should not be missed. Love not only makes the world go round; it generates the people who populate the world. It rescues individuals from isolation and connects them to families that persevere from generation to generation. The very thought of the tree and all it symbolized not only brought memories of the man's *"mother"* who *"bore"* (carried and endured labor pains) him but sparked within the bride fresh urges to intimacy. For reasons we do not know, the woman in the Song is much more conscious of the mothers' roles in their lives than of the fathers' (see on 1:6; 3:4, 11; 8:1–2), neither of whom is mentioned.

PLEDGE OF FIDELITY

6 Set me as a seal upon your heart,
As a seal upon your arm;
For love is as strong as death,
Jealousy as cruel as the grave;
Its flames are flames of fire,
A most vehement flame.
7 Many waters cannot quench love,
Nor can the floods drown it.
If a man would give for love
All the wealth of his house,
It would be utterly despised.

Song of Sol. 8:6–7

These magnificent words that pledge deathless love and then describe its power and worth are uttered by the bride. Her *formula of mutual possession* we have met before (2:16; 6:3; 7:10). Here it is expanded, elaborated, and decorated like a magnificent violin cadenza in the middle of a concerto. The orchestra's instruments are frozen in silence; the conductor joins the audience in rapt attention; the lone musician reaches for sweeter, brighter, stronger tones than even she thought possible. And the result is an outburst of love-poetry which is the artistic match of anything William Shakespeare or Elizabeth Barrett Browning ever put to ink.

Its similes and metaphors are brilliant. The dominant one is her self-description—a *"seal upon your heart"* and *"arm"* (v. 6). She may mean "value me as you would your own seal, that stone or metal stamp by which you label possessions as your own and ratify legal documents." More likely she is calling herself the seal, to gain the right to put her stamp on him and claim him as her own possession both inwardly (*"heart"*) and outwardly (*"arm"*).

The *"love"* (the word is the one by which he addressed her in 7:6) she describes is what *she* feels toward him. It is a love of ultimate power and duration, as *"death"* and *"grave"* (Heb. *Sheol*) signify. It is intensely focused (*"jealousy"* or "zeal") so that it will pay any price (*"cruel,"* that is "hard," "severe") for its survival and exact high tariff from all who threaten it. *"Its flames"* will keep burning under dampening and soggy circumstances and will threaten all who aim to douse them. *"A most vehement flame"* is a superlative expression, as strong as anything Hebrew can kindle, to show the brilliance and tenacity of love. *"Flame* of Yah," that is, of Yahweh, is one possible rendering. The chief role of the fragment of the divine name is to heighten the description of the flame, but a secondary role may be to remind us from Whom comes such love.

The *"flame"* imagery is sustained in verse 7 with the negative side of the picture: fire that bright, love that strong, was unquenchable no matter how much *"water,"* what great *"floods,"* descended upon it. *"Water"* here, as often in Scripture, is viewed as life-threatening not life-giving (see Ps. 88:6–7; Jon. 2:3; Isa. 43:2): water-filled pits in desolate places, stream beds suddenly flowing with terror from flash floods, the sea itself—all these put life in jeopardy for the Israelites. Millennia before the phrase became fashionable in our circles, the bride in the Song knew all about "tough love," love that endures, confronts, forgives, demands, and blesses.

Indelible as a seal sharply stamped, unquenchable as a fire with leaping flames, and unbuyable even at an exorbitant price—such is the *love* that she offers. No *"man,"* however great the *"wealth"* of the possessions and influence of his estate (*"house"*), could raise a "bride price" high enough to procure her affections. Indeed, such an overture would be greeted with the fiercest contempt (*"utterly despised"* is an emphatic construction in Hebrew in which the verb root is repeated to underscore the action): she would turn on her heels at best and spit in his face at worst. She belongs as exclusively to her lover (v. 7) as she entreats him to belong to her (v. 6).

343

TEST AND BOAST OF CHASTITY

8 We have a little sister,
And she has no breasts.
What shall we do for our sister
In the day when she is spoken for?
9 If she is a wall,
We will build upon her
A battlement of silver;
And if she is a door,
We will enclose her
With boards of cedar.
10 I am a wall,
And my breasts like towers;
Then I became in his eyes
As one who found peace.

Song of Sol. 8:8–10

Marriage is a family affair. The bride's pledge of fidelity (vv. 6–7) sparks in her mind recollections of conversations with her brothers (note 1:6) when she was a few years younger. Like other brothers in the Bible, they felt a keen responsibility to guard their sister's virginity and to give her incentives to do the same (Gen. 34:6–17; 2 Sam. 13:20, 32). They could have been part of the audience (note vv. 5, 13, which suggest the presence of family and friends) and would have delighted in her recital of their words. Five years or so may well have been the time span between *"no breasts"* (v. 8) and *"breasts like towers"* (v. 10). In the Mediterranean world, as in many other places, dramatic things happen to the female body between, say, ages ten and fifteen, which was about the typical time for marriage.

Dowry seems to be the subject broached in the brothers' question. Dowry was the contribution of the bride's family to the marriage transaction, as bride price (see v. 7) was the groom's part. *"Spoken for"* suggests the arrangements for betrothal and marriage (1 Sam. 25:39) in which brothers apparently took part (Gen. 24:29–60). Their treatment of her at that time would depend on her behavior in the meanwhile (v. 9). *"Wall"* and *"door"* I take to be contrasting not parallel terms, although scholars are divided on the matter. What tips the scales for me primarily is her response (v. 10) in which she chooses

344

only one of the terms, not both: *"I am"* ("was" is probably better; the past tense of *"I became"* is the clue) *"a wall,"* a phrase which allows her to describe her maturation—*"and my breasts like towers"*—and continue the architectural simile. *"Battlement* (literally a row of stones to defend soldiers who mount the wall to guard it) *of silver"* points to a generous dowry and may recall the poetic description of the tiered ornaments which decorated her neck (4:4). It is the reward for her virginity; she must remain a *"wall,"* impregnable, impenetrable until marriage. If this is not the case, *"if she is a door"* open and available to outsiders, their response will be to cut her off (*"enclose her"*) from family support. *"Boards of cedar"* connote strength and firmness (note 5:15).

With joy and pride, the woman boasts that she passed the test (v. 10). She came to the betrothal fully mature of form and figure, ripe and ready for marriage (note the signs of maturation in Ezekiel 16:7–8). The descriptions of her beauty have certainly confirmed this (4:1–5; 7:1–9). She also came to it intact, untouched, reserved for the one to whom she was pledged—a *"wall."* She deserves not only her brothers' praise but the family dowry. Yet it is not that of which she proceeds to speak. *"His eyes"* must refer to her husband; perhaps she nods or points to him as she says these words. The *"peace"* that she *"found"* (or "brought" if we read a different Hebrew root) seems to follow through on the fortress imagery of *"wall"* and *"towers."* It speaks of complete security, total well-being which she has discovered and carried with her to the marriage. The Hebrew *shālôm* may be a word-play on *"Shulamite," "Jerusalem"* (6:4, 13) and *"Solomon"* (8:11), which contain the same three consonants as *shālôm.* The joy of having passed the test and the delight in gentle boasting about it set the tone of this verse. She, not the *"battlement of silver"* (v. 9), is the true dowry. To the relationship she has brought beauty, purity, and strength like Jerusalem's (6:4). Any marriage with such assets is off to a golden start.

BOAST OF EXCLUSIVENESS

> 11 Solomon had a vineyard at Baal Hamon;
> He leased the vineyard to keepers;

Everyone was to bring for its fruit
A thousand pieces of silver.
12 My own vineyard is before me.
You, O Solomon, may have a thousand,
And those who tend its fruit two hundred.
Song of Sol. 8:11–12

It is now the husband's turn. Though the grammar gives us no hint
of the speaker's gender, the context seems to point to the *man* who
now calls the bride *"my own vineyard"* (v. 12) and gestures to her, as
she had to him (v. 10), as the one standing *"before* ("in front of," "in
the presence of") *me."* She had called her body, her person, *"my own
vineyard"* in 1:6. Now she belongs to him as permanently, intimately,
and exclusively as he belongs to her (vv. 6–7); his words seal the
promises of mutual possession, which she had so graphically eluci-
dated in verses 6–7.

To do so he changes the metaphor while deliberately linking the
language to what has just been said. Picking up on her word *"peace"*
(*shālôm*, v. 10), he compares the legacy he has gained in her with the
vast agricultural holdings of *"Solomon,"* whose Hebrew name rings
with notes of peace. He recounts the vast financial returns that flow
to Solomon—*"a thousand pieces* (perhaps *shekels) of silver"* (a link to v.
9), each year from each sharecropper (*"keepers"*). None of this does he
envy. His beloved was right: his love and hers are beyond price (8:7).
Solomon's vineyards are several day's journey to the north, if Ibleam
(also called Belemoth or Khirbet Balama), a town a few miles south of
Megiddo, is the correct site of *"Baal Hamon,"* otherwise unmentioned
in the Bible. But the lover's *"vineyard"* is right there before him, available and eager and committed. Let *"Solomon,"* who is addressed for
dramatic effect as though he were present, have his lavish income
and the sharecroppers who *"tend its fruit,"* their modest annual com-
mission of *"two hundred"* shekels. The shekel, originally nuggets or
dust of the metal, then minted as coins about 500 B.C., weighed just
under half an ounce; according to Isaiah (7:23), a thousand vines
were valued at a thousand silver shekels, but we do not know if this
was the total worth of the vineyard or its annual income. Such details
would not matter to the husband. His bride was to him a vineyard
beyond price. Her *"fruit"* no money could buy, and it was reserved
for him (4:13; 7:6–9, 13; 8:2).

13 You who dwell in the gardens,
     The companions listen for your voice—
     Let me hear it!

Song of Sol. 8:13

The final two verses sum up the themes of yearning and invitation which are threaded through the Song and which help bind it together (2:4–6, 16–17; 3:1–4; 4:8, 16; 7:7–9, 10–13; 8:1–3, 6–7). Especially do verses 13–14 provide a coda which is the counterpart to the woman's song of yearning in 1:2–4. There, at the beginning, she longs for their separation to conclude and their intimacy to begin. There, in the presence of her companions, she calls out to her absent lover. Here, at the close, he does the same. She has temporarily absented herself to stay awhile (*"dwell"* is too permanent sounding) *"in the gardens."* He intensifies the yearning (and perhaps does a bit of teasing) by mentioning that their friends (*"the companions,"* probably family members would be included, though the earlier use of the term refers to his fellow shepherds, 1:7) are lonesome for *"your voice"*; we remember how the voices were featured in Poem II—she thrilled at the *"voice of my beloved"* (2:8); he begged, *"let me hear your voice,"* He now repeats that plea: *"let me hear it."* His concern is much more for himself than his companions. He and they want to know that she, at the end of the ceremonies and the honeymoon, will still call to him for love.

CALLING FOR LOVE TO CONTINUE

14 Make haste, my beloved
     And be like a gazelle
     Or a young stag
     On the mountains of spices.

Song of Sol. 8:14

And call she does, in terms almost identical to the invitation of Poem II (2:17). There the initial imperative had been *"turn"*; here the note of urgency is sharper, *"make haste,"* or, more literally, "take flight," "flee," "run away from the friends to where I am."

The familiar tones of her affection that have sounded throughout the Song are present in her call in poignant summary. Her zeal for him again pushes her to take the *initiative;* the Song ends as it began, with her arms stretched out to him in invitation. Her *bondedness* to him reveals itself in her favorite name, *"my beloved"* (see on 1:13); she feels as close to him as can any kin to another. Her *openness* to him, her vulnerability to his passions, becomes plain in the imagery of the *"ga-zelle"* and *"young stag"* (see on 2:7, 8, 17); the strong eroticism of this language serves to ready both partners for their embrace. Her sense of the *beauty* of love's most intimate act is as alert as ever; she sees her body as more than flesh and bone—it's a veritable *"mountain"* range, alive with the fragrance of all the *"spices"* any palace could know (see on 1:12–14; 4:13–14). The *mutuality* of their desire is clear; what she wants is what he wants, as a comparison of 8:14 with 4:6 shows. Her commitment to the *permanence* of their love is signaled in what she does *not* say here; consciously she omits the night-to-morning time frames of the previous invitations (see on 2:17; 4:6).

The greatest Lover of all knew the significance of this permanency: "having loved His own who were in the world, He loved them to the end" (John 13:1). The couple in the Song would have admired that commitment. Their love reminds us to look to our own love and, more importantly, to draw upon His.

Bibliography

GENERAL

Alter, Robert, and Kermode, Frank, eds. *The Literary Guide to the Bible.* Cambridge, Mass.: The Belknap Press of Harvard University Press, 1987.

Kidner, Derek. *An Introduction to Wisdom Literature: Proverbs, Job and Ecclesiastes.* Downers Grove, Ill.: InterVarsity Press, 1985.

LaSor, William S., David A. Hubbard, and Frederick W. Bush. *Old Testament Survey: The Message, Form, and Background of the Old Testament.* Grand Rapids, Mich: Wm. B. Eerdmans, 1982.

ECCLESIASTES

Bergant, Dianne. *Job, Ecclesiastes.* Wilmington, Del.: Michael Glazier, Inc., 1982.

Crenshaw, James L. *Ecclesiastes.* Philadelphia: The Westminster Press, 1987.

Eaton, Michael A. *Ecclesiastes.* Leicester, England; Downers Grove, Ill.: InterVarsity Press, 1983.

Fox, Michael V. *Qohelet and His Contradictions.* Sheffield: Almond Press, 1989.

Ginsburg, Christian. *The Song of Songs and Qoheleth.* New York: KTAV Publishing House, 1970.

Gordis, Robert. *Koheleth—The Man and His World.* New York: The Jewish Theological Seminary of America by Bloch Publishing Co., 1955.

Hubbard, David A. *Beyond Futility: Messages of Hope from the Book of Ecclesiastes.* Grand Rapids, Mich: Wm B. Eerdmans, 1976.

Kidner, Derek. *A Time to Mourn and a Time to Dance.* Downers Grove, Ill.: InterVarsity Press, 1976.

Loader, J. A. *Polar Structures in the Book of Qohelet.* BZAW 152. Berlin: Walter de Gruyter, 1979.

————. *Ecclesiastes: A Practical Commentary.* Tr. by John Vriend. Grand Rapids, Mich: Wm. B. Eerdmans, 1986.

Ogden, Graham. *Qoheleth.* Sheffield: JSOT Press, 1987.

Scott, R. B. Y. *Proverbs. Ecclesiastes.* Anchor Bible. Garden City, N. Y.: Doubleday & Co., 1965.

Whitley, C. F. *Koheleth: His Language and Thought.* BZAW 148. Berlin: Walter de Gruyter, 1979.

Whybray, R. N. *Ecclesiastes.* New Century Bible Commentary. Grand Rapids, Mich.: Wm. B. Eerdmans, 1989.

Wilson, Gerald. "'The Words of the Wise': The Intent and Significance of Qohelet 12:9–4." *Journal of Biblical Literature* 103 (1984), pp. 175–92.

Two important works in French:

Glasser, E. *Le Procés du Bonheur par Qohelet.* "Lectio Divina" 61. Paris: Les Editions du Cerf, 1970.

Lüthi, Walter. *L'Ecclésiate a vécu la vie.* Tr. by Daniel Hatt. Geneva: Editions Labor et Fides, 1952.

Two recent works in German

Michel, Diethelm. *Qohelet.* Erträgeder Forschung 258. Darmstadt: Wissenschaftliche Buchgesellschaft, 1988.

Zimmerli, Walther. *Prediger.* Das Alte Testament Deutsch 16/1. Göttingen: Vandenhoeck & Ruprecht, 1962.

THE SONG OF SOLOMON

Carr, G. Lloyd. *The Song of Solomon.* Tyndale Old Testament Commentaries. Leicester, England; Downers Grove: Ill.: InterVarsity Press, 1984.

Dillow, Joseph C. *Solomon on Sex.* New York/Nashville: Thomas Nelson, Inc., 1977.

Falk, Marcia. *The Song of Songs: Love Poems from the Bible.* New York: Harcourt, Brace, Jovanovich, 1977.

Fox, Michael V. *The Song of Songs and the Ancient Egyptian Love Songs.* Madison: The University of Wisconsin Press, 1985.

Ginsburg, Christian D. *The Song of Songs and Coheleth.* New York: KTAV Publishing House, 1970.

Glickman, S. Craig. *A Song for Lovers.* Downers Grove, Ill.: InterVarsity Press, 1976.

Gordis, Robert. *The Song of Songs.* New York: The Jewish Theological Seminary of America, 1961.

Matter, E. Ann. *The Voice of My Beloved: The Song of Songs in Western Medieval Christianity.* Philadelphia: University of Pennsylvania Press, 1990.

Murphy, Roland E. *The Song of Songs.* Hermeneia. Minneapolis: Fortress Press, 1990.

Pope, Marvin H. *Song of Songs.* The Anchor Bible. Garden City, N.Y.: Doubleday & Co., 1977.

Schonfield, Hugh J. *The Song of Songs.* London: Elek Books, 1959.

Tournay, Raymond J. *Word of God, Song of Love: A Commentary on the Song of Songs.* Tr. by J. Edward Crowley New York, N.Y./Mahwah, N.J.: Paulist Press, 1988.

White, John B. *A Study of the Language of Love in the Song of Songs and Ancient Egyptian Poetry.* SBL Dissertation Series 38, Missoula, Montana: Scholars Press, 1978.